The
SHOW *and*
the GAZE *of*
THEATRE

Studies

in

Theatre History

and

Culture

Edited by Thomas Postlewait

The
SHOW *and*
the GAZE *of*
THEATRE

A European Perspective

ERIKA FISCHER-LICHTE

UNIVERSITY OF IOWA PRESS

IOWA CITY

Ψ

University of Iowa Press

Iowa City 52242

Copyright © 1997 by the

University of Iowa Press

All rights reserved

Printed in the United States of America

Design by Richard Hendel

http://www.uiowa.edu/~uipress

Printed on acid-free paper

Library of Congress

Cataloging-in-Publication Data

Fischer-Lichte, Erika.

The show and the gaze of theatre: a European perspective / by Erika
Fischer-Lichte

p.   cm.—(Studies in theatre history and culture)

Includes bibliographical references and index.

ISBN 0-87745-607-0, ISBN 0-87745-608-9 (paper)

1. Theater—Philosophy.   2. Intercultural communication.   I. Title.
II. Series.

PN2039.F57   1997

792'.01—dc21   97-24047

97 98 99 00 01 C 5 4 3 2 1
97 98 99 00 01 P 5 4 3 2 1

For sorrow's eye, glazed with blinding tears,

Divides one thing to many objects,

Like perspectives which, rightly gaz'd upon,

Show nothing but confusion — eye'd awry,

Distinguish form.

Richard II, act 2, scene 1, ll. 16–20

CONTENTS

ACKNOWLEDGMENTS

The following chapters appeared, in slightly different form, in these publications: "Theatre and the Civilizing Process: An Approach to the History of Acting," in *Interpreting the Theatrical Past: New Directions in the Historiography of Performance*, ed. Bruce McConachie and Thomas Postlewait, 19–36 (Iowa City: University of Iowa Press, 1989); "From Theatre to Theatricality: How to Construct Reality," *Theatre Research International* 20:2 (Summer 1995), 97–105; "What Are the Rules of the Game? Some Remarks on *The Yellow Jacket*," *Theatre Survey* 36:1 (May 1995), 21–36; "The Aesthetics of Disruption: German Theatre in the Age of the Media," *Theatre Survey* 34:2 (November 1993), 7–27; "In Search of a New Theatre: Retheatricalization as Productive Reception of Far Eastern Theatre," in *Non-literary Traditions in Modern Theatre*, ed. Günter Ahrends and Hans Jürgen Diller, 161–180 (Tübingen: Gunter Narr, 1990); "Familiar and Foreign Theatres: The Intercultural Trend in Contemporary Theatre," in *Tendenzen des Gegenwartstheaters*, ed. Wilfried Floeck, et al., 227–240 (Tübingen: Francke, 1987); "Intercultural Aspects in Postmodern Theatre: The Japanese Version of Chekhov's *Three Sisters*," in *The Play Out of Context: Transferring Plays from Culture to Culture*, ed. Hanna Scolnicov, 173–185 (Cambridge: Cambridge University Press, 1989); "All the World's a Stage: The Theatrical Metaphor in the Baroque and Postmodernism," in *New Directions in Theatre Research*, ed. Kirsten Gram Holmström and Willmar Sauter, 80–92 (Copenhagen: Munksgaard, 1990); "Passage to the Realm of Shadows: Robert Wilson's *King Lear* in Frankfurt," in *Understanding Theatre: Performance Analysis in Theory and Practice*, ed. Willmar Sauter and Jacqueline Martin, 191–211 (Stockholm: Almquist and Wiksell International, 1995); "Avant-garde and Postmodernism: Theatre between Cultural Crisis and Cultural Change," in *Zeitgeist in Babel: The Postmodernist Controversy*, ed. Ingeborg Hoesterey, 216–228 (Bloomington and Indianapolis: Indiana University Press, 1991); "Walter Benjamin's 'Allegory,'" *American Journal of Semiotics* 4:1–2 (1986), 151–168; "Signs of Identity: The Dramatic Character as 'Name' and 'Body,'" in *Approches de*

l'opéra, ed. André Helbo, 79–88 (Paris: Didier, 1986); "The Quest for Meaning," *Stanford Literature Review* 3:1 (Spring 1986), 137–155; "Written Drama/Oral Performance," in *Aspects of Oral Communication*, ed. Uta M. Quasthoff, 305–321 (Berlin/New York: Walter de Gruyter, 1995); "Theatre Historiography and Performance Analysis: Different Fields, Common Approaches?" *Assaph. Studies in the Theatre* (1995), 99–112.

All essays have been edited or translated by Jo Riley.

INTRODUCTION
Theatre Studies from a European Perspective

Theatre, in some respects, resembles a market. For, like a market, where an intense exchange of commodities takes place, an exchange of all kinds of cultural goods and products goes on between theatre and other spheres of social life — other institutions, cultural performances, art forms, and elements of everyday life. Stories, rituals, ideas, concepts, perceptive modes, conventions, rules, techniques, actions, behavioral patterns, objects, etc., circulate among the different spheres, traveling to and fro. Transgressing the boundaries of theatre, they leave an imprint, perhaps even an impact. In any case, they change the sphere they enter — sometimes slightly, sometimes considerably. And sometimes, in passing, they even change the sphere they leave behind. European theatre and cultural history are filled with such examples.

Many medieval Easter plays include a sequence of scenes devoted to devils' play, among which the most popular was the *Descensus ad inferos* (Descent into Hell). This scene was usually performed according to the same pattern — in Latin and vernacular plays, the scene opened with the Latin *canticum triumphale*:

> *Adam:* Advenisti, desiderabilis
> quem expectabamus in tenebris
> ut educeres hac nocte
> vinculatos de claustis,
> te nostra vocabant suspiria,
> te larga requirebant lamenta,
> tu factus es spes desperatis
> magna consolatio in tormentis.

> *Adam:* Much longed for, you have come,
> The one for whom we wait in the darkness,
> This night to lead us,
> The chained ones, out of the gaol.

It is you our sighs call upon,
It is you our loud complaints seek out.
You are the hope of all those without hope,
The comforter of all our tortures.

After this, the angels would sing the request three times:

Angels: Tollite portas, principes, vestras,
et elevamini portae aeternales,
et introibit rex gloriae.

Raise the gates, you noblemen,
And open the doors,
And the King of Glory shall enter in.

At this, the devil responds with the question, "Quis est iste rex gloriae?"
(Who is this King of Glory?), which he repeats three times, and the angels
thrice reply: "Dominus fortis et potens / dominus potens in proelio" (The
powerful and almighty Lord, almighty Lord of battle).

This formula is to be found as early as the Gospel of Nicodemus. It was
transferred into the Easter plays from other ecclesiastical rituals. By at least
the ninth century, the consecration of churches was performed with this formula, which is itself part of the large body and tradition of ecclesiastical exorcism formulae. The absorption of this formula into the Easter plays had a
profound effect on the performance of the plays as well as on the church.

That the formula was firmly upheld, even in vernacular plays, seems to indicate that it was actually used as a formula to exorcise devils and demons. By
employing "white magic," as allowed and practiced by the church, it became
possible to act out all the "obscenities" of the following merchandise scene —
by which the devils enter the human body — without arousing fear in either
the performers or the spectators. The use of the exorcism formula, thus,
turned the performance — at least partly — into a magic ritual. On the other
hand, this exchange deeply affected the church. For the "obscenities," which
were acted out on the basic condition that the exorcism formula would be effective, mainly originated in pagan spring and fertility rites which the church
strongly opposed and sought to eradicate.[1]

Whereas, in the case of the exorcism formula, the exchange of contexts
achieved important consequences for both sides, the transfer of the central
perspective from painting into theatre seems to have been a one-way transaction. It completely changed the conditions underlying visual perception in
theatre, without causing any remarkable reaction in the fine arts. The medieval and Elizabethan stage allowed the spectators to circle around, to move

to and fro, to follow the action from at least three different sides, from different angles and perspectives, without running the risk of suffering an obstructed or distorted view. However, the introduction of the Italian stage with a central perspective, at the beginning of the seventeenth century, resulted in a radical reduction of the spectator's possible movements and positions and, consequently, the viewpoints and perspectives open to the spectator. The central perspective provided by the painted flats required the spectator to take up the fixed position of an external observer, who alone is guaranteed a complete overview. Since, however, the painted buildings and landscapes could only be perceived without distortion from one place in the auditorium — the royal seat — the transfer of the central perspective from painting into the theatre also forced the majority of the spectators into positions which only allowed a distorted version of the central perspective. The only undistorted view open to the ordinary spectator was that directed toward the other spectators in the auditorium. The perceptive habits and behavior of the spectators were deeply affected by this transaction.[2]

Exchange processes do not only occur from outside theatre to within, but also in the other direction, from theatre to the outside world. In 1621, on October 21, Don Rodrigo Calderón, Marqués de Siete Iglesias, was publicly executed on Plaza Mayor in Madrid. He had ruthlessly exploited his position and privileges for his own benefit and was sentenced to death for corrupt administration. Though he was one of the most hated persons in Spain, he managed to become a popular hero and to turn the day of his execution into the "most glorious day of the century," as a contemporary wrote in his diary, by borrowing a theatrical gesture and performing it perfectly as he mounted the scaffold. Don Rodrigo elegantly threw the hem of his cloak over his shoulder — an action executed by contemporary actors after a brilliant performance before exiting to provoke the applause of the audience. The borrowed gesture was able to turn shame into fame. People no longer referred to Don Rodrigo as an immoral criminal, but as a man of honor, dignity, and noble self-control.[3]

As stated above, the history of European theatre and culture abounds in examples of exchanges that have taken place between theatre and other cultural domains. The exchange processes may be connected with, or, better, may be interpreted with reference to, a diversity of aspects and problems, as the few examples given above already intimate. The chapters in this volume focus on aspects of perception, body, and language. Although some draw on material from the seventeenth and eighteenth centuries, they are mainly concerned with problems that have become virulent in the twentieth century. Thus, the core of this book deals with exchange processes that have taken place in this century and have had an impact on perception, body, and language in (mostly Western) theatre and culture.

During the first decades of the twentieth century, a radical cultural change took place in Europe. It strongly shook the traditional modes, habits, and patterns of perception, thought, and action prevailing in everyday life as well as in science and in the arts. This change resulted in the emergence of totally new styles of thinking and models of behavior. Most of all, it deeply affected perception, body, and language.

Technological innovations of the nineteenth century such as the steam railway, telegraph, photograph, telephone, phonograph, film, and automobile were already increasingly erasing the difference between time and space. As a result, completely new conditions of perception arose, particularly through the process of progressive industrialization and urbanization. After the turn of the century, electrification and automation spread rapidly, to such an extent that they increasingly determined everyday life too — particularly everyday life in the big urban centers. It was mainly speed of movement (as embodied in the railway, the tramway, the automobile, etc.) and the simultaneity of most diverse sensory impressions so typical of life in a city (as shown in Walter Ruttmann's film *Berlin — Die Sinfonie der Großstadt* [1927; Berlin — Symphony of a City]) which forced a permanent and rapid change of perspective and focus and resulted in a perpetual concentration on, and treatment of, the senses, particularly seeing and hearing.

Even on the apparently solid ground of physics, new theories appearing at the turn of the century totally challenged the traditional ideas of absolute space, time, and reality, suggesting that the perception of these things depended on the position of the observer and overturning ideas which were widely accepted within the mechanistic worldview valid since Galileo. Albert Einstein's theory of relativity (1905) and Max Planck's quantum theory (1900) gave rise to the idea that the observation of events in space and time depends on the relative motions of the observer and the observed, so that the act of observation itself directly affects the observed. The classical concept of an observer whose — quasi-objective — observations are generally held to be valid and eternally reproduced by all other observers was shattered. For it is the relations between the observer and observed that determine the measurement of distance and time. One observer's measurement will be different from that made by another, since the object is changed by the very process of being measured. While such phenomena play a vital role when high velocity or microscopic objects are involved, nonetheless, the awareness of such occurrences has had its impact on human consciousness and the role of the observer. The observer is part of the system; the results of observations depend on the observer's own motion in relation to the observed object, with the result that the observed object will not remain the same as it was before.

At the turn of the century, perceptive modes of appreciating the fine arts and music were doubted — modes of perception which had "molded" ways of seeing and hearing since the Renaissance. Impressionism revolutionized the act of seeing by focusing on the optic experience, on the visualization of the moment. The impressionist picture consists of colors — light and dark, warm and cold — and lines, which are related to each other or which challenge the beholder to relate each to the other in order to be able to perceive the specific moment. Cubism went even further by destroying the perspectively structured picture space. Thus, the position of the beholder as a fixed external observer was undermined.

Almost contemporary with the emergence of cubism, a similar revolution took place in the realm of music. In *Entwurf einer neuen Ästhetik der Tonkunst* (1906; Toward a New Aesthetic of Sound) Ferruccio Busoni challenged the composer to break the boundaries of tone, to go beyond the restrictions of tonal music. Arnold Schönberg's first atonal pieces followed a little later in 1908/1909. Thus, modes of perception, which Europeans, for approximately three hundred years, had thought exclusively determined their view of themselves, the world, and their position in it, were fundamentally challenged.

As early as 1890, James G. Frazer published *The Golden Bough: A Study in Comparative Religion* in two volumes (which he expanded to thirteen volumes by 1936). Drawing on a wealth of diverse material, Frazer attempted to prove that striking analogies exist between the ideas and actions of so-called primitive peoples and the customs and institutions of Western culture and that these are deeply rooted in the collective unconscious. Thus, the belief that Western culture was naturally superior to other cultures, a vital assumption close to the hearts of Europeans in the nineteenth century, was obliterated at one blow. At the same time, the concept of one European view of the world, valid for all, was shattered.

This fundamental change in the perception of the world was accompanied by a change in attitude toward the body, bodily practices, body images, and movement patterns. In industry, the invention of the conveyer belt, refa-time measurement, Taylorization, and so on required the human body to adapt its movements to the given rhythm of a machine. At the same time, various societies such as the physical culturists, the Garden City Association, and the *Lebensreform* and *Wandervogel* movements claimed to liberate the body from its existing constraints. These, they believed, stemmed from an inappropriate sense of shame and from external conditions brought about by increasing urbanization and industrialization. Thus, such movements propagated a thorough reform of lifestyle in all spheres — in nutrition, hygiene, clothing, housing, leisure activities, sexuality. They believed vegetarianism and abstinence from alcohol and nicotine were as much a prerequisite for the development of a new attitude toward the body as was natural care of the body: bathing, taking a shower, massage, gymnastics, sports, and clothes which did not restrict movement.

> What we need is a natural feel for the body. And this can be gained through our care of it. Can a person who gets out of a bath, cleansed, refreshed, and filled with a deep, good feeling in all the limbs so that the body swells and the life in every part of him brings him alive — can that person bring himself to destroy such good feeling through tight, restrictive clothing? Will he want to do it, after he has discovered, in working, leisure activities, running, swimming, riding, gymnastics, fencing, or whatever, that his body is, as it is, good and beautiful? It will only torment him when this feeling cannot be expressed through his clothing.[4]

A declaration of war was made on bodices and corsets, gentlemen's ties and starched collars, and any other kind of restrictive clothing. As the loose-styled, casual clothing proposed by the reformists became popular, a new body image was introduced and widely accepted.

The hygiene movement won its first battles in housing. In Prussia a law was drawn up in 1903 which specified, for the first time, the minimum dimensions of accommodation, defining the minimum requirements of "air-space" and "floor-space" to which a person was entitled. In 1899 the Garden City Association was founded in Britain, and the first garden city (Letchworth in Hertfordshire) soon followed, with healthier housing a priority.

The liberation from restrictive and deforming clothes set the body, so long immobile, in motion. The Ramblers' Association promoted extensive hiking tours in the countryside surrounding the cities. Other associations encouraged different kinds of sports, and the motto "outdoor exercise" was particularly taken up by the many naturist and nudist movements. The new ideal of a "natural" body, moving freely in "air" and "light," was equally advocated for both sexes.

The newly evolving concept of a dynamic body was mainly practiced and propagated by gymnastic schools, which began to spring up across Europe from the turn of the century. In 1911 Emile Jaques-Dalcroze, a movement teacher from Geneva, opened a "College of Music and Rhythm" in Hellerau. His aim was to develop a new rhythmical consciousness in his students, which he understood to be "the power to re-present every sequence of, and relation between, units of time, in all their nuances of effort and speed." In order to acquire this ability, his students should learn how to move to rhythm. Movement of the body in certain rhythmic patterns was intended to develop the faculty of perceiving rhythm. Jaques-Dalcroze also strove for the development of the capacity to perceive different kinds of rhythms simultaneously. "In order to arouse the feeling for rhythm [in a child], it is vital that we do so by making different parts of the body execute movements which represent different time values."[5] The movement patterns advocated by Jaques-Dalcroze revolutionized traditional European forms of movement, in that they consciously followed a polyrhythmic structure. Before World War I, only very few artists could master such movement patterns, so that they represented a rather peripheral phenomenon. In the twenties, however, polyrhythmic music gained enormous popularity in the shape of the Shimmy and the Charleston, imported from America, which follow different rhythms simultaneously. These dances led to a broad acceptance of the new movement patterns.

In accordance with the new ideal of a dynamic body, dance gained a prominent position and particular relevance within the system of different art forms. Free Dance, as created and advocated by Geneviève Stebbins, Loïe Fuller, Isadora Duncan, and Ruth St. Denis, broke with the conventions of the classical ballet; it did away with dancing on point, pirouettes, and the inevitable "tutu." Instead of the movements fixed by the rhetorical code of the classical ballet, the individually interpreted movement patterns of Free Dance followed the "natural" body movement. In the beginning, such movements were modeled after body images represented on Greek vases, terra-cotta ware, and statues; nonetheless, they aimed toward a totally "new movement." "The dancer of the future will be a Woman whose body and soul have developed so in harmony that the movement of her body is the natural language of her soul."[6]

If the moving body was intended to become the language of the soul, then the implication was that language no longer fulfilled this function. Friedrich Nietzsche alludes to similar findings when he complains that language is "diseased," its strength "exhausted," incapable of expressing "strong emotional feelings."[7] Thus, as early as 1876, Nietzsche declared the crisis in culture, which would be much discussed at the turn of the century, to be a crisis of language. Hugo von Hofmannsthal's Lord Chandos describes it in his *Lord Chandos-Brief* (1902; *Letter of Lord Chandos*) as the inability of language to function as a tool which structures and controls perception, knowledge, and action: "the abstract words, which the tongue must naturally serve in order to bring any kind of pronouncement to the light of day, crumbled in my mouth like rotten fungus. It all crumbled into bits and the term came to describe nothing at all."[8] The language crisis, accordingly, affected the linearity of writing as well as logocentrism in general. Thus, it is small wonder that the change started from those two aspects.

In part, language ceded important functions — such as expressing emotions, communication, and information — to other media: to the body, painting, film. This loss of function and, implicitly, authority particularly affected written or printed language. The telephone, the gramophone, and somewhat later the radio and increasingly pictorial commercials also began to replace printed language in importance. In the context of urban life or of experimental art, language was used as pure graphic sign or as bits and pieces of dialogue which are then "mutated" into elements of a picture collage or sound montage. The simultaneity of the image and written texts, of noises, sounds, tunes, and linguistic sounds, broke through the linearity of writing and destroyed it. Even the reading process no longer followed a linear movement. The acoustic poems of the dadaists — for instance, Hugo Ball's *Caravan*— were designed as pictorial signs in a style later adopted by concrete poetry or as montages of textual parts which determined the structure of John Dos Passos' *Manhattan Transfer* or Alfred Döblin's *Berlin Alexanderplatz* and forced the eye to a nonlinear, multidimensional movement.

On the other hand, the language crisis also resulted in the construction of a multitude of "specialist languages" which, because of their particular terminology, were restricted in range. Since the terms of natural language were no longer able to "describe" the "whole," it became necessary to invent new terms for the "parts" as well as for the parts of the parts, and so on. Accordingly, natural language could no longer be understood and used as an "objective" representation of the world given by nature. Instead, it was assumed that language is only able to function as an instrument of description, knowledge, and communication in particular contexts.

The radical cultural change brought about by such alterations did not occur in consequence or as a sum total of single alterations which independently affected perception, body, and language. On the contrary, all the alterations mentioned above seem to have been interconnected. Thus, the accelerated speed of movement (the railway, tram, automobile) and the development of new movement patterns (reformed clothing, sports, gymnastics), combined with a change in the function of language and the loss of the fixed position of the external observer, caused new styles of perception, set the body in motion, and destroyed the linearity of writing. In other words, wherever change occurred in one of the three factors in question, the other two were also involved. It is as if they form a triangle in which each position depends on the other two and, inversely, affects them. Accordingly, cultural change can be described as a change in the triadic relation formed by perception, body, and language.

This triadic relation is unequivocally constitutive of theatre. In general, it is described as the relationship between spectator, actor, and dramatic text. Moreover, theatre has reshaped and reorganized these three factors and the relationship between them in a revolutionary way in the course of this century. Thus, it might be concluded that the tensile interaction between perception, body, and language works as a kind of focus point, where the different processes of change which have occurred in Western theatre and in Western culture during the course of the twentieth century meet and converge. Thus, theatre history can be understood and described as cultural history. Moreover, it follows that theatre studies should take cultural studies as the frame of reference, where the interaction between perception, body, and language is the focus of study.

This hypothesis seems all the more plausible when it is taken into account that processes of change have often been performed as processes of exchange. Different kinds of perception modes, body images, movement patterns, uses of language, etc., are constantly being circulated back and forth between theatre and the other media, art forms, institutions, cultural performances, and behavior patterns of everyday life. The aim of this book is to highlight and investigate such exchanges. From different perspectives and problems, the chapters examine the particular course taken by an exchange as well as its specific function within larger processes of change.

The chapters are grouped in four sections. The first section is devoted to exchanges within Western culture. Although some elements that have been transferred into European theatre from the non-Western cultures are considered, the question of exchange between cultures remains subordinate. This is the focus of the second section, which deals with theatre interculturalism. Here examples are taken not only from the Western stage, but also from the African, Chinese, and Japanese theatres. This section closes with a performance analysis of Tadashi Suzuki's production of Anton Chekhov's *Three Sisters* and introduces the third section, which highlights the individual performance as the place of exchange. The fourth section of the book comprises chapters which discuss different theoretical models of exchange.

This structure seems to suggest that three different approaches can be applied to the study of theatre — historical (represented by the first section and parts of the second), analytical (parts of the second and third sections), and theoretical (the fourth section). However, this impression is deceptive;

though in simple terms a shift of focus from the predominantly historical approach to a more analytical or theoretical approach can be determined, it is impossible to pursue theatre historiography without applying theoretical and analytical tools; to analyze performance without theoretical and historical context; to theorize on theatre without drawing on historical material and the analysis of one's own aesthetic experience of theatrical performance. Thus, it seems fitting to close this part of the introduction with some methodological reflections.

What is meant by the claim that the focus shifts to a predominantly historical approach?

Certain phenomena in the distant or even recent past of theatre history attract attention — a particular use of the body, place of performance, construction of space, a specific way of manipulating objects, a certain use of sounds and noises, some sentences of a review of a visiting performance. For various reasons, such things are so striking that they demand to be understood — their context, the conditions on which they are based, their function and meaning. Furthermore, they are able to arouse interest because they seem to refer to various theories always present in the back of the mind — theories to do with the civilizing process, cultural change, aesthetic perception, meaning constitution, the basic anthropological condition, the possibility of a universal language, etc. Whether such theories are implicitly or explicitly articulated, they condition and determine the perspective and methodology by which the various sources and documents (including video recordings of performances) will be analyzed. While even a historical approach aims to understand and explain the phenomenon concerned in its historical and cultural context, nonetheless, since there is no understanding *per se*, it will always be an understanding within a certain framework provided by a theoretical principle. And since these principles, in turn, may be challenged in the course of the investigation, historical research can even disprove the very theory which inspired and triggered it.

A similar dialectic works in performance analysis. Since it is not possible to analyze a performance by considering every detail, choices have to be made concerning the aspects on which the analysis is going to focus. If, for example, the activities of the performers in a particular space or the activities of the spectators have been chosen as the particular focus, it is impossible to refer to everything performed and displayed, since such things are performed and displayed in a permanent flow. In order to structure this flow it has to be segmented. However, the very segmentation depends on certain prerequisites such as the point of departure or the aims of the investigation. Thus, before embarking on the enterprise of even choosing a focus, the problem(s) to be tackled in the analysis must be formulated. These might be diverse: What is the function of the recurring allusion to Baroque theatre in Ralf Långbacka's *Don Giovanni* (1989)? What are the conditions under which an international audience is able to receive Robert Wilson's *King Lear* (1990) production? How, and in what respect, did the transformation of the genre of colonial exhibition in Coco Fusco and Guillermo Gómez-Peña's performance in *Two Undiscovered Amerindians Visit . . .* (1992) challenge the spectator? What is it that entitles artists like Hermann Nitsch, Joseph Beuys, or Marina Abramović to perform a ritual not only in their own eyes but also in the judgment of the other participants, the spectators? Clearly, such questions are formulated on the basis of particular theoretical premises and thus create a similar position as in historical research. Although the analysis aims to answer questions which are inspired by various theoretical premises, it may be necessary to modify or even abandon these very premises because the process of analysis is also shaped and organized by the concrete material of the performance under consideration, which, in its turn, has a certain history of its own.

Where a predominantly theoretical approach is taken, the aim is either to develop a new theory or to modify, confirm, or disprove an existing one, whether it be a theory of language, an aesthetic theory, a theory of dramatic dialogue, a theory of identity, or a theory of postmodernism. Thus, examples from theatre history as well as from contemporary performance are chosen which promise to promote such goals. The theoretical approach is usually founded on the results of both historical studies and performance analysis. However, it may happen that the theoretical involvement with the concrete historical and aesthetic material yields new insights on the historical or aesthetic phenomenon which not only shake the theory they were meant to support (or affirm a theory they were meant to disprove), but, moreover, challenge the state of theatre historiography altogether or identify a new mode of aesthetic perception.

Thus, the conclusion can be drawn that the traditional distinctions in theatre studies between theatre historiography, performance analysis, and theory are senseless. Theatre historiography is never without theory and seldom without performance analysis — just as there is no theory without theatre historiography and performance analysis and no performance analysis without theory and theatre historiography.[9] To label an approach historical, analytical, or theoretical, therefore, only indicates the prevailing tendency of a study. In this sense, the first seven chapters of this volume may be classified as historical, the following six as performance analysis, and the remaining six as theoretical.

Whichever approach prevails, each chapter in its own way, explicitly or implicitly, deals with the question of the boundaries which separate theatre from other art forms, media, cultural performances, institutions, and everyday life in twentieth century Western culture. For each exchange between another cultural domain and theatre which is discussed here challenges the established concept of theatre — each results in a shift of the boundaries between theatre and life. In this respect, all exchange can be regarded as an attempt to negotiate the limits between theatre and other cultural domains and to redefine them.

In the seventeenth century most Western European languages used the term *theatrum* or *theatre* to refer to a multitude of diverse activities — irrespective of an increasingly metaphorical use of such terms. The term *theatre* signified any raised space, where something worth being seen and observed was set up or happening — be it a fountain or an execution, a comedy or an operation, an exposition of rare *naturalia* or a funeral procession. Moreover, the term was used in the titles of many philosophical, theological, moral, literary, historical, biographical, scientific, technological, geographical, and medical treatises. An abundance of publications which took the term *theatre* or *theatrum* as part of the title flooded the European book market: *Theatrum Morum* (Prague, 1608), *Theatrum Veterum Rhetorum, Oratorum, Declamatorum quos Sophistes Nominabant Graeces* (Paris, 1620), *Theatrum Europaeum* (Frankfurt, 1634–1738), *Theatrum S. Casimiri quo ipsius prosapiae, vita, miracula pompa in eiusd. apotheos Vilnae Lith.* (Antwerp, 1604), *Theatrum Pacis, oder Friedensschauplatz aller fürnehmbsten Friedens-Instrumenten und Tractaten* (Nuremberg, 1663–1685), *Theatrum Chemicum* (Argentorati, 1613–1662), *Theatrum Florae* (Paris, 1622), *Theatrum Insectorum* (London, 1634), *Theatrum Machinarum* (Nuremberg, 1661), *Theatrum Orbis Terrarum* (Antwerp, 1570), to mention just a few. In Germany, it was not until the end of the eighteenth century that the term was restricted to a particular institution, its buildings, and its products. Thus, in the seventeenth century the term *theatre* not only implied a variety of diverse meanings, but even oscillated between different kinds of institutions and cultural performances. The limitation of the term at the end of the eighteenth century seems to be a result of intense negotiations on the concept of theatre, particularly on the future exclusion of certain exchanges from specific cultural domains into theatre.[10]

In the twentieth century the inverse process can be observed. Exchanges taking place between all kinds of media, art forms, cultural performances, institutions, everyday life, and theatre are renegotiating the concept of theatre. Each exchange discussed in the following chapters is part of an ongoing process, in which the boundaries between theatre and other cultural domains are permanently reassessed, a process which constantly redefines the whole concept of theatre.

ART STUDIES, CULTURAL STUDIES, MEDIA STUDIES? THOUGHTS ON THE "INTERDISCIPLINARY" NATURE OF THEATRE STUDIES

The redefined concept of theatre requires a particular kind of interdisciplinary research. For it contains three different, yet interrelated, meanings of the term *theatre*: theatre as an art form, as a genre of cultural performance, and as a medium. Each of these meanings entails and engenders different kinds of interdisciplinary and comparative approaches which, *in summa*, affirm and illustrate the idea of theatre studies as an "interdisciplinary" field *par excellence*.

As a particular art form, theatre can be defined as a performing art that unfolds in different kinds of spaces using heterogeneous materials such as the human body, voice, various kinds of objects, light, music, language, and sounds to create the theatrical performance as its product or work. Such a work is, of course, of a transitory, ephemeral nature. It does not dispose of a fixed artifact that could be conveyed and handed down to another generation. The product of theatre is consumed and vanishes in the very process of being produced. This seems to be one of the commonly acknowledged differences between theatre and all other art forms which create works of a more permanent nature — those which have a fixed and transportable artifact, such as the fine arts, literature, film, and, to a certain extent, music (musical scores).

However, this seemingly indisputable fact entails a certain inconsistency. On the one hand, it refers to the relationship between different art forms within a theatrical performance and, on the other, to the relationship between theatre as a performing art and other art forms.

It is widely believed that not only are different kinds of materials and sign systems used within a theatrical performance, but also different art forms, which are constituted by one of the material or sign systems used in a performance: the fine arts — because of the theatre building, particularly the stage, auditorium, set, and costumes; music — because of the musical sign; or literature — because of the linguistic signs. If this premise is accepted, the question arises as to how it may happen that the individual art forms participating in a theatrical performance create fixed artifacts whereas the performance itself does not. That is to say, how are the different art forms interrelated within a performance such that they do not play a role as fixed artifacts but as elements in a performative process? In one attempt to answer this question, Richard Wagner developed the concept of a *Gesamtkunstwerk* (total work of art) that was intended to be a general organizing principle according to which the different art forms were to be employed in order to make a performance. This concept, however, was fiercely attacked by Edward Gordon Craig half a century later: "How can all arts be combined to make one art? It can only make one joke."[11] Instead, Craig argued that a theatrical performance uses material elements which, though they may function as the smallest constitutive elements or units of other arts (such as line and color, words, movement), are, nonetheless, not to be identified with any specific art form.

If neither approach is wholly accepted the problem remains crucial. What kind of interplay between different art forms occurs in a performance that is able to transform their fixed artifacts into elements of a performative process? How does a theatre performance function as an "interart work"? This can only be appropriately dealt with in the context of comparative art or interart studies. Here the theatre performance can be taken as a model by which exemplary investigations into the ways and modes of interplay between the arts are made possible. Whatever the method of procedure and results may be, the performative mode will be focused upon as the fundamental category.

It will also play a key role concerning the second problem, namely, the question of the relationship between theatre and other art forms. I have suggested a certain consensus among scholars who regard the performative process as the basic difference between theatre and some other art forms. However, there seems to be good reason to question such a consensus — reason provided by research of recent years and by recent developments in the arts in particular.

Research on oral cultures and on European medieval culture has emphasized the fact that poetry did not — or did not originally — exist as written text but as part of an oral tradition — i.e., it existed by being performed in front of an audience. The voice and the body of the orator/narrator were the means of its realization and mediation. It was created in the performative process. In this sense, poetry was not defined by any written artifact but by the performative process in which it was recited and received.

This performative mode has regained enormous importance recently in the field of literature. Authors no longer restrict their activities to producing texts. They also travel extensively, reading their texts to various audiences eagerly gathered to listen to the voice of the poet, the novelist, the chronicler, and to enjoy the author live. Furthermore, some audiences not only flock to get in touch with the "real" author but also assemble for readings from the works of past authors performed by actors. Poetry readings clearly play an important part in contemporary Western cultural life. A particularly remarkable reading was organized and performed by the group Angelus Novus in Vienna in 1986 at the Vienna Künstlerhaus. Members of the group took turns to read the 18,000 verses of the *Iliad* in twenty-two hours, nonstop, to an attentive audience. The audience's attention was particularly attracted to the specific voice of each reader, foregrounded as each one succeeded the next, thus interrupting the flow of the hexameters only through the sudden marked differences in vocal quality. At such events, the mode of literary existence is, quite emphatically, displayed as a performative mode.

This is equally true of other contemporary art forms. In the fine arts, it is most obvious in terms of so-called body art. Here the live body of the artist is presented and displayed in front of an audience. But even in the field of landscape art, of light, video, and other installations, the performing mode dominates. In such cases, the beholder is challenged to move around the installation and to interact with it while other visitors may observe her/him doing so. The roles of performer and spectator alternate accordingly. Thus, visiting a museum or an art-site nowadays turns out to mean participating in a performance — partly as performer and partly as spectator.

This was all the more true for actions by artists like Joseph Beuys, Wolf Vostell, Yvonne Rainer, Ann Halprin, those of the "Fluxus" group, or the Viennese actionists who, in the sixties and early seventies, inaugurated the new genre of performance art.

Music can also be said to be a performative art — if the existence of musical scores is excluded. Before the invention of the gramophone, music was usually played before an audience. Contemporary music foregrounds and emphasizes this characteristic feature in quite a remarkable, even sensational manner. Take percussion music, for example. In recent times, the field of percussive improvisations has expanded to an extent that can hardly be surveyed anymore. Here the heart and core of contemporary music is to be found — from "avant-garde," "ethno," and "New Age" to "techno." Percussion music is generally characterized as music performed and received by the whole body. It includes permanent passages from the aesthetic dimension of music to the ritualistic and ceremonial one. Here the performative mode is absolutely constitutive.

From the examples listed above we can conclude that the performative mode can no longer act as the criterion by which theatre may be distinguished from other art forms. Rather, it seems as if the performative mode actually enables all the different art forms to be related to each other. This does not only mean that the interplay of different art forms in a theatrical performance and the relationship between theatre and other art forms are to be investigated by focusing on the performative mode but that the performative mode seems to be a fundamental category in itself in contemporary inter-disciplinary arts studies. Since theatre studies engaged as arts studies deals explicitly and at great length with the performative mode (particularly acting, singing, and dancing) and its unique aestheticity, it seems only natural that it should claim a leading part in future interdisciplinary arts studies for itself — at least, as far as the performative mode is concerned. For, as the perfor-mative genre *par excellence*, theatre can serve as a model when investigating other arts.

As a particular genre of cultural performance, theatre is characterized by the same fundamental features as other such cultural performances (for in-stance, rituals, ceremonies, festivals, games, sports competitions, political as-semblies, election campaigns, circus performances, colonial exhibitions, lec-tures, concerts, etc.). That is to say, events which include "a definitely limited time span, a beginning and end, an organized program of activity, a set of performers, an audience, and a place and occasion of performance."[12] The term *cultural performance* was coined by the American anthropologist Milton Singer at the end of the fifties. He introduced it in order to describe "partic-ular instances of cultural organization, e.g. weddings, temple festivals, recita-tions, plays, dances, musical concerts etc."[13] According to Singer, a culture articulates its self-image and self-understanding in the cultural performance, which it then represents and exhibits to its members as well as to outsiders. He defines cultural performances accordingly "as the most concrete observ-able units of a cultural structure."[14]

In terms of the characteristic features listed by Singer, theatre does not only differ from other genres of cultural performance, but also shares some features with others. That is to say, the borderlines between theatre and other genres of cultural performance are permanently redefined and, thus, highly permeable to different kinds of exchange processes taking place between them. While, for instance, the Elizabethan theatre strove to delineate itself clearly from all kinds of rituals such as the rites of May, exorcism, and chari-vari (cf. Shakespeare's *A Midsummer Night's Dream, Twelfth Night, King Lear* or John Webster's *The Duchess of Malfi*), the Puritans identified theatre with such rituals and this, in the end, resulted in the closing down of the theatres. On the other hand, at approximately the same time in France and Germany a process started which can be described as the theatricalization of other genres of cultural performance. Thus, for instance, the festivals at the court of Louis XIV or public executions, where, at least in Germany, such theatricalization was in effect until the end of the eighteenth century.

In this century the trend has been toward the annulment of rigid demarcations between theatre and other genres of cultural performance. In manifestos and through their own productions, theatre avant-gardists in the first decades claimed to transform theatre into a festival (for instance, Peter Behrens, Adolphe Appia, Emile Jaques-Dalcroze, Max Reinhardt), a ritual (Georg Fuchs and Antonin Artaud), a political assembly (Vsevolod Meyerhold and Erwin Piscator), or a circus performance (Boris Arvatov, Sergei Radlov, Sergei Eisenstein). Similar ideas were pursued and radicalized in experimental theatre from the sixties (for example, Jerzy Grotowski, Peter Brook, Ariane Mnouchkine, Dario Fo, Klaus Michael Grüber, Eugenio Barba, the Squad Theatre, the Bread and Puppet Theatre) as well as by a number of performance artists.

Conversely, an enormous theatricalization of other genres of cultural performance exists in contemporary Western culture. It can be traced back to political ceremonies in the twenties, for example, and it became most prominent in all the public events staged by the Nazis. It molds the character of sports competitions, not only the Olympic Games (noticeably the opening and the closing ceremonies), but also a number of specific genres such as figure skating and boxing and wrestling matches. The theatricalization of concerts, particularly pop, is also quite significant.

This means that the theatrical performance is to be investigated as *one* genre of cultural performance which is defined by its very position within a whole system of cultural performances that makes up a particular culture. Thus, it would seem wise to study a theatre performance of a given culture and epoch in relation and comparison to other genres of cultural performance effective at that time, to analyze similarities and differences and to retrace the processes of exchange going on between them which constantly shape and reshape the system of cultural performance as a whole, as well as identifying the position and function of any such genre, including the theatrical performance.

Thus, it is hardly surprising that defining theatre as a particular genre of cultural performance meant opening up perspectives and possibilities for interdisciplinary approaches in cultural studies. For it led directly to theatre researchers' beginning to explore different kinds of cultural performance: festivals (Fischer-Lichte 1990b and 1993; Lazarowicz 1981), religious rituals (Baumbach 1995), ceremonies of penance (Kotte 1994), political ceremonies (Das Gupta 1988; Schramm 1995), funeral processions (Fischer-Lichte 1990b), executions (Carlson 1995). A domain was entered that other disciplines had already claimed for themselves, even if only recently.

Traditionally, in dealing with Western cultures, studies in the humanities proceeded from the assumption that a culture articulates its self-understanding in texts and monuments which are believed to be the privileged if not sole object of research. Whereas in oral cultures the importance of the cultural performance was conceded, studies in the humanities have taken a long while to accept such premises with respect to Western cultures. Thus, it was — with rare exceptions — not before the eighties that the humanities took up the challenge proposed by the concept of the cultural performance and investigated festivals (Biver 1979; CRAR 1994; Davis 1975; Heers 1986; Jacquot 1956–1975; Moine 1984; Roberti 1980; Strong 1991), political ceremonies (Apostolidès 1981; Burke 1992; Cannadine and Price 1982; Kepplinger 1992 and 1993; Meyer 1992; Sarcinelli 1987), executions (Foucault 1975; Garland 1985; Muchembled 1992; Nye 1984; Van Dülmen 1988), funeral rites (Arce 1958; Giesey 1960; Huntington and Metcalf 1979), storytelling and concerts (Charles 1989; Schwab 1971; Zumthor 1983 and 1984).

The conclusion may be drawn that the cultural performance has only recently become the object of research in a number of disciplines. Besides theatre studies, it has also become a concern of history, sociology, political science, psychology, anthropology, philosophy, musicology, art history, archaeology, and communication science. This seems to indicate a change of paradigm in two respects. Whereas the majority of the disciplines listed above focus traditionally on texts and monuments as the objects of their research, here a shift has taken place to the transitory and ephemeral events of the cultural performance. On the other hand, while the identity of each discipline was formerly defined by recourse to certain texts and monuments only, the shift of focus to the cultural performance annuls such a definition. For the same genre of cultural performance may become the object of research in different disciplines. In terms of specific approaches to a problem, it would make good sense, for example, if public executions were investigated by historians, anthropologists, and theatre historians. Here a new kind of interdisciplinary approach is evolving.

In terms of developing adequate comparative and interdisciplinary approaches, theatre studies is in a good position to make a substantial contribution. For in order to investigate the cultural performance, four aspects dealt with in theatre studies at great length are indispensable:

1. the performative process itself (i.e., the performance in the narrow sense of the word);
2. its production (i.e., the devices of its staging and fabrication);

3. the employment of the performers' bodies; and

4. the spectators' behavior and perception.

All the approaches developed for and applied to myriads of studies on the art of using the body in theatrical performances, for example, can be made fertile when examining the use of the performer's body in different kinds of cultural performance. At the end of the nineteenth century the particular use of the human body seemed to be the only criterion for distinguishing theatrical performances from other genres of cultural performance. While in rituals, sports competitions, circus performances, and executions the performers actually perform certain bodily actions — such as mutilating the body, running, walking a tightrope, torturing the body and beheading it — the actor in a theatrical performance only pretends to execute them. Boris Arvatov's *Theatre as Production*, published in 1922, formulated this difference with respect to the circus as follows: "The difference between theatre and circus consists of the following: while in theatre the actor only pretends to be superior, skillful, sensitive, inventive, brave, and so on — in the circus he really is these things."[15]

Of course, this difference can only claim a very limited historical as well as cultural validity, if at all. First, actors in a theatrical performance usually execute bodily actions such as entering the stage, crossing it, sitting or lying down, gesturing, exiting. Additionally they may also perform acrobatics or even mutilate their own body — as in many performances nowadays — or execute torture (as in a medieval passion play — the reason why the performer playing Christ's part had to be replaced several times — or in the Living Theatre). On the other hand, there are a number of other kinds of cultural performance where performing an action also entails a certain "as if" — for example, in many festivals or even in wrestling. For this reason, it makes good sense to apply the model of how to describe and analyze the use of the human body onstage as developed in theatre studies to other cultural performances. Indeed, this is also valid regarding the other three aspects. That is to say, in the field of interdisciplinary cultural studies which deal with different genres of cultural performance, the potential contribution of theatre studies cannot be overestimated.

As a medium, theatre is defined by very specific conditions of perception and communication which are basically different from those of the printed media as well as the so-called new media. For theatre to occur, performers and spectators must gather together in a specific place for a specific duration of time. The printed media and the new media, on the other hand, liberate their users (readers/spectators) from space and time. Without having to move, events which are happening or have happened at different places at different times can be closely followed. Though physically immobile, the reader/spectator is able to travel at will through time and space with the help of the media. In theatre, production and reception are concurrent processes. While the physically present performers execute certain actions and present signs, the physically present spectators react directly by receiving the actions in one way or another and interpreting the signs in whatever way they choose. The performance is always realized in this sense as a process of face-to-face interaction between performer and spectator. Theatre, thus, is an event which happens in a community of physically present people, whereas the printed media and the new media are commonly used by individual people independently and in isolation from others (i.e., without any physical contact with either the producers or other recipients).

In terms of perception, it can be stated that the camera in the new media prescribes the focus and perspective to the spectators, while in theatre the spectators can let their eyes wander over the performance and choose the focus and perspective for themselves.

From its very beginnings, theatre studies has strongly emphasized this fundamental difference. One of the founders of German theatre studies, Max Herrmann, derived a first tentative program for the new discipline:

> The original meaning of theatre was derived from the fact that it was social play — played by all for all. A game in which everyone is a player — participants and spectators. . . . The spectator is involved as co-player. The spectator is, so to say, the creator of the theatre. So many participants are involved in forming the theatre event that the basic social nature of its character cannot be lost. Theatre always involves the social community. This point must not be neglected by theatre studies.[16]

This crucial difference has become constitutive for theatre studies.

However, theatre does not only demarcate itself from the other media. Even here various processes of exchange can be observed. On the one hand, theatre has incorporated the products of the new media into its repertory of theatrical signs. As early as the twenties Piscator, Eisenstein, and Meyerhold used film, radio speech, etc., in their productions as effective theatrical signs. Over the last thirty years such potential has multiplied through the electronic media. On the other hand, a certain theatricalization of the new media takes place when reality is not portrayed but, on differing levels and according to each different genre, is staged and fabricated in the news, a talk show, a political discussion, etc., or when the virtual space simulated by a computer is claimed to be theatre.

In terms of the function of the new media in theatre (i.e., the intermediality of a theatrical performance), the first question that arises is whether a basic difference can be found between the interplay of different art forms in a theatrical performance and its intermediality. Indeed, it seems that just as the fixed artifacts of other arts are transformed into theatrical signs and, thus, function as elements in a performative process, similar statements can be made regarding the use of other media in a theatre performance. They do not only function as theatrical signs, but also relinquish the particular conditions of perception and communication. For the spectators are able to let their eyes wander between the screen, or the monitor, and other places onstage. In this sense, the basic conditions of perception and communication in theatre are not affected. This is not to say that the introduction of the new media into theatre has not affected the spectators' mode of perception. Quite the contrary, it must be assumed that totally new perception modes were demanded in order to enable them to cope with the simultaneity of aural and visual perception as well as different kinds of visual perception. This may be similar to the contribution made by the fine arts when central perspective painting on a box-set stage was introduced, for example, or, in general, the introduction of a new type of space — proscenium, box-set, orchestra, *hanamichi*, etc. Thus, the question remains as to whether intermediality in a theatrical performance should be dealt with in a basically different way than merely the interplay of various arts. It would seem advisable to relate any research on intermediality in theatrical performance to relevant interart studies.

Theatre studies as media studies opens up another highly fascinating field of interdisciplinary studies — namely, processes of medial transformation. Since Denis Diderot's *Lettre sur les sourds et les muets* (1751) and Gotthold Ephraim Lessing's *Laocoön* (1766), there has been an ongoing discussion on the possibilities of medial transformation. In focusing on the relationship between the written text of the drama and the theatrical performance, theatre studies has taken an important part in this discussion and greatly contributed to it. Quite a number of theories — extensively based on semiotics — have been developed in order to explain this relationship and, in particular, the process of transformation from the script to the performance. Most scholars agree with the premise that a medial transformation cannot be described in terms of a process which transfers "content" from one medium to another without changing it (as milk can be transferred from a jug into a glass), for it results in a totally new product which is to be understood as a work *sui generis*, which can only be created under the conditions set by this specific medium.

Other than this rather "old" type of medial transformation, today there are quite a number of others: the transformation of a theatrical performance into a film or video recording, a film into a play, a play into a radio play or other forms of acoustic art. Whether, and to what extent, theoretical models which have been developed in the context of research on the transformation of the literary text of a drama into a theatrical performance can be applied to other types of medial transformations remains to be seen.

Another important aspect of interdisciplinary media studies concerns the change in function undergone by theatre in a media culture. Here two issues, above all, are at stake. It seems that contemporary theatre expressly reflects on the conditions of perception the new media have brought about either by incorporating them and experimenting with them, as, for instance, the Wooster Group does, or by totally renouncing them, as, for example, in productions by Peter Brook. Such reflections still remain to be taken up by theatre studies.

On the other hand, the media culture turns the particular situation of communication in a theatrical performance into a special event. Theatre appears to be one of the last residues where people can publicly communicate with each other. It is one of the very rare places where bodies can unfold their aura or even magic potential. In this context it seems highly relevant that theatre in contemporary Western culture also serves as a place of mediation between the past and the present. The bodily presence of the performer, in this sense, is endowed with a particular historical signature. For when plays of the occidental tradition are staged, from Aeschylus to Samuel Beckett, figures appear onstage whose history forms a part of our collective memory. However, they do not appear as in our dreams, imaginations, and memories or as in the new media — rather, they adopt a bodily appearance. The performance takes place as a nightly resurrection of the "dead." Moreover, because of the particular conditions of our media culture, it is precisely this aspect which is foregrounded and plays an important role in today's theatre. Such changes of function can only be observed and explained in the context of the role and function accorded to the new media in our culture. Even here an interdisciplinary approach is valid.

To sum up: whether theatre studies is pursued as art studies, cultural studies, or media studies, in each case it seems to represent an interdisciplinary field *par excellence*. There is good reason, therefore, to assume that theatre studies can serve as a paradigm as the humanities open up toward a new interdisciplinary approach.

PART I
Theatre as Culture

THEATRE AND THE CIVILIZING PROCESS
An Approach to the History of Acting

Theatre is a communal institution, representing and establishing relationships which fulfill social functions. The drama, the production, and the location of the performance all contribute to these functions. Of course, in general terms, we recognize this communal condition of theatre. Theatre historians regularly acknowledge that theatre and society are closely related.

Examples of this symbiotic relationship are more or less familiar. Aeschylus' *Oresteia* voiced new social and communal norms that were meant to define, if not control, the ways in which the Athenian citizens of different social strata were to live together. Shakespeare's *Richard III* demonstrated some of the consequences of Machiavellian politics, a method of stagecraft which, in its representation of statecraft, both fascinated and terrified the audiences of his time. Pedro Calderón de la Barca's *The Magnanimous Prince* presented the ideal action of a Christian martyr, thus polemicizing against any kind of apostasy from the true Catholic faith. Lessing's *Emilia Galotti* confronted the German audiences of the eighteenth century with the bourgeois ideals of a tender, sentimental father and his most virtuous daughter, both representatives of proper emotional and moral behavior.

As far as drama is concerned, all these cases prove the stage to be a highly appropriate arena for representing, or propagating, norms and ideas crucial to the given society. But to phrase the issue in this way may be misleading. We have to recognize that theatre is not just a medium for "transmitting" a play and its themes. Theatre expresses the society in which it occurs through a wide range of cultural systems: painting, music, costume, body movement, gestures, language, architecture, commentary, and so on. All these systems form an integral part of the culture as a whole, contributing to its norms and rules, expressing its signs and meanings. Even when transplanted onto the stage, they never cease to indicate their use and meaning in the general cultural context.

At the most basic level, everything in the theatre and the theatregoing process has meaning. Over the last twenty years, in particular, the field of semiotics has investigated these theatrical meanings, trying to distinguish the various codes at work in performance. Much valuable work has been done, although in the process, unfortunately, most theatre semioticians have separated theatre from history. In the process of breaking theatre into its many codes, semioticians have sometimes lost sight of one of the primary conditions of signs on the stage. A theatrical costume of a medieval king, for example, tells us that the person wearing this costume represents the historical and cultural conditions of a medieval king. The gestures and body movements of the actor have their cultural, not just theatrical, meanings. To a large extent, theatre depends upon the specific functions and developments of the cultural systems which it employs. Thus, we may say that not only the drama, which expresses in words and actions certain ideas and values of the society, but all the various cultural systems in the theatre contribute to its social functions. The theatre historian's challenge is to understand these interpretative cultural systems, to assess how the theatre shapes and is shaped by the fundamental ways of being and doing which constitute historical cultures.

In the case of drama, most scholars are aware that plays express a social perspective or worldview. Thus, we find books with titles such as *The Elizabethan World Picture, Shakespeare in His Own Age, Shakespeare and the Renaissance Image of Man*, and *The Artist and Society in Shakespearean England*. Sometimes they are too reductive in defining the supposed worldview, but at least the dramas are placed within a social picture. When we turn, however, to the other aspects of the theatre, almost nothing is written on how theatrical systems indicate, embody, or influence certain cultural systems. For instance, we need to investigate at the level of these systems how set relates to architecture and painting, how costume relates to clothing (not just "expresses a period style"), how acting represents and affects social and personal gestures, facial expressions, and body movements.

Works on acting do exist: *Acting Shakespeare, Elizabethan Acting*, or *The Performance Practice of Acting: The Eighteenth Century*. Up to a point, they explain certain aspects of historical acting, but they say little on how and why types of acting are related to, or derived from, a historically determined cultural context. Usually, the social context is merely assumed and circumscribed by a series of choice phrases and metaphors that are quite problematic. In turn, the historical changes in acting styles seem to be caused by very general aesthetic principles that guide the production of artworks within a given epoch, but have little or nothing in common with the historical and social situation in which they occur.

As a preliminary, let us consider the history of acting in order to illustrate some of the issues involved in a cultural history of theatre. At first sight, it seems appropriate to define acting as the ways in which the human body is shaped and presented on the stage. We say that the human body belongs to the realm of nature. It has organic traits; it has physical and physiological functions, needs, and purposes. It is a part of nature. Not surprisingly, all actor training puts great emphasis on these physical characteristics. The common aim is to strip away the superfluous or outer aspects (that inhibit expression) in order to discover the real, natural body.

Consequently, we would hardly be astonished to find that while the human body is defined in these terms, acting — the presentation of the body on the stage — is not primarily described or considered in historical terms. In fact, acting is primarily taught and learned in physical ways; cultural history, if taught and studied, is divorced from the idea of acting (and, thus, is perhaps considered by many actors to be insignificant or irrelevant). Acting teachers, for example, seldom know (or are prepared to teach) cultural history; they do not understand how to situate performance training within the cultural practices of history. Even history teachers when, and if, they consider acting tend to define it as a formal style (natural or artificial) rather than a cultural practice. History is but the overlay of "period styles," which can be taken care of by a costume, a few gestures, and some quickly learned methods of walking and sitting.

Yet the human body never exists as pure nature, apart from history. From the very beginning of life, culture starts to shape, restructure, and regulate the body and its physical needs and functions. The instinctual drives and the special modes of their articulation are formed by culture. Culture even has an effect on the shaping of the body development and adult form, through culturally determined factors, such as nutrition, hygiene, and public health. And, of course, each culture's ideas on valid, desirable, and ideal body types also exert extensive influence on the "natural" body. Thus, the human body should be seen as the result of a reciprocal process of the organic and the cultural, an interaction between individual nature and cultural context. The process begins at the moment of birth and continues until the moment of death. As a result, each individual body participates not only in the natural order but also in the symbolic order of culture. The body, like any other cultural phenomenon, is historically determined.

In *The Civilizing Process*, Norbert Elias has described and analyzed the history of the "European body" from the Middle Ages onward as a "structural change in people towards an increased consolidation of their affect controls, and therefore both of their experience (e.g., in the form of an advance in the threshold of shame and revulsion) and of their behaviour (e.g., in the differentiation of the implements used at table)."[1] He notes, for example, that in the Middle Ages people often walked and ran naked through the streets to the public bathhouse, where men and women had their weekly baths without any separation of the sexes. Medieval people ate from one common bowl, using their fingers not forks (which did not even exist yet as eating implements). The process of eating was accompanied by sniffing, belching, spitting, and farting. But from the Renaissance onward the threshold of shame and revulsion constantly advanced up to the early twentieth century, and people became more and more "civilized." Thus, the civilizing process transformed not only social practices but the very operation and manifestation of the body within society. As Elias points out, in great historical detail and with subtle analysis, this process was closely connected with a "long-term change in the social structure towards a higher level of differentiation and integration — for example, towards a differentiation and prolongation of the chains of interdependence and a consolidation of 'state controls.'"[2]

It seems plausible that these long-term changes in the structure and behavior of human personality were necessary prerequisites to certain cultural rearrangements and achievements in European history that promoted the general progress of culture. But Elias emphasizes that these changes cannot be judged or classified as the progressive march of history — at least not in the sense in which the nineteenth century understood and defined progress. Rather, the growth of "civilization" should be seen as the price, within elaborate conditions of order and control, that the European cultures had to pay for their technological, scientific, economic, and social changes. This argument, from a different perspective, is one that Michel Foucault also makes in his historical studies.

If we describe the European history of the human body in terms of the civilizing process, the question arises as to whether the history of acting might not also be investigated and explained in similar terms. For the actors' bodies, as presented on the stage, are likewise culturally conditioned in accordance with the actual state of the civilizing process. Moreover, the particular mode of their presentation onstage may contribute to this ongoing process by representing and propagating new models of self-presence and self-presentation for audience imitation. The actor promotes and ridicules modes of behavior both uncommon and common at the time. In such cases, acting not only mirrors but partakes in and contributes to the historical process of civilization and thus fulfills important social functions.

The connections between the art of acting and the social process of civilization can be seen by referring to the theatre of three different epochs, each marked by important social changes: the Baroque theatre; the bourgeois, illusionist stage of the eighteenth century; and the avant-garde theatre at the beginning of the twentieth century.

In examining some of the acting conventions of these three epochs, I shall draw upon handbooks and theories of acting instead of detailed descriptions or pictures of actual performances. I do not use these sources because they are especially privileged; nor do I rule out the value of detailed research on actual daily practices, from theatre to theatre, actor to actor. But for the convenience of quickly illustrating the issues here, these prescriptive materials provide us with clear definitions of the new norms and rules that were put forward and instituted. Needless to say, there is often a gap between theory and practice. While sufficient descriptive sources demonstrate that the prescriptions were not always followed or fulfilled, nevertheless, the use of key theoretical works can tell us much about an epoch and its cultural ideas. These works grant us a deeper insight into the intentions of acting and thus enable us to formulate a theory concerning possible connections between the art of acting and the civilizing process in European history of the last three centuries.

THE BODY AS A "TEXT" COMPOSED OF ARTIFICIAL SIGNS

The theory of acting in the Baroque period proceeded from the assumption that acting's aim was strong emotional impact. Emotional responses were excited by the representation of emotion onstage, and it follows that the representation of emotion was the most important task and function of acting.

In *Dissertatio de actione scenica* (Munich, 1727), the Jesuit priest Franciscus Lang summarized the rules to be observed in order to guarantee the most effective representation of emotions:

1. Admiration: Both hands outstretched above the chest and palms towards the audience.
2. Shame: The face turned away over the left shoulder and the hands calmly joined behind the back. This same result can be achieved by just the right hand when it is clenched and unclenched repetitively.
3. Entreating: Both hands upraised with the palms turned to the listener again and again. Also with the arms hanging down. Also with the hands clenched together.
4. Weeping and Melancholy: Both hands joined in the middle of the chest, either high on the chest or lower about the belt. Also accomplished by extending the right hand gently and motioning towards the chest. . . .
5. Reproach: Three fingers folded and the forefinger extended. . . .

6. Imploring: Both hands extended towards the one being spoken to as if about to embrace him. . . .

7. Repentance: Pressing the hands to the breast.

8. Fear: The right hand reaching towards the breast with the four digits visible while the rest of the body is bent, relaxed and bowed.[3]

Performing such gestures, the actor had to take care not to give up the so-called *crux scenica*, an angle of 90 degrees formed by his feet. Such a stance was interpreted as the correct representation of a firm ego which may be attacked by strong emotions but never overwhelmed as, for example, in the case of the Christian martyr or the ideal courtier. The gestures are rather complicated and required long and thorough training; the actors who mastered them became living examples of emotional and physical control. By imitating these models, members of the audience could adopt the approved behavior and complete self-discipline in their everyday lives.

When we look at the rules of acting laid down by Lang in the context of the sociogenesis of the seventeenth-century court society, as described by Norbert Elias, some striking parallels are revealed. Elias notes that, for the formation of this new society, the individual was required to learn self-discipline, calculation of future aims and purposes, and control of not only the emotions but the whole body:

> In tracing the sociogenesis of the court, we find ourselves at the centre of a civilizing formation that is both particularly pronounced and an indispensable precondition for all subsequent spurts and counter-spurts in the civilizing process. We see how, step by step, a warrior nobility is replaced by a tamed nobility with more muted affects, a courtly nobility. Not only within the Western civilizing process, but as far as we can see within every major civilizing process, one of the most decisive transitions is that of *warriors to courtiers*.[4]

It need scarcely be said, as indeed Elias notes, that "there are widely differing stages and degrees of this transition, this inner pacification of a society," but that gradually a more complex social order of expressing power and controlling behavior develops:

> Competition for prestige and royal favour is intense. "Affaires," disputes over rank and favour, do not cease. If the sword no longer plays so great a role as the means of decision, it is replaced by intrigue, conflicts in which careers and social success are contested with words. They demand and produce other qualities than did the armed struggles that had to be fought out with weapons in one's hand. Continuous reflection, foresight, and cal-

culation, self-control, precise and articulate regulation of one's own affects, knowledge of the whole terrain, human and non-human, in which one acts, become more and more indispensable preconditions of social success.[5]

The qualities and proprieties of the required social behavior coincided exactly with those promoted by the contemporary art of acting. Thus, the comportment of the actor could be presented and perceived as a generally acknowledged model that should be copied.

In turn, the actor responded to the ideal versions of behavior in the court society. Accordingly, the character presented by the actor who followed the rules was clearly marked as an ideal. Should the actor break the rules by running across the stage, falling down and rolling on the floor, lowering his hands below the waist, or standing with his feet parallel to each other, he indicated to the audience that the character he embodied had a weak identity — as in the case of a fool, madman, or tyrant. Undoubtedly, the tyrant and the madman acted as negative examples, not to be copied; the fool served to grant the spectators a feeling of superiority, to relieve them — at least temporarily — of the enormous pressures caused by the rigorous demands of self-control. The theatre, thus, assumed the cultural function of conveying an ideal behavior pattern which individuals then had to internalize and practice in order to adapt to the challenges of everyday court life.

THE BODY AS A "TEXT" COMPOSED IN
THE "NATURAL LANGUAGE OF THE EMOTIONS"

The growth of middle-class society in the eighteenth century was paralleled by the formulation of a new concept of art in general and of theatre in particular. Art was expected to be an imitation of nature (*imitatio naturae*) in accordance with the development of a materialistic culture. The new ideal of life and art was "naturalness." The behavior of aristocrats was criticized and reproached as artificial and even unnatural. Increasingly, if not exclusively, the tasks, functions, and aims of the theatre were to be redefined: the stage should imitate nature and so create an illusion or semblance of reality. Accordingly, the greatest German actor of this epoch, Conrad Ekhof, defined the task of acting thus: "The art of acting is to imitate nature through art and to approach it so closely that probabilities must be taken for truth, or to present events as naturally as if they were taking place right now."[6]

The development of a new art of acting was closely related to the contemporary discussion on original and primitive language. After Etienne de

Condillac claimed that human language was first a *langage d'action*, consisting of gestures and movements, it was a common and widespread idea that gestural language was a universal human language. Accordingly, most theoreticians of the period agreed that acting should be an imitation of this natural language. For instance, Georg Christoph Lichtenberg argued that actors should model themselves on the "involuntary language of gesture which passion, in all gradations, uses throughout the world. Man learns to understand it completely, usually before he is twenty-five. He is taught to speak it by nature and this so emphatically that it has become an art to make faults."[7] Nature's language had to be transferred to the stage in order to provide actors with desired patterns of natural behavior.

But in which ways could this be accomplished? Rémond de Sainte Albine suggested in *Le comédien* (1747) that the actor should identify with the dramatic character he enacted. For, as Sainte Albine argued, the actor who senses the emotions felt by the dramatic character would produce the appropriate gestural signs for this emotion automatically. Lessing, however, objected to this argument:

> Mr. Rémond de Sainte Albine, in his whole book, proceeds from the implied assumption that the external movements of the body occur as natural consequences of the internal condition of the soul, and thus follow spontaneously. Admittedly, it is true that everyone without special training is able to express to some extent the state of his soul by means of signs which can be perceived through the senses — in one way or another. Onstage, however, we want to see sentiments and passions expressed not just in a partial manner, not just in the imperfect way in which an individual would express himself in the same circumstances. We want rather to see them expressed as perfectly as possible, leaving no room for further improvement.[8]

As Lessing — and, along with him, Diderot — concluded, empathy could not be taken as a method for creating the natural signs of emotion onstage. Nor could the observation of people's gestures in everyday life serve as a method, because education spoils people by teaching them either to hide or to exaggerate their true emotions. Where, then, should actors find the natural language of emotions which was to be imitated? Two possible solutions were offered. The actor should search for them where they preserve their original expressiveness — in "savages," children, and the common people. The natural language of emotions might also be reconstructed with reference to the "Law of Analogy" whereby anything that occurs in the mind has its analogue in the body.

On the basis of the Law of Analogy, Johann Jakob Engel attempted in *Ideen zu einer Mimik* (1785–1786; Ideas on Mimesis) to make an exhaustive list and detailed description of all possible gestural signs which might represent character and emotion. He deduced and described the perfect representation of a sluggard as follows:

> Very significant is a head not carried erect on the shoulders; parted lips leaving the chin drooping; eyes with half of the eyeball hidden behind the eyelid; tottering knees; a belly stretched forward; feet turned inward; hands reaching straight into the pockets of the jacket, or even arms swinging freely. Who will not, at first sight, recognize there a limp and inactive soul, incapable of any attention, any interest, a soul, not really awake, without even enough energy to flex the muscles necessary to carry the body properly and to hold its limbs properly? Only a sluggard, being extremely dull and lazy, can present a posture so meaningless and soulless.[9]

Engel proceeds in a similar manner by deducing and describing the gestural representations of different emotions. Since, for example, happiness opens the soul wide, a person experiencing happiness will open the mouth with a smile and accelerate every movement. The body in this view serves as a perfect and natural means for expressing psychic experience.

The actor who observes the Law of Analogy transforms the human body into a perfect natural sign which expresses each emotion and psychic state of the dramatic character. Employed in this way, however, the body ceases to be perceived as sensual nature. The actor's body is thus presented as a cultural system which nature itself has created and defined as such: it becomes a composition of signs constituted by nature as a "text" which is "written" in the "natural language of emotion." While attempting to "read" and understand this text, the spectators supposedly forget that the actor's body is sensual nature and perceive and interpret it as a texture of signs which represent most adequately the emotions of a dramatic character.

Such treatment of the human body on the bourgeois illusionist stage corresponded very closely with certain tendencies which were fundamental to the formation and establishment of middle-class society, in part because eighteenth-century society claimed to restore the lost naturalness which court society had despised and neglected. Thus, middle-class society reestablished the "original" parallelism between nature and society. In that the theatre aimed to restore the original language of gestures in the art of acting, it served as a corrective force in the civilizing process which, under the influence of court society, had spoiled and deformed this language to the point that it had been almost completely lost in European culture. In turn, the demand for naturalness, while paying homage to the child and the "savage," served as a pretext for pushing ahead the civilizing process: the repression of instinctual drives (of the "animal" nature of humans) in order to assert a rigorous concept of virtue.

Thus, certain values that were basic and vital to middle-class society were passed off as demands made by nature itself. The theatre not only adopted this concept of nature but also explicitly propagated it: the positive dramatic characters — mostly the daughters, as in George Lillo's *The London Merchant* or Lessing's *Emilia Galotti*— were shaped as models of virtuous behavior and self-denial, while the actors who embodied them were supposed to present their bodies not as sensual nature but as a text composed of "natural signs" of goodness. The spectators should identify with the dramatic characters, copy their behavior, and thereby develop the individual sensibilities and the required new standards of virtue and renunciation that were prerequisites to the progress of bourgeois society.

THE BODY AS RAW MATERIAL FOR SIGN PROCESSES

At the beginning of this century, the representatives of avant-garde theatre across Europe unanimously negated the principles underlying the bourgeois illusionist stage as formulated in the eighteenth century and realized in the nineteenth century, which culminated in the realist and naturalist movements. Although one line of modernist theatre, from Anton Chekhov and Konstantin Stanislavsky to Harold Pinter and Peter Hall, continued to carry forward a realist tradition (usually treated ironically), most modern theatre turned away from it. The actor's body was no longer perceived as a text composed of natural signs for emotions but as raw material for sign processing with a wider field of reference than the emotions of a dramatic character. In order to realize their particular aims, the avant-gardists turned to the art of acting as developed and employed in the theatre of the Far East, in Japan, China, Bali, and India. Instead of creating an illusion of reality, they intended to lay open the conventional nature of the theatrical process, to foreground and theatricalize it, as Meyerhold explains:

> Neither the antique stage nor the popular stage of Shakespeare's time had any need for the scenery which the striving for illusion demands nowadays; nor was the actor merely a unit of illusion in those days. It was the

same in medieval Japan. From descriptions of Japanese theatrical performances, we know that special stage-assistants, known as *kurogo* and clad in
special black costumes resembling cassocks, used to prompt the actors in
full view of the audience. When the costume of an actor playing a woman's
part became disarranged at a tense moment in the drama, one of the *kurogo*
would quickly restore the graceful folds of the actor's train and attend to
his coiffure. In addition, they had the task of removing from the stage any
objects dropped or forgotten by the actors. After a battle, the *kurogo* would
remove fallen helmets, weapons and cloaks. If the hero died on the stage,
the *kurogo* would quickly cover the corpse with a black cloth and under the
cover of the cloth the "dead actor" would run off the stage. When the
course of the action required darkness on stage, the *kurogo* would squat
down at the hero's feet and illuminate his face with a candle on the end of
a long stick. To this day the Japanese preserve the acting style of the days
of the creators of Japanese drama.[10]

As can be gathered from this statement, which reveals the fascination of
the avant-gardists with the theatre of non-European cultures, the interest was
mainly focused on the abundance of nonrealistic modes and conventions.
The non-European theatres provided an art of acting and production which
was not meant to express the emotions of an individual — let alone a European middle-class individual — a point strongly emphasized by Antonin Artaud, who denied, uncompromisingly, that the individual was relevant in any
way to the theatre:

> The theatre must side with life, not with the individual life, that aspect of
> life where the CHARACTERS triumph, but with a kind of liberated life in
> which human individuality is brushed aside and man is no more than a
> reflection. The true object of the theatre is the creation of myths, the
> translation of life under its universal and immense aspect, and the extrac-
> tion of images from life, in which we desire to find ourselves again.[11]

Avant-gardists assumed that the acting in Japanese and Chinese theatre did
not promote any kind of identification between the spectator and the embodied character onstage in the manner of the realistic acting in the European
theatre. According to Bertolt Brecht, for example, the Chinese art of acting
seemed to be a perfect model of a form of acting which creates the effects of
alienation:

> The peculiarity of the artist watching himself, which is an artistic and
> ingenious act of self-alienation, prevents the total identification of the

spectator — that is to say, an identification bordering on self-abandon-
ment — and brings forth a wonderful distance from the events. . . . The
artist presents processes of great passion, but his performance does not become heated. In moments of intensity for the portrayed person, the artist
puts a lock of hair between his lips and bites it. But that is like a rite, there
is nothing eruptive in it. . . . The artist shows that this character is beside
himself, and he does this by indicating the signs of the emotional condition. . . . The controlled effect is due to the fact that the artist in this manner keeps his distance from the character he portrays.[12]

The fascination with non-European cultures was not limited to theatre
artists. It was common to avant-gardists: in poetry, the novel, painting, and
sculpture. This condition begs additional explanation. In 1890, for instance,
James George Frazer published *The Golden Bough: A Study in Comparative Religion* in two volumes. By 1936 it had been extended to thirteen volumes.
Frazer had compiled an enormous amount of material taken from different
cultures in order to demonstrate striking analogies between the thoughts and
customs of the so-called primitives and the manners and institutions of the
European culture, similarities that are supposedly rooted in a collective subconscious. He thereby paved the way for relinquishing the idea of Europe as
the center of the world, so typically assumed in Western culture. In this light,
the devotion of the European avant-gardists to non-European issues can be
seen as an attempt to escape or revolt against a European civilization which
had repressed human nature and to return instead to the unspoiled, "original"
state of culture.

It follows that the approach to the Asian and African cultures entailed a
certain ambiguity. On the one hand, it expressed the desire for an escape
from Western civilization. On the other hand, it promoted the ongoing
process of civilization. For there is no doubt that such highly codified alien
forms of acting were enormously appealing to the avant-gardists and resulted
in a high degree of stylization in the modern theatre. Gestures no longer pretended to be natural expressions; instead, they were openly declared to be abstract articulations. The body no longer functioned as a natural sign for human emotions and psychic states but, rather, as material to be shaped and
used in order to signify other things. The actor presented the body not as a
natural expression of the mind or soul of a dramatic character, but as raw material by means of which a sign was formed that represented whatever needed
to be expressed. Formulating these tendencies in "The Actor of the Future"
(1922), Meyerhold wrote: "The actor must train his material [his body], so

that it is capable of executing instantaneously those tasks which are dictated externally [by the actor, the director]."[13]

Although the avant-gardists often differed in their particular aims and styles, sometimes considerably so, they all understood the actor's body to be raw material that could be reshaped according to artistic intentions. Proceeding from this assumption, they elaborated new techniques of acting such as Meyerhold's bio-mechanics, Artaud's theatre of cruelty, and Brecht's alienation effect. In spite of their appraisal of Far Eastern acting, however, they did not copy either its particular techniques or its repertory of theatrical signs, although they sometimes borrowed single elements for special purposes (Alexander Tairov, for example, used elements of the Indian theatre in *Sakuntala* by Kalidasa).

In formulating and elaborating his theory of bio-mechanics, Meyerhold referred to working processes:

apart from the correct utilisation of rest periods, it is equally essential to discover those movements in work which facilitate the maximum use of work time. If we observe a skilled worker in action, we notice the following in his movements: (1) an absence of superfluous, unproductive movements; (2) rhythm; (3) the correct positioning of the body's centre of gravity; (4) stability. Movements based on these principles are distinguished by their dance-like quality; a skilled worker at work invariably reminds one of a dancer; thus work borders on art.[14]

Accordingly, Meyerhold defined the actor as being equivalent to the constructor:

$N = A_1 + A_2$
where N = the actor,
A_1 = the artist who conceives the idea and issues the instructions necessary for its execution
A_2 = the executant who executes the conception of A_1.[15]

The actor became an engineer and the body a machine or part of a machine. This tendency is more obviously dominant in the theatre of the Russian constructivists. Nicolai Foregger was particularly successful with his so-called machine-dances based on a special technique of acting called *tafia-trenage*. The technique was acquired by using "acting machines" which were at the disposal of the spectators during the breaks. Foregger proclaimed: "Actors! Directors! Don't look for inspiration. There is but one teacher: The Machine!"[16] Thus, the mechanization of movement which could be reproduced at all times and without depending on the individuality of the actor became the new ideal for acting (not just, we might note, in the case of certain avant-garde theorists but perhaps most tellingly in the widespread practice of film, which made all movement a machine dance of signs).

Regardless of the differences in programs and styles, the avant-gardists employed mechanical motion in order to place the actor's body not only in the more comprehensive context of the surrounding space and the often technical objects structuring it, but also in the totality of movement (i.e., the movement of all bodies, objects, and, just as significantly, light). The body of the actor was no longer considered and exploited as a natural sign exclusively indicating the psychic states and processes of an individual but as an arbitrary sign. It was presented as a machine which functioned according to mechanical laws (as with the constructivists and cubo-futurists) or as constituent of a ritual which was performed according to a determined pattern (as with Artaud and, partly, Oskar Schlemmer).

By means of the increasing semiotization of the body, the actor produced movements in the modern theatre which pointed to the total integration of the once-natural human organism into a nonhuman, unnatural "superior" order: either into a world of technique — an everlasting process made possible by the second industrial revolution — or into a metaphysical order formed by transindividual, mysterious forces. That is to say, the treatment of the human body by the avant-gardists was marked by ambiguity. On the one hand, they employed the actor's body as raw material, as a precise and easily moldable instrument. In this respect, their acting techniques both supported and promoted the civilizing process by rigorously repressing or distancing the immediate sensual nature of the body. On the stage and in film, the body became objectified (even in the service of the sexual appeal of the actor's body). On the other hand, by remaking (and defamiliarizing) the actor's body, the avant-gardists aimed at creating a "new human being" beyond the limits of contemporary Western civilization: "man" as "producer of new meanings" (Meyerhold) or "man in harmony with the universe" (Artaud).

Thus, we can conclude that the avant-gardists are to be seen as both the culmination of the civilizing process and the expression of the revolt against it. They were contradictory, ironic, and "grotesque" (Meyerhold's key term for the yoking together of unexpected opposites). They stood against bourgeois individualism, yet, as revolutionary artists, they asserted the artistic integrity of the individual artist who operates as the defining and controlling producer or director of meaning. This dynamic, fulfilling and revolting against the civilizing process, is an integral part of the ambiguity with which the avant-gardists treated the actor's body.

Before drawing any methodological conclusions regarding the consequences of a possible connection between the art of acting and the civilizing process, let us summarize.

Each of the three theatre periods and formal modes under consideration came into being in a time of social upheaval or fundamental transformation. Each negated the aims and purposes of the preceding theatrical form. Each developed a new style of acting which paralleled the formation of new behavior patterns in society.

From the seventeenth century onward, there was a growing tendency on the stages of Europe to repress the body as sensual nature. During the Baroque period, the human body was presented both as a text of artificial signs (when the actor followed the rules) and as a representation of disordered sensual nature (when the actor broke the rules, particularly when enacting uncivilized or fitful behavior, as in the case of the fool). On the bourgeois stage of the Enlightenment, however, the body ceased to be represented and perceived by means of this codified system of sensual nature. It was, rather, employed as a natural sign system organized for the expression of individual emotions. Subsequently, in the avant-garde theatre the human body was understood and employed as raw material which the actor might organize and transform into a well-functioning mechanism or work of art. In fact, the tendency to repress the body as sensual nature, as unproblematic physical presence, is manifested in an ever-increasing semiotization of the actor's body.

As a consequence of these findings, it may be argued that theatre has contributed to the civilizing process by employing and interpreting the actor's body as a sign system. By gradually transforming the human body from an image of sensual nature into a system of arbitrary signs, Western theatre has continually confronted actors and spectators alike with changing cultural systems that express, interpret, and control human nature — and this is really what characterizes the civilizing process.

More recently, in the contemporary theatre of the neo-avant-garde (or postmodern) movements which arose in Europe and in the United States during the 1960s, the connection between the art of acting and the civilizing process has been reinterpreted. Although they have different presuppositions and aim at different ends, all these movements have concurred in their attack on the body concept inherent in the Western theatre of the last century: "What we have tried to liberate was the actor's body!"[17] While, for example, Robert Wilson accomplished the desemiotization of the actor's body and "liberated" it from meaning, the Living Theatre "revived" the sensual nature of the actor's body. Thus, the neo-avant-garde theatre can be seen as an attempt to free the human body from the pressure brought about by the Western civilizing process.

If such a close connection does exist between the art of acting and the civilizing process, as this brief overview suggests, we have to consider some methodological consequences. Whatever these may be, the history of theatre has to be related to social history. This does not mean that one will be reduced to a mere result of the other, to the status of an effect. It is impossible to prove decisively that acting initiated the social conventions or, contrariwise, that social conventions influenced acting. There is only evidence of congruence between acting and social behavior, between theatre and other aspects of social life. But this connection is sufficient reason to argue that theatre history cannot be explored in all its aspects without regarding social history. The historians should strive for a precise, detailed, and exhaustive description of all theatrical signs that are elaborated and employed by the theatre of a certain epoch — or at least of the general principles guiding their elaboration and use. The functioning of these signs — that is, the constituted processes of meaning which were performed onstage and introduced to the audiences — can only be explained and understood when they are related both to the cultural context and to the social situation in which the theatre took place. The theory of the civilizing process, as developed in the analysis of Norbert Elias, is just one such attempt. Theatre history as social history remains an uncultivated but certainly fertile field of research and interpretation.

DISCOVERING THE SPECTATOR
Changes to the Paradigm of Theatre in the Twentieth Century

At the beginning of this century, the structure of theatrical communication in Europe experienced fundamental change. While since the end of the eighteenth century focus had been centered on the characters onstage and the internal communication between them, the focus of interest now shifted to the relations between the stage and the spectator: the external communication between stage and audience.

Thus, Georg Fuchs defined the "purpose" of theatre as "dramatic experience."[1] He emphasized that

> it is in the spectator that the dramatic work of art is actually born — born at the time it is experienced — and it is *differently* experienced by every individual member of the audience. The beginning of a dramatic work of art is not upon the stage or even in a book. It is created at that moment when it is experienced as movement of form in time and space.[2]

Similarly, Meyerhold lamented the passivity of the audience in bourgeois theatre in his early work *On the History and Technique of Theatre* (1909):

> The spectator experiences only passively what happens onstage. The stage acts as a barrier between the spectator and the actor dividing the theatre into two mutually foreign worlds: those who act and those who watch — and there are no veins that could bind these two separate bodies into one circulatory system. The orchestra brought the spectator close to the stage. The stage was constructed where the orchestra had been and separated the audience from the stage.[3]

The passivity of the spectator in the traditional theatre overtly contradicted Meyerhold's idea of theatre. He considered the four fundamentals of theatre to be the author, the director, the actor, and the spectator. Meyerhold showed the communication between them in the form of an equilateral triangle.

On the one hand, this "triangle theatre" showed the communication between the "traditional" participants — between actor and author, director and author, director and actor. But, on the other hand, the "internal" communication described by the triangle forms the prerequisite of external communication between the triangle itself and the spectator. This communication can only succeed, however, if all the participants concerned — including the spectator — are active. Thus, Meyerhold defined the spectator as the "fourth creator."[4] The new "stylized" theatre he developed should create productions "in which the spectator can creatively complete, in imagination, that which the stage only indicates."[5]

This seemed a distant possibility, however, in the bourgeois theatre. For, as Platon Kershentsev diagnosed in *The Creative Theatre* (1918):

> The entire development of bourgeois theatre has brought with it the absolute passivity of the spectator. . . . The theatre is no longer a place of creative forms and experiences but a place of recuperation in which one need do nothing at all. . . . This is typically characteristic of the bourgeois order: politics are controlled and ruled by a small group of politicians while the great masses of the people remain passive.[6]

Kershentsev made this diagnosis of the bourgeois theatre and society after the October Revolution and formulated his ideas for reform with a view to the development of a proletarian theatre. The Italian futurists had succeeded in gaining similar insights into their own bourgeois society and theatre even before World War I. They saw only one way of conquering the notorious lethargy and passivity of the bourgeois spectators and of activating them: "to consistently invent new ways of shocking the spectator."[7] In *The Variety Theatre* (1913), Filippo Tommaso Marinetti made the following suggestions:

> We must shock and force every spectator in the circle, boxes, and galleries to act. Here are a few suggestions how: mud is smeared over a few seats so that the spectator, male or female, sticks to it and causes general hilarity. . . . One seat shall be sold to ten people, which will result in jostling, bickering, and strife. Those ladies and gentlemen whom we know to be slightly mad, easily irritated, or eccentric shall be given free seats so that they provoke confusion by their obscene gestures, pinching the ladies or other mischief. The seats shall be sprinkled with itching or sneezing powder etc. . . . We must systematically prostitute the whole classical art on the stage. We shall perform the entire Greek, French, Italian tragedies, for example, in reduced form in a comical mix in one evening.[8]

The change of the paradigm from internal to external theatrical communication was carried out with particular consequence in the revolutionary theatre of the Soviet Union. Meyerhold's notebook for his production of Emile Verhaeren's *The Dawn* at the first theatre of the Soviet Russian republic (premiered December 28, 1920) contains the following entry: "The audience has changed so much that we are also forced to readjust our own frame of reference. The new spectator cannot stand much — now that each spectator imagines the same model of Soviet Russia. . . . Now we do not monitor the author's interests but rather those of the spectator."[9]

Similarly, Meyerhold's student Eisenstein, a representative of the leftist radical proletarian movement to which Kershentsev also belonged, defined anew the role of the spectator in the theatre in his programmatic work *The Montage of Attractions* (1923): "The basic materials of the theatre are derived from the spectator as well as from guiding the spectator in a desired direction (or a desired mood)—which is the main task of every functional theatre."[10]

Although far-reaching ideological, political, and aesthetic differences existed between the various representatives of the theatre avant-garde (ca. 1900–1935), such artists were nonetheless widely in agreement in their conviction that the shift of the dominant from internal to external communication could win back the basic social and cultural functions of theatre — something that the bourgeois theatre had lost. It was for this reason that the spectator was at the core of their reflection and activities. For, in changing the spectator, the theatre could be brought out of its deep crisis, which they diagnosed as the illness of the times, which was generally assigned to either the misguided development of Western culture or the specific lifestyle within capitalist bourgeois society.

Georg Fuchs, for example, hoped that his theatre of the future would be in a position to produce a "systematic and well-organized technique for the satisfaction of that atavistic urge — the primitive greed for the intensification of life."[11] Theatre should transport the spectator to a particular state:

There is a strange intoxication which overcomes us when, as part of a crowd, we feel ourselves emotionally stirred. Scientific investigation may perhaps determine from what distant ancestors we inherit the proclivity for such intoxication. But whether it springs from primitive orgies or from religious cults, this is certain: there is an emotion which runs through each of us when, as part of a crowd, we find ourselves united in an overwhelming passion.[12]

Clearly referring to Nietzsche, who in *The Birth of Tragedy Out of the Spirit of Music* (1872) spoke of the "hope . . . for the rebirth of Dionysus which should now be ominously understood as the end of individualisation,"[13] Fuchs hoped that theatre would provide the birth of a "new" transindividual being who would revoke the self-estrangement of modern individuals and the restrictions of class society. As Fuchs localized the transindividual in a state of intoxication, however, in an atavistic regression to the primitive, the archaic, and the naive, it is hardly surprising that he believed that the "redemption" of the individual through the cultish monumental theatre in the 1920s and early 1930s was only possible in the lap of the *Volksgemeinschaft*. His critique of culture led seamlessly into fascist ideology.[14]

Antonin Artaud also took the awareness of a deep crisis in Western culture as a starting point. In *Third Letter on Language*, he writes:

> We live in probably the most unique moment in the history of the world in which the much tested world watches its general values fall apart. Calcified life disintegrates from all sides. In moral and in social terms, this is expressed in a monstrous unchaining of desires, in the liberation of the basest instincts, the crackle and flicker of a burning life, that bursts prematurely into flame.[15]

Among the "misconceptions of life . . . inherited from the Renaissance" so deeply destructive to humankind, Artaud especially emphasized logocentrism, rationalism, and individualism.[16] In order to overcome these, Western theatre must return to its prelogical, prerational, and preindividual origins. It should bring about a "state of trance" in the spectator[17] and, through direct influence on the subconscious, enable a "making conscious and a taking possession of certain dominant strengths . . . which direct and guide all."[18] Theatre should be retransformed into a magical ritual that brings about an exorcism, a *rite de passage* in the spectator: it should heal those Westerners who are suffering the disease of civilization in that it should reconstitute "life" and "man" to the spectator,[19] not as "psychological man with his very different emotions and characteristics," nor as the "social man who is subjected by laws and distorted religion and regulations," but instead as the "total man."[20]

While Artaud believed that theatre alone should be capable of curing the ills of the time, the theorists and practitioners of the new theatre in the Soviet Union saw the October Revolution as an important prerequisite to the development of a new kind of spectator. The passive bourgeois spectator was now a thing of the past, and the new proletarian spectator should be activated in theatre from the start. Thus, Kershentsev determined the task of the proletarian theatre to the effect "that we provide the path to the creative, artistic instincts of the broad masses."[21] Theatre should liberate creativity in every spectator and develop that creativity: "When the spectators of the future go to the theatre, they will not say, 'We shall go and have a look at this or that play,' they will express themselves differently: 'We're going to take part in this or that play,' for they will literally 'take part,' they will no longer be spectators who only watch and applaud, but 'actors' who take part in the play."[22]

This creative spectator will be capable, on the one hand, of "invoking or creating anew kinds of theatre of which we do not yet even dare dream" and, on the other hand, of advancing in a creative way the construction of the new socialist society.[23] Meyerhold expressed a similar vision. His theatre should provoke the spectators to permanent activity which would thus help creativity to break through: "For through the play, they will define themselves as a participant and *creator of new meaning* because for them as active members (the new, the already converted communist comrades), the whole essence of theatre consists of proclaiming time and again in a reflective excitement the *joy of new life.*"[24]

Despite some differences between, and the various directions taken by, the many representatives of the theatrical avant-garde, the theatre was conceived and defined by them all unanimously as the place where the chasm between art and life, so characteristic of bourgeois society, could be bridged, where art could be brought into life. Whether the theatre was to become a festival, cult, or rite of agit-prop in the process was, in this respect, of no consequence: all that mattered was that it should be capable of provoking the spectators into activity and thereby transform them into — variously determined — "new" beings.

Since this "transformation" should be brought about by basic changes in the existing patterns and habits of reception, by opening of new ways of perception,[25] the stratagems developed by different members of the avant-garde to achieve these various goals can be usefully compared: they changed the traditional concept of space handed down by the illusionist box-set stage and/or formulated a specific mode of sign system whose dominant was on the pragmatic level.

OTHER SPACES

"According to their nature and their origin, player and spectator, stage and auditorium are not in opposition. They are one unity."[26] This conviction, first formulated by Fuchs in 1904 in *The Stage of the Future*, was unreservedly shared by members of the avant-garde of widely differing schools. The theatre of private boxes and the box-set stage developed in the seventeenth century was thereby given merciless sentence. For, on the one hand, the stage obviously separated the acting space from the auditorium and, on the other, created unnecessary barriers between the spectators. New theatres, in which the unity of the player and the spectator was given appropriate attention, were the demand of the moment. Richard Wagner, in his festival theatre at Bayreuth (opened 1876), had already devised a unified auditorium in the shape of a segment of a circle sloping gently as an amphitheatre. In place of the Greek orchestra, or the more contemporary stage, he built a pit where the orchestra would be hidden from view, thus creating the "mystical abyss" which would separate the "ideal stage world from the reality represented in the auditorium."[27]

The new theatres aimed to annul exactly this separation. The Art Theatre in Munich (opened 1908), devised by Max Littmann in close collaboration with Georg Fuchs, largely conformed to Fuchs' reform ideas. The unity of the stage and auditorium was achieved by a proscenium that projected far into the auditorium and by the fact that the auditorium itself rose around the proscenium like an amphitheatre as far as the back wall. The stage was divided into three parts: the large proscenium, whose height and width could be altered; a main stage similarly flexible in terms of height; and an upstage area. The proscenium was also to allow the action onstage to be brought well into the auditorium.

A similar conception formed the basis of Henry van de Velde's Werkbund Theatre in Cologne in 1914, which was demolished soon after in 1920. Here, too, alongside innovations such as the cyclorama or the tripartite stage, which were to solve the problem of time-consuming scene changes, an auditorium formed like an amphitheatre was created and a proscenium stage mediating between auditorium and stage. In both these theatres, the proscenium acted as the architectural guarantee and expression of the unity existing between players and spectators.

For Max Reinhardt, however, the new function of the proscenium alone did not go far enough. He aspired toward a "people's theatre" with an arena stage. After World War I the architect Hans Poelzig rebuilt the Circus Schumann of Berlin for him. The open auditorium, which was conceived for 3,200 spectators, curved, in a semicircle from the arena, around a thrust stage on four levels with orchestra, two movable front stages, and a main stage with a *Kuppelhorizont*.[28] The plans for a total theatre designed by Walter Gropius for Erwin Piscator in 1927 went even further than Hans Poelzig's Großes Schauspielhaus. Piscator, who firmly believed in the idea of a political-proletarian theatre, was convinced that the spectator could only be activated when the constellation was no longer "stage against auditorium" but "rather one single, enormous meeting hall, one single, enormous battle field, one single enormous demonstration."[29] To this end, Walter Gropius designed for him a flexible theatre which could seat 2,000: the stage and open auditorium could be moved in relation to one another so that an arena, proscenium, or tripartite, dropped stage could be built as desired. Moreover, a so-called acting circle, which flanked the whole audience area, was planned as a further potential acting space. In setting up the theatre as an arena stage, canvas flats could be unrolled from fourteen points around the single room of the theatre and could be used for film projections. According to Gropius' designs, the architecture and technical equipment of his total theatre explicitly served the goal of "shackling the audience out of its intellectually based apathy, to assault it, to take it by surprise and to make it participate in the play."[30] However, no sponsor was found, and the designs were never realized.

Meyerhold's plans for a new theatre suffered a similar fate. He too raised the challenge of devising wholly new theatres in a conversation with young architects in 1927:

It has been the norm till now to divide the theatre into auditorium and stage. We believe this deeply rooted idea is wrong. Today, we must say: there is only one building, one whole — one theatre. The passive spectator and the active actor do not exist. . . . If the theatre were not divided into stalls, dress, and upper circle, if the orchestra did not stand as a chasm between the stage and the auditorium, if there were no stage, if the theatre were one whole, and a natural incline linked the acting space with the audience, then I would frighten off this passive, immobile mass, shake them awake, before I would allow them, after making them walk over the acting space, to return to their seats.[31]

Meyerhold's challenge was never met. Even Artaud's relatively modest ideas were never actualized. In order to recreate a "direct contact between audience and show, between actor and spectator,"[32] he wanted to transform the theatre into a simple hall in which the audience would take their seats on swiveling chairs in the center of the room. The "action" should be played without any "stage in the normal sense of the word," all around them "in all four cardinal points" as much in the room itself as on a gallery running around it.[33]

Since, however, appropriate new theatres which could provide the architectural preconditions for the demand for unity of actor and spectator, stage and auditorium, were only built in a few cases, the theatre reformers were forced to make do with other solutions. One possibility lay in the temporary remodeling of already existing theatres.

The Japanese *kabuki* theatre, with its *hanamichi* or entrance bridge running at right angles into the auditorium, was considered by many members of the avant-garde to be an admirable model of the unity between the spectator and the actor. Thus, Fuchs wrote, as early as 1904, "The Japanese theatre preserves this unity by means of the bridge across which the actor comes forward to the stage from the auditorium itself."[34] Similarly, Kershentsev recommended the development of a proletarian theatre:

> In the beginning it will be more practical to accommodate the old theatres to the new demands by taking the Japanese model. The Japanese theatre uses a platform at the same height as the stage which, like the aisles in our theatres, passes in-between the blocks of the seats. . . . In most cases, it will not be difficult to build a platform such as this in the center, joining the stage near the prompter's box. The platform must be 2 or 3 meters wide and of course have no rails; it must slope evenly toward the floor of the auditorium. This platform will not only serve to open, as it were, the door of the fourth wall to the actors in their entrances and exits, but also serve as arena for the dramatic action. I have often had the opportunity of observing how, in Japanese theatre, the most dramatic moments of the play (persecution scenes, chance meetings, pleading for mercy, deaths) are played on this platform so very close to the audience. . . . The first technical innovation of the new theatre will be the demolition of the stage through the construction of this central platform.[35]

Max Reinhardt had already put this innovation to use as early as 1910. In the 1909/1910 season, he directed at the Munich Art Theatre, where he felt that the open proscenium did not sufficiently include the spectators in the action. For the production of *Sumurun*, by Friedrich Freksa, he used a "flower path" (*hanamichi*) running through the auditorium. Its unprecedented success with the audience allowed him to use the *hanamichi* again in his production of Jacques Offenbach's *La belle Hélène* (1911). Lion Feuchtwanger, who was at first opposed to these innovations, now wrote in the *Schaubühne*: "Then he extended the limited stage at the Art Theatre fortuitously, gave new possibilities of adding nuance to the entrances and exits of the chorus, and finally allowed the director to increase or decrease the power of the illusion as he pleased. Lightness of movement was all."[36]

Meyerhold made use of the *hanamichi* in his production of *Earth Rampant* (1923). He placed it, as Kershentsev had recommended, at the center of the auditorium and widened it considerably so that cars, or even trucks, could drive along it to the stage. But the anticipated excitement from the audience was not forthcoming: "Our audience was uncomfortable. The vehicles pumped out fumes, they could have hit someone, run someone over."[37]

Meyerhold was consistently forced to experiment within the framework of the traditional theatre building. His "stylized" theatre, in some ways conceived as the "rebirth of the antique theatre,"[38] abolished the apron-stage in favor of a proscenium. In his production of *The Dawn*, the apron-stage was put aside altogether in favor of the orchestra. Meyerhold's dreams went even further: "Above all, we also want the modern spectator to escape out of this constrictive shell of theatre into the freedom of the different levels of the stage."[39] At the start of the Theatre of the Revolution, however, such dreams proved too daring. He was only able to get rid of the apron and the curtain and experiment with different concepts of space.

Reinhardt, on the other hand, fled from the "constrictive shell of theatre" even before World War I. In the summer of 1910 he produced Sophocles' *Oedipus Rex* in the Festhalle in Munich, which he redesigned as an arena. In November of the same year the production was taken to the Circus Schumann of Berlin. Here, a year later, Reinhardt directed Aeschylus' *Oresteia* and Hugo von Hofmannsthal's *Everyman*. Similarly, in 1911, Reinhardt's stage designer, Ernst Stern, transformed London's Olympia Hall into a spired Gothic cathedral in which spectators and actors were united in a performance of Carl Vollmoeller's *The Miracle*. In the 1920s Reinhardt devised the board platform for *Everyman* in front of the Salzburg Cathedral (1920) and produced Hofmannsthal's *Salzburger Großes Welttheater* (1923; The Salzburg Great Theatre of the World) actually inside the Kollegienkirche in Salzburg.

In all the above examples, Reinhardt tried to present and guarantee the unity of stage and auditorium, of actor and spectator, by setting the play, on the one hand, in spaces which were directly related to the lives of the spectators and, on the other, in spaces which stressed the festive nature Reinhardt aimed to communicate in festival halls and the circus, places of boisterous and thrilling entertainment, just as in the market square in front of the church, the locus of religious festival since the Middle Ages.

At the start of the 1930s Reinhardt turned to somewhat contrary means: he pulled the spectators out of everyday reality and enticed them, as it were, to the "original site of the event" of the drama. In May 1933 he directed *A Midsummer Night's Dream* in the Boboli Gardens in Florence and in summer of the same year in the meadows of South Park, Headington, in Oxford. In 1934 his *Merchant of Venice* played in San Trovaso Square in Venice. In that the spectators gathered at the "original site of the event" they became, at the same time, part of the theatrical event. Reinhardt's goal to make the boundaries between illusion (*Schein*) and reality as permeable as possible led to a blurring of each in the other so that they became almost indivisible. In a true Baroque manner, the spectator and the actor were united in the illusion of play in which the spectator was fully incorporated.

A similar vision in the search for new spaces was undertaken by the proletcult movement. On the one hand, space should be created to allow the theatre to endorse the daily reality of the proletarian audience. For this reason, for example, Eisenstein set his production of S. M. Tretyakov's *The Gas Masks* (1923) in a gasworks. On the other hand, the new spaces should function as sites for huge revolutionary festivals. To this purpose, town squares and streets were employed. On May 1, 1920, the proletcult organized the first mass play as part of anniversary celebrations in the Soviet Union. It took place among the colonnades of the former stock exchange in Petrograd. *The Storming of the Winter Palace* won special fame as a similar mass play following this model. It was performed on the anniversary of the October Revolution under the directorship of Nikolai Evreinov in 1920 in Petrograd. Several stages were constructed. The spectators stood in the former Alexander Square between the Winter Palace and the Military Command. Two terraces were built next to the Military Command, a white one on the right and a red one on the left. They were linked by a bridge on which several different scenes took place. The action played partly in the square and partly at the windows of the Winter Palace. And, as at the time of the October Revolution in 1917, the cruiser *Aurora* was anchored on the River Neva firing salvos over the theatrical event — as it had during the actual historical event.

Thus, here too, the dramatic action occurred at the original place of the event. And this was not all. Among the ten thousand or so actors who participated in the production were many who had actually been part of the overthrow of 1917. In this case, however, the choice of the original site of the event was not intended to draw the spectators into an illusion. The theatrical reenactment of the historical event at the site of its real happening functioned far more to provoke the spectators toward a kind of self-reflection, making them aware of their own realities as material that they might activate and create.

From within the bourgeois society, it was the dadaists who earned the merit of having radically attempted the rejection of theatre buildings and the bringing of theatre directly into the lives of the audience. From the happening-like actions of the Berlin "Oberdada" Johannes Baader, the dada chronicler Raoul Hausmann writes:

On Sunday, 17 November 1918, Baader attended the morning mass in Berlin Cathedral. As Dryander, the court priest, began his sermon, Baader shouted out at the top of his voice, "Just a moment! Tell me, what do you care about Jesus Christ? Not a fig . . . !" He couldn't go on anymore, there was a terrible tumult. Baader was arrested on the charge of blasphemy. They couldn't do anything to him, though, since he was carrying the complete text of his outcry with him in which it said, "for they do not care for his laws, etc." . . . Later, in 1919, Baader went to Weimar. . . . Once again, he interrupted the proceedings from a tribune amongst the congregation and handed out huge numbers of pamphlets that he edited, *The Green Corpse*. . . . But among other things, in the pamphlet was also REFEREN-DUM — "Are the German people prepared to give 'Oberdada' a free hand? If the referendum answers yes then Baader will create order, joy, freedom and bread . . . we shall blow Weimar to pieces, Berlin is the home of Da-Da!"[40]

The theatrical actions of the dadaists at the original sites of bourgeois ritual such as the church and government thus exposed the rituals themselves — religious service, parliamentary session — as theatrical processes. In that theatre was introduced into life in this way, life was denounced — or discovered? — as theatre.

A NEW PERCEPTION

The new spaces which should recreate the unity of actors and spectators thus provided the preconditions under which the spectators might be transformed into "new" beings — to transport them into a state of "intoxication" or "trance," to liberate their creativity and develop it or simply to shock them. In either case, the powers of vision and hearing as practiced in the bourgeois theatre, and, moreover, in the whole of Western culture for more than three hundred years, were to be destroyed.[41] A new kind of perception should provoke the variously desired effects in the spectator.

While the box-set stage presented the spectator with a perspectively organized picture frame which could only be seen from one viewpoint without distortion, the proscenium and the arena stages, the *hanamichi* and various stage platforms in front of and behind the audience, the circle of acting space embracing the spectator on all sides, and the podiums flanking the audience on either side totally destroyed a perspectival view of the acting space. Here it was replaced by different kinds of aperspectival views. Moreover, the spectator was no longer presented with a *picture frame* stage, but rather with a *spatial* stage. And this space did not represent one defined space — a room or a forest — but served varying functions. It should, for example, create specific preconditions and possibilities as well as serve the various requirements of the movements and actions of the players. This function was even achieved by the rhythmical spaces that Adolphe Appia designed for Jaques-Dalcroze in the Festspielhaus at Hellerau (opened 1912), where the acting space was composed of different flights of stairs linked to one another or by the scaffolding that the constructivist Lyubov Popova set on the bare stage for Meyerhold's production of *The Magnanimous Cuckold* (1922). This consisted of two platforms linked to one another, of stairs, ladders, slides, revolving doors, wheels, and a kind of mill. It organized the space in such a way that the actors used the stage as a working apparatus that allowed many different forms of movement. Neither Appia's steps nor Popova's scaffolding represented anything to which one could accord a specific meaning. They were, uniquely, stairs and scaffolding that remained, as such, dumb objects to the spectator. Only through the movements and actions of the players were they brought to life and meaning communicated to the spectators, according to the changing meanings of the processes and actions. The Russian theatre critic Boris Alpers described the process thus:

> At this time, an actor at the Meyerhold theatre would usually enter the stage at the beginning of the play just as the lights in the auditorium faded, with the springy, sporty step of the mime artist. The stage was randomly strewn with single, silent, neutral, nonexpressive objects. He would stand still and wait until the lights illuminated him and the various objects onstage. After a short pause, he would begin to act and immediately this object world around him came to life and began to undergo a series of innumerable and unexpected transformations and changes. A simple wooden structure became, according to the actor's will, the miller's house and each single episode literally opened a string of different rooms and sections of the spacious building.[42]

The design of the stage floor, the stage, and the various objects strewn around it had, in this case, no fixed meaning. Far more, they presented an open system of possible meanings that would only be actualized through the player's actions and the corresponding active relations provided by the perceptions and interpretations offered by the spectator.

The new stage space could also, however, fulfill one function without any reference to the actor at all. The multidimensional spatial stage employed by the futurists could make do without the actor altogether. The function of the actor was completely replaced by space itself. The core of the theatrical space was constructed of an electro-dynamic, polydimensional architecture of moving, plastic elements of light. As Enrico Prampolini explained, this form of construction enabled "the perspectival view to be drawn beyond the horizontal line, turn back on itself, and to create, though this simultaneous penetration, centrifugal rays of infinite perspectives and emotions toward the perspectives onstage."[43] The futuristic stage forced the spectator toward a wholly new kind of perception which was brought into line with the newest discoveries in physics as formulated by Einstein's teaching on relativity.[44] Consequently, every performance, as Prampolini demanded, became, through the specific design of the space, "a mechanical rite of the external transcendence of painting . . . it is the magical exposure of a spiritual and scientific secret."[45]

Quite another function was served by abstract stages without actors created by the Bauhaus movement. Where the actors appeared at all, they were no longer recognizable — at least not as interpreters of specific historical, social, or psychologically determined individuals. In some cases, their outward appearance denied any kind of attribution of identity because all the actors wore the same clothing, whose potential meaning was only activated by their actions (for example, in Meyerhold's production of *The Magnanimous Cuckold* or Brecht/Engels' *Man Is Man*). In some cases, their costumes and the sets served as a dash of color (as Gordon Craig used them), and still other actors appeared as geometrical figures (as Oskar Schlemmer used them), to mention just a few.

The actors became aesthetic tools which must satisfy different functions. Their outward appearance simply provided the preconditions that made these various functions perceptible. It was only the specific performance art which enabled the actors to realize the relevant functions.

In the bourgeois theatre, the actor performed movements and gestures which were familiar to the bourgeois audience in daily life. Thus, the spectator could relatively unquestioningly identify, and assign meaning to, the theatrical signs as theatrical signs of the specific volitional and emotional state of the role being played.

In the theatre of the avant-garde, on the other hand, the actors performed movements and gestures which either were wholly unfamiliar to the spectators or were extracted from totally other contexts. This resulted in a provocation: acrobatic sequences of movement or gestures from the *commedia dell'arte*, the functional movements and gestures of stage assistants dressed in black, borrowed from the Japanese theatre, who brought props onto the open stage or who adjusted the folds of a protagonist's costume, movements such as those performed by the dancers in Balinese theatre, as well as mechanical and wholly "abstract" sequences of movement.

In all these cases, the spectators are not in the position to perceive elements *ad hoc* as theatrical signs and interpret them — that is, on the basis of a theatrical code known to them or even on the basis of their own social experience. A different kind of reception was now needed.

The body of the actor was used as a material in which, with which, wholly new theatrical signs could be produced. It was to this end that Meyerhold developed his "bio-mechanics." Through special training, the actor's body should be transformed into an economic and efficient malleable "working machine" which was capable of effortlessly producing any desired movement on demand. These movements would now challenge the creativity of the spectators, since the spectators are only able to accord meaning by relating them to the movements of another actor or to the structure of the stage design and so on. In this way, the spectators are forced into a permanently creative activity by the play itself.

Artaud, in contrast, wanted to use the "human body" as "hieroglyphic characters" and thus "compose exact symbols on the stage that are immediately legible."[46] The actor should perform as a "living hieroglyph" which has a direct impact on the subconscious of the audience. Artaud took the performer in the Balinese theatre as the model:

> In fact, the strange thing about all these gestures, these angular, sudden, jerky postures, these syncopated inflexions formed at the back of the throat, these musical phrases cut short, the sharded flights, rustling branches, hollow drum sounds, robot-creaking, animated puppets dancing, is the feeling of a new bodily language no longer based on words but on the signs which emerge through the maze of gestures, postures, airborne cries, through their gyrations and turns. . . . These mental signs have an exact meaning that only strikes one intuitively, but violently enough to make any translations into logical, discursive language useless. . . . [They seem to move] with the very automatism of the unleashed subconscious.[47]

The movements and gestures of the actor were so structured, according to Artaud, that the immediate perception of them was able to influence the subconscious directly.

It follows from Artaud's description that the movements and gestures of the actors, the colors and shapes of their clothing, were, as isolated elements, not capable of accomplishing their potential effect. Far more, they formed relations with each other and with the different sounds: the syncopated inflections formed at the back of the throat, the musical phrases, rustling branches, drum sounds, creaking, cries.

In bourgeois theatre, the word formed the dominant by which, or under which, all other theatrical sign systems were ordered. Once the spectators understood the speech of the characters onstage they had already grasped the most essential part of the performance. Artaud, on the other hand, relinquished "our Western ideas of speech" and turned words into "incantations,"[48] whose magical effect was supported by random sounds. For his production of *Les cenci* (1935), Artaud had prepared various recordings of the cathedral bells at Amiens, machine sounds, fanfares, walking, a metronome, birds' chatter, and voices calling in increasing and decreasing volume "cenci." These were supported by an electronic instrument with monodic claviature. The recordings were played in different directions on loudspeakers in the theatre; a loudspeaker was installed in each of the four corners of the room so that the spectator was surrounded by the noises and could be brought into a hypnotic state. The performance won no special response from the spectators, however, and was utterly ripped apart by the critics: the acoustics were so poor that the text was unintelligible, the sounds atrocious, the music a cacophony. No one was prepared even to begin to attempt the new kind of reception proposed by Artaud.

This reaction might seem astounding when one considers what the futurists and dadaists had begun twenty years earlier when their *parole in libertà*, bruitism, onomatopoetic poems (such as Ball's *Caravan* and *Gadji heri bimba*), and simultaneous poems had shocked the bourgeois audience and vigorously upset the acquired habits of listening and comprehension of the spoken word. The dadaist simultaneous poems constantly resorted to all the "six families of sound of the bruitist orchestra" as the founder of bruitism, Luigi Russolo, categorized them in 1913:

1. Roars, thunderings, explosions, hissing roars, bangs, booms.
2. Whistling, hissing, puffing.
3. Whispers, murmurs, mumbling, muttering, gurgling.
4. Screeching, creaking, rustling, humming, crackling, rubbing.
5. Noises obtained by beating on metals, woods, skins, stones, pottery, etc.
6. Voices of animals and humans: shouts, screams, shrieks, wails, hoots, howls, death rattles, sobs.[49]

The acting space, linked through architectural elements, light, and movement, is here intersected and overlaid by a "sound-space": thus a four-dimensional stage was realized. The perception of such a stage clearly challenged its bourgeois audience too severely until well into the 1930s.

These few examples might suffice to illustrate what radical new powers of perception the avant-garde required of their audience. The goal of transforming them into "new" beings seemed to justify this drastic action. The ultimate test, however, could not be made: fascism and Stalinism stopped short the experiments of the theatrical avant-garde for a very long time. Until the 1960s the historical avant-garde movement in theatre was submitted to brutal repression and almost complete oblivion.

THE SPECTATOR AS SPECTATOR: EUROPEAN THEATRE
AT THE TURN OF THE CENTURY

Western theatre of the last twenty-five to thirty years seems, in some respects, to have resumed the experiments started by the historical avant-garde movement and developed them even further. It cannot be overlooked that the two stratagems devised to throw open new spaces and find a new mode of employing signs where the dominant is situated on the pragmatic level, as discussed above, are now advocated by the representatives of advanced contemporary theatre.

Modern theatres are usually equipped with a flexible stage and auditorium so that they can be used as box-set, proscenium, or arena stage, provide several performance areas, and much more. Already existing theatres are frequently remodeled to fit the same demands. In addition, many very different kinds of buildings are used as theatres: abandoned factories and slaughterhouses, tram depots, film studios, and so on. There is scarcely one kind of space in town where theatre has not already been performed: on the streets, in market squares, in parks and circus tents, in the shop windows of department stores, in sitting rooms, against the facade of a high-rise block of flats. And even outside the town new performance sites are forever being discovered: in the ruins of a castle, on cliffs, on a lake, in the clearing of a forest, on Haft Tan Mountain, in Shiraz at the tomb of Xerxes, in an abandoned quarry, and so on. There simply is no place where, in principle, theatre could not be performed.

In a similar way, the repertoire of theatrical signs has been enlarged. The theatre consistently incorporates elements from the giant fund of theatrical and cultural histories of all peoples and all times and uses them as theatrical signs: samurai armor with *allonge* wigs, leather masks from the *commedia dell'arte* with Chinese painted face masks, African drums with Japanese flute, and so on.[50] Alongside these, modern technology has opened up wholly new potential in the creation of theatrical signs such as those realized by computer-driven lighting equipment, video-sizing, laser beams, and holography. Fundamentally, there is no culture and no cultural system within it from which today's Western theatre cannot borrow elements for use as theatrical signs. Since the spectators are not usually familiar with the original form, function, and meaning of these elements — which are usually not touched on — and the elements familiar to them are used in such a way that recourse to their original context renders no intelligible meaning, reception can in no way be carried out as the recognition of the familiar and its classification into familiar contexts. The activity and creativity of the spectator are explicitly provoked.

One might then reach the conclusion that contemporary theatre — and, above all, postmodern theatre — brings the aims of the historical avant-garde movement full circle, picking it up and fulfilling it. Thus, it is hardly surprising that at least one representative of the historical avant-garde movement came to this conclusion. When Robert Wilson presented one of his own productions for the first time in Europe, with a performance of *Deafman Glance*, it was followed by an "open letter" in the *Lettres françaises* by the surrealist Louis Aragon addressed to one of his fellow combatants, André Breton, who died in 1966. In this letter, Aragon told Breton that "the miracle . . . has happened . . . the one we have been waiting for, the one of which we once spoke" and that it had "happened" when "I had long given up believing it possible"[51]— postmodern theatre as the extension and completion of the theatre of the historical avant-garde?[52]

Such a conclusion overlooks one fundamental difference between the avant-garde theatre of the first decades of this century and postmodern theatre. The development of the stratagems which postmodern theatre not only furthers but also greatly radicalizes was carried out by the avant-gardists with an ultimate goal in mind. Such stratagems functioned solely as the instrument by which this goal could be reached: to bring art closer to life, which is to say, to shock the spectators, or to liberate their creative potential and transform them, thus, into the longed for, yearned after — even if differently defined — "new" beings.

There can be no question of a similar objective in postmodern theatre. Here the spectators are not cultivated into "material" for specific purposes from which, with all the means available to theatre, "actants" should be produced. Far more, the spectators are given back their right to *spectate*. Postmodern theatre elevates the spectators to absolute masters of the possible semioses without, at the same time, pursuing any other ultimate goal.[53] The spectators are free to associate everything with anything and to extract their own semioses without restriction and at will, or even to refuse to attribute any meaning at all and simply experience the objects presented to them in their concrete being. Here it is understood and taken for granted that looking on is a creative act. The most appropriate expression of this new approach is found in Heiner Müller's "Bildbeschreibung" (1985; Description of a Picture): the reception of the image is executed as the production of a text — reception *is* production, looking on *is* acting.[54]

The stratagems which the avant-gardists evolved to operate and carry out their goals thus obtained a quite different function in postmodern theatre. While the avant-gardists tore down the stage in order to, as they believed, recreate the original unity of acting space and spectator and removed to new spaces in order to bridge the gap between art and life, the postmodern theatre can expand to accommodate all possible spaces because the spectators no longer need the stage as a reminder that they are watching a performance; instead they erect the stage in their own consciousness. While avant-garde theatre extended the repertoire of theatrical signs with elements it believed capable of having a direct impact on the spectator, the postmodern theatre is able to adopt elements from any cultural system of any culture it chooses. This is because the spectators are now in a position to keep an aesthetic distance from the objects and sequences put before them as well as to receive them purely from an aesthetic point of view.

In this way, postmodern theatre reflects on one anthropological constant which Helmuth Plessner formulated long before Jacques Lacan's pathfinding discovery and explication of the so-called mirror stage (*stade du miroir*): on one's distance from one's own Self and the eccentric position. As Plessner revealed, one finds the Self through forming relationships with the Other. By viewing the Self in the mirror as the Other or even in the mirror of the Other, an image of Self is composed.[55] The theatrical signs presented on the stage are part of the mirror that the spectator reflects back as the image of the Other. In that the spectators, for their part, reflect this image, they enter into relation with their own Selves.[56]

The mirror which postmodern theatre shows to its spectators may seem, in some respects, a shattered one. It consists of numerous disparate elements which, even as a whole, render no meaningful unit, can reveal no unifying image. The image reflected by postmodern theatre is one of many "Others": "TO LIVE INSIDE THE MIRROR; the man dancing the step, I, my grave his face, I the woman with a wounded neck, right and left in the hands a split bird, blood on mouth, I the bird, the one who shows the murderer the way in the night writing with my beak, I the frozen storm."[57]

The oneness of the recipient, the "I," is dissolved in the very act of receiving. The recipient becomes the thing received, the man, the woman, the bird, the storm, the many "Others" which are presented, and constitutes, at the same time, the new unity of his or her own "I," in that the many "Others" are observed from a distance. In the mirror of the postmodern theatre the spectator experiences the Self as a decentered subject that ascertains its own identity by observing and becoming aware of just that decentering. The act of looking on proves here to be a creative act that gives birth to the identity of the onlooker.

The stratagems developed by the theatre of the avant-garde in the first third of this century, to transform the spectator into one who acts, function in postmodern theatre in the opposite way as the condition of the possibility of recognizing the spectator as spectator and returning the rights of spectatorship. In the theatre, the fact of looking on is an action.[58]

The radicalization of avant-garde stratagems in postmodern theatre has, however, led to certain consequences which, although they do not qualify as the transfer of theatre into life, can nonetheless be seen as the transfer of life into theatre. For if it is left to the individual spectators to segregate the space by an imaginary stage and to perceive the objects and processes presented in specific sections of the segregated space with aesthetic distance, the spectators also apply this method even where theatre is not performed: every conceivable space can be perceived with aesthetic distance as a theatrical one; the spectators can place themselves before an imaginary stage and observe the objects lying beyond it and the processes engaged there as theatrical. Here too the spectators may creatively undertake new associations and interpretations of meaning, or the perceived object may be experienced in its concrete sense, from a purely aesthetic point of view. Such a theatricalization of reality and aestheticization of life must not allow the spectators to forget, however, that, outside theatre, looking on is nothing more than just looking on and thus cannot be equal to acting, nor can it replace acting.

The theatre metaphor reanimated by the concept of the *mise en scène* in postmodern theatre proves somewhat deceptive here.[59] Although one may speak of *mise en scène* in nearly all cultural spheres today with some justification, the equation of theatre and world or human life—*theatrum mundi, theatrum vitae humanae*—proposed here is only true precisely in the opposite sense. The Baroque prince was the ideal spectator in the theatre—the only one whose view of the scenic world of the stage was not distorted by perspective—as well as at the same time the ideal actant in the social, economic, and political world—because he was both as God's representative. But the individual in secular, plural, democratic nations can only lay claim to and perform the sovereignty of the Baroque prince as a spectator in the postmodern theatre. For here theatricality adopts a fundamentally different quality from that in social reality, which, nonetheless, can be explained and analyzed appropriately by this term. This problematic provides future interdisciplinary theatre research with a wide field of exploration.

FROM THEATRE TO THEATRICALITY
How to Construct Reality

At the end of the nineteenth century, the dominance of language, so typical of Western culture since the Renaissance, was increasingly challenged. As early as 1876, Nietzsche wrote on Richard Wagner in *Thoughts Out of Season*:

> He was the first to recognise an evil which is as widespread as civilisation itself among men; language is everywhere diseased, and the burden of this terrible disease weighs heavily upon the whole of man's development. Inasmuch as language has retreated ever more and more from its true province — the expression of strong feelings, which it was once able to convey in all their simplicity — and has always had to strain after the practically impossible achievement of communicating the reverse of feeling, that is to say, thought, its strength has become so exhausted by this excessive confusion of its duties during the comparatively short period of modern civilisation, that it is no longer able to perform even that function which justifies its existence, to wit, the assisting of those who suffer in communicating with each other concerning the sorrows of existence. Man can no longer make his misery known unto others by means of language; hence he cannot really express himself any longer. And under these conditions, which are only vaguely felt at present, language has gradually become a force in itself which with spectral arms coerces and drives humanity where it least wants to go.[1]

The disease of language which Nietzsche here diagnoses can be described as a degeneration of language from the state of being a polyfunctional, ambiguous, flexible semiotic system that allows people to express their feelings, to constitute their selves, and to communicate with each other into a restrictive technical language. Such "terminology" was capable neither of expressing strong emotions nor of serving to communicate between human beings anymore. Rather, it estranged them from themselves as well as from one another.

However, this focusing of language on its denotative-conceptual, logical-grammatical capabilities does not seem to have enhanced its cognitive qualities, as Hugo von Hofmannsthal's "Letter of Lord Chandos" (1902) shows. Here Lord Chandos complains:

> At first I grew by degrees incapable of discussing a loftier or more general subject in terms of which everyone, fluently and without hesitation, is wont to avail himself. I experienced an inexplicable distaste for so much as uttering the words *spirit*, *soul*, or *body*. I found it impossible to express an opinion on the affairs at Court, the events in Parliament, or whatever you wish. This was not motivated by any form of personal deference (for you know that my candour borders on impudence), but because the abstract terms of which the tongue must avail itself as a matter of course in order to voice a judgement — these terms crumbled in my mouth like mouldy fungi. . . . For me, everything disintegrated into parts, these parts again into parts; no longer would anything let itself be encompassed by one idea. Single words floated round me; they congealed into eyes which stared at me and into which I was forced to stare back — whirlpools which gave me vertigo and, reeling incessantly, led into the void.[2]

On the one hand, the "abstract words," the terms — the tools of cognition — decompose the very moment they are about to be used to formulate a judgment. On the other hand, the forms dissipate, so that the terms cannot refer to them any longer. In the process of total disintegration, the crisis of language turns out to be a crisis of perception and of cognition as well. Since language is not able to structure or control perception and cognition anymore, the world seems to fall apart. The single words appear as turbulences that do not lead to the perception or interpretation of reality but, instead, to a complete void.

The "cultural crisis" at the turn of the century, thus, seems to have sprung from the absolute dominance of language over the other semiotic systems; it was sensed the moment the crisis of language became apparent. In order to overcome the cultural crisis it was necessary to restructure not just the individual semiotic systems — particularly language — but also their interrelationships. The "retheatricalization of theatre" as proclaimed by the twentieth-century theatre world can be described and understood as the attempt to deconstruct the traditional system of semiotic systems employed in Western culture and to restructure the whole system as well as its individual subsystems in order to open up possible solutions to this crisis.

Here I shall not take the proclamations and theories of the avant-gardists as my point of departure, but instead a popular production by Max Reinhardt which ran from 1910 to 1912 in Berlin, London, Paris, and New York: the pantomime *Sumurun* by Friedrich Freksa. This production deviated in many respects not only from the usual productions of dramatic theatre of the time, but also from other — innovative — productions by Reinhardt.

The action of the pantomime takes place "in an imaginary Orient, perhaps in the legendary Samarkand."[3] It consists of a string of somewhat unrelated situations, unconnected by the logic of action or by psychology. The individual situations feature scenes of passion (love and murder), on the one hand, and, on the other, comical scenes dealing with the Hunchback (his suicide, his corpse, his resurrection). In order to achieve a rhythmically structured sequence from these more or less independent scenes, music (by Victor Hollaender) was introduced. The music, however, was not supposed to distract the attention of the spectators from the mimical play of the performers and thus ceased at "the very great moments," as Freksa put it. Accordingly, the coherence between the scenes was not established, nor was it guaranteed any longer by the mere linearity of their succession (i.e., it was not based as usual on logical connections between them or on the psychology of the dramatic figures); rather, it depended solely on the rhythm of the succession, emphasized by music.

The production was, even in other respects, planned as an experiment. In place of language, the performer's body should dominate. Not, however, like "the old pantomime which replaces the words by stereotypical gestures, so that one wonders why the people do not rather speak." On the contrary, scenes were to be created "that, basically, could do without words."[4]

The shift of the focus from language to the body had already been discussed and advocated for some years by Edward Gordon Craig and Georg Fuchs. In his article "The Dance" (1906) Fuchs defined dance as the basis of the theatre since, in principle, "dance and acting are one and the same art . . . rhythmical movement of the human body in the space, caused by the creative impulse to represent an emotion by the expressive means of one's own body, and with the intention of pleasurably releasing this inner drive by setting other people in the same or similar rhythmical vibrations."[5]

Fuchs even went so far as to proclaim the culture of the body as the foundation of a new culture. That is to say, he did not restrict his reflections on the dominance of the body to the realm of theatre; rather, he tended to think of the body as a means to overcome the crisis of culture. To a certain extent, the body was meant to replace language. Accordingly Fuchs, a disciple of Nietzsche, propagated the development of a physical culture. In "The Dance" he wrote:

> The culture of the naked body is the presupposition of the culture of the dressed body. . . . Our childcare, hygiene, massage, our gymnastics, physical

exercises and sports and whatever else related to that are being permanently refined, so much so that they are being transformed into aesthetics, quasi by themselves and without any explicit artistic intention. The strata of the most refined, in fact, already enjoy again the appearance of a perfectly developed human body and its movements.[6]

Fuchs held the development of such physical cultures to be a prerequisite to the process which transforms "the body into a means of artistic creation" and, in this way, the dancing body into a perfect semiotic system that will be able to realize all the tasks and functions language can no longer fulfill. Thus, the focus, as well as the dominance, shifts from language to the body.

In *Sumurun* Reinhardt brought about another radical innovation: for the first time, he employed the *hanamichi* from the Japanese *kabuki* theatre, the "flower-path," as he called it. Reinhardt was informed about the *hanamichi* and its particular possibilities by one of his stage designers, Emil Orlik. Orlik had lived in Japan for about a year in 1900–1901 in order to study the art of the wood block print. When he told Reinhardt about the *hanamichi*, its concept was already quite well known and discussed among theatre reformers.

Information about the *hanamichi* was available through many publications that had appeared on Japan and the Japanese theatre since the 1880s. In "Le théâtre au Japon" (1888) Alfred Lequeux, for example, describes the spatial conception of the *hanamichi* as well as the actors' use of it: "The life of the drama gains tremendously from this procedure. The whole auditorium participates, so to speak, in the action. What great proportions the scene adopts as it thrusts out over the spectators' heads as far as the entrance to the stalls."[7]

This spatial conception allowed the simultaneous representation of different actions taking place on the path and a subplot evolving on the stage. Lequeux concludes: "So everyone participates in the drama and therefore becomes more interested in it."[8] He interprets the *hanamichi* as a device which creates a totally different kind of interaction (compared to Western standards) between actors and spectators. This point is also made by Adolf Fischer in his article "Japans Bühnenkunst und ihre Entwicklung" (Japanese Stagecraft and Its Development): "Often two scenes unfold before the eyes of the spectators at the same time: one on the stage and the other on the *hanamichi*. You will not believe to what extent the audience, sitting between both parties, becomes emotionally involved and wrapped up in the action, and sometimes, carried away by its mood, even participates."[9]

Thus, the activity of the audience seemed, from a Western point of view, the most remarkable trait of the *kabuki* theatre.[10] It is small wonder, therefore, that the avant-gardists turned to the spatial conception of the *kabuki* theatre. In *Die Schaubühne der Zukunft* (1905; The Stage of the Future) Georg Fuchs also considered this device:

> And it is of great importance never to forget that drama, by its very essence, is *one* with the festive crowd. For it comes into existence the very moment it is experienced by the crowd. Performer and spectator, stage and auditorium, are, in origin, not opposed to one another, they are a *unity*. The Japanese theatre has kept this unity right up to the present time by use of the bridge along which the actor proceeds out of the auditorium onto the stage.[11]

The dissolution of the architectural separation between stage and auditorium which, from the very beginning of the century, theatre reformers such as Peter Behrens, Fuchs, Reinhardt, and Meyerhold never tired of postulating and trying out was not meant to be just another spatial device but also a change in principle in the communicative conditions underlying theatre. While from the end of the eighteenth century the focus of interest lay on the dramatic figures onstage and the internal communication between them, it now shifted to the relationship between stage and auditorium. The external communication between actor and spectator was emphasized and marked. Accordingly, Fuchs proceeded from the assumption that "drama" is created by the spectator in the process of his/her experience. Thus, the very act of looking on was understood as an active, creative process which is actually obstructed by the external spatial conditions of European theatre: box-set and raised stage. Accordingly, the avant-gardists held the abolition of both to be a necessary prerequisite for setting free the process of looking on as a creative activity.[12]

The conclusion drawn from the reports on the *kabuki* theatre was that its spatial conception seemed to provide ideal conditions for emphasizing external theatrical communication. Adolf Fischer had already suggested such "an experiment with the *hanamichi*."[13] It was Reinhardt who actually executed this experiment in *Sumurun*. The play was the beginning of a series of experiments which opened up totally new theatrical spaces such as the *hanamichi*, circus arena, marketplace, church, parks, meadows, woods, and many others.

The production *Sumurun* opened on April 24, 1910, in Berlin, was recast in London in 1911, and toured to Paris and New York in 1912. Wherever it went, it was an overwhelming box office success, although the critics' response was quite different. Nonetheless, whatever stance was taken, the reviews provide us with a wealth of information concerning the structure and the effect of the production.

Most critics noted the dissolution of the linear structure. Oskar Bie, who was somewhat unhappy with the production because of its "Stillosigkeit" (restlessness), wrote in the *Neue Rundschau*: "Towards the end, Reinhardt has set the prominent murder scenes in the manner of the Japanese: it is striking and, rhythmically, tightens up the play. During the second half, in the love and murder scenes (love and murder are silent), my impression was one of strong intensity."[14]

Bie refers — in rather positive terms — to a totally new experience of time. The replacement of a tension caused by the action and/or the psychological development of the dramatic characters with an intensity released and fore-grounded by one single independent moment annuls time as an unbroken continuum. Instead, time is realized as a rhythmically structured, discontinu-ous sequence of single moments of different intensity. Because of their inten-sity, the moments gain a time quality of their own which, ultimately, is based on the subjective experience of each spectator: depending on the degree of intensity, one moment can even stretch into eternity. Thus, we can conclude that the particular structure of the performance brought about a subjectifi-cation of time: it realized time as the subjective experience of intensity.

The dominance of the body as means of expression in the production was given general attention and lengthy description. Bie emphasized the accom-plishments of the dancer Grete Wiesenthal. She "is the true future unity of acting and dance, i.e., of psychic representation and plastic elaboration in an independent sequence of postures and excitations, which overlay the play like a corporeal melody which, moreover, is sweet as such."[15] Wiesenthal did not employ her body in such a way as to produce clearly delineated and well-known signs, to which the spectators could attribute more or less the same meanings. On the contrary, she presented an "independent sequence of pos-tures" as a sequence of rhythmically structured asemantical elements. This procedure resulted, on the one hand, in drawing the attention of the specta-tor to the pure materiality of the elements, to their corporeality that must be perceived as such, and on the other hand — following from this — it allowed each and every spectator to bestow his/her own subjective meaning on the element in question according to his/her own presuppositions. Thus, the em-phasis on the materiality of the body presented onstage went together with a shift from the tendency toward clarity in the signs of acting to a tendency to-ward ambiguity. It is small wonder, therefore, that most critics received the acting as "telling a story,"[16] interpreting the perceived gestures and move-ments as signs of a story they themselves superimposed. The critic of the *New York Review* even went so far as to discuss the effect of the production in the context of physical culture theory:

Sumurun is a great feather in the cap of the physical culturists who hold that the body is the instrument of the soul and mind, designated by the creator solely for the purpose of expressing its emotions and thoughts and all that. . . . The physical culturists have possibly never before had such an excellent demonstration made for them as this *Sumurun*. It proves, better than all the books on the subject ever written, or all the lessons in "bodily expression" ever given by teacher or professor, "how eloquent is silence." [17]

Since this eloquence of the body, however, was not realized according to a given code, the process of meaning-generating referring to its elements (gestures, postures, movements) was open to different results depending on the different subjective presuppositions of the spectator in each case.

The emphasis on materiality determined not only the use of the body but the use of color as well. The New York critics stated that the use of color was "not only beautiful, but novel and refreshing. . . . Reinhardt seems to have studied the soul of each color. He gets his effect of Oriental wealth by getting each color to a glow and then adding other colors but sparingly until he gets the effects he wants." [18] That is to say, in *Sumurun* only those theatrical sign-systems prevailed that either did not have a coded meaning, such as music and color, [19] or were used in a way that divested the system of any coded meanings, such as acting. Thus, the materiality of body, color, and sound was stressed, a materiality that was *per se* asemantic. As a result, the two processes of perceiving and of meaning-generating were related to each other in a new way. First, the spectators perceived the presented elements in their particular materiality. Then, depending on their perception and their universe of discourse, the spectators could attribute meanings to the elements they perceived. That is to say, perception determined the constitution of meaning or, to put it even more radically, perception was interpretation.

The process of perception, moreover, was emphasized by the introduction of the *hanamichi*.

In *Sumurun* there is a narrow runway reaching from the back of the orchestra floor over the tops of the seats and on to the stage. Along this runway most of the characters of *Sumurun* cross from the back of the theatre over the heads of the audience and on to the stage. This is a daring device for one who is working on your imagination to create the effect of delusion. And it is all the more tribute to the acting of the German company, who present *Sumurun*, and to the staging that, although some of the audience could put out their hands and touch the garments of the actors as they passed them, none of the spell that enveloped the actors on the stage left them as they crossed the runway at the end of the play and made their way back.[20]

This positive judgment of the *hanamichi* is decidedly contradicted by another critic, who writes that the *hanamichi* "distracts the audience's attention," because "the actors make their entrances at some vital point in each scene of the play." This is fatal, since no spectator is able "to resist the temptation of turning round or looking skyward as a flock of very fat eunuchs or a bevy of gaily fledged ladies of the harem come clattering down the center of the theater just two feet above your head." The critic comes to the conclusion that the *hanamichi* was not only totally superfluous, but directly counterproductive: "It destroys a great deal of the illusion and it makes the audience miss many points of the play."[21]

What can we gather from these two reviews about the function and the effect of the *hanamichi*? First we learn that the spectators did "not resist the temptation of turning round." They looked toward the stage as well as toward the *hanamichi*. The spectators had two different levels of interest and two different perspectives. They were able to let their eyes wander not only over the stage but between stage and *hanamichi* as well. Since the actors made "their entrances at some vital point in each scene of the play" the spectators who turned around in order to see who was coming missed what was happening onstage at that moment. On the other hand, if they chose to keep their eyes fixed on the stage, they missed what was happening on the *hanamichi*. Thus, whatever the spectators elected to watch, they missed something that their neighbors — deciding otherwise — would perceive. Since it is quite impossible to let the eye rest at two different points in space at the same time, each and every spectator was bound to perceive something different and following his/her own perception was obliged to make an individual selection and combination of the elements presented onstage and on the *hanamichi*. In the end, therefore, everyone brought forth an individual production.

The subjective conditions underlying the process of reception were marked by the *hanamichi* in yet another respect, since the characters appeared "from the back of the theater over the heads of the audiences." The critic from the *Erie Dispatch* describes the *hanamichi* as "a flower-decked path, illuminated by colored lights." The characters "in the wordless drama came apparently from nowhere and walk upon the stage over this symbolic pathway to take their places in the moving scenes of the amusing melodrama."[22] The colored lights established relations between the *hanamichi*, the costumes of the actors, and the stage space. The flowers on the path — the pictorial translation of the word "flower-path" — indicate that the dramatic figures do not reach the stage via the hard boards of reality, even if they come from the same direction as the spectators when they enter the auditorium. However, they do not appear from "nowhere": in making their entrance "over the heads of the audience" they seem to have sprung from their heads; they appear as the creatures of their imagination, as the creatures of their dreams.

Most New York critics underline the fact that the production had an "atmosphere of unreality," that "seeing *Sumurun* . . . is like looking on in a tense, vivid dream," that "there is a quality of unreality, a rich mysteriously exotic spell which the pantomime weaves about the spectator as he sits looking at it, that is like nothing as much as the feeling in a heavy dream."[23] Bearing this in mind we can conclude that the *hanamichi* also functioned as a connecting path between the spectator's imagination and the dream world onstage. Thus, the *hanamichi* brings the awareness that the dream world onstage is not to be taken and understood as a representation of an objectively given reality somewhere else, but instead is constituted as a subjective creation of the spectator's imagination. It is the spectator's reception — as perception and meaning-constitution — that brings the world of the stage into being as the world of his/her own dreams. Whoever appears on the *hanamichi* emerges from the imagination of the spectator and, via this path, enters the world of the stage — of the dream — where his/her desires and fears are acted out.

Thus, our investigation suggests the following findings:

1. The continuity of linear time is displaced by a discontinuous sequence of independent moments, structured rhythmically.
2. Noncoded theatrical sign systems dominate. In this way, the materiality of the theatrical sign is emphasized, particularly the materiality of the actor's body.
3. The spatial conception realized by the device of the *hanamichi* invites the spectator's eye to wander between different points in space.

Such deviations from the "norm" of contemporary theatre (naturalist as well as symbolist) result in a radical subjectification of the process of reception: of experiencing time, of perceiving, of generating meaning. These processes depend on the subjectively determined conditions of each spectator and, thus, differ from spectator to spectator. Not only does the process of reception turn out to be a process of production but each and every spectator brings forth her/his own performance. The process of reception is realized as a subjective construction of theatrical reality.

The semiotic systems and their interrelationships are restructured in several respects. First, the relationship between the semiotic systems is fundamentally changed: language is excluded and the dominance shifts to the materiality of the body. Second, the relationship between the semiotic levels is altered: the semantic level is no longer dominant; the focus shifts to the sign bodies, on the one hand, to the materiality of the theatrical signs employed and to the pragmatic level, on the other. Third, the principles underlying and ruling the combination of signs are changed: instead of linearity, causality, logic (of action), or psychology (of dramatic figures), rhythm governs the combination of the theatrical signs chosen. These basic changes result in another alteration regarding the general function of the theatrical signs: for the most part, they no longer serve a representational function but an expressive and relational function instead. In this way, the traditional sign systems and their interrelationships, typical and determining of European culture, at least since the eighteenth century, are deconstructed and, at the same time, reconstructed in a completely new manner.

This restructuring of the semiotic systems deeply affects the process of perception and cognition. European theatre, from the Renaissance to the naturalist and the symbolist theatre, realized the performance as a representation of a given "other" reality—whether as its illusion or as its symbol. Theatrical reality was intended as the representation of another reality. In this respect, theatre functioned as a model of reality. It demanded that the spectator should look and listen carefully in order to understand the model presented. Accordingly, it was assumed that the spectators would not differ essentially in their understanding of the performance, as long as they were able to recognize it as a model and to interpret it by relating it to the represented — objectively given — other reality.

Sumurun, however, disregarded such assumptions. The performance did not represent any objectively given reality. Rather, it functioned as a model of the process of how to construct reality. The factors most fundamental to this process highlighted by the performance were the experience of time and the perception and constitution of meaning as, basically, subjectively determined experiences and processes. Theatrical reality turned out to be the result or product of the spectator's subjectively executed construction.

European theatre up to the beginning of the twentieth century presupposed a clear-cut difference between the subject of cognition (the spectator) and its objects (the representation of reality onstage as well as the represented reality). As far as *Sumurun* is concerned, this difference no longer existed: it was the subject of cognition who brought forth his/her objects in the process of cognition. The role of the spectator was no longer to recognize and understand one representation of reality but, instead, to create his/her own reality. As a consequence, theatre was not to be defined anymore through its representations but through the processes of construction which it triggers. Since this capacity is not restricted to theatre (or art in general), yet is explicitly focused and marked by it, I call it theatricality.

Theatre proclaimed and established a new kind of relationship between the subject and the object of perception and cognition, as well as between theatre and reality. As early as 1886, Ernst Mach had shown that the psyche and the physical are not essentially different and that, consequently, the assumed dualism between subject and object is no longer valid:

> In popular speech and philosophy, we are used to setting *reality* opposite *appearance* [*Schein*]. I observe the pencil I hold to be straight, but placed at an angle in water, I see it as bent. In the latter case, we say: the pencil *seems* bent, though in *reality* it is straight. What justification have we, however, for saying *one* thing is real and *the other* is merely appearance? In both cases, certain facts exist which represent different relations of elements determined by different causes. The pencil is *optically* bent because of its surroundings; *haptically* and metrically, however, it is straight. . . . If no opposite exists, the difference between . . . appearance and reality is utterly superfluous and worthless. . . . The opposition between the self and the world, as that between the senses or appearance of things and object, dissolves completely.[24]

It seems as if *Sumurun*, by emphasizing its own theatricality, exemplifies or even verifies Mach's insight. There is no opposition between a given reality and its representation (illusion) onstage; rather, there are as many realities as the different spectators can construct by relying on their own perception of the performance. Since they are not forced to follow a logic of action or a psychology of character, they are allowed — invited even — to delve into the "turbulences" of single sign bodies — to look down onto that which made Lord Chandos' head reel — and, arriving at the "void" of their sheer materiality, to allow totally new meanings to emerge, well aware that these are their own subjective meanings and not meanings inherent in the sign bodies.

By restructuring the semiotic systems in a way that made it possible for each and every spectator to perceive the presented material independently of his/her own conditions and to generate meaning accordingly, the process of "retheatricalization" foregrounded the subjective conditions of perception and cognition. These are, as Mach discovered, generally valid. There can be no difference between theatre and "reality," or everyday life, for in theatre as well as in everyday life we construct our own reality, proceeding from our perception of more or less the same kind of material (human beings in an environment). In any case, reality is the product of a subjectively conditioned and performed process of construction.[25]

That does not mean, however, that there would be no difference between everyday life and going to the theatre. Whereas in everyday life we construct reality without being aware of it and without reflecting on it because we are kept busy realizing our intentions and reaching our goals, in the theatre the focus of our attention shifts to the very process of construction and the conditions underlying it. While constructing a reality of our own, we become aware of doing so and begin to reflect upon it. Thus, theatre turns out to be a field of experimentation where we can test our capacity for and the possibilities of constructing reality.

The retheatricalization of theatre during the first decades of our century has paved a way out of the cultural crisis so virulent at the turn of the century. At that time, only a rigorous stance against language, a turn to noncoded theatrical signs, and a liberation of these signs from the chains of linearity, causality, logic of action, and psychology were able to bring about a radical shift of the focus from any given reality and the problem of how to represent it to the subjective conditions underlying perception and cognition and, consequently, to the problem of how to construct reality.

The theatre of the avant-garde movement as well as the much later postmodern theatre sought to accomplish this shift by opening up new theatrical spaces which invited the spectators to let their eyes wander and/or by predominantly employing noncoded signs that allowed the spectators to attribute whatever meaning they chose. In this way, they emphatically stressed theatre's faculty to serve as a field of experimentation where each and every spectator can experience and test her/his possibilities of constructing reality.

This faculty of theatre, however, neither depends on nor is advanced by forms of postmodern theatre alone. Awareness of the process of constructing was awakened in the spectator by avant-garde theatre in the first decades of this century and is constantly being heightened by postmodern theatre, with the result that even today, on a box-set stage on which a so-called realistic performance is unfolding, the spectator is aware that he/she is in the process of constructing theatricality as well as how he/she is constructing it. Even under such conditions, by reflecting theatricality, the spectators reflect on the conditions underlying and guiding the process by which they construct reality.

WHAT ARE THE RULES OF THE GAME?
Some Remarks on *The Yellow Jacket*

The Ceylon exhibition which Carl Hagenbeck describes in *On Animals and Human Beings* (*Von Tieren und Menschen*, 1909) as one of the absolute highlights of his career was part of an institution which nowadays seems quite incredible to us: the "colonial exhibition" (*Völkerausstellung*).[1]

> The vast caravan out of Ceylon . . . arrived safely in Europe in April 1884. . . . There were sixty-seven people, twenty-five elephants . . . and a great many oxen of various kinds. The ethnographic exhibition included hundreds of different shows, and even the plant world was represented in numerous exhibits. . . . My Singhalese troupe was veiled in the ancient wondrous world of India; not only had we captured the vibrant, picturesque, outward appearance of India, but also the shimmer of its mystique. The colorful, captivating sight of the caravanserai, the majestic elephants, partly bedecked in golden saddles, partly in work harnesses and pulling gigantic loads; the slim, attractive, doe-eyed dancers with their sensuous movements and, last of all, the great religious Perra-Harra procession — conjured up a magic web which subjected the public entirely. . . . The exhibition was opened in Hamburg. . . . After Hamburg came Düsseldorf, Frankfurt, and Vienna. . . . From Vienna it went to Berlin. . . . In the following years, 1885 and 1886, I traveled with the same exhibition through southern Germany, Switzerland, and Vienna a second time, and finally set out for England. . . . It was in Paris, at the height of its success, that the Ceylon exhibition finally came to an end. The average number of visitors to the Jardin d'Acclimatisation on a Sunday was 50,000–60,000. Throughout the two and a half month duration of the exhibition, the number of visitors was nearly one million.[2]

In 1874 Hagenbeck suffered serious financial loss in the animal trading business and, in order to make up for it, opened the first exhibition of this kind on everyday life in Lapland. It was such an overwhelming success that he continued to organize colonial exhibitions throughout Europe until 1931. Similar exhibitions took place in the form of world and international exhibitions. It seems that from the very beginning this kind of event strongly appealed to European audiences. So it is small wonder that very soon a number of other entrepreneurs followed Hagenbeck's example and profited from the growing public hunger. Colonial exhibitions all over Western Europe attracted extremely broad audiences right up to World War I.[3]

In this respect, it does not come as a surprise that two official discourses claimed to inspire and even legitimize the colonial exhibition: the discourse of colonialism and the discourse of science. In Germany, for instance, such exhibitions undoubtedly served the function of winning over a large population in support of German colonial interests. And in France the colonial exhibition seemed to propagate and justify controversial current colonial politics.[4] By "staging and presenting a comparative relation between 'primitive' and 'civilized' men,"[5] such exhibitions seemed capable of suggesting to European audiences their own superiority as "civilized people" over the "primitive races" on display. By this device, it was hoped that a sense of the civilizing mission might be emphasized in justification of colonial politics. In accordance with these aims, sites where the colonial exhibitions were shown were carefully chosen: zoological gardens and panoptica.[6]

The discourse of science, on the other hand, procured a rather curious legitimization for the colonial exhibition: it guaranteed the application of genuinely scientific principles to the exhibitions — including the shows — and claimed the absolute authenticity of everyone and everything displayed. Thus, the "scientific value" of such exhibitions seemed secure. Accordingly, scientists recommended them as highly instructive and informative. Rudolf Virchow, an anthropologist from Berlin University who cooperated closely with Hagenbeck, advertised the colonial exhibitions in the ethnographic journal *Zeitschrift für Ethnologie* in a special section called "Verhandlungen der Berliner Gesellschaft für Anthropologie, Ethnologie und Urgeschichte" (Report of the Berlin Society of Anthropology, Ethnology and Prehistory). In an issue of 1898, for example, we read:

From the second of this month, the Vienna Zoological Gardens will be holding an exhibition in the Fairy Palace. It will include an Ashanti village and a Javanese village. Both "villages" are filled with numerous natives who practice their various crafts, display their dances, and provide a lively vista of native life. The countless children who attend special schools there are an exemplary additional exhibit, and these alone merit a visit.[7]

On the last pages of the same issue the following jumble of advertisements for events in Berlin is to be found:

1. On the 9th of May, Castan's Panopticum, where an unusually large and learned Orangutan and the pleasing snake-charmer Salembo are to be seen. 2. On the 10th of May, the passage-Panopticum, where a huge troupe from Togo are gathered. 3. On the 14th of May, Carl Hagenbeck's India is at the Kurfürstendamm, where a whole Indian city is reproduced and native Indians display their crafts and skills. Mr. Maas will give a talk on the Togo people after the meeting.[8]

The proclaimed "authenticity" of the colonial exhibitions seemed to allow an approach similar to that applied in field research. Virchow carried out some anthropological assessments of some members of the groups, and the photographer Günther took photographs of them. The anthropologist Franz Boas, who worked as an assistant at the Museum of Völkerkunde in Berlin, collected linguistic samples of the Bella-Coola Indians from the American Northwest coast, and the musicologist Carl Stumpf investigated their chants and music. Detailed descriptions of the extensive ethnological findings which accompanied colonial exhibitions were published in the *Verhandlungen*.

Moreover, the "didactic value" of the colonial exhibitions was stressed by pointing to the fact that in former times the experience of a foreign culture was limited only to those privileged persons who could afford to travel. The colonial exhibitions, on the contrary, made this experience accessible to everybody, particularly by introducing special rates on Sundays. Thus, it was argued, it became possible for millions of Europeans to "travel" to the foreign worlds of an "Ashanti-village" or an "Indian town" or a Lapp family.[9]

Hidden behind and intertwined with the two official discourses of colonialism and science, both exploited by them and exploiting them, another discourse nourished and controlled the colonial exhibitions — the theatrical discourse, the discourse of show business. Hagenbeck engaged the "troupes" from abroad on the basis of a contract which guaranteed them a certain profit — usually in the form of material assets. In this respect he was not unlike directors or managers of circuses, music halls, or theatres, who engage a company of acrobats, dancers, actors, or showpeople of whatever kind because they are convinced that the hired company will be able to attract audiences. This was exactly the case with Hagenbeck when he undertook the project of the colonial exhibition.

Preparing his first colonial exhibition in 1874, Hagenbeck proceeded from the assumption that the everyday life of an alien people — the Lapps — would prove sufficiently spectacular to appeal to the spectators:

It was very interesting to watch the little people, who grow only to a height of 1.3–1.6 meters, at their work. They dismantled their tents and then put them up again as if they were at home. . . . It was a pleasure to watch how the deer were trapped by their slings, how cleverly the sledges were driven, and how smooth the process of erecting and collapsing the tents was. A great interest was always shown when the deer were milked, and a little Lapp woman was the center of attention when she naïvely offered her infant the breast, quite undisturbed by the public.[10]

As for later exhibitions, Hagenbeck quite intentionally chose items that promised to emphasize the spectacular. For the Kalmuck Exhibition (1883) he invited "two Buddhist priests . . . to come along as well, who made no poor impression in their ornate robes."[11] Moreover, in this case, alongside the everyday activities, "prayers, singing, dancing, wedding processions, and wrestling were performed."[12] The Bella-Coola Indians (1885–1886) carved masks (which are still preserved in the Berlin Völkerkunde Museum), produced a totem pole, and performed dances, chants, games, and a shamanistic exorcism. Their "hametzen" or cannibalistic dance, by which the Bella-Coola initiate new members into their secret union, was received as something quite sensational. But the most spectacular event ever shown in a colonial exhibition was, without doubt, the "Ceylon-Caravan." It even incorporated Tamil actors who "performed the stories of the old epics."[13]

It seems somewhat naïve to believe that European audiences only poured into the colonial exhibitions because they were supposedly "authentic," in order to "learn" something about foreign cultures. Certainly, such exhibitions were "authentic" insofar as all elements presented — such as costumes and makeup, actions, objects — were actually to be found in the respective cultures. But in order to be presented in the context of a colonial exhibition, these elements were taken out of the context of the culture in which they functioned as particular meaning-generating elements. Moreover, they were selected and combined according to principles imposed by the organizers — whether this was intentional or unintentional is not relevant.[14] Hagenbeck's remark on the attention which the nursing Lapp mother attracted entails a first unmistakable hint. Even more revealing seems his phrase concerning "the slim, attractive, doe-eyed dancers with their sensuous movements" or, to give another example, his note concerning the Nubier exhibition (1876): "A youthful, giant Hamran hunter who, despite his tender age of 19, ranged over 6 ft. tall and inspired veritable admiration in the hearts of our European ladies."[15] From such statements we may conclude that the fascination European spectators felt in the presence of the performing foreigners was, to a certain extent, sexually motivated; their voyeuristic curiosity was directed toward the exposed bodies of the non-Europeans.

On the other hand, "the devil dancers with their grotesque masks," the Indian snake-charmers, the cannibalistic dances of the Bella-Coola, and, from Dahomé, "the stronghold of ancient African barbary, a true kingdom of horror," the king's amazons, "those semi-wild Megars, blood-thirsty and hungry for war," with their sword-dances also strongly appealed to the audiences.[16]

Thus, the elements to be presented in the colonial exhibition were selected and combined in such a way that their presentation would appeal to the suppressed sexual desires and archaic fears of the audience — to all that had been expelled from official discourse in the late nineteenth and early twentieth century. As a consequence, a rupture emerged between perception and meaning-attribution: perception was directed toward often almost naked dancing bodies, to which the perceivers were unable to attribute any meaning that the discourses they disposed of would provide. In this sense, the perceived bodies and their movements — although strongly appealing to the spectators, perhaps working on their subconscious — remained meaningless to them. They were, so to speak, "empty signs." Here the discourses of colonialism and science tried to interfere by imposing their own meanings. But this could only mask the rupture, not actually close it.

The "natural" bond between perception and meaning which the ruling discourses established and sought to maintain did not function in the colonial exhibitions; they rather seemed to be dissolved.

At the turn of the century, such dissolutions and ruptures proliferated in different cultural fields. The proverbial "cultural crisis" of that time may be quite adequately described as the consequence of an enormous dissemination of ruptures between the process of perception and meaning-generating. Modris Eksteins, in his pioneering study *Rites of Spring*, argued that World War I exploded as the result of or at the climax of this crisis.[17]

On the eve of World War I, in the theatrical season of 1913–1914, one play became the hit of the season by apparently serving the official discourses of colonialism and science and, in so doing, reflecting on the rupture between perception and meaning-attribution: *The Yellow Jacket*.

The play was written by George C. Hazelton and J. H. Benrimo as an adaptation of various Chinese plays. It was compiled from some of the most popular scenes of Cantonese opera and thus exposed — particularly in act 3 — a number of possibilities and opportunities to introduce a wide range of Chinese stage conventions to the Western stage. Indeed, the conventions chosen were such as might have appeared rather peculiar, if not absurd, to European audiences of the time. These conventions were laid down in the dramatic text either in the *dramatis personae* — as in the figures of Chorus and Property Man and his assistants — or in the stage directions for the stage designer, the musicians, and particularly the actors.

The play seemed to draw on the discourse of colonialism by making fun of the foreign — in this case, the Chinese — and exposed the foreign to the laughter of European audiences by ascribing to foreigners a ridiculous way of expressing themselves in word and action. It referred to the discourse of science by pretending to teach to European audiences the "strange" conventions of the Chinese theatre.

The play was produced in New York, London, Madrid, Düsseldorf, Berlin, Vienna, Budapest, St. Petersburg, and Moscow by leading stage directors such as Max Reinhardt (Kammerspiele Berlin, March 31, 1914), Gustav Lindemann (Schauspielhaus Düsseldorf, March 3, 1914), and Alexander Tairov (Moscow, December 1913). Wherever it was performed, it was a box office success.

This comes somewhat as a surprise. For — as far as we can judge from reviews and descriptions — these productions meticulously followed the stage directions and thus realized the strange theatrical conventions spelled out in the written text of the script. The question arises as to whether this success was due to a possible recourse to official discourses — such as colonialism and science — or whether it sprang from another source. I am going to tackle this question by referring to the four most prominent performances: the London production in the Duke of York Theatre (April 7, 1913) and the productions by Tairov, Lindemann, and Reinhardt.[18]

CHORUS: AGENT OF EXTERNAL THEATRICAL COMMUNICATION

The play and the performances under investigation open with the appearance of Property Man and Chorus and an introduction by Chorus:

> The Property Man enters indifferently from the opening at center of curtain, strikes thrice on a gong and exits. The Chorus then enters, bows right, left and center. His costume is that of a rich Chinese scholar, the dominant note being red. His manner is most dignified. His actions are ceremonious.

CHORUS: Most honorable neighbours, the bows, which I so humbly and solemnly divest myself of, are given in reverence to the three powers — Heaven — Earth — Man. I have been appointed by my humble brothers of the Pear Tree Garden to conduct you through a story of our celestial land to be played upon our most unworthy stage.[19]

Through this introduction a certain frame of reference is established: the place where the performance is going to unfold is defined as a Chinese theatre; the actors are announced as "brothers of the Pear Tree Garden" (i.e., members of a Peking opera group, who are all male; nonetheless, in the productions I know of, the female parts were played by actresses). This frame of reference sets the conditions which, in the course of events, will determine the process of meaning-generating. All that is to be perceived and interpreted has to be related to this frame.

The crucial and dominant function of the frame is constantly reinforced throughout the performance. In his introduction, Chorus goes on to explain the history of the theatre of the Pear Tree Garden and the offstage actions that his brothers are now undertaking — such as the burning of costly incense before the God of the theatre.

In this way the spectators are explicitly reminded that they are sitting in a — Chinese — theatre. What follows will be, as a matter of course, a theatrical performance. As a theatrical performance, it has some underlying rules and conventions which the spectator must know in order to be able to follow and fully understand the performance. And since it is introduced as a Chinese theatrical performance, it cannot be assumed that the spectators have *a priori* knowledge of rules gathered from other cultural fields. That is to say, the performance does not presuppose the existence of a "natural" bond between perception and meaning as established by a common, generally accepted discourse or an effective theatrical norm such as, for example, the norm of realistic theatre. Accordingly, the rules which regulate how to relate perception and meaning to each other — which meaning to attribute to which perception — have to be spelled out. Chorus continues his introduction by explaining some of these rules, such as the particular use of colors in the painted face-masks or the convention of the Property Man: "Ere departing my footsteps hence, let me impress upon you that my Property Man is to your eyes intensely invisible."[20]

Once the rules are introduced, the play can start to unfold. But the work of Chorus seems not yet done, his main function not yet made completely clear. For the setting of the frame only entails some general rules. In order to remind the spectators constantly of the given frame and to provide them with more detailed rules, the Chorus acts as an ongoing guide throughout the performance. In serving these functions, Chorus realizes quite a number of different devices. One such device is the announcement of the places where the action will be held, such as "'Tis the garden of Due Jung Fah, the second wife of Wu Sin Yin the Great,"[21] or "'Tis in a courtyard in the palace of Wu Sin Yin the Great,"[22] without anything changing onstage. Or Chorus announces an event: "'Tis a snow-storm," and his announcement is followed by the action of Property Man and his assistants: "Property Man's assistants enter doors right and left with white flags rolled with cut paper, which they shake out. They come down stage, cross, and exeunt opposite doors from which they enter. Property Man walks to center with tray of cut paper which he throws into the air, over his shoulders, then crosses to left again."[23]

Chorus lays bare the rules according to which the following actions are to be perceived and interpreted and thus controls the various processes: throwing cut paper, for instance, is to be perceived and interpreted as the sign of a snowstorm. Similarly, Chorus explains the actions of the dramatic characters. When, for example, Git Hok Gar is dead — which is indicated by the white cloth Property Man has spread over him — he "throws off the white sheet. Rises, goes up center, turns — looks at Wu Hoo Git, smiling and with gesture of blessing, climbs ladder to Heaven." Chorus adds the remark: "He ascends to Heaven!"[24] Climbing up the ladder, in this way, is explained as a sign of the figure ascending to Heaven.

The announcements and explanations of Chorus expressly serve to endow the spectators with the knowledge of the rules which control the processes of perception and meaning-production to be executed by them while watching this very specific performance. It is not a question here of whether or not these rules actually underpin the theatrical conventions effective in Chinese theatre in general or in the Peking opera specifically.[25] What interests us here, on the contrary, is the fact that these rules were introduced in performances which were shown to European audiences, which had no knowledge of such conventions. That is to say, in this case, the function of establishing a particular frame, of introducing specific rules, mainly consisted of pointing to the special conditions that should be considered regarding perception and meaning-generating in this one production.

Accordingly, at the end of the performance, Chorus cancels the specific rules of the play which have been in effect from their introduction onward. The actors are again referred to as actors, playing the part of dramatic characters: "And now, most august and honorable neighbors, you may bestow your kindly recognition upon my brothers as I nominate them each in turn and they will personally augustly thank you."[26] When the company is lined up across the stage, Chorus points out each member, beginning with Chee Moo and ending with Property Man: "And now quite visible to your eyes, our Property Man."[27]

The cancellation of the rules underlying the performance of the play, however, does not imply an annulment of the general frame of reference, namely, that the performance takes place in a Chinese theatre. This presupposition is upheld until the very end — as shown for instance in referring to the actresses as brothers from the Pear Tree Garden. It provides the justification for the enterprise of confronting the audience with a performance which issues its own rules of perception and meaning-generating without any regard to the set of rules the spectators dispose of already (because they have acquired their knowledge beforehand either in the theatre or in other cultural systems). However, the general frame alludes to this set of rules inasmuch as it introduces the performance in a certain respect as an "illusion of reality" — a rule which is familiar to the European spectators from their own theatrical experience. But in this case the illusion of reality which is to be created onstage is proclaimed to be the reality of another stage, namely the Chinese stage.

Whether the spectators actually need this common basis in order to be ready to accept a totally new theatrical model of perception and meaning production I am not in a position to judge. However, it seems that the critics took recourse to this hint. The critic in the *Sketch*, for example, writes of the London production: "*The Yellow Jacket* is a Westernised Version of a Chinese chronicle play of hatred, adventure and love, presented, as far as reasonably may be, after the fashion prevailing in the theatres of Canton." This critic, as well as some of his German colleagues, seeks to further the understanding of the performance by pointing to some similarities between the Chinese and the Elizabethan stage and, in this way, to explain the obvious deviation from the rules realistic theatre has established. He continues: "The theatres of Canton, the scenic arrangements of which bear curious resemblances to those of the Elizabethan theatre. . . . Fundamentally, it is very interesting because it shows how needless is realism, how prodigiously an audience is capable of make believe."[28] The critic in the *Frankfurter Zeitung*, writing on Lindemann's production, argues more or less the same way: "It became obvious that we may expect anything from our imagination."[29] And his colleague Richard Elchinger concludes in his review on the same production in the Munich *Neueste Nachrichten* that the devices as elaborated and demanded by the Chinese stage may be seen as "the complete emancipation from illusionistic mechanics of our occidental box-set stage."[30]

These examples show convincingly that the critics at least — and probably the spectators, too — accepted the general frame described by Chorus as the basic condition underlying their involvement in the process of laying down and following new rules on how to perceive stage space, the actors' bodies, movements, and objects onstage as well as which meanings to attribute to them.

Thus, we are now in a position to draw the following conclusions concerning the relation between perception and meaning-attribution proposed and realized by the various productions of *The Yellow Jacket*.

1. The functions fulfilled by the dramatic character Chorus operate on the level of external theatrical communication. One such function is to emphasize the fact that the theatrical process is realized as an interaction between stage and auditorium. Hence it follows that the meanings which are constituted within this process depend on the "agreements" actors and spectators alike make during their interaction. They are brought forth by both parties as the product and result of their interaction, to be more precise, of their particular "agreements." That is to say, in this case, meaning does not spring — quasi-automatically — from the general knowledge and universe of discourse possessed by the spectators when they enter the theatre. Rather the principles and rules guiding and controlling the process of meaning-constitution are to be negotiated in the interaction between actors and spectators. As a consequence, such principles and rules cannot claim general validity. They apply solely — and exclusively — to the process of meaning-production to be realized during this one performance.

2. The rules that are agreed upon refer to two fundamentally different levels. The first level is established by introducing a common frame of reference, namely the agreement that the performance is to be seen as taking place in a Chinese theatre. This frame explains the rules that follow as "Chinese" (i.e., as "strange" and unfamiliar to European spectators). In this respect, it forms the basis of the second level on which Chorus introduces specific rules that explain which place is meant by the almost empty stage, which event is indicated by an action of Property Man, and which action is signified by a particular performance of an actor. These rules are effective under the condition set by the frame. The spectators are able to learn them while watching the performance and to apply them in the course of the performance — to play the game of the performance according to its constitutive rules (set by the frame) as well as according to its particular regulative ones.

Tairov gave particular emphasis to the function of Chorus by connecting stage and auditorium through a flight of broad steps. As Alice Koonen remembers, "At the beginning as well as at the end of each act Chorus climbed down the steps to the spectators in order to explain to them what was happening onstage."[31] The London Chorus, "who explained everything and nothing, who announced the changes of the scenery that did not exist, who put the actors into their proper places from the point of view of the author," is declared by the critic of the *Sketch* "our greatest pleasure." Walter Turzinsky, the critic of the *Breslauer Zeitung*, describes the Chorus in Reinhardt's production "as prologue, epilogue, and explaining everything," as "the mediator between stage and audience."[32] Thus, it seems, in all productions under investigation here, the role of Chorus was realized as agent of the external theatrical communication issuing the rules on how to relate perception and meaning to one another.

PROPERTY MAN: MANIPULATING OBJECTS OR INVENTING THEATRICAL SIGNS?

The stage is described in the play as an almost empty space: "There are two doors, one stage left for entrance and one stage right for exit. In the center at the back is an oval opening surrounded by a grill, within which the musicians sit. Above this opening is another, square in form, which represents Heaven. About the walls of the scene are Chinese banners and signs of good cheer. Huge lanterns hang from above."[33]

There are no objects distributed in the stage space in order to indicate the particular place for which it stands. Rather, the objects are displayed in a curious manner: "At the left is a large property box, and above it are chairs, tables, cushions, etc., in fact all properties used in the play."

This stage direction was realized by all of the productions under investigation here and aroused a novel theatrical experience in the spectator. In the European theatre of the time, an object onstage functioned as a theatrical sign for the object it denoted: a table meant a table on which the dramatic figure could put a letter or a plate or could thump, sit, or whatever else, a seagull meant a seagull, indicating perhaps the vicinity of a seaside or — as a shot seagull — an action by a dramatic figure. Alternatively, the object was used as a theatrical sign for something which could be symbolized by it (for example, the seagull in Chekhov's *The Seagull*, which could mean the subject of a tale to Trigorin or a symbol of destiny to Nina). No such possibility was realized in the case of *The Yellow Jacket*. The objects lying in, on, or around the property box were to be perceived merely as objects and not as theatrical signs at all.

This prerequisite was abolished whenever Property Man walked to the box, took out one or more of these objects, and introduced them into the action. What happened then Koonen describes with regard to Tairov's production: "Property Man was seated center stage, and in the course of the play he took the necessary objects out of his box: he set a pole on the floor, which was supposed to represent a tree; he held a ladder, on which the hero, decapitated by the wicked Emperor of China, ascended to Heaven; he blew confetti from a bowl, thus representing a snowstorm."[34]

As for the Property Man in Reinhardt's production, we read something very similar in the *Badische Presse*: "Property Man on the open stage continuously procured props: a flagpole stands for a willow tree; cut paper, thrown in the air, is a terrible snowstorm; four chairs, put one on top of the other, mean an almost insurmountable mountain; and so forth."[35]

The objects in and on the property box are objects of everyday life and not yet theatrical signs: tables, chairs, cushions, etc. The moment Property Man introduces them into the action of the play they are transformed into theatrical signs. When put back into the box they are no longer to be perceived as theatrical signs but again as objects known from everyday life. It is the particular action of Property Man as he introduces an object into the action of the play which transforms it into a theatrical sign. This distinction points to the fact that it is the particular use of an object that turns it into a theatrical sign. Accordingly, it functions as a theatrical sign only as long as it is used.

Hence we can conclude that the meaning of an object on stage depends on two conditions: *that* it is used as a theatrical sign and *how* it is used as a theatrical sign.

Let us inquire into these two conditions more thoroughly: What does it mean when we say an object is used as a theatrical sign? When Wu Hoo Git has bought the girl Chow Wan, we read the following stage direction: "Property Man's assistants push four stools together, then bring four chairs and place them back of stools, touching them. The assistant exits right but returns immediately with two bamboo poles to be used as oars. He hands one to another assistant and they stand a little above to the right of the chairs. Property Man gets drapery and places it over the back of chairs. Then he places two cushions on the stools which he gets from left near property box."[36]

Up to this point, the use of the named objects as theatrical signs is not recognizable. They are manipulated in a way that could prepare for a number of different uses. When Chow Wan escapes from Wu Hoo Git, who tries to embrace her, "Property Man makes a gesture to Chorus, who rises" and announces: "'Tis a flower boat which floats upon a silver river of love." Chow Wan then refers to the objects as to a boat by action and speech: She "seats herself on a cushion in the boat and invites Wu Hoo Git to board it by saying: 'Come with me in the flower boat.'" Finally, the action of the two assistants reinforces the meaning "boat": "two assistants with poles pretend to row the boat. Musician rubs two pieces of sandpaper together in time with the strokes." [37]

As long as Property Man's assistants have manipulated the objects without Chorus attributing a meaning to them, they function as objects of everyday life, as stools, chairs, bamboo poles, drapery, and not as theatrical signs. The very moment Chorus attributes the meaning "flower boat" to them and the actors refer to them by gestures and speech as to a boat, they function as the theatrical sign of a flower boat.

In this way the process and the conditions under which an object or some objects are transformed into theatrical signs are expressly marked — so much so that it was noticed and spelled out by the critics. In the *Sketch*, for example, this sequence in the London production is described and interpreted as follows: "A long rug spread over some seats to represent a bark, a couple of boatmen some distance behind the incredible craft, the scratching of something against wood, sensuous sounds produced mainly by the scraping of catgut, a pair of lovers . . . and behold, a gorgeous pleasure-barge almost as beautiful as Cleopatra's and the melody of Shakespeare, music of Gounod, and a momentary surrender by all of us to elementary instincts of passion." [38]

Thus, we can conclude that it was not the meaning of the objects which suggested the meaning of the respective theatrical sign but rather the act of expressly attributing that meaning and the particular use the actors made of it. Chorus' statement clearly classifies the object as the theatrical sign of a boat and, in accordance with this statement, the actors refer to it as to a boat.

This brings us to the second condition: the particular use that allows the spectator to ascribe a specific meaning to a manipulated object. While in the example given above the chairs and stools function as elements of the theatrical sign "boat," in other scenes they were employed to signify quite different objects. Before Wu Hoo Git declares: "I will build a mountain that shall kiss high Heaven, and on the top of it I will cone ten thousand thousand peaks, till topping the highest with my dainty foot," Property Man and an assistant "bring table on which are two stools to center. Wu Hoo Git takes one stool, places it right, at table, the other stool remaining on table." Wu Hoo Git now announces: "I ascend" and "climbs on table impulsively." Then he "climbs to the top of chair on table, back to audience." [39] Although Property Man and his assistants have brought the table and the chairs to center stage, they do not yet function as theatrical signs. They are, however, not objects in the same way as they were when they were on and beside the property box. When they are placed center stage, one could perhaps classify them as "virtual theatrical signs." The moment Wu Hoo Git takes one stool from the chair, places it to the right of the table, and announces "I will build a mountain" he refers to the table as to the theatrical sign of a mountain. When he climbs on the table he transforms it into the theatrical sign of a mountain and, by climbing to the top of a chair on a table, transforms the chair into the theatrical sign of the upper part of the mountain and its top into the theatrical sign of the peak that touches Heaven.

By referring to the same object with different actions or by establishing different relations between the objects, the actors not only transform the objects into theatrical signs. They also attribute to them different meanings. That is to say, one and the same object may be used as a theatrical sign for different objects, actions, or processes. Its semiotic function does not depend on its everyday function, its possible resemblance to another object, or its metaphorical relation to an idea. Rather, the semiotic function is attributed to the object by means of the actions which an actor executes as it is taken up. Its possible semiotic functions and meanings, when used as a theatrical sign, are not to be derived from the everyday function and meaning of the object. The dissolution of the "natural" bond between perception and meaning, the rupture between them, seems to serve as a prerequisite for their employment as theatrical signs. In this way the principle of polyfunctionality, multifariousness, and ambiguity of theatrical signs is stressed.

While the actors who represent a dramatic character in the play quite regularly transform an object into a theatrical sign when manipulating it — as Wu Hoo Git transforms the table into a mountain and Chee Moo transforms a stick into a baby — Property Man relates to the objects he manipulates in two different ways. As long as he is simply procuring the objects onstage, they remain objects from the everyday world such as table, stools, cushions, and poles. The moment he introduces them into the action of the play by handing them over to an actor, or by letting Chorus name their now actual meaning, they are transformed into theatrical signs.

In their reviews of the different productions, the critics all emphasize that Property Man showed absolute indifference toward the action of the play. The Property Man in the London production handed the actors "the swords, or the weeping willow tree, or the snowstorm, or any little thing like that needed by them, with an air of the profoundest contempt or boredom — not even the youngest of our dramatic critics could show a profounder scorn for actors and acting than this Property Man, who was rendered perfectly by Mr. Holman Clark."[40] And of Reinhardt's Property Man, Rudolf Schildkraut, we learn that "he sat in a corner, his back to the audience, smoking cigarettes or reading a paper or chewing rice and only took part in the action quite unwillingly, when he had to provide the actors with the props they could not do without."[41] Without the slightest effort to move unobtrusively (having been introduced as invisible!) and without any pretense of interest in the action of the play, Property Man presented himself, in both cases, as a man who does not take part in the world of the stage play, who, instead, belongs to everyday life. However, he has to transfer some objects from the everyday life into the stage world in which, by means of the play of the actors, they adopt ever changing functions and meanings. Thus, Property Man acts as a kind of *Grenzgänger* between the two worlds of everyday life and theatrical reality, and his crossing of the border between the two worlds directs the spectator's attention to the peculiar capacity of the theatrical process to transform any object and any action into the theatrical signs of other objects and other actions.

Any relationship between perception and meaning in *The Yellow Jacket*, thus, is established and controlled by very specific conditions:

1. Perceiving an object onstage does not entail the need to interpret it as a particular theatrical sign. Its presence onstage only allows for the assumption that, in the course of the ongoing performance, it will be used as a theatrical sign, without suggesting a particular meaning which might be attributed to it. It could be labeled a virtual theatrical sign. An object onstage is transformed into a theatrical sign as a consequence either of its being handed by Property Man to an actor, who plays the part of a dramatic figure, or of its being declared a theatrical sign by Chorus. That is to say, the perception of an object onstage does not necessarily result in the perception of it as a theatrical sign and the attribution of the appropriate meaning to it.

2. When the object is used as a theatrical sign and, accordingly, is perceived as such, its possible meanings are not to be derived from the function and meaning of the respective object in everyday life or from any other similarity that may be assumed between the object and another object to which it might refer as its theatrical sign. In *The Yellow Jacket*, two in principle different ways of ascribing meaning to an object, when it is employed as a theatrical sign, are realized. It may be declared to be a sign of X. In this case, its meaning is the result of an agreement. Alternatively, the meaning of the object emerges as a result of a particular relationship which the actors establish between the object and a gesture or a movement or a sound, in acting. Accordingly, the semiotic function of the object as a theatrical sign cannot be determined as descriptive or representational; rather it is to be described as relational.

3. Since the meaning of any object used as a theatrical sign emerges here as the product of a particular relationship, any change of relations will lead to

an alteration of meaning. That is to say, the relation between an object used as a theatrical sign and its meaning is not a stable one. In situation *A*, a table may be introduced as the theatrical sign of a mountain; in situation *B*, however, it can be used in order to represent a cave. Thus, the spectator learns the basic rule, during the performance, of how to use an object as a theatrical sign and how to proceed in order to attribute a meaning to it, rather than learning the fixed relation between an object as signifier and another object as its signified. Any object may be used in order to signify any other object.

TAKING PLEASURE IN THE RUPTURE:
A THEATRICAL EXPERIENCE ONLY?

The productions of *The Yellow Jacket*, we may conclude, not only proceeded from the experience of a rupture between perception and meaning; they also sought to intensify this experience by radically separating the processes of perceiving and meaning-generating from each other. Usually, to perceive a certain shape and a certain color means to perceive a certain object. That is, perception and meaning-constitution are performed almost simultaneously. For to perceive an object means to attribute a certain meaning to a certain shape and a certain color — for example, the meaning "table." On the basis of different cultural discourses, some additional meanings may also be attributed to the meaning "table"— for instance, the meaning "Bauhaus furniture," which is almost synonymous with the meaning "work of art," or the meaning "King Arthur's dinner table," or whatever. In the case of *The Yellow Jacket*, however, the object which is perceived as a table does not mean "table," but instead (i.e., not as well as) "a mountain" or "part of a pleasure barge." And these meanings are not attributed on the basis of common cultural discourses but as the result of a particular relationship which is established between the perceived object and a performed/perceived movement and/or speech onstage, as well as with the spectator. Thus, perceiving a table is the same here as perceiving an "empty sign"; for all the meanings provided for it by the effective cultural discourses do not apply. In this case, the actual meaning emerges, as explained, as the consequence of a particular relationship between perception, movement, and speech, which not only the actors, but the spectators must establish as well.

The reports on the overwhelming success of the productions give rise to the idea that the audiences greatly enjoyed establishing such relations. They seem to have interpreted the emphasis on the rupture between perception and meaning which caused "empty signs" as a request to establish new and unexpected relations between perception, movement, and speech established by the actors onstage, and in this way they allowed ever new meanings to emerge in order to fill the "emptiness." And, as we can guess from the reviews, they took an extreme pleasure in doing so.

This seems somewhat puzzling. For, as I have stated in the beginning, the proliferation of ruptures between perception and meaning elsewhere resulted in a "cultural crisis" — in other cultural fields the experience of such ruptures and the abundance of "empty signs" which they produced was felt to be disquieting, disintegrative, and disorienting. Why did the audiences enjoy in performances of *The Yellow Jacket* that which they abhorred in everyday life, where it caused deep anxieties?

One answer to this question is determined by the rules of the game. At the beginning of the performance Chorus' introduction establishes a common frame of reference, namely the agreement that the performance is to be held to take place in a Chinese theatre. This frame explains the following rules of how to relate perception and meaning to each other as theatrical (i.e., not applying to everyday life) and as "Chinese" (i.e., "strange"). In this way, the rules are explained as working exclusively within this framework, not claiming any further validity. They are introduced as nontransferable. Thus, one might argue that the spectators accepted the rules as constitutive for this one performance — this one game — only and played the game with great pleasure without feeling the need to transfer the experience caused by this game to other "games" — to other performances or even to other cultural fields than theatre.

However, this argument does not appear watertight when seen in the light of the reviews. By comparing the rules spelled out in the performances of *The Yellow Jacket* to the rules effective in realistic performances, some critics concluded that realism is "needless,"[42] that "we may expect anything from our imagination,"[43] that an "emancipation from all illusionistic mechanics of our occidental box-set stage" is overdue.[44] That is to say, they were ready to transfer the rules of *The Yellow Jacket* to other theatre productions and, thus, to understand *The Yellow Jacket* against the background of the realistic theatre as a new model of theatricality. In *The Yellow Jacket* they found the theatrical process redefined as a process of meaning-production which is performed in the particular frame of reference of being theatrical — and not an imitation of "the real world" (here "Chinese" and not "European") — as well as in a particular configuration of perception, speech, and movement. A theatrical performance, accordingly, may be redefined as a game in which any object may be used to signify any other object or action by relating it to a specific speech and/or movement.[45] In this way, some of the critics and, supposedly, some of the spectators too were willing and able to transfer the rules of this game to other games of the same genre: theatrical performances.

On the other hand, they seem to have accepted the fundamental difference between theatre and everyday life. That which appears possible, even desirable and enjoyable, in theatre was not held to be appropriate in everyday life. Taking pleasure in the rupture remained then, at least, a purely theatrical experience.[46]

THE AESTHETICS OF DISRUPTION
German Theatre in the Age of the Media

RETURN TO THE AVANT-GARDE?

In the early 1960s certain new developments in Western theatre occurred which, in some ways, seemed to complete the process of redefinition of theatre that was initiated by the historical avant-garde movement at the beginning of this century. In a decisive move against the long- or reestablished bourgeois, educational, and commercial theatre, now theatre was explicitly being defined as the "detailed investigations of the actor-audience relationship."[1] As before, this new definition led to the search for new theatre spaces and genres and a new manner of using signs where the focus shifted from the semantic to the pragmatic level. Performances were held in a workshop (Richard Schechner's Performance Garage in New York), a factory (Ariane Mnouchkine's Théâtre du Soleil in a former ammunitions factory in Vincennes), a slaughterhouse (Bremen), cinemas (Bremen and Bochum), an exhibition hall (the Schaubühne Greek project), a film studio (the Schaubühne Shakespeare project at the Halleschen Ufer 1976–1977), a tram depot (Frankfurt), and the 1936 Olympic Stadium in Berlin (Grüber's *Winterreise* [1977; Winter Journey]). Either a new concept of space was created for each production (Jerzy Grotowski, Schechner, Mnouchkine, Peter Stein, Einar Schleef) or a different location was found for each production. Theatre was performed in the street, in market squares, parks, circus tents, department store windows, living rooms, even on the façade of skyscrapers, in ruined castles, on cliff tops, at a lake's edge, and in a forest clearing. Peter Brook directed his first "intercultural" production, *Orghast*, at the theatre festival in Shiraz in 1972 at Xerxes' tomb, and Robert Wilson's *KA Mountain* and *GUARDenia Terrace* played seven days and seven nights in and around Haft Tan Mountain. Since the beginning of the 1960s, theatre has continued to create for itself new performance spaces. There is nowhere on earth which is not, in principle, a potential performance space.

In the same way that Lothar Schreyer founded his Sturm- und Kampfbühne after World War I with a group of initiated amateurs, so-called independent companies sprung up throughout the Western world which — in part living and working communally — experimented with new forms of theatre. Indeed, it was mostly such groups — Eugenio Barba's Odin Teatret founded in 1964, for example — that realized and spread the idea of a street theatre reverting to ancient theatre traditions such as processions, market fair spectacles, acrobatics, fire-eating, fooling, and clowning. Other groups, such as the Lindsay Kemp Company founded in 1962, drew on such diverse traditions as classical and modern dance on the one hand and the music hall, circus, pantomime, and striptease on the other, mixing trivia, kitsch, and art at random.

It was not only independent companies that broadened the idea of what theatre could be. Solo performers such as the "clowns" Jango Edwards and Dario Fo created highly individual styles of one-man theatre. Another example is the transvestite Craig Russel, who dressed in the glittering robes of show business and presented the female stars of entertainment from Marlene Dietrich to Judy Garland in a broad range of styles including satire, parody, travesty, and mimicry, from total identification to critical persiflage.

The happening and Action Art developed — out of the fine arts as a kind of re-edition of dadaism — as new theatrical genres. From 1959 on, happening artists such as Allan Kaprov, Michael Kirby, and Wolf Vostell dispensed with the idea of theatre as a finished product in actions and performances which were not intended to be interpreted but only experienced. The demarcation between actor and spectator was no longer clear; instead, the spectator experienced the action by becoming an actor. In his *Abreaktionsspielen*, the Action artist Hermann Nitsch used real objects and real events: the sign character, the meaning-potential, of props and stage events was negated, and in their place the real character of the plot, the objectness of things, was displayed and experienced.

Further borderline phenomena took root at the very edges of this already fringe idea of theatre: the exhibition *Inszenierte Räume* (Staged Spaces) by Karl-Ernst Herrmann and Erich Wonder (Hamburg, 1979), for example, presented rooms which the two stage designers had created for the spectators to walk through and experience, rooms in which the visitor to the exhibition became the actor. Another example is the Theater im Schaufenster that the actor Heinz Schubert discovered in the shops along the city streets and photographed — the advertising "scenes" that window dressers created with their dream people.

When Ivan Nagel set up the Theatre of Nations in Hamburg for the International Theatre Institute in the spring of 1979 he put together a program which impressively documented the whole breadth of this extended idea of theatre, a concept of theatre so expanded over the previous twenty years that it had become almost unrecognizable. In the program notes, Nagel wrote on the different forms of theatre performing alongside one another:

> They do not complement each other in one harmonious idea of world theatre; indeed, their aims, methods of working, the performances themselves, are all mutually exclusive. . . . One performance questions the next. If theatre can be defined as what the young clown Jango Edwards does alone onstage for two hours when he releases all the savagery of the body, all the fury and rebellion of the heart, can the beautiful, intelligent performance of the Burgtheater Ensemble so gently re-interpreting Goethe's *Iphigenia in Tauris* also be called theatre? Each genre accuses the other. Can art be created in lethargic prosperity, representational snobbery, and political tangle, or is only pseudo-educational diversion and appeasement possible under such circumstances? And can the exhibition of all the powers of one single artist, cut off from the community of a professional ensemble, lead anywhere but to destructive aggression and bitterness?[2]

This uncertainty concerning the idea of theatre that Nagel stresses so emphatically and that prevailed from now on seems to be a consequence of a devastating erosion of the whole traditional cultural system. The breaking of the boundaries of theatre corresponds with an extensive theatricalization of everyday life: the Theater im Schaufenster found its equivalent, that is, its continuation in "lecture hall theatre," "church theatre," and "department store theatre" as Peter Handke contested as early as 1968.[3] A strict or at least "clean" division between the spheres of high and subculture, art and the everyday world, theatre and life, was no longer possible.[4] It seems as if this kind of theatre has, since the 1960s, increasingly fulfilled the cultural-revolutionary demands set forth by the historical avant-garde movement to close the gap between art and life, to bring art into life.

Now, just as at the beginning of this century, theatre's self-reflection is carried out as a process of questioning the aesthetics of theatre. Once again the repertoire of potential theatrical signs is considerably extended. Theatre in Western cultures has consistently absorbed new elements from the enormous wealth of theatrical and cultural histories of all peoples of all times and used them as its own signs. The repertoire of theatrical signs is a super-supermarket of cultural practices and items which can be invoked and employed at will. Alongside this, modern technology has opened thoroughly new potential in the creation of theatrical signs such as those which can be realized by computer-controlled lighting, video-sizing, laser beams, and holography. There is basically no culture and no cultural system within it from which Western theatre cannot "borrow" elements to be used as theatrical signs. The most important aesthetic procedure thus lies in the choice of particular elements and in determining the principles underlying their simultaneous and successive combination.

Consequently, in this respect, too, the theatre seems to have taken up the aims of the historical avant-garde movement and, since the early 1960s, developed them. Indeed, one of the members of the historical avant-garde came to this conclusion. When Robert Wilson presented one of his plays, *Deafman Glance* (Paris, 1971), for the first time in Europe, an "open letter" appeared shortly afterward in the *Lettres françaises* by the surrealist Louis Aragon addressed to his former colleague in arms André Breton, who died in 1966. In the letter, Aragon informed Breton that "the miracle . . . has happened . . . the one we have been waiting for, the one of which we once spoke," and that it happened after he had long given up hope.[5] Are we, therefore, to see the theatre of the neo-avant-garde (or postmodern) as a continuation and completion of the theatre of the historical avant-garde?

However close this conclusion may come to the truth, it is nonetheless deceptive.[6] This is because the general circumstances under which the "revolution of theatre" occurred in the first decade of this century are radically different from those of the last thirty years. The theatre of the historical avant-garde set out to destroy the bourgeois cultural system oriented toward bourgeois individuals, their ideals, and their needs. It aimed to create a new culture oriented toward the needs of the masses, a mass culture, and, in particular, a people's theatre. The growing automation and technicalization of communications, work, and everyday life, the new media of film, radio, and gramophone, had just begun to have an effect on the perceptive habits of the spectator so that the perceptive ability that Eisenstein, Meyerhold, and Piscator anticipated for their theatre was certainly too great a challenge.

In the 1960s a new mass culture was already long established — not, however, through the creation of a people's theatre, but through the distribution of the new mass media, film, radio, the gramophone, and television. The technical reworking of perceptive ability was already so advanced in everyday life that an endless, simultaneous, and multidivergent appeal to the eye and ear is considered "normal." In this situation, theatre wanted to "cure" the individual of a sense of isolation and anonymity as well as total absorption into the masses, both of which are consequences of mass culture, and to provide the individual with the opportunity of experiencing "authentic situations." The growing self-reflection of theatre and its questioning of theatre aesthetics were accordingly carried out in deliberate confrontation with the culture of the media. An examination of the theatre of the last thirty years should, therefore, consider its *media-theoretical* aspect.

Between theatre and the new media of film, television, and video exist, as is well known, fundamental phenomenological differences. For theatre to occur, the actors and spectators must gather together in a specific place for a specific duration of time. The new media, on the other hand, free their users (spectators) from space and time; without having to leave the house (the room, the bed) they can follow events which are happening or have happened at different places at different times. Though physically immobile themselves, the spectators seem to be able to travel at will through time and space with the help of the new media. In theatre, production and reception are concurrent processes: while the physically present actors execute certain actions, present signs, the physically present spectators react directly by receiving the actions in one way or another and interpreting the signs in whatever way they choose. The performance is always realized in this sense as a process of face-to-face interaction between actors and spectators.

The new media, on the contrary, work with images of human bodies, objects, and events which are created by technology or electronics and which can be reproduced at will. Interaction between the user and the representation of a person (whether one who acts a fictive persona or the real person) in the receptive process is as impossible as interaction between the user and the producer of the images. In fact, the producer communicates with the spectator along a one-way track. The new media use technology to transmit technologically created products (communicants) as mass communication to the individual user. Theatre, on the contrary, is an event that happens to a group of physically present people.

Moreover, while the camera prescribes the focus and perspective,[7] the theatre spectators can let their eyes wander over the performance and choose the focus and perspective for themselves. Thus, the main differences refer essentially to three aspects: the actor-spectator relationship, the modes of perception and reception, and the materiality of the signs employed.

While the theatre of the historical avant-garde was still dreaming of a theatre for the masses and even saw its ideal in a filmicization of theatre (Meyerhold, for example), theatre since the 1960s has increasingly focused on the phenomenological features of theatre, displaying them provocatively or, at the very least, making them obviously apparent.

The happening *In Ulm, um Ulm und um Ulm herum* (In Ulm, round Ulm, and round about Ulm) created by Wolf Vostell in November 1964 together with the Ulm Theatre Company (artistic director Ulrich Brecht, dramaturgy Claus Bremer) dealt with the idea, among others, that theatre is a bodily *going through* of an experience. Instead of gathering, as usual, at one place for the event, the approximately three hundred participants were asked to pass through twenty-four stations one after the other (they were brought to each by bus): an airfield, a carwash, a multistory car-park with an underground garage, an open-air swimming pool (at night), the inner cloisters of a monastery (Wiblingen), a field, the city slaughterhouse, the slaughterhouse sauna, a cowshed. The last station should have been a garbage dump, but since the second aspect of the theoretical agreement, not only to be at a specific place but also to be there at a specific time, could not be fulfilled because of inevitable delays, the additional elements of "set" (such as the televisions) were already dismantled and this station was dropped. Against all intent, the second condition of a theatre experience was inevitably stressed.

> "Usually" the spectators only need fulfill the prerequisite of being in a certain place at a certain time if they intend to watch theatre — where perhaps several different scenes are presented to them on one stage — but here, the spectators had to continually shift physically from one place to the next. As they entered each new theatrical space they themselves became actors: in the multistory car-park they wrapped in blankets "dead" bodies that were lying around and moved them offstage, grabbed apparently abandoned tires from the walls, and generally larked about. In the field, they stood freezing in the dark, holding hurricane lamps, telling each other their life stories. In the slaughterhouse they pounced upon a lavishly set table where the actors had just begun a feast and tidied the dishes away.[8]

While here the participants were turned into actors (and at the same time spectators of the action — as in everyday life) the first Frankfurt Experimenta (1966) concentrated on negotiating forms of interaction between actor and spectator. The question was raised: who, under what conditions, may transgress the dividing line between stage and auditorium. At the premiere of Peter Handke's *Publikumsbeschimpfung* (Offending the Audience; directed by Claus Peymann), which not only challenges the basic relationship in theatre between actor and spectator but formalizes it, the actors directed their verbal attack from the stage at the audience.

> Between outbursts of applause, a young man at the front stood up and left the theatre shouting: "I know your game. I'm off." . . . Another spectator in the middle of the second row stood up as the question of standing up and sitting still was being discussed onstage. He declared that he did not want to sit down again, to which the actors spontaneously replied "Better sit down," which seemed to help. But on the second evening — or so we

hear — it came to a far livelier reaction in the audience. Finally the director had enough of playing along and tried to push those who had climbed up from the auditorium off the stage.[9]

The chaos that occurred here was the result of different assumptions concerning the process of theatrical interaction. While the director and actors assumed that the roles of the actor and the spectator were already acknowledged and that the appropriate places (stage and auditorium) were fixed from the start, some members of the audience no longer accepted these traditional conventions. They carried out an exchange of roles (from spectator to actor) and transgressed, to a certain extent, the border between auditorium and stage. The distribution of roles and the process of interaction were open to negotiation.

While the Frankfurt Experimenta, both in this production and in others (e.g., Bazon Brock's *Theater der Position*; Theatre of Position), was unable to find a balance, the Living Theatre (which emigrated from the USA and finally settled in Berlin 1965) came down on the side of audience participation. In different productions, the actors consistently crossed the dividing line and entered the auditorium, moved among the audience, and turned directly to individual spectators both verbally and physically, while the audience reacted to a certain extent and became, in a limited way, participants.[10]

In the 1960s and early 1970s the question of a potential role exchange from spectator to actor — the question of audience participation — was the main focus of interest among experimental productions, but in the course of the 1970s it came to be understood that the act of watching itself had, in the process of theatrical interaction, a specific quality of its own which actually constitutes and defines the very process. While happenings and audience participation sought to fight the lethargic acceptance, the passive consumption of audience behavior made habitual or strengthened by and through the new media, the act of spectating was now conceived and emphasized as a form of active doing.

In 1976 the Schaubühne at the Halleschen Ufer, under Peter Stein's direction, created a production in preparation for their version of *As You Like It* (1977) entitled *Shakespeare's Memory I & II*: memories of Shakespeare as well as Shakespeare's memory. In one of the halls at the abandoned CCC (Central Cinema Company) film studios in Spandau, the actors presented approximately three hundred spectators with seven hours of lectures (on astronomy or the Spanish armada), readings (from poems to Elizabeth I by Walter Raleigh and the earl of Essex), demonstrations (of models of the world and the movements of the stars), tableaux (Elizabeth I in the royal carriage), market and fairground entertainment (acrobatics and sword-dance), short scenes from Shakespeare's plays, and much more. Several pieces were presented simultaneously.[11] The spectators were free to walk to and fro among the various action spaces, to choose this piece and reject another, and in this way — following their own preference, curiosity, or simply their noses — they put together their own program from the broad palette of pieces on offer. The production systematically marked the characteristics which fundamentally differentiate the reception of theatre from the new media under so-called experimental conditions, that is, through isolation and "exaggeration": for even if the spectators are seated before a fixed stage, they are nonetheless required to direct their gaze and attention to one of the elements presented simultaneously and thus "miss" the rest. In this sense, all spectators in theatre compile their own performance.

This sense of the creative act of spectating was overtly stressed, fought for, and realized in the late 1970s and 1980s, over and over again. Either various excerpts of the "environment" onstage were played simultaneously, a practice used to a great extent by the Schaubühne — from Klaus Michael Grüber's *Bacchae* (1974) and *Winterreise* (1977) through Stein's production of the *Trilogie des Wiedersehens* by Botho Strauss (1978; Three Acts of Recognition) and from Aeschylus' *Oresteia* (1980) to Andrea Breth's production of Arthur Schnitzler's *Der einsame Weg* (1991; The Lonely Way). Or a new spatial design was found for each production which actually provoked the spectators into letting their gaze wander or choose between scenes: the quasi-amphitheatre stage for Hans Neuenfels' Frankfurt production *Medea* (1976) which extended into the auditorium, for example, or Frank-Patrick Steckel's square, surrounded on all sides by the audience, where he produced *Penthesilea* (1978, Frankfurt), or the wide "catwalk" that Einar Schleef built in the cellar of the Frankfurt Depot where his *Götz* (1989) and Lion Feuchtwanger's *1918* (1990) were played.

Now that the productive power was released and lay in the gaze of the spectators, the box-set stage could be revived again. For even here the creative gaze of the spectator is the condition which enables theatrical interaction: in the theatre, spectating is equal to acting. Just as in Heiner Müller's "Bildbeschreibung" (1985; Description of a Picture), where the reception of a picture is realized as the production of a theatrical text, so reception in theatre is always a productive process. To have recalled this medial condition of theatre and brought it back into public consciousness is the achievement of experimental and aesthetically advanced productions of the last twenty years.

In the course and wake of its self-reflection in the last thirty years, theatre has developed such different aesthetic devices that each attempt to reduce them by description or analyzing function to a common denominator is doomed to failure. In one sense, however, they are noticeably alike. Each stresses the specific materiality of theatrical communication, which is itself, to various extents, provocatively exhibited: its specific spatiality, corporeality, and sound quality.

The stage no longer represents a real place (living room, grove before Diana's temple, forest, or cave), nor is it symbolic of an idea (archetypal world, suppression of people, consciousness). Rather, it presents, above all, an artificial space as stage space. This is as much true of the almost empty stage in Peter Zadek's *Othello* (Hamburg 1976), with its shoulder-high red curtains around a box-set stage explicitly marking the theatrical space, as it is of the Esplanade Hotel refurnished by Antonio Recalcati for Grüber's production of *Rudi* (1979). The surviving rooms among the ruins next to the Berlin wall between no-man's land and the barbed wire fence refer, with little or nothing added, to Bernard Brentano's novella, which is broadcast via loudspeakers as the spectators wander through the rooms.[12]

Independently of which space is chosen and what stage format is used within it, the stage space represents an artificial space, an environment which can be entered and played, whose single segments or elements (details) can be loaded with different meaning-potential by individual spectators depending on the actions of the actors and/or the extent of the spectator's capacity to remember, associate, and fantasize.

In Wilfried Minks' *Maria Stuart* (Bremen, 1972), for example, the meeting between the two queens takes place in a room so completely filled with Elizabeth's state robe that it is defined by it. Elizabeth (Margit Carstensen) rises out of the tip of an eight-meter-high state gown while Leicester, who is to rescue Maria, hangs like a tassel from it. Maria (Ute Uellner) stands below in a green meadow. She runs toward Elizabeth as against the face of a cliff and, as she runs, Elizabeth lifts her skirts, exposing the green meadow under Maria's feet as the hem of her dress. The procedure can of course be interpreted directly according to the text, but it has meaning even beyond this relation. Its polyvalence allows it to be coupled with different chains of image and association.[13]

Another example: on the second evening of the Greek Project at the Berlin Schaubühne for Grüber's production of *The Bacchae* (1974), a huge planked area marking the playing field in the exhibition hall was lit by bright neon light (stage designers Gilles Aillaud and Eduardo Arroyo). Immediately after the bacchae made their entrance, they inspected the room, fingered the walls which closed the playing area at the back and the ventilators, turned off the light, and began to tear the boards from the floor. Clumps of soil, fruit, lettuce, and wool were thrown up. Finally, they unearthed the elderly Cadmus (Peter Fitz) and Tiresias (Otto Sander), thoroughly covered in slime. Then, simultaneously with the entrance of Pentheus (Bruno Ganz), a road-sweeping machine that had been parked in an opening in the wall on the left side drove onto the stage. It was manned by figures in yellow plastic suits. The machine swept away the "filth" created by the bacchae, the yellow figures replaced the boards, and Pentheus ordered the neon light to be turned on again. In this example, one could certainly interpret the actions as direct "translations" of the text. But the actions are not understood by their relation to the text alone and instead open dimensions that go far beyond the text so that they actually refer to the text in only one or another respect.[14]

A third and final example: Hans Neuenfels designed a stage for his Frankfurt production of *Iphigenia in Tauris* (1980) that basically consisted of two parts: on the right half of the stage stood a group of chairs from Goethe's time, in front of folding screens with an opening. The left half of the stage, on the contrary, was covered in water with a sandy island and two tall trees in the middle. Lying in the sand on the island was a glass shrine with a life-sized doll in it (the statue of Diana). At the beginning of the performance, Thoas (Edgar M. Böhlke) sits on a chair in the right half of the stage. He is dressed in a modern suit, wearing glasses and reading a book. After Iphigenia (Elisabeth Trissenaar) turns down his proposal, he crosses the stage, wades through the water to the left half of the stage, takes off his jacket and shirt, revealing tattoos on the upper half of his body, kneels down in the sand, unearths an ancient animal skull from beside Diana's "shrine," places it on a column at medium height, and prays to it with fervent muttering. Thoas' relapse from civilization to barbary thus suddenly becomes obvious without even remotely exhausting the potential of meaning of the actions onstage through this reduction.[15]

The productivity of the theatrical space seems, in this way, almost limitless. Although it is spatial relations that are presented, these spatial relations prove to be, at the same time, political and anthropological, interpersonal and introspective, mythical and historical, grammatical, syntactic, or semantic: indeed, relations of all kinds can be wholly externalized in the performance area as spatial relations.

True, the spectator may often put together a whole chain of such relations even before the actor has created, revealed, or even suggested specific relations through change of position and action. Thus, the spectator will find relations in the environment of the *Bacchae* between the sweeping machine and the horses standing behind another opening in the wall, between the figures in yellow plastic suits and the man in the tuxedo, who can also be seen in yet another opening in the wall, drinking champagne. These might be relations of opposition (animal vs. machine; animal vs. human; work clothes vs. formal dress) or relations of equivalence (agile animal that stands still/active machines standing still/live people standing; machines/space suits/neon lights/ventilators). In a similar way, the spectator may discover the opposition of nature and culture on Neuenfels' stage or perhaps the opposing pair: Goethe's Weimar/ancient Greece. The specific theatrical productivity of the space is, however, generally only revealed by the physical actions of the actors. The changing spatial relations created by moving in and through an environment can stimulate a whole wealth of associations to explode in the spectator's mind.

Thus, it is above all these changing relations between space and body made possible by the environment which emphatically stress and clearly mark the spatiality of theatrical communication as well as its corporeality. Such enormous productivity is only unveiled when two conditions are met: the stage is presented as an art space (see above) and the actors present the body as material for an art figure.

This second precondition demands wholly new ways of using the body onstage. Accordingly, since the late 1960s, widely differing practices of bodily discovery and bodily training for the actor have been developed and tried out. In most cases the demand for "authenticity"—for authentic bodily discovery and authentic bodily expression—took priority. Artaud and Grotowski were deemed to be pioneers in this sense, as was Lee Strasberg's Method, which built upon Stanislavsky's "system," Zen yoga, and Tai Chi and other Far Eastern practices of bodily discovery and use of bodily expression. The new bodily awareness that grew from this enabled the actors to present their bodies onstage in such a way that the materiality of the body — corporeality — was explicitly marked.

This was as true of the dressed (costumed) bodies as of the naked ones. Even though the naked body, as potential for cultural-revolutionary protest, does not play so prominent a role in the Federal Republic of Germany as it does in the American avant-garde culture of the late 1960s and early 1970s, the presentation of the naked body onstage increasingly gained meaning even there. However, nakedness was not foregrounded as pure materiality — as pure nature — rather, the naked body appeared as culturally worked upon and fixed in different semantic relations.

Nakedness was, for example, set in relation to specific aspects of character. Thus, in Ulrich Heising's production of Franz Xaver Kroetz' *Stallerhof* (Hamburg, 1972; Stallerhof) the — dramaturgically founded — nakedness of Beppi (Eva Mattes) stressed the vulnerability of the bare physis — her unprotected exposure, externalizing Beppi's particular situation.[16] In Zadek's *Lulu*, on the other hand, (Hamburg, 1988), Susanne Lothar demonstrated Lulu's nakedness as the sensuousness of her physis, which is unwilling to be domesticated, and thus, at the same time, the limited potential of the body as material for art, which can only be made up for by overlaying this moment with an aspect of the artificial figure on display.[17]

In his *Bacchae*, Grüber constructed a whole system of producing meaning from the opposition of naked and dressed bodies: the men were all naked except for a G-string, the women were all dressed — each differently, each highly individual. When Dionysus (Michael König) and Pentheus (Bruno Ganz) meet for the first time they come very close to one another, greet each other with an intimate kiss, touch each other, and almost melt into one person. While Dionysus persuades Pentheus to put on women's clothes, so that he can observe the women in Cithairon safely, Pentheus puts on the lady's shoe which Dionysus held in his hand when he was pushed onto the stage on a hospital trolley to deliver the monologue of his first appearance. After Agave (Edith Clever) kills her son, there is no dismembered body lying on the stage. Instead of Cadmus putting together the (naked) body of his grandson, Agave sews together pieces of the suit that the man in the tuxedo wore — stand-up collar, tails, white shirt, gray lacquered shoes. There is a whole sequence of equivalences and oppositions which can occur in this process (e.g., naked Dionysus vs. clothed Bacchae; naked Pentheus vs. clothed road-sweepers; naked Dionysus, naked Pentheus vs. man in white suit in the doorway; naked Dionysus vs. Pentheus dressed as a woman; the text version of a naked Pentheus vs. elements of a tuxedo). It not only releases an enormous meaning-potential, but also consistently stresses the various specific materiality of the bodies appearing onstage.

In a completely different fashion, Zadek exposed the nearly naked body of the actor in his *Othello* as material for the production of theatrical signs. Othello (Ulrich Wildgruber) was painted with a dark color that began to run as the first beads of sweat appeared. When the nearly naked protagonists, Othello and Desdemona (Eva Mattes), embraced, Othello's black color rubbed off and left marks on Desdemona's stomach. The "noble Moor" was thus revealed as a theatrical blackface representing all the contemporary prejudices and stereotypes of the Europeans toward the concept of "black." When Desdemona gave herself to him, something of him rubbed off onto her — the color stained her.[18]

Although toward the end of the 1960s and beginning of the 1970s the materiality of the body was spectacularly prominent in the naked body of the actor, since this time, it has been aimed at generally and accorded systematic precedence. Peter Stein's *Tasso* production as early as 1969 in Bremen, for example, ended with a "thrilling final cipher . . . in expressive signs": "Tasso, squatted on the grass for [his] . . . last monologue, stretched out on his back in front of Antonio, raised himself to standing on straddled legs, touching Antonio's body all the while as if climbing up him, and clawed into Antonio's shoulders as if hanging there, gawking around with idiot satisfaction and jerky movements of the head: a chimpanzee who is carried from the ring by his master after performing his turn."[19]

Stein further varied the methods he first tried out here in his early productions at the Schaubühne. In *Tasso* he exploited the opposition between the human body and ape behavior; in *Peer Gynt* (1971) it was the opposition between living body and dead body/corpse: "At the end, Peer Gynt died in Solveig's castle after she had spent her life waiting for him. The co-workers of the button molders brought them both down from the mountain, placed them in front of a photographer's camera which committed them per photo to posterity in a Pietà-like picture of almost 'supernatural' love — like a devotional picture."[20]

In *Prinz Friedrich von Homburg* (1972; The Prince of Homburg), Stein achieved the appropriate effect by dividing the figure between the actor's body (Bruno Ganz) and a puppet, while in the *Trilogie des Wiedersehens* he created a final tableau with the opposition: living face vs. face encased in bandages as part of a work of art.[21] Each of these final images was created and displayed as a complex sign which referred back to the previous production with specific meaning. At the same time, it emphatically brought into view the general problem of theatrical signs and meaning-production: the signs presented through the actors' bodies are not absorbed by the meanings that may be attributed to them. Rather, they are signifiers — sign bodies — with a kind of necessary surplus of meaning that is the result of their particular materiality.

Theatre since the end of the 1960s has continually thematized and reflected upon this problem in new and different ways in its various representations of

the body. Pina Bausch, for example, confronts specific sequences of movement with kinds of speech which "concretize" them:

> A group of men fawn upon a woman standing in the center with small ges-
> tures of stroking, tickling, caressing, which, due to increasing frequency,
> are exposed as being intrusive, possessive, and selfish. The woman col-
> lapses silently so that the men don't even notice her reaction. They con-
> tinue to fondle her as she lies on the floor. Positive expressions such as "to
> shower someone with kindness" or "to love someone to death," "to take
> someone under one's wing" prove to be rigid, tyrannical actions when
> physically concretized. Bluebeard dressed Judith in the clothes of all the
> dancers — Bluebeard's wives — until she is numbed into unconsciousness,
> delivered up to his whims as a puppet.[22]

Pina Bausch also employs techniques which one can find today in the work
of many choreographers and directors (among others, Jan Fabre and Robert
Wilson): the endless unchanging repetition of a series of movements or the
contrasting repetition of a movement sequence performed in "normal time"
and in slow motion. As a result of this technique, the gestures and movements
of the body forfeit their sign character — they appear as nothing more than
gestures and movements.

This "sweet materiality" of gestures where "running . . . is just running," as
Grüber put it, is also stressed in many of his productions.[23] In *Empedokles:
Hölderlin lesen* (1975; Empedocles: Reading Hölderlin), for example, the tramps
in the waiting room, constructed on the side stage, execute each movement
with precision, slowly and thoroughly: buttoning the coat, putting away the
remains of a meal, tying on a scarf, shaking out a cloth. While Brecht used
similarly concrete actions to clarify aspects of the figure, here they appear for
their own sake. A gestural action that everyone recognizes from everyday life
according to the context does not refer here to the plot or help create character; it simply refers to itself. Since, however, it is realized as a concrete
identifiable action, it qualifies as a "sign" that should nonetheless remain
"meaningless."[24]

A borderline case — in many ways — is offered by Robert Wilson's productions created, since 1979 (*Death Destruction & Detroit* at the Schaubühne
in Berlin), in German municipal and state theatres. Wilson's point of departure is the individual corporeality of each actor: "I watch the actors, observe
their bodies, listen to their voices and then I try to make a play with them."[25]
While insisting on their individual corporeality, he makes the actors execute
minimal movements: they enter and walk across the stage, they stand still or
sit down, they sit immobile on a chair or hang from a rope from the flies, they

lift a hand, an arm, a leg, and lower it again, they draw their faces into a smile. That is, on the one hand, they execute movements which, in a way, form the basic vocabulary of the stage: entering, walking across the stage, standing, sitting down, sitting, lying down, lying, standing up, exiting. On the other hand, they adopt decidedly unusual positions: they hang on ropes (*Golden Windows*, Munich, 1982); they balance on a ladder (*the CIVIL warS*, Cologne, 1984). All movements are executed in rhythmic, geometric patterns, predominantly in slow motion.

The actor's body and movements do not function here as signs: the body is simply present onstage, going through the motions without meaning anything. When in *Hamletmaschine* (Hamburg, 1986; The Hamlet Machine) a woman sits at a table and scratches her head and smiles, this does not mean that a figure — Ophelia, for example — is sitting at a table, scratching her head and smiling; it simply shows an actress sitting at a table, scratching her head and smiling. When in *Parzival* (Hamburg, 1987) Christopher Knowles enters balancing a plank on his head and turns in a circle on the spot, this says nothing about Parzival; what is presented is just how Christopher Knowles balances a plank on his head and turns round on the spot.[26]

The moving or static body of the actor is displayed as a moving or static body with its own specific characteristics, its own particular materiality. It is not to be perceived as a sign; rather attention is focused on its concreteness — the positions it adopts, the movements it executes in slow motion. The actor's body is not used here as material for an art(ificial) figure, but in its materiality itself as an artwork. The individual moving and immobile bodies of the actors in Wilson's theatre become the "true" work of art. The exposition of their specific being onstage achieves what Arthur Danto called the "transfiguration of the commonplace."[27] Through being exposed on the stage, the actor's bodies are transfigured into works of art. In this way, the emphasis on corporeality as the *sine qua non* of all theatrical communication is pushed to its furthest limits.

Wilson's theatre, however, operates in precisely the contrary borderline area where the actor's body is continually threatened with "disappearance." Wilson works mostly with a flat backdrop, often a canvas, which serves as a projection screen for film (e.g., *CIVIL warS*) or lighting reflections (e.g., *Lear*, Frankfurt, 1988) or which shows abstract pictures (e.g., *La maladie de la mort*, Berlin, 1992; Disease Death). Since Wilson gives prominence to his actors and their movements through space and generally has them execute their movements parallel to the forestage and the backdrop, the impression arises that the corporeality of the actor melts into the flatness of the picture. Since Wilson also lights the actors with a *contre-jour* and overhead light, however, their three dimensionality, plasticity in space, is explicitly emphasized. That is, his theatre reflects, stops, perpetuates, as it were, the very moment at which the actor's body prepares to pass from the stage space into the flat surface of the picture, in which the three dimensionality of the body is on the verge of disappearing into the surface of the picture — the moment in which theatre yet again stops and confirms its specific materiality before it melts into the medium of the picture in which it will completely dissolve without trace.

However multifarious, different, or even in part contradictory contemporary theatre may be, by forcefully emphasizing spatiality and corporeality in theatrical communication, it not only reflects — quasi self-sufficient — on its specific materiality, but actually puts it provocatively on display. Stubbornly insistent, it continually directs attention to the fundamental difference between theatre and the technical-electronic media — a difference which will only be annulled with the disappearance of the theatre into the new media — or with the disappearance of spatial bodily reality in the computer.[28]

As for the sound quality in theatrical communication, this kind of difference is barely evident. Quite the contrary — here theatre has very clearly profited from developments in the new media. The theatrical sign systems of sound and noise can be expanded through the media in ways of which avant-gardists such as Meyerhold, Leopold Jessner, and, above all, Artaud only dared dream. The overwhelming effect of the sound of wind and barking dogs in Grüber's *Empedocles*, for example, is as much in debt to sound technology as was the acoustic space designed by Hans Peter Kuhn for Wilson's *Lear*, in which the spectator was accosted with sounds coming from all directions: whirring sounds that swelled up and faded, the beats of drums, bird calls and twitterings, barking, calls from afar and a babble of voices, the clattering of cutlery, flute music, the sound of dripping water, banging metal, and ever-recurring audible silence. In this, as in other productions, it was precisely these noises, these sounds, which sensuously represented strange and distant, even transcendent, spaces to the spectator. The sound quality of theatre both confirms and negates at the same time the spatiality of theatre: it is confirmed, in that the space presented to the eye is extended by that which the ear is presented; it is negated, in that it absorbs the visual space into the acoustic space and destroys it.

This brinkmanship of sound quality, directly on the border between affirmation and negation, on the one hand of the spatiality, on the other of the corporeality in theatrical communication, is consistently taken up in productions of the last few years — despite the great risk of failure. The human voice is given precedence as the field of play where, in highly individual ways, corporeality and sound quality clash against each other: in making sounds, the corporeality of the voice manifests itself and at the same time is released from the body, to which, however, it returns through the ear.[29] This exciting tension between the sound quality and the corporeality of the voice can, however, be disrupted or even distorted by language: when the signifieds of the spoken text are forced into the foreground in such a way that they seem to detach themselves from their signifiers, the sound quality, the speaking voice, is reduced to its pure mediality; its specific materiality evaporates.

For a theatre that aims to reflect on and emphasize the materiality of theatrical communication, a serious, apparently insoluble problem arises, particularly in the so-called spoken theatre. Here it is essential to devise techniques which clearly mark the materiality of the voice even when speaking language. Grüber sought to achieve this by having the actors speak very quietly, Hansgünther Heyme, by having the actors shout. But the signifieds were frequently swallowed up by the signifiers and obliterated almost uncompromisingly.

Einar Schleef, however, found a way of giving prominence to the signifieds by marking the materiality of the signifiers, by binding space, body, and voice directly to one another. He employed a technique that the avant-gardists from Georg Fuchs and Meyerhold to Jessner and Jürgen Fehling repeatedly put at the heart of their discussions on the retheatricalization of theatre: rhythm. In his Frankfurt productions from *Die Mütter* (1986; Mothers) to *Faust* (1990), Schleef had the actors noisily stamp their feet in steel-capped boots as they descended a huge staircase or cross a wide catwalk while speaking words and sentences in chorus, in continuous repetition to the rhythm of the strides. The synchronous rhythmicization of space, bodily movement, and speech brought the specific materiality of theatrical communication, in an expressively sensuous way, to the fore. In space, corporeality and sound quality were prominent; in body, spatiality and sound quality; in sound, spatiality and corporeality. The seemingly indissoluble union created by rhythm resulted in a direct semantification of specific materiality.[30]

The devices that Wilson uses prove, to a certain extent, to have taken the opposite path to emphasize the sound quality of the speaking voice. Amplified by a microport, the actors' voices simultaneously resound from loudspeakers, apparently detached from the actors' bodies. Together with other sound material — noises, bangs, sequences of notes — they form a kind of sound collage which establishes its own acoustic space. Since it is barely possible to establish a relationship between the spoken text produced in this way and the movements executed by the actors at the same time, the specific materiality of voice and gesture is given additional emphasis. From his early productions to *CIVIL warS* (including act 1, scene A) Wilson employed specially chosen fragments of everyday speech, bits and pieces of dialogue as speech material. When the sounds of these linguistic ready-mades were concentrated, by electronic amplification or alienation and insertion, into one sound collage, speech was often reduced to pure noise. Since the beginning of his collaboration with Heiner Müller (*CIVIL warS*, act 4, scene A), on the other hand, Wilson has predominantly used poetic speech material. He emphasizes sound by having sentences enunciated slowly, clearly, and in continuous repetition, in part together with distortions of sound and overlapping of other sounds. The acoustic space created in this way — as in *Hamletmaschine* or *La maladie de la mort*—is, above all, a linguistic space. Its pronouncedly exposed materiality seems to allow the meanings of the spoken words and sentences to evolve directly from the sound quality.[31]

Heiner Müller further developed this technique of splitting voice and body in his own production of *Mauser* (Berlin, 1991) to such an extreme that it touched upon an ancient theatrical tradition. He separated the speakers of the text from the players. While one group of actors, clearly in view onstage and in the auditorium, continually repeated the text, another group of actors executed gestural actions in silence, which, as in Wilson's theatre, bore no recognizable relation to the simultaneously spoken text. In this, Müller was drawing on the methods of the Japanese puppet theatre of which Brecht had already made his own use. While in the Japanese *bunraku*, as in Brecht, the spoken text and gestural action refer to the same thing and thus clearly correspond with one another, here the lack of such a correspondence was emphasized. Sound quality and corporeality were strictly isolated from each other so that their respective materiality was given focus. This focusing gained particular emphasis in that all technological-electronical means of production were dispensed with and the process of separation was carried out as an eminently theatrical one of display: when speaking and acting on the stage are divided between different actors, the spectators know, as in Japanese *bunraku*, that they should exclude the clearly present and visible body of the speaker as absent from their aesthetic perception. In that Müller, however, destroyed any recognizable relationship between spoken text and gestural action, both sound quality and corporeality stood emphatically in the fore.[32]

In Müller's production, the typical dominance of body over language, characteristic of the 1970s and early 1980s, was annihilated. Body and language were used as equally valid and equivalent, though as basically different materials. In their production of *Homer lesen* (1986; Reading Homer), however, the Vienna group Angelus Novus moved toward a gray area in which the spoken text became the sole protagonist, advancing the idea of language as the dominant theatrical material.[33] In the Vienna Künstlerhaus, the members of the group took turns reading the 18,000 verses of the *Iliad* in twenty-two hours, nonstop. Copies of the *Iliad* were laid out in other rooms, inviting the listeners wandering around to read along with the sound of the reading voice. It was not the individual corporeality of the actors performing that attracted attention but, rather, the specific materiality of their voices that was clearly present as each reader succeeded the next, which interrupted the flow of the hexameter only through the sudden marked difference in vocal quality.

By fixing the materiality of theatrical communication as language and thus theatre as a space in which language is sensuously experienced in the sound of a voice in this production, the theatre clearly separated itself from the technological-electronical media, which — as predominantly image media — allow language to decay into background noise. Theatre is clearly demarcated from this in that it can be described and defined as the place in which space, body, and language meet in their various specific materialities.[34]

ANTHROPOLOGICAL THEATRE

The "electronic age" is characterized, as Paul Virilio rightly comments, above all by technological developments which are opening the way to "a new visual perception . . . that has become independent of man: satellites are always in the process of filming, mapping, locating objects, computers ceaselessly analyse the situation automatically so that a new, eccentric view of the world has come into being."[35] Because theatre never tires of directing attention toward its very own theatricality, exposing it in a provocative way, it confirms, on the other hand, the fact that aesthetic perception is the same as sensuous perception: it is tied to the body of the perceiver, only made possible and determined by that very perceiver. The simultaneous physical presence of the actors and the spectators in the same room, the *sine qua non* of theatre, thus appears to mark the special condition of the possibility of aesthetic perception altogether — theatre becomes the paradigm of aesthetic experience as sensuous, bodily experience. The self-reflection of theatre, its constant recourse to its own special phenomenology, is thus carried out as reflection on the conditions which create the possibility of aesthetic perception and aesthetic experience.

The aesthetics which theatre achieves in this way — by uncompromisingly insisting on its materiality and its permanent, demonstrative display — can perhaps be most appropriately described and identified as the "aesthetics of disruption." The freely wandering gaze of the spectator suddenly halts, transfixed by a gesture, a look, a beam of light, a ray of color, a thing, before wandering off again. The path of the spectator's gaze, the points where it rests, and the length of these rests are decided by the interaction of the material presented onstage with the spectator's individual, subjective capacities to perceive, to memorize, and to fantasize, with the spectator's own particular structure of needs. Reception is thus completed as the various subjective disruption of the space-time continuum. It allows individual subjective spaces and individual subjective times. The aesthetics of disruption thus marks peculiarities which are valid in a general sense for theatrical reception.

Such disruption has little in common with the process of montage employed by Piscator or Brecht, for in this case not only were the "cuts" predetermined, but also the single elements all referred to complex themes (foundering revolution, inflation, and so on), or referred to the "fable" or the plot. Here, however, the spectator's eye is in charge of the "montage"—it creates its own production. Equally, this theatrical aesthetics of disruption is not derived from so-called zapping, switching back and forth between television channels. For here the spectator cannot let the eye wander—it remains unmoving, focused on the same point in space. On the contrary, one could characterize zapping as the process by which the spectator in front of the television set seeks to simulate the wandering eye of the theatrical experience without having to, or being able to, actually move it.

The disruption created by the gaze of the spectator in theatre, on the contrary, is a direct result of its free movement within the time-space continuum. When the spectator's gaze disrupts this continuum, it presents—as Heiner Müller in his "Bildbeschreibung" put it—"the breach in the flow, the other in the return of the same" ("die Lücke im Ablauf, das Andere in der Wiederkehr des Gleichen"). Theatre takes place at each moment in which "the observation slit [of the eye] in time opens between one look and the next" ("der Sehschlitz in die Zeit sich auftut zwischen Blick und Blick").[36]

The self-reflection which contemporary theatre performs in its experimental and most aesthetically advanced productions has quite a different thrust from the self-reflection of theatre of the historical avant-garde movement. For the former contemplate the possibilities and conditions that are the "givens" of humankind and expose them to the reflecting gaze of the spectator. Today theatre is no longer interested in psychology or sociology, but rather, above all, in anthropology.[37] In fact, Marshall McLuhan's statement, coined in the age of the technological-electronical media, is valid for contemporary theatre: "the medium is the message."

In this process, the "rediscovery of the human body" stands at the core and appears possible because "the body is no longer socially necessary. It is no longer used in the work process, and less and less is it needed for social presence, because social presence is largely determined by telecommunications. But that opens the chance to rediscover the human body that still exists in the shadow of our technical world."[38]

This rediscovery of the body occurs in everyday life through employing a wealth of (principally) "Eastern style schools of bodily practices which have gripped a broad spectrum of the population."[39] The body stands at the center of regulations concerning nutrition, clothing, cosmetics, and movement; spare time not occupied by the technological-electronical media is dedicated to the body. In theatre, the rediscovery of the body has occurred over the last thirty years through reflecting on and displaying its particular materiality. The body, which has become superficial to society, becomes here, solely through focusing on this aspect of its particular qualities (i.e., corporeality), a work of art.[40]

While in the 1970s and early 1980s the focus was on the actor's body, in recent years signs are growing that the rediscovery of the human body goes hand in hand with a rediscovery of language. Events such as the *Homer lesen* by the Angelus Novus, Müller's *Hamlet* (1990) and *Mauser* productions, and even the recent *Julius Caesar* production in Frankfurt by the Needcompany (1992) have employed text exclusively as material for speaking. The words and sentences pronounced by the various individual voices of the physically present actors appear here in their specific sound quality as the true theatrical work. If these signs have been interpreted correctly, then it is highly likely that aesthetically advanced theatre in the near future will, in this new sense, develop as a theatre of language. But one cannot say for sure. It seems unwise to formulate a prognosis.[41]

The separation of speaking and acting, the marking of their relative materiality in contemporary theatre, directs attention to the body and to language as the most fundamental anthropological givens. Whether this turn toward anthropology is to be seen as a last stand against the ruling trend of the media to replace "reality by the image" and against the media's "preparation for computerization," as a last halt before the moment "when the computer takes over,"[42] or whether it is to be seen as a liberation of possibilities which, it is true, were always available, but can only now be unfolded *because* the computer is taking over — this question cannot and should not be decided here.

The dissolving of the borders of theatre and the corresponding theatricalization of reality that results that can be observed everywhere in the West over the last thirty years can, in the light of this controversy, hardly be understood as the simple solution to the demands made by the historical avant-garde in reaction to bourgeois culture, to build a bridge over the gap between art and life so typical of the bourgeoisie and draw art into life. The "fusion of theatre and reality" that occurs today has quite a different thrust.[43] By marking and reflecting on the fundamental conditions of human existence, which the process of civilization increasingly buries almost to the point of suffocation, the aesthetics of disruption aims to uncover them in everyday life, returning them again — or finally? — to their inborn rights. When the theatre, in its aesthetically advanced productions, calls out to reality "Ecce homo!" a far distant echo sounds back from reality, "Ecce homo!"

PART II
Theatre Cross-Culture

IN SEARCH OF A NEW THEATRE
Retheatricalization as Productive Reception
of Far Eastern Theatre

WHAT IS RETHEATRICALIZATION?

"Retheatricalization," proclaimed at the beginning of this century,[1] was above all aimed at countering naturalist theatre, the prevailing form at the turn of the century. In place of a realistic-psychological theatre of illusion, dictated by literature, members of the historic avant-garde movement throughout Europe (ca. 1900–1935) wanted to propose an "other" theatre, different in every way from what had gone before: a theatre freed from the chains of literature, constituted as an autonomous art form; a theatre which did not imitate a reality which actually existed, but which created its own reality; a theatre which nullified the radical split between stage and spectator and which developed new forms of communication between them, so that the chasm between art (theatre) and life, so typical and characteristic of bourgeois society, might be bridged.

To this extent, the retheatricalization of theatre implied the development of a wholly new, determinedly anti-illusionist, theatrical code which was not only to propose a different repertoire of signs, but also to present other syntactic, semantic, and pragmatic rules; which was not only to produce new relations between the signs used on the stage, but also to establish a fundamentally new relationship between stage and spectator. The code to be created for this "retheatricalized" theatre was to initiate wholly new rules, for both internal and external theatrical communication.[2]

In developing this new code, members of the theatre avant-garde turned to various traditions of nonillusionist theatre.

1. Greek theatre offered an important point of reference. As early as the nineteenth century, it had provided a significant impulse toward the reform of theatre. In 1849, in both his works *Die Kunst und die Revolution* (Art and Revolution) and *Das Kunstwerk der Zukunft* (The Artwork of the Future), Wagner developed and explained his concept of the *Gesamtkunstwerk* as the art of the future by drawing on the *polis* and theatre of the Greeks.[3] This association was to remain constitutive for him. The ground plan of the festival theatre in Bayreuth (the foundation stone was laid on May 22, 1872) is clearly

modeled after the Greek theatre. In the same year Nietzsche, whose admiration for Wagner at this point knew no bounds, concluded his work *Die Geburt der Tragödie aus dem Geist der Musik* (The Birth of Tragedy Out of the Spirit of Music), which was the source of much inspiration to many theatre reformers at the beginning of the twentieth century.

2. In very different contexts, members of the theatre avant-garde were drawn to the great folk theatre traditions of the sixteenth and seventeenth centuries, principally *commedia dell'arte* as well as Elizabethan theatre, the Spanish Siglo de Oro, and the early period of the Vienna *Volkstheater* under Anton Stranitzky.

3. A third reference point was drawn from various indigenous folk cultures in a broad sense, with their festivals and customs. Most frequently employed were elements of the market fair, puppet and marionette theatre, conjurers and tightrope walkers, show booths and market cries, as well as circus clowns and acrobatics.

4. A "contemporary" reference point was found in modern folk culture, which can partly be described as popular culture. This strand of tradition is composed of music hall, boxing, revue, cabaret, and, not least, film.

5. A further reference point seldom observed by previous research was provided by the various forms of Far Eastern theatre such as the Japanese *no* and *kabuki* theatre, Chinese opera (notably its best-known form, Peking opera), Indian *kathakali*, and Balinese *barong*.[4] It is the recourse to these traditions that is the theme of this chapter.

These multifarious and in part strikingly divergent traditions were not explicitly taken up for their literary elements, but rather for their widely differing nonliterary elements such as theatre architecture and costume, ritual and mask, bodily movement and music, and so on. In this sense, the retheatricalization of theatre means the process of productive reception by which modern European avant-garde theatre adopted elements of nonliterary traditions from utterly dissimilar European and non-European traditions and fertilized the development of a new theatrical code.[5]

RETHEATRICALIZATION AS PRODUCTIVE
RECEPTION OF FAR EASTERN THEATRE

Models for a New Theatre

The function and meaning of the productive reception of Far Eastern theatre for the development of a new theatrical code are examined here with a few examples drawn solely from Japanese theatre.

The opening of Japan in 1868 was the start of lively travel from Europe to Japan. Returning travelers published more or less accurate and detailed reports on the foreign culture. Beginning in the 1870s, one already finds isolated reports in English, French, and German on Japanese theatre; at first only in newspaper articles,[6] but after the 1880s in book form.[7] For a long time, these reports were the most important source materials from which one could gain knowledge of Japanese theatre. In any case, they sufficed to convey to the European reader/spectators, who were tired of naturalism, the impression that Japanese theatre might provide a countermodel to a European theatre they felt to be developing in the wrong direction.

The initial highpoint of enthusiasm for Japanese theatre was reached with a tour to Europe by Otojiro Kawakami's troupe, starring Kawakami's wife, Sada Yakko. The troupe was not a "real" *kabuki* troupe, but belonged to the *shimpa*, a school attempting to modernize *kabuki*. Nevertheless, even this school only admitted male actors, since the ban of 1630, totally forbidding women on the stage, was still in force. Sada Yakko, who was trained as a geisha and thus as a dancer, first took over the leading roles during the troupe's tours abroad (1899 in San Francisco). The troupe was the first to travel through Europe and America offering a larger Western audience the opportunity of seeing Japanese theatre — even if it was not authentic traditional Japanese theatre. Sada Yakko was a sensation at the World Exhibition in Paris (1900) as well as in London (she performed twice in front of Queen Victoria, in 1900 and 1901) and in Berlin (1902). The audiences were captivated and, despite feelings of estrangement and at times arrogance, the critics aptly pointed out the originality and remarkable aspects of a performance art which might stimulate European theatre — in which the literary theatre of illusion dominated: "To us, the plot seems naïve. It is, I repeat, a pantomime libretto. But it is through mime that they principally convey and express passion, and not merely passion alone, but also the nuances of emotion. It is just as in Wagner's music where the voice sometimes only serves to narrate the dramatic situation in a simple melody while the orchestra expresses all the nuances of feeling borne by that situation. Mime is the essential art of the Japanese artists."[8]

There are two aspects of Henri Fouquier's critique worth mentioning. On the one hand, by referring to Wagner, it explicitly points out that theatre does not serve to imitate reality, but creates its own reality, a reality of "emotion." On the other hand, it also unmistakably acknowledges the fundamentally different formation of the dominants; the position occupied by language (the literary text) in European theatre is taken over here by the art of acting.

The dominance of the performance art, particularly in Sada Yakko's death scenes, seems to have totally overwhelmed the European audience. The Paris critics even went so far in this respect as to place her above their national treasure, Sarah Bernhardt:

> An incomparable spectacle. Without contortions, without grimaces, she gives us the impression of a death that is physically progressive. We see life slowly abandoning the little body, almost second by second. . . . Our Sarah Bernhardt herself, who so excels in dying, has never given us a stronger feeling of artistic truth.[9]

> After her temptress smiles, what eyes deep with anger! Her nose dilates, her cheeks become hollow, fright convulses her whole frame, and she dies with a sort of supernatural realism.[10]

When the troupe performed the two plays *Kesa* and *Shogun* in Berlin in 1902, however, Franz Blei wrote somewhat mockingly, "The whole world in Paris went to be charmed by 'Sada's death'; the accommodating Japanese changed this scene, so that what only took a minute in New York when I saw it lasted the whole play in Paris and in Berlin seemed endless."[11]

One can, however, easily understand the addiction of the European audience to Sada Yakko's death scenes. It was precisely in such scenes that the Western spectator experienced a theatre which could dispense with language to a large extent, a theatre which, solely by means of its performance art, through bodily movement, was capable of creating a reality of "emotions." One can thus assume that at least part of the audience and critics received the theatre practiced by the Japanese troupe as a countermodel to the dominantly literary theatre of Western culture, which only sought to imitate reality: "What a spectacle for the imagination, what a feast for the eyes," as the French critic Arsène Alexandre excitedly exclaimed in *Le théâtre*.[12] Indeed — a "theatrical" theatre that in no way required "retheatricalization."

The concept of a countermodel was strengthened by the second visit by Sada Yakko to Paris in 1908 as well as by performances by the dancer Hanako in Berlin, Paris, and London between 1905 and 1908. On the occasion of the latter's performance in Berlin, René Schickele wrote:

> Above all, in the precise grace in everything she does, therein lies Hanako's greatness. She maintains her grace as she dies with the quivering and hoarse death-rattle of a great bird. In the movement where she sinks softly, wave-like, onto her face from an upright position, she achieves a great bright stillness after the dull thud of the body which makes death so

shocking. But then she is attractive, like a flower. . . . Read the chapter on the Japanese smile in Lafcadio Hearn's book.[13]

Here again, it is the negation of the imitation of reality and the extraordinary skill of the dancer to create and express the reality of death entirely with her body that Schickele emphasizes in Hanako's death scene — exactly those characteristics which set Japanese theatre most radically in opposition to European theatre of the time.

The final sentence in the critique quoted above suggests, however, that it is not just the idea of Japanese theatre as countermodel to European theatre that is engaged, but, more generally, Japanese culture as a countermodel to Western culture. Accordingly, Schickele introduces his critique by recommending to his readers Lafcadio Hearn's books on Japan, which, in the meanwhile, had been translated into German. For "they provide information on the happiest of exiles, they are the diaries of a romanticist fleeing Europe, who found a home of breathtaking beauty in the land of young Hanako and because he was as happy as only a man can be who, sick of the all pervading spiritual ugliness of corpulent communities, found a people that can be consumed, with a smile, by the cult of blossom-like beauty."[14]

The recourse to Japanese culture occurred throughout Europe, but, especially in Germany, it was associated with the hope of finding a way out of the widespread and virulent crisis in Western culture.[15] It is therefore not surprising that even the performances by the Japanese troupes were received, at least to a certain extent, with this view in mind. Nonetheless, it is indisputable that their performances principally fulfilled the function of presenting the Western audience with a countermodel to its realistic-psychological theatre of illusion and of demonstrating the possibility of a "theatrical" theatre more or less *ad oculos*. To this extent, these performances provided theatre reformers and audiences with vital stimulation toward the development of a new theatrical code.

Reorganization of the Relationship between Stage and Spectator (External Theatrical Communication)

The Russian theatre avant-gardist Vsevolod E. Meyerhold (1874–1940) developed a new theatrical code to counteract the passivity of the spectator in bourgeois theatre, a phenomenon all too familiar in his own experience. Meyerhold began his career as an actor at the Moscow Arts Theatre, where he played Treplev in Stanislavsky's well-known premiere production of *The Seagull*. Despite his acting success, he was soon dissatisfied — as much with his own work as with the fundamental ruling principles of the Arts Theatre. He thus withdrew from the ensemble and, from 1905, developed his "conditional" theatre, which aimed to overcome the shortcomings of the naturalistic stage and realize a "theatrical" theatre. Meyerhold believed that the distinct separation of stage and auditorium was the greatest obstacle hindering such a "theatrical" theatre. In his early work *On the History and Technique of Theatre* (1907) he complained:

> The spectator only experiences passively what happens on the stage. The border between actor and spectator is drawn by the platform stage that divides the theatre into two foreign worlds: those who only act, and those who only receive, and there are no arteries which might bind these two separate bodies in one circulatory system. The orchestra brought the stage closer to the spectator. The platform stage arose where once the orchestra stood and distanced the spectator from the acting space again.[16]

Meyerhold aimed to determine fundamentally new relations between the stage and the spectator. His concept was not compatible either with the spatial conventions of the box-set or raised platform stage or with the principle of "true to life" on the naturalistic stage:

> Naturalistic theatre teaches the actor to express only the obviously salient, specific elements, never to leave something to suggestion, nor consciously not play something out to the full. That's where this frequent overexaggeration in naturalistic theatre comes from. . . . In his imagination, the spectator is capable of completing that which is only implied. . . . Naturalistic theatre clearly denies the spectator this ability to continue drawing, to continue dreaming, as he does when he listens to music.[17]

Accordingly, Meyerhold saw the need to dispense with these conventions and to replace them by devices that might free the spectators from passivity and engage them in activity. He experimented with elements of different, nonillusionist theatre forms. In the end, he found the most promising course was to turn to Japanese theatre.

> In Japanese art, we might see that the Japanese, knowing the conventional nature of theatre, are not shy of playing without a curtain, or of building a "flower path" through the auditorium. They are not concerned, if, during a monologue, a neutrally clothed man holding a candle on a long stick approaches the actor quietly to light the actor's face so that his expression is more clearly seen. The spectator is not amazed; he knows that it is just a "stage assistant" who simply lights the actor's face.[18]

Here Meyerhold addresses two particularly salient and typical conventions of *kabuki* theatre: the *hanamichi*, or flower path, and the *kurogo*, or stage assistant.

The *hanamichi* is a path approximately one and a half meters wide on the left side of the auditorium, which links the back of the auditorium with the stage and runs through the audience. It is said that it was originally developed as a passageway on which the audience might offer the actors *hana* (presents). However, in the architectural development of the *kabuki* theatre, the extension of playable areas was determined by the development of turning the action of the actors toward the audience. In this sense, the introduction of the *hanamichi* can be explained as a solution to the problem raised by this fundamental impulse. Earle Ernst describes the main *kabuki* stage as "the more formal of the two acting areas, while it is on the *hanamichi* that more intimate acting is performed. The *hanamichi* does not bring about intimacy by any significant change in the actor's technique of expression, but by its unique function as an acting area."[19] In any case, the introduction of the *hanamichi* seems to have created a convention which specifically concerns the relationship between the stage and the spectator. Its function can be described as lending this relationship a special proximity.

The *hanamichi* is used for entrances and exits as well as for especially important moments and phases of performance. The most significant acting area is the *shichisan*, a point seven-tenths of a meter along the *hanamichi* away from the stage.

As the actor moves forward on the *hanamichi* he is first concerned . . . with the expression of the essential nature of the character (if this is his first entrance in the play) as well as with the present mood of the character. He moves forward a distance of some forty feet to the *shichisan*, and during the whole of this distance (which is as great as the width of the stage in the average Western theatre), he is concerned with only two things: establishing the nature and present state of the character and establishing rapport with the audience. His proximity to the audience and the audience's reorientation from the stage to the *hanamichi* separate the character from involvement with the field of theatrical interest on the stage and thus the actor is enabled to bring the character into a sharp focus, over a considerable acting area. Pausing at the *shichisan*, his new mood, attitude, or direction of thought is clearly indicated by his pattern of movement. . . . He is not bound at any point on the *hanamichi* . . . by realistic considerations of time and may prolong his actions throughout the length of the *hanamichi* as long as is necessary to strengthen the impact of the character upon the audience. As he leaves the *shichisan*, he enters into the psychological area of the play, his progressive delineation of the character and its relation to the play firmly established in the mind of the audience.[20]

Ernst's comments explicitly demonstrate the fact that the *hanamichi* refers, in multifarious ways, to the relationship between the actors (the stage) and the spectators. It not only establishes a special proximity and intimacy between them, but, far more, it offers the actor the opportunity of developing the character of the role as well as the current mood or emotional state. On the other hand, it thereby provides the spectators with the possibility of concentrating on single characters and building a relationship with them. In fulfilling this function, the *hanamichi* is directly related to the specific formation of the dominants in the code of *kabuki* theatre: the art of acting always functions as the dominant.

The second convention noticed by Meyerhold, the *kurogo*, or stage assistant, also refers to this formation of the dominants. Each actor is accorded a stage assistant whose task it is to bring and remove props, to rearrange the folds of a costume, to wipe away perspiration, to bring tea or water for refreshment, to light the actor's face, and so on. The *kurogo* is usually dressed in black, though in winter scenes, when the stage is covered with a white cloth, the *kurogo* wears white. In *kabuki* aesthetics the word *kuro* (black) means "nothing"— the black clothing makes the stage assistant invisible according to the aesthetic conventions of the Far East.[21] The *kurogo* moves quickly and silently and stands behind the actor, a wall, or a tree. When the set offers no such discreet hiding place, the *kurogo* kneels down facing the back of the stage. In *kabuki* aesthetics, this position makes the stage assistant nonexistent. To this extent, the spectator does not see him or his actions. The convention of the stage assistant focuses the audience attention exclusively on the actor's art in representing a character.

> The stage assistant in the *kabuki* does not efface himself because he is a nonrealistic intrusion into the stage picture. He does so in order that he will not detract from the total design. . . . He is indispensable to the *kabuki* on both utilitarian and aesthetic grounds, for without him the actor would be obliged to arrange or change his own costume, to procure his own properties at the appropriate moment, and would thus lose, to a damaging extent, his expressiveness. The stage assistant in freeing the actor of these obligations enables the actor to perform his true function — that of acting.[22]

Meyerhold transferred both these conventions into his own theatre. As is clear from the statements quoted above, he did not receive and interpret them for their specific functions in *kabuki*, but rather out of his experience with the naturalistic theatre of illusion.

Meyerhold first used the figure of the stage assistant dressed in black in his production of Molière's *Dom Juan* (1910). He based the introduction of this device on the idea that it was the task of the *mise en scène* to pierce through the "soul of the work" in order to bring out the "essence of its architectural character." While Meyerhold felt that it would be wrong to aim at "an exact copy of the stage in Molière's time,"[23] he saw the introduction of the stage assistant as a suitable means of achieving his goal. For it would allow "the whole drama to be shown through the veil of the perfumed, over-gilded royalty of Versailles":

> Blackamoors, who enshroud the stage in narcotic clouds of spices by sprinkling perfume and glowing platinum from crystal flasks, blackamoors who flit across the stage to pick up Don Juan's lace handkerchief, or pull up a chair for a tired actor, blackamoors who tie the laces of Don Juan's shoes while he argues with Sganarelle, blackamoors who bring the actors lanterns when the stage sinks into semidarkness, blackamoors who remove their cloaks and daggers from the stage after the bitter fight between Don Juan and the robbers, who crawl under the table when the statue of the commendatore appears, who summon the audience with silver bells and announce the interval on the open stage.[24]

Meyerhold used the stage assistants in a very specific way: they served to confirm that the world in which the characters lived was, in fact, the "perfumed, over-gilded royalty of Versailles." In order that such a function could be fulfilled, however, Meyerhold changed them back into actors playing a part, in this case, blackamoors. While in *kabuki* theatre the stage assistants are not "seen" by the audience, Meyerhold draws direct attention to them: the actors dressed in blackamoor costumes step out of their roles and turn — as, for example, in announcing the interval — directly to the audience.

Meyerhold's stage assistants do not refer to the art of acting as the dominant, but rather establish a new relationship between actor and spectator. Through the productive reception of this element of Japanese theatre, the external theatrical communication undergoes a fundamental change: the spectator is no longer a passive *voyeur* of the illusion of reality, but instead becomes the active recipient, whose "collaboration" is essential to the completion of the performance.

Meyerhold employed the *hanamichi* in a similar way. In autumn 1920 he announced his "October Revolution in the Theatre" and began to develop a new, radical audience-related theatre. First he removed the raised platform stage. Meyerhold's "conditional" theatre aimed toward a "rebirth of antique theatre,"[25] and though Meyerhold had removed the raised platform stage in favor of the proscenium stage, he did away with the idea of "stage" altogether by using the orchestra in his premiere *mise en scène* in the Soviet Russian republic's first theatre — a production of Emile Verhaeren's *The Dawn* (December 28, 1920). In his production of S. M. Tretyakov's *Earth Rampant* (1923) Meyerhold used the *hanamichi*. He set it, however, in the middle of the auditorium and widened it considerably so that not only motorbikes and cars, but even trucks might have access to the stage. Critics felt that its most important function was to allow moving vehicles onstage: "A bridge of communication cut right across the auditorium and columns of cars, motorbikes, and bicycles sped unswervingly along it throughout the whole performance."[26]

In Meyerhold's own words, it was "agit-prop" theatre, whose task was to shake the audience awake and to enthuse them with the goals of the revolution: "Instead of aiming at an aesthetic effect, the set should move the spectator to the point where he no longer sees the difference between this and such events in real life, such as maneuvers, parades, street demonstrations, war, and so on. . . . The play is closely related to contemporary achievements: the triumphs of technology."[27]

Even though the audience did not react with the anticipated enthusiasm,[28] the function attributed to the *hanamichi* was fulfilled: the relationship between stage and spectator was fixed and regulated so that the chasm between art and life was bridged and art could be carried over directly into life. While in *kabuki* the *hanamichi* should bring actor and spectator closer together and should underline the art of acting as the dominant of the theatrical code, Meyerhold used it solely to inspire the audience with the triumphs of technology, thus to motivate them toward constructing a new reality — the modern industrial state. If the productive reception of elements of Japanese theatre in Meyerhold's prerevolutionary phase was to activate the spectator toward the creative completion of the performance — or the work of art — in the October Theatre phase it was accorded the task of motivating the spectator to the creative reorganization of himself or herself and of social reality.

In both cases, the productive reception of elements of Japanese theatre in Meyerhold's theatre was given the function of engaging the spectator in permanent activity, thereby regulating the relations between the stage and the spectator in a fundamentally new way. At the same time, this change effected a shift of the dominants: while in the realistic-psychological theatre of the 1900s interest was concentrated on the internal communication between the figures onstage, the focal point now shifted to the external communication:

the communication between stage and spectator was accentuated and accredited as the dominant.

The Constitution of One's Own Reality (New Regulations of Internal Theatrical Communication)

Jacques Copeau (1879–1949) was, to a large extent, in accord with the ideas of reform proposed by the avant-garde. In one significant area, however, he differed: he held to the idea that the function of theatre was to interpret the classics of dramatic literature. He wanted to achieve this kind of interpretation by a *mise en scène* derived from a new anti-illusionist aesthetic:

> By *mise en scène*, we mean the sketch of a dramatic action. That is, the collaboration of movement, of gesture, and of pose, the accord of facial expression, speech, and silence; it is the totality of the spectacle on stage which stems from a single idea which it sketches, orders, and harmonizes. The director develops a hidden but visible string with the actors — an alternately sensitive and relative relationship, the absence of which would cause the drama to lose the essence of its expression even if it were performed by actors of outstanding quality.[29]

The *mise en scène* should actually present an interpretation of a literary text — as was the case in Meyerhold's production of *Dom Juan*. In the process, however, it was not to imitate reality but to create the "essentials" of the drama as a reality onstage by its own means. Thus, language in Copeau's *mise en scène* would no longer function as the dominant. Copeau far more wanted to realize the *mise en scène* as the "totality of the spectacle onstage."

The special demands that such an aim enforced not only on the director but also on the actor could not be fulfilled by actors trained in the school of naturalism. Therefore, Copeau founded the Vieux Colombiers Theatre School, to teach the students the attitudes, behavior, and, not least, special techniques required. The students of this school worked on the production of a *no* play in 1924.

Jacques Copeau's notebooks prove that he studied extensive reports dealing with Japanese theatre. Many pages are dedicated to books and newspaper articles on Japanese theatre, where he engages in purposeful comparisons to European theatre. He felt that *no* theatre satisfied, in a special way, the Japanese need for idealism, nonreality, and poetry. Such a theatre was certainly above "the logic that has de-poeticised our Occidental theatre."[30] Copeau chose this theatre form for working with students because "this form is the strictest that we know and demands exceptional technical skills from the actors."[31]

Clearly, Copeau's interest in Japanese theatre was based on two main ideas. One was that this theatre was possibly the furthest removed from any kind of imitation of reality; each performance created its own poetic reality which obeyed only its own laws. Another reason was that *no* theatre had developed a performance art whose signs served neither to communicate a plot — for example, a character enters a village — nor to convey the expression of an individual emotion — such as the character's happiness. They far more carried a highly symbolic value and were in accordance with the ideal of Zen: they comprised the essence of plot and emotion in the most reduced form. In order to produce this kind of sign, a special technique was needed which could only be acquired through many years of training.[32] Thus, the *no* theatre realized completely the ideal that Copeau proposed for the *mise en scène*.

Copeau did not prepare the *mise en scène* himself, but delegated it to his colleague Suzanne Bing. Madame Bing taught the students the basics of *no* in the summer of 1924, relying heavily on collections of texts and commentaries by Arthur Waley and Noël Péri.[33] They were surprised by the similarities between the dramatic "rules" of *no* theatre and those that Copeau had begun to develop and employ in his own work. "The Noh appeared to be the application of the musical, dramatic, and plastic studies upon which, for three years, we had nourished our students, so much so that their various improvisations, the goal of these studies, were related in style to the Noh much more than to any contemporary work."[34]

The play chosen was *Kantan*, often ascribed to Zeami but probably written after his time. It tells the story of Rosei, who leaves his village in search of happiness. In the town of Kantan, he sleeps on a special pillow which allows the sleeper to see his whole future in a dream. After several minutes, in which he experiences his whole life, Rosei wakes up, realizes that life is just a dream, and returns to his village.

The choice of play is interesting to the extent that it evokes thematic associations with the tradition of European "classics." The metaphor of life as a dream can be found in many of Shakespeare's dramas; it also underlies the Baroque theatre in a similar way, as does the metaphor of world theatre. Both are employed as structural elements of drama and theatre in an exemplary way by Calderón in his *El gran teatro del mundo* and *La vida es sueño*. Thus, *Kantan* can easily be associated with a nonillusionist European theatre tradition.

Madame Bing wanted to avoid a mechanical imitation of the *no* play and its theatrical conventions as much as a Europeanized adaptation. She aimed at a productive reception:

We would present as best we could the work as it is, seeking our inspiration in the Noh and in the style of Japanese art. We would attempt to see just what this art and this style are made up of. We would take as the base of our movement and our *mise en scène* all the traditional restrictions instead of rejecting a single one; we would confine ourselves within their narrow limits, rather than attempting to escape them. It is within this framework, depending upon this solid base, that we would allow ourselves the liberty of transposition.[35]

The conditions determined by the *no* theatre fertilized the development of a "totality of the spectacle on the stage." Thus, lyrical, emotional sections were accompanied by the flute, while drums (one soft, one rather harsh) were used as if they dictated the actors' movements. In this way the relationship between music and bodily movement was emphasized.

While Meyerhold had turned to the Japanese stage assistant in order to present a new relationship between the stage and the spectator, Madame Bing used the stage assistant to highlight the autonomy of the stage reality. The stage is ruled by other laws than those in reality. Thus, although the stage assistant was reassigned his "original" task of bringing props when needed and arranging costumes, in this case his function was also quite different. While the Japanese spectator does not "see" the stage assistant, in Madame Bing's production the stage assistants should actually emphasize their presence to the audience at the Vieux Colombiers, thereby underlining the unique rules of the stage.

The rehearsal work clearly led to the desired result of developing a wholly new style of the art of acting. Madame Bing describes the results of their efforts in this way:

Faces are impassive, gestures slow and solemn; a fine discretion, a fine control order the expression, so that the simple gesture of a father posing his hand on the shoulder of his lost son gives enough intensity of emotion to bring tears to the eyes. We chastened our gestures.

We ennobled our postures, attempting to make of them a melody of noble and beautiful poses, one engendering the next according to the logic of the drama. A little more daring and obedience, and we composed the dances, one slower, another faster, as required.

The Noh actor must never forget that he is *acting* a poem; he must refuse to call on facile personal emotion, which works directly on the emotion of the audience. The emotion must arise from the poetry itself, a hard discipline for the very young actors full of the impatient ardour of self-expression. The Noh actor leaves the stage exhausted by this constraint.[36]

This style of performance did not contain a single trace of naturalism or psychology. It did not imitate reality, but exposed the actors to the possibility of creating their own reality. The internal communication between the figures on the stage no longer operated according to the laws of social reality, but entirely according to laws which were introduced by the performance itself, valid for that performance only. The productive reception of the *no* play *Kantan* resulted in the development of a new anti-illusionist theatrical code whose repertoire of signs and syntactic, semantic, and pragmatic rules could in no way be deduced from the dominant system of Western culture (costume, movement, interaction, etc.).

Although the production was not performed publicly because the leading actor twisted his knee in the dress rehearsal, the rehearsal work had nonetheless wholly fulfilled its goal, as can be seen from Copeau's concluding judgment: "This Nô, as it appeared to me in the final rehearsal, in its profound scenic harmony, the rhythm, style, and quality of its emotion, remains for me one of the jewels, one of the secret riches of the production at the Vieux-Colombiers."[37]

The New (Western) and the Foreign (Traditional) Theatre

The productive reception of elements of Japanese theatre in both examples examined here contributed enormously to the proposed "retheatricalization" of theatre. In Meyerhold's case, it enabled a restructuring of the relationship between the stage and the spectator, as well as the shift of the dominant from internal to external communication. For Copeau and Bing it provided the conditions under which the performance could be constituted as an autonomous reality.

The path opened by the productive reception of Japanese theatre was further explored and developed through the productive reception of other traditions (as, for example, by Copeau, whose newly founded Compagnie des Quinze began to perform in the style of *commedia dell'arte* at folk festivals and market fairs in 1930) as well as through the development of a new style of the art of acting (as exemplified by Meyerhold, who began to experiment with the idea of "bio-mechanics" in 1920). By the end of the 1920s, this development was flourishing so strongly that the different avant-garde movements, though disagreeing heavily with one another, had all in their own way realized the "retheatricalized" new theatre, the goal that had been the object of search since the turn of the century.

How profoundly the situation actually changed during this period is shown by the reaction to the performances of Japanese troupes in Europe in the 1920s. In 1928 Sadanji Ichikawa's *kabuki* troupe performed in various Russian cities. In 1930–1931 Tokujiro Tsutsui's troupe performed in Western Europe. Unlike Ichikawa's troupe, this was not a *kabuki* troupe. Although their repertoire contained several *kabuki* plays, they did not cultivate the classical style of *kabuki*.

In Moscow Meyerhold's student Sergei Eisenstein was among the audience. In the early 1920s Eisenstein had worked in Meyerhold's theatre and had also participated in his "bio-mechanic" experiments. During this time, he conceived his theory of the "montage of attractions," which was later to be of prime significance in his career as film director.[38] In 1928 Eisenstein clearly received the *kabuki* performance with this theory in mind, as well as with the experience he had gathered partly in Meyerhold's and Nicolai Foregger's audience-oriented theatre and partly as film director. In his work *Behind the Scenes* (1929), he remarked on the special relationship between Japanese performance art and the art of montage:

> The first thing which jumps to our attention is, of course, the purely filmic method of "performance without transition." The Japanese performer uses mimic transitions which he has thoroughly refined next to the exactly contradictory method. In a specific moment of his performance, he stops and holds a pose. The *kurogo*, disguised in black, hides him officiously from the audience. And look! his makeup is transformed, and he has a new coiffeur. Now another phase of his emotional state is characterized. . . . Another outstanding feature of *kabuki* theatre is the principle of "disintegrated" performance. Socho, who took the main female roles at the Moscow performances, performed the role of the dying daughter in *Yashao* (The Mask Maker) by using an utterly disintegrated concept of the art. Acting with the right arm alone, acting with one leg, acting with the neck and head only. (The whole process of the death agony was disintegrated into a solo performance of each single limb whereby each played its own role: the role of a leg, the role of an arm, the role of the head.) Disintegration into single shots. The single sections gradually became shorter the closer they came to the tragic end.[39]

If one compares this description of the death scene with comments by the Paris critics or René Schickele at the beginning of this century, one is struck by its immense professional content. While reviewers of Sada Yakko or Hanako simply quoted single gestures and concentrated principally on describing impressions which the death scene had provoked, Eisenstein analyzes in detail the artistic methods employed to win specific effects. Eisenstein's knowledge of the new Soviet theatre and film enabled him to make a careful dissection and structural analysis of the art of acting of *kabuki* and thus expose the process by which something was "made" or a specific affect achieved.[40]

At the start of the 1900s, Japanese theatre performances in Europe were received as a countermodel to the ruling naturalistic theatre, which opened up the exciting possibility of a different, "theatrical" theatre. Later, after this new theatre had been developed, Japanese performance art was received in terms of a professional comparison of different artistic methods.

This change is not only apparent among the theatre artists; it also affected the theatre critics. When Tokujiro Tsutsui's troupe visited Berlin on their way to and from Paris (in October 1930 and January 1931), Herbert Ihering spoke of their performances in the following way:

> These actors perform mimic stations. Just as the stations on a holy pilgrimage remain the same, the same holy pictures, the same stages of the story of suffering, all pilgrims must pass by them with the same gestures, with the same kneeling down and standing up again, so all the stations in these plays and roles seem fixed. Generations of actors must pass by them. . . . Another play: *Over the Border* (*Kanjincho*). The same Kiyoshi Mimasu, here in the role of a border guard, performs in the rigid mask play, wearing cothurns, self-absorbed and — with disguised, screwed-up voice. Not in order to characterize a different role, not to confirm an individual interpretation, or to overact, but in order to satisfy the fixed tone of the role, of the play, of the inviolable tradition. . . . The actor is nothing. The performance art is everything. For us, the reverse is true: the actor is all, the performance art nothing. Here new generations of actors arise to serve the eternal laws. The poles of world theatre are Max Reinhardt and the Japanese. . . . The Japanese who always enter according to the same unshakable law. And most incredible: they fulfill this law, keep it alive, they keep it fluid.[41]

Ihering's critique testifies, on the one hand, to the clear recognition of the principal differences between the Western and the Japanese theatre traditions and, on the other hand, reveals the ability to acknowledge and understand the unique nature of the foreign theatre tradition. The critic attempts here to discover a starting point for an intercultural theatre hermeneutic. He is in a position to do this simply because of the level of development in avant-garde theatre, which had significantly heightened a broader awareness of different artistic approaches. Ihering himself finally points to this connection when, at the end of his argument, he draws on the relationship between the Japanese theatre and the theatre of Brecht:

> But we ourselves stand to win a different approach toward the German stage, if we view it from the enormous tradition and the huge achievements of Japanese theatre. We realize the aims of many experiments, as for example those of Brecht. Not toward the individual disintegration of the stage art, but toward the creation of a basic style, of a basic behavior, of a form, of a tradition. The fundamental situation and the mimic stations in Japanese theatre show what we are lacking and what we must yet achieve.[42]

The productive reception of elements of Japanese theatre could now be purposefully carried out as experiments toward finding the solution to specific artistic problems which had arisen in the development of this new theatre. This was, however, only possible toward the end of the long journey, not at its start.

This was the kind of productive reception that Brecht favored in practice. According to Elisabeth Hauptmann, Brecht also saw Tokujiro Tsutsui's troupe perform. Among his papers one finds the following fragmentary note, which was probably written down as a direct reaction to the Japanese performance:

"ON JAPANESE PERFORMANCE TECHNIQUE"

we should attempt to examine certain elements of foreign performance art for their usefulness. this attempt will be carried out within the very specific situation of our theatre, where our own theatre is not sufficient to accomplish its tasks (tasks of a new kind). these are the tasks demanded of the performance art by the epic dramatic structure. now the above mentioned foreign technique has long since been in the position to accomplish similar tasks — similar, but not the same ones. the technique must be separated from those highly essential prerequisites, transported and subjugated to quite other conditions. in order to undertake such an analysis, one must take the viewpoint that there is a kind of technical standard in art, something which is not individual, not already developed, but something one can build in, something transportable. this statement should suffice to show that we are convinced of this. anyway, this technique cannot be considered to be that "form . . . which is only valid insofar as it is the form of its own content." japanese performance technique . . . can naturally only mean something to us insofar as it is able to know our problems. the "japanese" in it, moreover, its whole "character" or "individual worth," etc., is irrelevant to this analysis.[43]

Unfortunately, such an analysis was never carried out. Nonetheless, this fragment suffices to clarify Brecht's approach to the reception of foreign elements. He faced a concrete problem that his own well-developed theatre was unable to solve, because it was not endowed with the means to do so. The foreign theatrical forms and elements were now only received in terms of whether they might provide something toward the solution of the problem, for example, by offering specific new means. The foreign, in this case the Japanese, was not interesting for its "individual worth," nor as countermodel, but only as one possible strategy toward the solution of specific problems interesting to Western theatre. The productive reception of elements of Far Eastern theatre thus entered a radically new phase.

FAMILIAR AND FOREIGN THEATRES
The Intercultural Trend in Contemporary Theatre

THE INTERCULTURAL TREND AS A PRODUCTIVE FACTOR
IN THE HISTORY OF THEATRE

In recent years, theatres of widely differing cultures have engaged in an ever increasing tendency to adopt elements of foreign theatre traditions into their own productions. Thus, Ariane Mnouchkine used elements of Japanese and Indian theatre in her Shakespeare productions: costumes, masks, music, individual gestures, steps and dance sequences; Robert Wilson borrowed many elements from the Japanese theatre in his work; and Peter Brook experimented to a great extent with the Indian dance theatre *kathakali*. The *kathakali* theatre traditionally consists of dramatized episodes of the two great Indian epics, the *Mahabharata* and the *Ramayana*. Its precisely determined costumes, masks, dance steps, mudras, and gestures have been fixed for centuries, handed down through the generations. Now a *kathakali* troupe has used these traditional means to present the story of *Dr. Faustus*. In *Hayavadana*, the Indian dramatist Girish Karnad referred directly to Thomas Mann's story *The Transposed Heads*, a tale Mann was inspired to write after an original Sanskrit story. Thus, Karnad returned, in this roundabout way, to the original Indian source. After the Cultural Revolution in China, experiments were carried out to try to combine Chinese and Western theatre traditions. These experiments ranged from the introduction of specific elements of Chinese opera (such as the conception of space) into the spoken theatre (originally imported from the West) and the systematic attempt to unite the principles of classical Chinese theatre with elements of Stanislavsky and Brechtian techniques in *China Dream* to experimenting with Western dramas wholly transposed into the classical Chinese opera forms such as Shakespeare's *Macbeth* as *kunju* opera and Brecht's *The Good Person of Sezuan* as Sichuan opera. A similarly radical experiment was Gao Xingjian's play *Bus Stop*, which was based on the Western tradition of absurd theatre. In Japan Yukio Mishima has used the traditional form of the *no* play to touch on Western themes and subjects. Yukio Ninagawa and Tadashi Suzuki have both directed Greek tragedy,

Shakespeare, and Chekhov in a performance style derived from traditional Japanese theatre forms.

English- and French-speaking theatre in Africa has also turned to European theatre — in this case, to represent themes from African history and mythology. John Pepper Clark drew directly from Greek tragedy in his play *A Song of a Goat*. In a similar way, Ola Rotimi alludes to *Oedipus the King* in his *The Gods Are Not to Blame*. Wole Soyinka has transposed Euripides' *The Bacchae* into Yoruba culture and set the god Ogun in place of Dionysus; *Opera Wonyosi* was adapted according to Brecht's *Dreigroschenoper* (*The Threepenny Opera*), which is itself an adaptation of John Gay's *Beggar's Opera*. Such contact with elements of the old African theatre has led, in part, to the evolution of a completely new form of theatre.

This development, which in no sense began simultaneously in all the different cultures, can be observed worldwide from the 1970s. This raises some important questions. Did these obvious coincidences happen randomly (made possible because of the speed of the communication flow provided by the mass media, international theatre festivals, etc.)? Have the productive associations of the theatre of one culture with elements of foreign theatre traditions fulfilled quite different functions in each case, rendering any comparison between them senseless? Or might there be a similar approach employed by all that would expose an underlying similarity, which would make the comparison of different kinds of intercultural production not only useful but also fruitful?

The productive association of the theatre of one culture with the theatre of a foreign one is neither entirely new nor unique. It has instead a long history which, in Western culture, reaches as far back as antiquity. It became a conscious program when Goethe proclaimed the birth of an age of world literature: "National literature means little nowadays, the era of world literature is at hand, and each of us now must help to hasten its arrival."[1] While Lessing still believed the development of a German *Nationaltheater* a matter of urgency, Goethe saw a more important task in the preparation and realization of a repertoire that would consist of the most significant plays in world literature. He began, therefore, to develop a repertoire for his own small, somewhat provincial, theatre in Weimar which would encompass the most important dramas of European theatre history alongside advanced, literary contemporary plays (principally his own and Friedrich Schiller's) and the unavoidable trivial "daily bread" productions. Thus Sophocles' *Antigone* and Shakespeare's *Hamlet, Henry IV, Romeo and Juliet, Macbeth, Julius Caesar,* and *Othello* were played alongside Calderón's *The Constant Prince* and *Life's a Dream*, Pierre Corneille's *Cid*, Jean Racine's *Phèdre*, Molière's *Miser*, comedies by Carlo Gozzi and Carlo Goldoni, and tragedies by Voltaire and Lessing. Theatre became the agent of mediation between Goethe's own culture and the foreign.

In order that such mediation be achieved, Goethe did not consider it important to produce the plays deriving from foreign cultures as they appeared in their original textual form. He was far more eager that the contemporary audience feel the full effect directly. To that end he was prepared to make far-reaching alterations to the original texts and was energetically supported in this by Schiller. Out of consideration for the moral standards and expectations of the Weimar audience, for example, Schiller cut the porter scene from *Macbeth* entirely, finding it obscene and ugly. He replaced it with a pious *aubade* (dance song). Goethe revised *Romeo and Juliet* for similar reasons and to such an extent that his version was described by a later Shakespeare scholar as an "amazing travesty."[2]

Goethe explained his approach in a letter to Charlotte von Wolzogen: "The maxim that I have followed was to concentrate on the interesting parts and to harmonize them, for Shakespeare was forced by his genius, his age, and his audience to add much disharmonious confusion in order to reconcile the ruling theatre genius."[3]

Through this approach, Goethe thoroughly succeeded in bringing the works of a foreign culture to his audience and in making them a vibrant component of the theatre of his time. On his production of *The Constant Prince*, he wrote to G. Sartorius: "This time we have a play that was written nearly 200 years ago in quite a different climate, for people of quite different culture, and it is produced in such a fresh way that it might have come hot from the oven."[4]

The repertoire at the Weimar theatre was exclusively made up of European dramas despite the fact that Goethe had expressly wanted to bring about a theatre that drew from world literature. Such a contradiction is not the result of Eurocentricity, however, as is often the criticism aimed at Goethe, nor does it stem from a lack of knowledge about theatre traditions outside Europe. Not only had Goethe read the drama *Sakuntala* by the Indian poet Kalidasa in a German translation of 1791 by Georg Forster, but his acquaintance with it had "a very great influence on [my] whole life."[5] He showed his enthusiasm in the now famous distich:

Wouldst thou the blossoms of spring, as well as the fruits of autumn,
Wouldst thou what charms and delights, wouldst thou what plenteously
    feeds,
Wouldst thou include both heaven and earth in one designation,
All that is needed is done, when I *Sakuntala* name.[6]

Goethe's enthusiastic reception also found expression in his own work. He took the idea of the "Prelude in the theatre" in *Faust* from Indian drama. Despite this, he shied away from adapting and incorporating it into his Weimar theatre. With regret he decided "that our sensibilities, customs, and ways of thinking have developed so differently from those in this Eastern nation that even an important work such as this . . . can have little success here."[7]

The limitation of dealing solely with European theatre traditions which Goethe so lamented was first challenged by the historical avant-garde movement. By calling for the retheatricalization of theatre, which they felt was long overdue, they rejected the form of bourgeois theatre of illusion so dominated by language and turned to theatre traditions from non-European cultures to fertilize and advance European theatre.[8]

Edward Gordon Craig proposed the introduction of masks as he observed them used in African and Asian theatres. Max Reinhardt experimented with the Japanese *hanamichi*, or flower path, leading from the stage through the auditorium. Meyerhold also turned to the Japanese theatre, seeing in it a model of artistic conventions which he wanted to set in place of the theatre of illusion with its representations of reality (in 1910 he engaged Japanese artists to teach his actors the art of gesture). Jacques Copeau primarily advocated the art of *no* theatre; he wanted to teach his actors this art through a production of the *no* play *Kantan* (1924). Alexander Tairov turned to various elements of costume and gesture from Indian theatre in his production of *Sakuntala*, and he and Reinhardt also produced the Chinese drama *The Yellow Jacket* (Tairov 1914/Reinhardt 1913). In 1935 Brecht saw the famous Peking opera female-role actor Mei Lanfang and, in evolving his theory of *Verfremdungseffekt*, looked to the example of Chinese performance art. Artaud believed he had discovered essential archetypes in Balinese theatre, which he wanted to represent in "the exact symbols" he saw in its "hieroglyphics."[9]

The most profound changes which the European avant-garde achieved in theatre were aimed against the literary, psychological realistic theatre of illusion; they directly affected the status of the literary text and language, performance art, conception of space, and quality of spectator perception. The discussion of these innovations at the time, and the need of introducing them, drew its basic arguments from reports of Far Eastern theatre, as well as from the rare guest performances by actors and troupes from the Far East such as Sada Yakko and the Otojiro Kawakami company in London, Paris, and Berlin (1900–1902), the dancer Hanako in Berlin, Paris, and London (1907–1908), the Ichikawa Sadanji *kabuki* company in Russia (1928), the Tokujiro Tsutsui company in Western Europe (1930–1931), and Mei Lanfang in Moscow (1935). The significance of Far East Asian theatre for the European avant-garde and its conception of a new theatre form cannot be overestimated.[10] The fundamental and far-reaching renewal of European theatre which occurred in the first decades of this century appears to be, not least, the consequence of a conscious and productive encounter with theatre traditions of foreign cultures.

At approximately the same time as the avant-garde sought to adopt elements of Far Eastern theatre, a new form of theatre arose in Japan which was based on the model of Western realistic theatre. The process was preceded by a first encounter with European theatre in a series of Shakespeare productions. In 1885 *The Merchant of Venice* was thoroughly reworked and produced in the style of *kabuki* theatre (the same basic principles laid down by Goethe in his adaptations were also adhered to here). *Julius Caesar* followed, in 1901, in a carefully precise translation and *Hamlet* ten years later in a wholly "Western" production initiated by the Literary Society (Bungei Kyokai). As early as 1909, Tsubouchi had founded a theatre school in which the study of Shakespeare and Ibsen played an important part. In 1909 the first Ibsen play in Japan was staged, *John Gabriel Borkman*, and in 1911 *Nora*, which was an overwhelming success. This early movement initiated the emergence of Japanese spoken theatre —*shingeki* (new drama).[11]

By the 1920s this wholly new theatrical form, *shingeki*, was fully established. The Literary Society and the Tsukiji Little Theatre founded by Kaoru Osanai in 1924 took the realistic theatre of Western culture as their model. In general, contemporary European dramas were produced; Ibsen and Chekhov were especially favored. Stanislavsky's was held to be the authoritative directing style. The aim was to reproduce as close a copy as possible of Stanislavsky's productions at the Moscow Art Theatre. The members of the *shingeki* movement believed that traditional theatre forms such as *no* and *kabuki* were outdated and sterile, no longer in touch with the problems of contemporary Japanese society. In turning to realistic European drama, they tried to stimulate the development of modern Japanese society by offering a model.

Since Japanese theatre had considerable influence on Chinese students and political refugees living in Japan, a similar development in theatre can also be seen in China.[12] In 1906 Li Xishuang founded the Spring Willow Society in Tokyo, which aimed to introduce spoken theatre into China. The troupe won initial success with dramatizations of Harriet Beecher Stowe's *Uncle Tom's Cabin*, *La dame aux Camélias* by A. Dumas *fils*, and V. Sardou's *La Tosca* (1909). In Shanghai in 1914 the Friends of the New Theatre opened the Spring Willow Theatre, which was dedicated to furthering the development of spoken theatre. Members of the May 4th Movement (1919) took Ibsen's dramas as their model; *Nora* and *Enemy of the People* acquired special significance. Hu

Shi, who translated *Nora*, wrote: "Ibsen describes the actual relationships within domestic life, and thereby shocks the spectators into realizing how dark and rotten the foundations of domestic life really are. He inspires those caught in domesticity to revolution and renovation. This is Ibsenism."[13]

While the leading members of the European avant-garde were discovering the theatrical traditions of the Far East as a potential source of innovation for their own theatre, Japanese *shingeki* and the Chinese Spring Willow Society seized on the possibilities provided by realistic theatre and drama of Western origin. Just as in Japan and China, the various avant-gardists in Europe maintained that their own inherited theatre forms had become sterile and neither satisfied the new aesthetic dictates or ideals nor were able to react appropriately to the changing social situation. In sum, the adoption of theatrical elements, or particular theatre forms of foreign cultures, effected two quite specific changes in East and West in aesthetic-theatrical methods of approach to a production and in sociocultural developments. In the West, it was a question of the renovation of theatre, the key issue being the retheatricalization of theatre, while in the East it was the demand for a theatre which should "mirror" life. However, it was also a question of fundamental cultural change. Most European avant-gardists were critical of the state of contemporary civilization and wanted to overcome the logocentrism of the Western world, to depose the image of the human being defined as an individual personality and to break the limiting conception of space. Others, such as Artaud, wanted to attack the dominance of rational argumentation. The Japanese and Chinese innovators, on the contrary, wanted to popularize the representation of the individual in society, as well as to introduce rationalism and to demand further modernization. Interculturalism in theatre thus served as much primarily aesthetic and theatrical goals as predominantly sociocultural ones.

The deliberate and productive encounter of one theatre with theatre traditions of other cultures thus has a long history during which it has exposed and satisfied varying functions. For Goethe, the main aim in mediating the foreign was to expose its humane content as "universally valid." The historical avant-garde movement, on the other hand, was concerned to reanimate European theatre; it took recourse to foreign theatre cultures largely for reasons of theatre aesthetics. Finally, members of the Japanese *shingeki* aimed, by establishing a Western-realistic style of theatre, to introduce a new style of life, to Westernize Japanese society.

The simple statement that the intercultural trend dominates contemporary theatre worldwide ignores the various functions of each case and even the question of useful comparison between them. The following discussion deals with these issues by drawing on examples from Europe (Robert Wilson, Peter Brook), India, and Nigeria (Wole Soyinka).

THE INTERCULTURAL TREND IN CONTEMPORARY THEATRE

Both the "international" and "intercultural" phenomena are particularly evident in the work of Robert Wilson and Peter Brook. Not only has Robert Wilson, for example, produced a mammoth project, *the CIVIL warS*, in many foreign cities—Marseilles, Cologne, Rotterdam, Milwaukee, Lyon, Nice, Rome, and Tokyo—but in each of these individual sections he picked out the dominant elements of history, theatre tradition, and culture in the country in which he was working. The section devised in Tokyo contains a sequence of steps, gestures, and sounds taken from Japanese theatre, particularly *no* and *bunraku*. The section conceived in Cologne, where Heiner Müller was creatively involved, not only calls for the appearance of Frederick the Great, but also refers directly to the history of German literature and theatre with literary quotes from Goethe, Friedrich Hölderlin, Franz Kafka, and Heiner Müller and musical quotes from Frederick the Great, Franz Schubert, and Hans Peter Kuhn. The quotations from historical figures, literature, and music are juxtaposed in a giant collage of cultures, including the figural quote of Abraham Lincoln, literary quotes from Shakespeare, the Bible, and American Indian prophesies, music quotations from Philip Glass and David Byrne, and excerpts of film.

Both the elements of one's own culture and those from the foreign culture are ripped from their various contexts. They can neither refer back to the context from which they originate, thereby offering coherence and meaning, nor enter into a relation with one another, to produce meaning. In Wilson's theatre, elements deriving from different contexts actually show a random juxtaposition of cultural fragments, set scenes, and ready-made images. It is made up of isolated bits of information, whose very accumulation prevents the production of meaning. The actors' bodies, objects, and scraps of language, sound, and music are no longer offered as signs that should represent something, mean anything, but rather as objects which refer only to themselves and which delight in their very objectness.

One might view performances such as these as products of a thoroughly networked and interconnected postindustrial society so crisscrossed by a flood of disconnected moments of communication—pure bits of information—that it is no longer able to bring together any meaningful association of signs. The single sounds and images, meaningless in themselves, deny any reference to their origin and background and finally point dumbly back to themselves. There is no longer a sign process, meaning, or orientation.

This approach can, however, be interpreted quite differently. Since the audience is presented solely with objects that are not culturally bound to a specific meaning, any spectator from any culture can receive the objects presented in the context of his or her own culturally specified experience and deduce meaning. The refusal to implement a sign process onstage thus appears to be the precondition for allowing the process to be carried out inside the spectator's head, regardless of the culture to which the spectator belongs. Wilson's presentational theatre (it almost avoids representation of any kind) could, to this extent, be seen as the renunciation of a Western cultural imperialism that tries to force its own meaning on other cultures through its own products. As a theatre of pure presentation, Wilson's theatre exposes itself to the possibility of being a cultural factor in cultures of other origins as well as its own.

Peter Brook exacts similar demands with his "cosmopolitan theatre," by taking quite a different path, however. He also works with elements deriving from very different cultures, but he chooses these according to their suitability to afford meaning in cultures other than the original one. Peter Brook attempts to filter out elements of theatrical traditions of different cultures which seem to him to mobilize a theatrical communication between members of different cultures. This approach is characteristic of productions such as *Orghast* among the ruins of Persepoli in 1971; *The Iks*, the story of a dying African tribe, devised in Africa; *The Conference of the Birds* (1977), an adaptation of an original medieval play by the Persian mystic Attar; and — to particular effect — the dramatization of the Indian epic the *Mahabharata*. The *Mahabharata* traditionally represents, in countless episodes, an infinite source material for the many different forms of Indian theatre and Javanese and Balinese shadow puppet theatre. Peter Brook presented his adaptation at the theatre festival in Avignon in an abandoned quarry.

Brook accords much importance to the idea that his productions can be performed in many widely differing cultures. He takes the view that every theatrical tradition is composed of elements which can be employed in the context of other traditions. Brook is working toward a theatre of the future in which the individual elements, though they may derive from different traditions and cultures, can function, be understood, and be assigned meaning as theatrical elements in any chosen culture. This conscious and productive encounter with foreign theatre cultures must lead — in Brook's theatre programmatically, in Wilson's rather implicitly — toward the development of a "universal language of theatre."

It is perhaps hardly surprising to find the phenomenon of the combination of elements of their own and foreign traditions in the theatre of the Third World countries. But this superficial analogy should not lead one too hastily to draw parallels. For in the case of Third World countries, the combination of cultural elements is accorded a fundamentally different value than in Western cultures. While in the West it is to be seen as the result of a deliberate desire to extend one's own culture, in the Third World it is the result of colonization. Thus, it functions more frequently as a kind of transitional phase by which the imposed foreign will be gradually eliminated.

In India and Africa, theatrical interculturalism of the same period (1900–1940) is significantly different because it was not the outcome of a conscious choice and free adoption of foreign theatre forms by theatre artists, as it was in Europe, Japan, and China, but must be seen as directly related to European colonization. In both India and Africa, the Western theatre was introduced as a model of the colonizing society and was implemented in the consciousness of the native people as the instrument of colonization. Despite this basic parallel, however, there are important differences in the developments in India and in Africa.

From 1821 Indian spectators also attended the English theatre in Bombay. The foreign melodramas, so popular among British spectators, were also well received by the Indian public. When Indian theatre was first established in the second half of the nineteenth century, it drew extensively from this kind of theatre in preference to any other. These Indian troupes, the so-called Parsee Theatre (because it was founded and principally performed by the Parsee), toured towns in northern India until 1940, giving regular performances. The form of theatre they played was "intercultural" — the proscenium arch and painted backdrop were copied from the English theatre, as were the fantastical scenic effects, storm and battle scenes, explosions, and all the necessary machineries of theatre, sumptuous costumes and makeup, the front curtain, and tableaux and choral singing at the beginning and close of the play. The dance sections, on the contrary, had their origins in Indian dance traditions, and classical Indian music was the base for the songs, which were mostly directly lifted from different regional theatre traditions. Similarly, the sources from which the dramas drew their themes came directly from folk theatre: Parsee romances, Hindu legends and mythology. The Parsee theatre relied on a conservative view of society and propagated the moral values of the middle class. Since these moral values and ideals were mixed with nationalism, the target of the Parsee theatre was, at least partially, colonialism. In complete contrast, the fight against colonialism which the Progressive Writers' Association of India (PWA) and the Indian People's Theatre Association (IPTA) led in the development of an Indian drama and theatre in the 1930s and 1940s was not only explicitly antifascist, but also directly anticolonialist. In order to reach workers and farmers with a new patriotic goal, they increasingly looked back to their own folk theatre traditions, without, however, consciously evolving the precepts of an intercultural theatre form.[14]

In Africa, in schools principally organized by missionaries and colonial authorities, the illusionist box-set stage (developed in Western drama in the nineteenth century) was introduced as the prime model. On the one hand, students were encouraged to perform European dramas styled on the Western model in order that they adopt and imitate the foreign lifestyle. In these productions, African traditions were partly touched on (for example, the use of space in an open air theatre, narrative gestures, and cultural traditions such as music, dance, and ceremony) in order to ease the learning and internalization of the foreign model. On the other hand, the students were asked to write their own dramas based on the European model. The Ecole William Ponty in Saint Louis, Senegal, spearheaded the movement in the 1930s in this way: the students were given the vacation task of collecting and noting down the themes and stories in the oral traditions of their native homelands such as myths, legends, narratives, and traditional customs. The theme of the play that the students would then write was chosen from these findings. The goal of this school drama was predominantly, if not exclusively, to instill Western values in the students and to encourage a Western attitude and behavior insofar as it was of benefit to the colonizing authorities.

Alongside this theatre form, which was enforced by the Western, principally European, model, other forms of intercultural theatre that evolved out of African theatre were also engendered. In the 1920s, in many towns, the so-called concert party was established. This genre of music-theatre made use of revue style, North American minstrel shows, English music halls, and Hollywood films in a free dramaturgy close to traditional African theatre in which music, dance, song, addressing the spectators, dialogues, and slapstick numbers alternated within one performance. The concert party consisted mainly of themes on contemporary urban life and the problems surrounding it. The critical flexibility and openness of this theatre made it a valuable and important instrument of the anticolonial movement.

In Nigeria, alongside the concert parties, which were aimed at town spectators, the Yoruba traveling theatre, which mainly toured rural areas, also gained enormous influence. This theatre was created out of the cantata and choral works of the Christian church during the 1930s and 1940s and also refers back to the Alarinjo traveling theatre tradition that can be traced back in Yoruba culture as far as the sixteenth century. The first troupe was founded in 1946 by Hubert Ogunde and the second significant troupe in 1948 by Kole Ogunmola, an outstanding director, author, and theatre artist from West Africa. The traveling theatre spoke in the language of the Yoruba people; the action was set to traditional music and dance forms; and an acting style was developed which was oriented toward the movement styles of traditional arts and ceremonies as well as forms of native comic theatre. The plots were created out of the legendary stories and mythologies of the Yoruba people. This traveling theatre achieved a great deal in strengthening and confirming the cultural identity of the Yoruba.[15]

Nigerian dramatists also turned to elements of European theatre. John Pepper Clark adapted the story of Ozidi, which is narrated and performed by the Ijaw in a seven-day festival, into a full-length drama in English. In *The Song of a Goat*, he employed the "goat song" device of Greek tragedy in a programmatic way, as does Soyinka in his dramas. Soyinka works with the form of drama as it has evolved in European theatre history, and he also writes in English. But he ties these elements of Western culture to elements of African culture — themes and characters of Yoruba history, mythology, and religion, poetic devices from orally transmitted poems, and the methods of characterization and structure that are employed in traditional rituals such as the Obatala Festival and others. In this way, he combines elements of European and African tradition quite freely. Unlike many other African writers, Soyinka does not employ elements of his own culture to romanticize precolonial history and the traditions of that era. With *A Dance of the Forest*, for example, written for the celebrations on gaining national independence but rejected by the committee in charge of the performances, Soyinka exposed the dialectical relationship to his own tradition as it mediates between self-conscious adaptation and critical rejection. The reference to Troy and European antiquity seems, in this relatively early drama, explicitly programmatic. Since history, according to Soyinka, constantly repeats itself because of human stupidity, incompetence, and wickedness, it is the task of theatre to sustain a vision of humankind according to the various culturally determined ideals and to help realize this vision. In Soyinka's dramas, African culture does not solely appear in place of the European but far more — despite its innate weaknesses — as an effective potential with which to correct the dehumanizing tendencies of European culture.

This intention, which determines the mediation between elements of European and African traditions in all Soyinka's dramas, is given special priority in his adaptation of Euripides' *The Bacchae* and *Death and the King's Horseman*, which he wrote in 1976.

In his version of *The Bacchae*, Soyinka transposes the action to Yoruba mythology: the god Ogun takes the place of Dionysus. This transposition results in important shifts which particularly affect the end of the tragedy. While in Euripides' play the dismembered body of Pentheus remains onstage after the return to barbarism, thus ending the dramatic action with the suggestion of hopelessness and the despairing surrender to the meaninglessness of life, a "communion rite" takes place at the end of Soyinka's version, as proposed in the play's subtitle: *The Bacchae of Euripides: A Communion Rite*. A fountain of wine spurts from Pentheus' head as a source of strength for the community. The dismemberment of Pentheus thus appears to have been a sacrifice and a true transformation of the king, who in this way becomes one with the same power he once opposed, Dionysus, the god of wine. It ends with the return to world order which Pentheus had destroyed.

The responsibility of the individual toward the community, especially when that individual holds a position of power, is stressed even more forcefully in *Death and the King's Horseman* as a correction to the European tradition which concentrates on the fate of the individual, the hero. Here Soyinka employs the strict form of the drama in five acts in which the fate of one individual is usually presented: Phaedra or Britannicus, Iphigenia or Wallenstein. But this form, which drives toward the hero's catastrophe in action and opposing action, is undermined by Soyinka. Following the European tradition of five acts, he shows the fall of the titular hero Elesin Oba, who, by committing ritual suicide four weeks after the death of the king, must try to ensure that the worlds of the living, the dead, and the unborn remain harmonious. He fails to do so, however, seduced by life, and under pressure from the opposing action in the person of the English District Officer, Pilkings. In opposition to this movement, which follows the traditional development of classical European drama in exposition, complication, climax, peripeteia, and catastrophe, Soyinka places a second movement at the beginning of act 2, centered on Elesin Oba's son, Olunde. Against his father's wishes, Olunde goes to England to study medicine. In his encounter with the foreign culture he has found a conscious identification with his own culture. He returns in order to show his father, whose suicide he approves, his last respects. When his father withdraws from his duty, Olunde takes his role. He kills himself in his father's place in the hope of securing the prosperity of his people after all. The Praise-Singer rightly accuses Elesin Oba of having placed his own ego above the needs of the community, of having used them for his own aims and thus having failed:

Elesin, we placed the reins of the world in your hands yet you watched it plunge over the edge of the bitter precipice. You sat with folded arms while evil strangers tilted the world from its course and crashed it beyond the edge of emptiness — you muttered, there is little that one man can do, you left us floundering in a blind future. Your heir has taken the burden on himself. What the end will be, we are not gods to tell. But this young shoot has poured its sap into the parent stalk, and we know this is not the way of life. Our world is tumbling in the void of strangers, Elesin.[16]

European theatre, in Soyinka's view, has long since forfeited its cosmic, universal dimension and has sunk to the level of a moral institution in which only punishment and reward are of value. He thinks theatre should be instead

a constant battleground for forces beyond the petty infractions of habitual communal norms or patterns of human relationships and expectations, beyond the actual twists and incidents of action and their resolutions. The stage is endowed, for the purpose of that communal presence which alone creates it — and this is the fundamental defining concept, that the stage is brought into being by a communal presence — so, for this purpose, the stage becomes the affective, rational and intuitive milieu of the total communal experience: historic, race-formative, cosmogenic.[17]

Only in a theatre in which the individual consciously accepts responsibility toward the community can the charismatic powers of a humanist image of humankind unfold.

Soyinka is thus not only interested in providing African culture with an African theatre instead of a European one; rather he addresses the question of what theatre might bring to a humanely driven culture, as indeed to the whole world. The conscious and productive mediation between European and African theatre traditions thus indicates the utopia of a world culture based on humanist and humane traditions, a utopia to which many different national cultures can all, in their own specific ways, contribute.

Even though the starting point, program, position, method of approach, and goal of the theatre artists in Europe, Japan, China, India, and Africa are individually wholly divergent, the conscious and productive encounters with elements of foreign theatre cultures, in general, serve similar functions: to create a "universal language of theatre" and to mobilize communication between members of different cultures.

The idea underlying the intercultural trend in contemporary theatre across the world is that the path of permanent mediation between the cultures will, in the many different ways described above, gradually lead to the creation of a world culture in which different cultures not only take part, but also respect the unique characteristics of each culture and allow each culture its authority.

This concept of a world culture is diametrically opposed to the idea of a unified, one-world culture in which all differences are eliminated — in its ugliest form, a cultural monopoly like Coca-Cola, television, and McDonald's. The somewhat utopian concept of a world culture which theatre seems to be working toward in the productive encounter with elements of foreign theatre cultures is seen more as a communal task of the theatrical avant-garde in the different cultures and is projected in these terms. The intercultural trend in world theatre aims to fulfill this demand, whether implicitly or explicitly.

The perspectives arising in the context of the idea of a future world culture should not at the same time cloud the vision of the various concrete functions that the intercultural trend has for one's own culture. The use of foreign elements or the adoption of them in a production is thus always to be understood as a process of cultural transformation in which the components extracted from the other culture are embedded in one's own culture so that their special potential can unfold in the here and now. Even in contemporary intercultural theatre, the intercultural phenomenon fulfills a wholly concrete function in each culture which refers to its own culture alone, before it can be individually analyzed or described. Undoubtedly any examination of the intercultural brings to light aspects which can only be explained and understood in the context of the culture concerned. For it is quite natural that Wilson, Brook, and Soyinka all direct their work primarily at the audience of their own culture and the concrete social situations in which they live — just as before them Goethe, Meyerhold, Brecht, Artaud, and Osanai have done.

Unlike the previous era of theatre history in which Goethe lived, however, interculturalism in contemporary world theatre cannot exhaust itself through culturally specific functions. It is aimed far more at the same time toward the idea of a future world-culture-to-be, which will be won by these means. In this respect, theatre functions, in one sense, as the aesthetic *Vor-schein* of utopia.

CHANGING THEATRICAL CODES
Toward a Semiotics of Intercultural Performance

The adoption of elements of foreign theatre traditions in intercultural performances in the last fifteen to twenty years seems, in all the multiplicity of its forms, tasks, and goals, to fulfill a significant and far-reaching function which is shared by all the cultures in one important respect: all the performances are unanimously described and evaluated as the instrument or vehicle of recreation in the traditional, native theatre form and repertoire of an established theatre which had been the norm until the 1960s.

In Nigeria, theatrical interculturalism has led — as much in the English spoken drama as in the different forms of the Yoruba traveling theatre — to a diversity of previously unheard of developments whose various individual and, in part, regional functions cannot as yet be adequately assessed since they devolve upon special historical conditions and developments.

In India, intercultural performances have made the cross-fertilization of theatre in rural and urban areas possible: city theatre, strongly influenced by the West, resorted to the various regional theatre forms and thereby opened up wholly new perspectives for itself; the traditional theatre in rural areas experimented, on the contrary, with problematic dramatic texts, among which Brecht's drama played a significant role. It thus expanded its expressive and effective potential. In that interculturalism has brought town and rural theatres closer together, the possibility of creating a pan-Indian theatrical language seems to have emerged for the first time in the history of modern Indian theatre.

In China, the traditional opera forms were cast aside by intellectuals in the 1920s and 1930s as sterile and antiquated and, after the founding of the People's Republic, as feudal and outlived. However, the same traditional opera forms experienced a profound recreation after the Cultural Revolution: the staging of Western dramas in traditional opera forms initiated the development of its potential and also proved its intrinsic vitality, productivity, and elasticity most spectacularly. Westernized spoken theatre, on the other hand, was given new impetus when the alternately promoted Western techniques (Stanislavsky and Brecht) were combined with elements of the traditional performance style of Chinese opera, so that a new form of "ideographic" theatre emerged.

In Japan, the Western-realistic theatre introduced in the 1920s (*shingeki*), which experienced a new blossoming after World War II, lost its audience almost completely in the 1960s, at least as far as young spectators were concerned. The "Little Theatre" movements which were established at this time attempted to revitalize *shingeki* by recourse to elements of traditional Japanese theatre and even *shinto* rituals, thereby making it more attractive to young spectators. In contrast, the *kabuki* theatre adopted some Western "show" elements, whereby it became accessible to new spectators and secured a fresh popularity.

In European theatre, interculturalism has led, on the one hand, to the expansion of already existing theatre forms, and, on the other, to the introduction of wholly new ones. The potential range of expression in Ariane Mnouchkine's epic-folk theatre has been considerably broadened by the adoption of Japanese and Indian theatre elements. For Peter Brook, interculturalism has directly provided the conditions toward achieving a "cosmopolitan theatre," which aims to create a kind of universal language of theatre. Eugenio Barba's theory of the actor's pre-expressivity is exclusively based on observations of Far East Asian theatre. Finally, for Wilson, the recourse to foreign theatre forms becomes the constitutive factor in the development of a new kind of performance, relatively independent of text, which can largely be described as the collage of cultures. Here intercultural theatre and postmodern theatre merge easily.

Clearly, where a specific disposition toward the appropriation of the "foreign" exists, the aesthetic function of an intercultural performance in the recreation and revitalization of its own theatre is fulfilled in a particularly enduring, multidivergent, and successful way. This is most evident in the reception of Brecht in Nigeria, India, and China. Since a great number of structural equivalents exist between Brecht's epic theatre and the traditional theatres of Nigeria, India, and China, Brecht can be put to use in a unique way to fructify and make the revival, and particularly the renovation, of these theatre forms functional. While Brecht plays a more secondary role in contemporary Western and Japanese theatre, his positive contribution to the current developments in Nigerian, Indian, and Chinese theatre should not be underestimated. Brecht seems to have been given the role of catalyst through which the ultimately religion-based traditional theatre forms (at least in India and Nigeria) can be bound to the modern form of political theatre. The aesthetic function of intercultural theatre here forms the basis of the realization of a specific sociocultural function.

While, despite the many differences between the various cultures, the aesthetic theatrical function can consistently be described and evaluated as a renewal of their own theatre, opinions as to the sociocultural function of interculturalism in contemporary theatre are widely divergent. Here profound differences in the cultures are discernible.

In Nigeria and India, the problem of cultural identity seems to stand in the foreground. In the majority of cases, foreign theatre traditions are only appropriated inasmuch as they seem qualified to act as a medium between the demand for modernization and industrialization and maintaining traditional ways of life. The awareness of the high value of their own culture (forcibly repressed by colonialism) sharpens the desire for a critically selective use of Western elements in the theatre world, whereas in the world of mass media one can observe a less discriminating imitation.

In China, after the Cultural Revolution, a new evaluation of the traditional culture was initiated. The traditional theatre forms which, until then, had been cast aside as the expression of feudal or bourgeois principles were reevaluated as the product of centuries of cultural creativity in the Chinese nation which could be made fertile again, once they were given the new content relevant to the changed social situation. The vital function of theatrical interculturalism as intermediary can especially be noted in the production of Western dramas, such as *Macbeth* or *The Good Person of Sezuan*, in the style of classical Chinese operas.

In Japan, various intercultural performances seem to satisfy almost self-contradictory cultural functions. On the one hand, they present — as rejection of the purely Western *shingeki*, and through an intensified return to traditional theatre forms — a sharp criticism and refusal of the Westernization of Japanese society (opposed to such Westernization, Suzuki and Shogo Ota attempt to validify an authentic Japanese cultural identity in their productions); yet, on the other hand, these same directors raise the demand for a universally comprehensible theatre; whether, as Suzuki maintains, by returning to the universal human expressions in body and speech, or as Ota maintains, by going beyond speech in sacrificing language to develop theatrical images which are relatively open to interpretation and which can therefore be construed differently and defined by spectators from different cultures.

In this respect, interculturalism in modern Japanese theatre comes close to interculturalism in the West: Robert Wilson exhibits nonrelated elements from widely different cultures on the stage and thus creates images to which wholly arbitrary meanings can be assigned or which can be received as images without meaning. Peter Brook heralded the age of a "cosmopolitan theatre" which chose elements which it found to contain universal validity for, and comprehension by, all possible or known cultures. In this case, theatrical interculturalism is not concerned with specific cultural identities, but aims toward the "universal," the whole human homogeneity beyond the differences determined by one's own culture. No consensus of opinion can be reached as to how this desire for universality should be evaluated. Is it to be seen as a countermand to cultural imperialism (because one culture's own product can no longer be supplied with its own interpretation of meaning, it is rather left to the members of the other culture to decide which meanings to construe)? Or is it rather to be viewed as an opportune revival of cultural imperialism and cultural exploitation, since the demand for universality negates the demand by the non-Westernized, nonindustrialized cultures for their own identity (their culture is plundered in the search toward universality), so that the merging of all differences is legitimized by a "universally valid" centralized culture, which is actually defined and dominated by Western culture?

Similar fundamental differences are also seen in the evaluation of the procedure of creating intercultural theatre in this way (the arbitrary adoption of elements from different foreign cultures and the use of them in one's own theatre). While members of the Western culture are generally indifferent as to what is made out of their own traditions (music and text) in the theatres of other cultures, the intellectual elite of the so-called Third World, on the contrary, resist such cultural exploitation and even the interpretation of their own culture in Western theatre (as was most notable in the case of Peter Brook's *The Mahabharata*). Thus, theatrical interculturalism has a political aspect concerning the actual power relationships between cultures which should not be overlooked.

COMMUNICATING THE FOREIGN OR PRODUCTIVE RECEPTION?

Every intercultural performance builds a net of relations between its own theatre and the foreign theatre traditions from which it has taken elements. The relative positions accorded the familiar and the foreign in the performance depend entirely on the structure of this net. Thus, it must be noted that this net is structured on one side by the function of the adoption and on the other by the actual process of adoption.

I have described and defined the aesthetic function of interculturalism in contemporary theatre as the revitalization of traditional theatre forms and, in general, as the recreation of theatre. This can further be exemplified through the use of two examples taken from European and Chinese theatre: Ariane Mnouchkine's production of *Henry IV* and Brecht's *Good Person of Sezuan* staged in the traditional form of Sichuan opera.

The Théâtre du Soleil can generally be characterized as epic-folk theatre. Its dominants are the complex signs "character" and "situation": typified characters are presented in key situations which suggest nuances in their psychology and which, at the same time, situate them in a distinct historical era. This formulation of the dominants is supported by *Verfremdungseffekte* (in a Brechtian sense) of widely different forms and techniques, extensively emphasized with the help of masks and fixed costume types which are as much newly invented as they are lifted from other theatre forms such as the *commedia dell'arte*.[1]

The problem that Mnouchkine faced in her project to stage Shakespeare was how to preserve the foreignness of his dramas. She commented on this in an interview in the following way:

> No, Shakespeare is not our contemporary. For, if you really suppose that he is one of us, that his language is as much our own, that he deals with precisely those problems which also concern us . . . then he seems even more strange. . . . If we agree that Shakespeare . . . went very far, further than any other, then the actors and the spectators require a great deal of courage to follow him into this far-away country that is really our own selves. . . . And then he remains foreign, as foreign as we are.[2]

The troupe felt that if they used the methods of expression they had developed so far (which were already extremely familiar to their spectators) this foreignness could be neither expressed nor communicated. They turned, therefore, to the signs used by the Japanese theatre — wholly foreign to their own spectators. They took the masks, costumes, steps, gestures, style of speaking, and music as well as the Japanese conception of space (for example, the *hanamichi*). The function of all these foreign elements thus guaranteed the typical techniques and formulation of dominants intrinsic to Mnouchkine's epic-folk theatre.

The Third Sichuan Opera Troupe from Chengdu (Sichuan) set themselves the task of dealing with and presenting the problematic relevant to and underlining the actual social situation in the People's Republic of China within the traditional form of Sichuan opera. This form of opera, like all the classical Chinese opera forms, is not only strictly codified, it is also limited to a traditional repertoire which can hardly be seen as having any relevance to the contemporary social situation. Thus, the real, lifelike problematic of a Western drama was approached — in this case, Brecht's *Good Person of Sezuan*. The function of the foreign text served, therefore, to secure social significance and topicality of performance within the form of the Sichuan opera tradition.

The process of adoption in both cases transformed the actual elements adopted to a great extent. In Mnouchkine's *Henry IV*— as indeed earlier in *Richard II*— the elements deriving from *no* and *kabuki* changed in form in the process in such a way that connoisseurs of Japanese theatre felt they were even further removed from their original context. For the European spectators who perhaps had seen Akira Kurosawa and Kenji Misogushi films, it provided associations uniquely referring to the Japanese Middle Ages, and the elements simply lost all original meaning. In the context of the production in which this metamorphosis took place, the elements acquired new meanings. In combination with the Shakespeare text and other elements of the production, the Japanese elements could satisfy many different functions: the "Japanese" wooden masks, which were worn by the former power holders, were assigned meaning through their opposition to the white painted faces (which had been used since *1789*) of the young rebels or the painted faces of Falstaff's buffoon drinking companions (in use since *Les clowns*). These greatly enhanced the build up of plot and characterization. The Japanese elements further signified very specific situations: the entrance of the court was marked by "Japanese" music, the court ceremonies by mimelike "Japanese" gestures, the uprising of the nobles against Henry, in contrast, by pantomimic "Japanese" gestures. Not least, finally, the Japanese elements were employed in psychologically extreme situations: for example, the ever increasing pirouettes used to express the obsession with battle of Hotspur and the enemies of the king.

The foreign elements here have taken over a considerable function which is related to the dominants of the underlying theatre form: as the medium of *Verfremdung*, they specify the characterization and situation of *Henry IV*. The spectator is in a position to identify the foreign elements as "Japanese" (relating them to Japanese theatre or film) or as referring to the Japanese Middle Ages and, by way of external decodification, to apply them to Shakespeare and receive Shakespeare as estranged. Similarly, by referring to other elements of the performance — internal decodification — the spectator can assign meaning to the foreign elements. The Japanese elements thus enrich the form of epic-folk theatre and expand its potential means of expression.

The Brecht text, when produced as Sichuan opera, also underwent far-reaching change. It was fitted to the aesthetic principles and existing repertoire of categorization of role-types; the plot was strengthened by its concentration on the love relationship between Shen Te and Yang Sun and the opposition between good and evil set in accordance with the familiar role-types.

On the other hand, through these very changes to the foreign text, even the established theatrical form of Sichuan opera was changed. While Chinese opera generally (with the exception of what could better be described as props) does not employ a set, the directors in this case felt they must make the basic idea of the play explicitly clear to the spectators through the stage design. The basic idea was held to be the distortion of humankind through capitalism. In order to symbolize this, the set designers created larger-than-life deformed masks which were hung from the flies on ropes in varying numbers throughout the play. In this way, a new medium of expression (stage design) was introduced into Chinese opera that it had not known before. The chosen formulation it took, nevertheless, followed the well-established principles of this species of theatre: a certain aspect is located as the most interesting or salient point, one which can be clearly and quickly understood by the spectator as *pars pro toto* and which can be interpreted as the representative of the whole.[3] From this aspect (in this case the deformation of human nature), one element is isolated (here the distorted masks), which will then function as the sign for the whole proceedings — the distortion of humankind.

A similar transformation can be observed in the gestures used. The directors decided it was important to bring out the process of the battle between good and evil within Shen Te/Shui Ta. For the two basic positions which Shen Te and Shui Ta represent, the directors turned to preexisting role-types. The psychological battle in Shen Te seemed, however, impossible to present within the given repertoire of gestures. Thus, quasi-realistic, slightly stylized gestures never seen before in Chinese opera were developed instead.

The foreign text had therefore initiated changes in the traditional theatre form, making it productive (where it was once only reproductive), thereby revitalizing it and fitting it to the needs of the changed social situation.

In both these cases, the adoption of the foreign is sparked off by a problem which has arisen in the traditional theatre (and in extreme cases in the culture). This problem cannot be solved within the scope of the existing theatrical forms. The recourse to foreign theatre forms serves above all, therefore, the function of changing the underlying theatre forms in such a way that they are then able to solve the indigenous problem. The starting point of intercultural performance is not primarily interest in the foreign, the foreign theatre form or foreign culture from which it derives, but rather a wholly specific situation within one's own culture or wholly specific problem originating in one's own theatre. The net of relationships which an intercultural performance weaves between the familiar theatre and culture and the foreign theatre traditions and cultures from which it adopts elements is thus clearly dominated by the "familiar."

In the intercultural performance, therefore, the communication of the foreign does not occupy foreground interest. The goal is not to bring the spectators closer to or familiarize them with the foreign tradition, but rather that the foreign tradition should be, to a greater or lesser extent, transformed according to the different conditions of specific fields of reception. It is far more the fundamental question of the particular problem that has evolved in one's own culture, in one's own theatre.

Thus, it seems useless to refer to the theoretical concepts and vocabularies of translation to describe and assess intercultural performances. This is because the intercultural performance does not take the foreign text or even the foreign culture as the point of departure to be communicated by its own theatre culture. Rather, it stems from the needs and demands of its own theatre and culture. That is to say, the foreign text or the foreign theatrical conventions are chosen according to their relevance to the situation in question, transformed and replanted. It makes little sense, therefore, to speak of the source-text and the target-text, even less of a source-culture or target-culture, as should be the case when the foreign is to be communicated in translation. This is due to the fact that the source culture and the target culture are one and the same thing: its own culture. The path toward foreign traditions which the intercultural performance treads appears to be a tactical strategy toward solving specific aesthetic-theatrical and sociocultural problems, toward bringing together town and rural theatres, toward capturing a new section of the public, toward affirmation of one's own cultural identity, toward promoting modernization and industrialization, toward the call for a universal communication, and so on.

The adoption of elements from foreign theatre traditions in the intercultural performance is consequently not to be seen and understood as the process of a translation, but is perhaps better measured as the process of *productive reception*, as defined by Gunther Grimm:

> The field of *productive reception* embraces all the production processes of a work which are either occasioned by or strongly influenced by reception. Through the emphasis and activity of the subject dealt with, the aesthetic aspect of reception predominates in contrast to the productive aspect,

since the reception clearly serves the production. . . . The research of productive reception or receptive production is different from former influential research in its reversal of the perspective.[4]

An intercultural performance productively receives the elements taken from the foreign theatre traditions and cultures according to the problematic which lies at the point of departure. The potential, particularly the special 'uslovnost' (conventionality — Lotman) of the underlying system of performance (of the theatrical form), as well as the specific restrictions of production and reception and the impending problem are decisive in the answer to the question as to which culture or theatre tradition will be approached, which elements will be chosen, in what ways these will be altered, and how they will be combined.[5] As we have seen, this kind of productive reception is, in many cases, in a good position to provide the underlying theatre forms with the power to revitalize the original, antiquated functions long since beyond repair or at the same time to realize and satisfy newly arisen functions which have occurred because of specific recent developments in society.

THE CHANGE IN THEATRE CAUSED BY PRODUCTIVE RECEPTION

The renovation of theatre, which the intercultural performance effects on its way to productive reception, does not present a return to an earlier condition of theatre, but rather a qualitative change: either as the expansion of the potential means of expression and impact of an established theatre form (*kabuki*, Chinese opera, Indian folk theatre, Yoruba theatre, and Mnouchkine's epic-folk theatre) or as the establishment of an entirely new theatre form (Suzuki, Ota, Brook, and Wilson).

Intercultural performance initiates a change in theatre to a degree that is significantly unlike any previous process of theatrical change. Crudely simplifying, we can identify two basic kinds of processes of change in the history of theatre:

1. Changes in the context of an all-embracing cultural change which can be described and understood as the overthrow of an era;
2. Punctual changes occurring in individual productions which then over a long period accumulate and lead to a gradual change in the existing theatre form.[6]

In the first instance, the governing or rising social class cannot, or can no longer, identify itself with the existing theatre forms, and so a new theatre emerges which is patterned to fit the needs of this class. Among changes that can be ascribed to this category would be the establishment of the court theatre with its mythological feasts and Italian opera in the seventeenth century, the emergence of the bourgeois theatre of illusion in the eighteenth century, or even the constitution of a retheatricalized, nonliterary, "total theatre" at the start of the twentieth century. The birth of *no* theatre in Japan in the Muromachi period (1392–1568), the development of *kabuki*, the art of "riverbed beggars," for a city audience in the Edo period (1600–1868), and the introduction of *shingeki* in the Meiji period (1868–1912) can also be added to this heading. In each of these examples, a new theatre form was evolved for a specific stratum of society and, on the whole, remained in use for a long time — even if greatly modified by punctual changes.

In the second instance one can list, for example, the various changes made to *kabuki* described above: the discovery and introduction of flying machines for the actors (1701), the revolving stage (1758), the adoption of gas light (1878) and electric light after World War II, or the reworking of a new kind of *kata* through the psychological interpretation of a role, introduced by Ichikawa Danjuro IX (1839–1903), which had previously been unknown in *kabuki*.

In European theatre, there are also many such punctual changes in evidence as, for example, in the case of the theatre of illusion, which between 1750 and 1900 underwent an ever increasing number of modifications — changes which were triggered by other new dramatic forms, by technical innovations, or by a change in theatrical conventions (for example, the darkened auditorium in the second half of the nineteenth century).

The change in theatre that the intercultural production can effect on its way to productive reception is thus partly comparable to changes of the second type: an established theatre form — Mnouchkine's epic-folk theatre or the Sichuan opera — is subjected to punctual changes which then expand its power of expression and impact, without challenging the unique theatrical form (its individual syntactic, semantic, and pragmatic rules). Theatrical change brought about by an intercultural performance, however, differs in one fundamental respect from punctual change, for in cases of punctual change one can only begin to speak of change after a long period, since the changes introduced punctually in individual productions are continuously integrated and only gradually accumulate. However, the process of productive reception effects a far more profound change in the underlying theatre form, within one single intercultural performance. Thus, in one production alone, a kind of time accelerator operates, allowing a process which would otherwise extend over several years, or even decades, to take place in a highly condensed form.

On the other hand, the theatrical change instigated by the intercultural production can also partly be compared to the change of the first kind: wholly new theatrical forms are created side by side with the already existing theatre forms. The question remains unanswered as yet, however, as to what extent this change is bound to the overthrow of an era, as was the case in eighteenth-century Europe and in Japan in the Meiji period. One can simply affirm that the new theatrical forms were not patterned on, or aimed at, a new stratum of theatre-oriented society: the spectators for whom Ota, Suzuki, Brook, and Wilson work stem principally from the middle classes — and have constituted the mainstay of theatre audiences for a very long time.

Thus, the changes that intercultural performances effect seem to bind together the two forms of change, a cohesion unknown till now in the long history of European and non-European theatre cultures. This raises a whole string of questions which at present we are not even close to answering. The simple fact that the possibility of such rapid change in theatre, created through the process of productive reception of the "foreign," is currently evident in widely divergent theatre cultures presents a remarkable coincidence that can only be clarified through recourse to an all-embracing process of cultural change.

Productive reception allows any elements of any number of foreign cultures to undergo cultural transformation through the process of production, thereby making one's own theatre and culture productive again. This process changes the form, use, and function not only of the adopted elements, but also of the adopting theatre and, in the long run, perhaps even the adopting culture. In that the theatre adjusts itself to elements of foreign traditions (cultures), it can become a *permanent dynamic* which, although it may concern foreign elements in the first instance, is also concerned with itself and its own culture. The intercultural production in contemporary theatre is, therefore, not uniquely to be interpreted as an aesthetic indicator of a potential social change in the existing culture. It functions far more as the place of execution and instrument of such cultural change.

INTERCULTURAL ASPECTS
IN POSTMODERN THEATRE
The Japanese Version of Chekhov's *Three Sisters*

THEATRE BETWEEN CULTURES

Transferring plays from one culture to another has a fairly long tradition on the European stage. Omitting Roman adaptations of Greek drama, we can date it back to the late sixteenth or early seventeenth century, when English, Dutch, and Italian groups of actors were moving from one country to another all over the continent. They introduced plays of their own tradition to the theatres of their host countries and initiated a process of cross-pollination among different European cultures. The process of consciously intended mediation between the cultures grew into a theatrical program when Goethe proclaimed the era of *Weltliteratur*: "A national literature has little left to say; the age of world literature has dawned and each of us must contribute to hastening its arrival."[1]

On his small provincial stage in Weimar, Goethe established a repertoire that comprised the most important dramas of the Western world, including, for instance, Sophocles' *Antigone*; Shakespeare's *Hamlet, Henry IV, Macbeth, Julius Caesar*, and *Othello*; Corneille's *Cid*; Racine's *Phèdre*; Molière's *The Miser*; Calderón's *The Magnanimous Prince* and *Life's a Dream*; and comedies by Gozzi and Goldoni, as well as plays by Lessing, Schiller, and Goethe himself. Since Goethe was convinced that the audience would neither understand nor appreciate the dramas of foreign cultures if he staged them without any alterations, he did not shrink from shortening and even changing them considerably. Any given production of a foreign play proved to be a mixture of elements taken from two cultures: the one in which the play originated and the one in which it was staged. It was the aim and function of such intermixing to promote intercultural understanding.

Although Goethe's Weimar theatre may be considered an important step toward the proclaimed goal of a world theatre, it was limited to European drama: taking a play out of its original context was carried out within the confines of European culture as a whole.

Interest in foreign theatrical traditions went beyond the boundaries of Europe for the first time with the avant-gardists. Meyerhold, for example, used elements of the Japanese theatre,[2] Brecht borrowed from the Chinese,[3] Tairov from the Indian theatre,[4] and Artaud took the Balinese as his model for a new theatre.[5] However, these artists did not intend to employ theatre as a means of mediating between their own cultures and those of the theatrical forms they were adopting and adapting: rather, they were in search of a new theatre. Each wanted to exploit Asian theatrical forms in order to accomplish his particular purposes. They simply borrowed those principles, texts, and styles of staging which they considered to be useful in achieving an avant-garde theatre style. Thus, the mixing of elements from at least two different theatrical traditions aimed at, and resulted in, the development of a new theatre. Nevertheless, by proceeding in this manner, they did introduce aspects of some Asian cultures into Europe.

The Japanese audience became acquainted with the European theatre tradition for the first time some decades earlier. As early as 1885 an adaptation of *The Merchant of Venice* was performed in *kabuki* style. However, a consciously intended mediation of European theatrical culture did not begin until 1901, when the first faithfully translated text of a Western play was staged in Tokyo: Shakespeare's *Julius Caesar*. Ten years later, this performance was followed by a completely Westernized production of *Hamlet* staged by a company called Bungei Kyokai (the Literary Society).

The Bungei Kyokai and the Tsukiji Little Theatre (established in 1924 by Kaoru Osanai) were the first to initiate and systematically develop a special Western-oriented theatre known as *shingeki* (new drama). This was a theatre which totally cut itself off from traditional Japanese forms such as *kabuki* and *no*, devoutly subscribing to Western models. Its repertoire consisted exclusively of Western — usually contemporary — plays, the favorites being those of Ibsen and Chekhov. The acting style strove for a realistic, even naturalistic, reflection of reality as developed by Stanislavsky, the admired master. *Shingeki* did not intend to form a mixture between Japanese and European theatrical traditions, but rather to present a purely European theatre.[6]

At the same time as avant-garde theatre directors in Europe were abandoning the illusionist theatre as antiquated and unable to produce a stimulating and really artistic performance and were discovering the innovating possibilities inherent in the highly stylized theatre of the Far East, literary societies in Japan were praising the innovative potential of Western drama because they were bored with the rather uniform texts of *kabuki* and *no* and were no longer able to appreciate the theatrical values of these old traditional theatre forms. For them, modern theatre had to be Western theatre. Like the European avant-gardists, the *shingeki* hoped to renew the theatre by referring to a totally different, and therefore exotic, theatre tradition.

After World War II, *shingeki* flourished again in the wake of the progressive Westernization in all phases of Japanese culture and society. This period lasted until the late sixties. The "modernization" brought about in the theatre by *shingeki* companies was, in fact, Westernization. The genuinely Japanese theatre tradition was not only neglected but expressly negated for the sake of an illusionist, lifelike, and realistic theatre. The *shingeki* claimed to be the only modern — that is, legitimate — theatre in Japan.

It was against this status quo of *shingeki* that the "little theatre movements" exploded in the late sixties. They strove neither for an exclusive return to Japanese theatre traditions nor for a complete denial of Western drama. Instead they protested against an elitist theatre which was nothing but a copy of an antiquated Western model and not in the least related to contemporary Japanese society and its problems. They demanded a theatre which would be able to respond to the current social situation in Japan and which would also address a nonelitist audience.

One of the most prominent and influential representatives of the little theatre movements is the Suzuki Company of Toga (SCOT), led by Tadashi Suzuki. Suzuki's productions often derive from Western plays, mainly Greek tragedies (such as Euripides' *The Trojan Women* and *The Bacchae*), but also from a favorite of *shingeki*, Chekhov's *Three Sisters*. However, the company has developed a special style of acting which can be considered a particular offspring of the traditional Japanese acting schools. "Suzuki . . . sucked much of his nourishment from the traditional and popular theatre forms of Japan. No other director has learnt and stolen so much from *no* and *kabuki*, and certainly none has utilised so effectively the popular folk songs which have entered the unconscious mechanism of the psyche of the Japanese nonelitist populace."[7]

Thus, Suzuki's productions form particular "mixtures" of elements from Western (foreign) and Japanese (indigenous) theatrical traditions, as did Goethe's stagings and those of the European avant-gardist stage directors.

Suzuki's work raises some interesting questions. In which ways and to what purpose does Suzuki employ dramatic texts stemming from the Western tradition, and what is the function and aim of these particular "mixtures"? I shall attempt to answer these questions using his production of Chekhov's *Three Sisters* as my text.[8]

Suzuki's production of *Three Sisters* did not take more than one hour to perform, and this is the usual length of his productions. Chekhov's text, therefore, had to be shortened drastically: more than half the dialogue was cut. The four acts were revised into ten scenes. There was nothing left of Solyony, Fedotik, Rhode, and Ferapont, and only one line of Kulygin's text remained. With the exception of Andrei, Suzuki merged all the male characters together (i.e., the military people) and distributed their speeches between two characters called "Man 1" and "Man 2." In the main, they were given the philosophizing passages of Tuzenbach and Vershinin as well as Tuzenbach's expression of his faith in the coming of a new era (act 1), Vershinin's reflections about a better future (act 1, act 2), and the confessions of love to Masha (Vershinin) and Irina (Tuzenbach). The other texts of Man 1 and Man 2 were taken from Vershinin's complaint about his personal situation (act 2) as well as Chebutykin's refusal to work (act 1) and his announcement that he is going to leave (act 4). Although most of Vershinin's text was given to Man 1 and what was left of Tuzenbach's to Man 2, this principle was not consistently observed. Sometimes Man 1 spoke Tuzenbach's or Chebutykin's lines and Man 2 Vershinin's or Chebutykin's. On the other hand, some speeches were given to both of them at once, such as Vershinin's departing phrases to Olga (act 4), Irina's yearning call "Moscow! Moscow! To Moscow!" (act 2), and Olga's last long passage at the end of the play. The text was certainly not distributed between Man 1 and Man 2 according to any individualizing principle.

On the other hand, the text of the sisters was shortened without limiting its effectiveness in molding their separate individualities. Olga's constant complaints about her work at school and the headache it causes her, as well as her warnings and admonishments to her siblings, survived in Suzuki's version: "Don't whistle, Masha" (act 1); "Stop that, I can't bear it" (act 3); "Let it rest, Andryusha" (act 3); "Calm yourself, Masha" (act 4). Masha's text concentrated on the topics of her unhappy marriage and her love for Vershinin (act 2). Irina was characterized by her desire for work in the beginning (act 1), her refusal to allow Tuzenbach to talk to her of love (act 1), her complaint about her work at the telegraph station (act 2), and her desperate outburst about the misery and failure of her life (act 3). The shortened text sufficed to shape the individuality of each character clearly as well as to delineate the traits all three of them have in common: their memories and their dreams of Moscow as the symbol and guarantee of a better life.

Apart from the three sisters, Man 1, and Man 2, the characters of Andrei, Natasha, and Anfisa also remained intact. The love-scene between Andrei and Natasha from the end of act 1 here formed scene 4: it presented both of them full of hope and happiness. Andrei had his second and last appearance in scene 8, first asking his sisters to respect his wife, Natasha, and confessing to them his debts (act 3), but then complaining to Man 1 and Man 2 that his wife was a "small, blind sort of thick-skinned animal. In any case, she's not a human being" (act 4).

Natasha appeared again in scene 7: "carrying a candle; she enters from the door on the right and crosses the stage without speaking" (act 3). She appeared for the last time at the end of scene 9, where, satisfied that all were going to leave the house, she shouts to the maid: "What's a fork doing here, I'd like to know? Hold your tongue!" (act 4). Only enough of Andrei's and Natasha's dialogue was left to show their initial circumstances and what had become of them.

Anfisa, the old nurse from the country, was presented as a friendly woman caring for the three sisters, providing them with food and tea. The text originally spoken by Olga — "If we only knew, if we only knew!" — was here given to Anfisa as the last lines of the play. The division of characters into three groups (the three sisters, Man 1 and 2, and the others), as suggested by Suzuki's adaptation of Chekhov's text, was further emphasized by certain scenic components and arrangements. Whereas the three sisters and Man 1 and 2 stayed onstage all the time or, in the latter case, almost until the end, Andrei, Natasha, and Anfisa appeared and left alternately. While the three sisters and Man 1 and 2 wore almost exclusively European clothes, Andrei, Natasha, and Anfisa were dressed in traditional Japanese garments. Through the sign-systems "entrance/exit" and "costume" an opposition was formed between the three sisters and Man 1 and 2, on the one hand, and Andrei, Natasha, and Anfisa, on the other.

Within these larger groups another opposition was constituted through the sign-system of movement. Whereas Andrei and Natasha walked erect, Anfisa crossed the stage in a squatting position. While the three sisters moved on, or between, three European armchairs set side by side upstage and three Japanese straw mats lying side by side downstage, Man 1 and 2 were "imprisoned" during the first nine scenes in two huge wicker baskets upstage (reminding the spectator of the dustbins in Beckett's *Endgame*), just able to raise their heads over the edge. Only in the last scene did they leave the baskets, move across the stage, and, finally, depart.

Among these different oppositions, that between the three sisters and Man 1 and 2 seemed to be the most important. According to the deindividualizing tendencies of Suzuki's text version, Man 1 and 2 were dressed totally alike, in black suits and shoes, with huge sunglasses and umbrellas, which they put up when leaving the baskets. As long as they stayed in the baskets, they were engaged in philosophizing. It was made very clear that philosophy was nothing but a compensation to them. After scene 9, all the stanzas of the Horst Wessel song were sung in German and, suddenly, Man 1 and 2 seemed to revive. They jumped out of the baskets and rushed across the stage, making their departure for real life, the war. These men were without any individuality—theorizing about a better life as long as they were kept immobile and hurrying eagerly "to arms" and violence when war and destruction were about to break out.

The three sisters, on the other hand, were presented as three individuals who, nonetheless, had some features and properties in common. Each was dressed differently: Olga had a Japanese hairstyle and her clothes were a mixture of European and Japanese elements. Masha's head was covered with a *topi* and she wore a long European dress with a knitted multicolored shawl around her shoulders. A large red ribbon was tied in Irina's hair; she wore glasses, a long skirt, a blouse, and a jacket. None of the three had shoes—their feet were encased in white woolen socks. Each carried a handbag: Olga, a patterned paper bag; Masha, a wicker bag with long handles; and Irina, a dark leather bag. Each held an open umbrella in her hand at all times. Olga's umbrella was broken.

The significance of these umbrellas derives from the fact that, during the 1930s, middle-class women in Japan used to carry open umbrellas when shopping. As Suzuki explained in an interview, even their pet dogs were fitted out with smaller versions. The umbrella was understood as a sign of the "modern," that is, Westernized, attitude of its possessor.

In the production, the umbrellas functioned as a symbol of the dreams to which the sisters constantly clung, dreams of "Moscow" or of a Western way of life. As they are all alike in this respect, the gestures they performed with the umbrellas, both at the beginning and end of the play, were precisely synchronized. At other times, their gestures were used to characterize their different individualities: Olga's rather resigned attitude toward life; Masha's briskness and desire for both love and escape, as well as her sense of humor (in the meal scene); and Irina's growing desperation at the failures in her life.

The space within which the three sisters moved was marked by the European armchairs upstage and the Japanese mats downstage. In the beginning they sat or squatted on the armchairs and in the end they stood on them, clutching their umbrellas as if hoping to levitate. At the end of scene 3, the three sisters left the chairs and went forward to the mats, where they sat down in the Japanese manner and had the meal which Anfisa brought them on three small tables.

The world in which the three sisters live, between the armchairs and the straw mats, was also characterized by music. Movements, gestures, and words were accompanied by instrumental music, partly of European romantic origin (with the violin and piano dominating), partly as though taken from the soundtrack of a Hollywood film. The music pointed to the dreams and desires, hopes and illusions, which determine and ruin the sisters' lives.

Since the stage-architecture was basically Japanese, it can be assumed that what was happening onstage could be understood as occurring within the context of Japanese culture. In this respect, Suzuki's production of Chekhov's *Three Sisters* can be seen as a harsh critique of Westernization as it has taken place in Japan after World War II. The process is shown to entail a dehumanization of life; to men it has brought the philosophy of a better life in the future which, nonetheless, has been unable to keep them from aggression and violence. To women, Westernization introduced dreams and hopes of happiness (in love) and self-fulfillment (in work) which cannot be realized in the current situation.

Whereas *shingeki* companies used Chekhov's plays as the image and model of a desired Western life which was to be copied and taken as a guide even if it had nothing to do with the actual Japanese situation, Suzuki adopted the opposite point of view and staged Chekhov in order to demonstrate critically what happens when this model is followed unconditionally. This does not mean that Suzuki preaches a return to traditional Japanese culture. By presenting Andrei and Natasha as thoroughly Japanese, he renders such a conclusion impossible. Besides, the question of the traditional Japanese ways of life is not dealt with in this production, but rather the problems brought about by unquestioning and excessive Westernization. Paradoxically — at least from the point of view of *shingeki*— Suzuki succeeded in responding to the current situation in Japan by staging a European play.

RISE OF A "WORLD THEATRE"?

Above all, the enormous impact of Suzuki's productions was created by specific techniques of body movement. He has even elaborated a special kind of physical training to help actors acquire the necessary abilities. Essentially, the training consists of stamping the ground without letting the upper half of the body move. Suzuki explains his method as follows:

Of course, emphasising the fact that the construction of the human body and the balance of forces which support it are centred on the pelvic region is not thinking unique to my method; but almost all the performing arts invariably use such thinking. Only, I believe it is specific to my training that first of all the actors are made to feel conscious of this by stamping and beating the ground with their feet. In our daily life, we tend to disregard the importance of the feet. It is necessary for us to be aware of the fact that the human body makes contact with the ground through the feet, that the ground and the human body are inseparable, as the latter is, in fact, part of the former, meaning that when we die we return to the earth — to make the body, which usually functions unconscious of its relationship, aware of this fact by creating a strong sense of impact through the beating of the ground with the feet.[9]

Suzuki's method and its theoretical foundation are deeply rooted in Japanese culture. In traditional forms such as *no* and *kabuki* actors very often convey the feeling that the feet are planted firmly on the ground. This is symbolized in such movements as "sliding steps" (*suriashi*) or stamping (*ashibyoshi*), which are meant to express the affinity with the earth. Suzuki's actors perform many of those movements which were developed in *no* and *kabuki*, which originally stem from ancient rituals.

In all traditional Japanese performing arts, the performers use the stamping movement to signify the trampling down of evil spirits, as the late anthropologist Shinobu Origuchi explained. The movement might also imply the arousal of energy which activates human life. This interpretation is represented in the Opening Ritual of the Heavenly Stone Wall in the Japanese creation myth, where a goddess named Ameno Uzumeno Mikoto dances on a wooden tub. Origuchi describes her dance as follows: "Perhaps the tub symbolised the earth. The goddess stomped on it and struck it with a stick while making loud noises; actions supposed to wake up and bring out the soul or spirit that was believed to be under the tub, whether sleeping or hiding, in order to send it to the unseen sacred body of the god near by."[10]

In this context it becomes understandable why ancient Japanese stages were built on "places closely bound up with the sense of danger we feel whenever we are confronted by a sense of our own destruction: for example, in a cemetery, at the frontier between two villages, at the line of demarcation between two kinds of space. . . . In these places local spirits (*genii loci*) are said to reside."[11] By stamping on the stage floor, *no* and *kabuki* actors conjure up such spirits in order to acquire their energy.

Even though Suzuki is deeply aware of the Japanese origins of the acting technique he has developed, he claims that it is founded on a condition basic to all human beings: "Perhaps it is not the upper half but the lower half of the body through which the physical sensibility common to all races is consciously expressed; to be more specific, the feet. The feet are the last remaining part of the human body which has kept, literally, in touch with the earth, the very supporting base of all human activities."[12]

This means that the special way in which Suzuki's actors use their bodies is meant to be performed and understood in all cultures without any regard to their differences and peculiarities. This technique, together with Suzuki's insistence on combining European dramatic texts with an acting style derived from the Japanese theatre, forms the basis for the realization of a "world theatre." This world theatre is supposed to be received and understood in all cultures because it is based on universals of human expression. These universals are, in Suzuki's opinion, language and the human body. Since language is developed to the highest degree of expressivity in European drama, and the human body as a means of expression is similarly exploited in the traditional Japanese theatre, he aims to combine them in order to create and establish an intercultural form of theatre, a theatre which would have a strong effect on audiences all over the world.

In this respect, Suzuki's endeavors concur with those of other leading stage directors in Europe and in the United States. For years, Peter Brook has argued for the realization of what he calls "cosmopolitan theatre," for the elaboration of a "theatrical language" understandable in all cultures.[13] To this end, he has looked for elements that could be used in different theatrical traditions: European, African, Asian, American. The most convincing results of this procedure have been the productions of *Orghast*, performed in the ruins of Persepolis in 1971; a little later *The Iks*, a story of an African tribe about to die out; *The Conference of the Birds*, in 1977, an adapted version of a medieval play written by the Persian mystic Attar; and most recently *The Mahabharata*, performed in a deserted quarry near Avignon.[14]

Another striking example is Robert Wilson's gigantic project of *the CIVIL warS*, which consists of different parts being produced in Cologne, Rotterdam, Marseilles, Lyon, Nice, Rome, Tokyo, and Milwaukee. It was originally planned to bring these parts together on the occasion of the Olympic Games in Los Angeles (1984) in one enormous performance that would take about twenty-four hours. It is a characteristic feature of at least those parts with which I am acquainted (*The Knee Plays*, Milwaukee, and the German part, act 1, scene A; act 4, scene A and epilogue) that elements of different cultures are used simultaneously — for example, images from German and American history (Frederick the Great and Lincoln) or physical movements from the Japanese *no* and those imitating human gestures outside any gravitational field. This is not the place to discuss whether Wilson's undertaking involves an exploitation of cultures rendering their essentials into insignificant elements which only serve to present something "new" or "exotic."[15] In the context of this chapter, I merely wish to emphasize the fact that the project was planned, produced, and performed not only as an international but also as an intercultural enterprise.

Ariane Mnouchkine's stagings of Shakespearean plays (*Richard II*, *Henry IV*, and *Twelfth Night*) might also be considered attempts to realize similar tendencies. In these productions she combined a European text with elements taken from Asian theatres, mainly from the Japanese *no* and *kabuki*, such as costumes, music, gestures, and movements. By proceeding in this manner, Mnouchkine wanted to "estrange" the Shakespearean text, which proves ultimately to be no less strange than the Japanese theatrical elements and, thus, achieves a hyperrealistic mode of representation. The point she was trying to make was that European dramatic texts of past periods may seem just as strange to us as any material taken from a foreign culture. We have no immediate access to either a foreign culture or the past of our own culture. It was the aim of Mnouchkine's "hyperrealism" to make the spectator aware of the "fact" that our own past culture is as alien to us as the tradition of a foreign culture. It may be, as some critics argued, that the employment of Japanese elements served only a decorative purpose (mainly in *Richard II*) and that the proclaimed hyperrealism was not actually achieved.[16] Nonetheless, it should be stressed that Mnouchkine's intention was founded on an intercultural perspective.

There are a number of other examples (for instance, the Odin Teatret of Eugenio Barba), but those mentioned above will suffice to emphasize that intercultural awareness forms an essential part of postmodern theatre.[17] It seems that many leading stage directors would support the demand for "world theatre"—not a world theatre in the sense of Goethe, promoting intercultural understanding by the way of mediating between cultures, but rather a world theatre conceived as an "intercultural" mode of theatrical expression and representation which is accessible to spectators all over the world. Goethe was convinced that the products of a foreign culture can only be made understandable to the members of our own culture by way of a conscious mediation: by translation or adaptation. The above-mentioned stage directors of today, on the other hand, strive toward a theatre that will be enjoyed and understood by members of different cultures, because it uses an "intercultural" (i.e., a universal)—theatrical—language.

While I have certain doubts as to the theoretical plausibility of such a world theatre, it is equally worthy of reflection and investigation. Here I have endeavored to show that postmodern theatre seems to be characterized and dominated by intercultural tendencies in a way that is unknown in the history of Western, as well as Japanese, theatre. It may well be that this kind of interculturalism reflects a general development in the culture of postindustrial societies (and even in some societies in the Third World): one can observe a certain tendency in different cultures to merge into one world culture. Whether such a world culture will in fact arise and what it will look like is, for the time being, impossible to predict. Perhaps the search for a universal theatrical language in postmodern theatre indicates that the theatre has already passed into this new era.

Scene from Vsevolod Meyerhold's *The Magnanimous Cuckold*, Moscow, 1922.

Bella-Coola in Berlin, 1886. Archives Preußischer Kulturbesitz.

Hagenbeck's Singhalese-Caravan. Original illustration by L. Beckmann.
From *Die Gartenlaube: Illustriertes Familienblatt* 54 (Leipzig, 1884), 565.

The Yellow Jacket: "The intensely invisible! Mr. Holman Clark as the Property man."
From *The Sketch*, April 9, 1913, 11. Courtesy of the British Library.

The Yellow Jacket, production: Max Reinhardt, Kammerspiele Berlin,
March 3, 1914. Max Reinhardt-Forschungs- und Gedenkstätte.

Bacchae, production: Klaus Michael Grüber, Berlin, 1974. Photo: Helga Kneidl.

Robert Wilson's *The Hamlet Machine*, Thalia-Theater, Hamburg, 1986. From *Theater heute* 12 (1986), cover photo. Photo: Elisabeth Henrichs.

Sada Yakko in *The Geisha and the Knight*. Act 1: The battle for Katsuragi's head.
Loïe Fuller Theatre, Paris, 1900. From *The Sketch*, June 26, 1901, 389.
Courtesy of the British Library.

Tokujiro Tsutsui (right) in *Kanjincho*, the Globe Theatre, London, 1930.
From *The Sketch*, July 2, 1930, 29. Courtesy of the British Library.

Westmoreland's "Japanese" wooden mask in opposition to Henry's white-painted face in Ariane Mnouchkine's *Henry IV* in Paris.

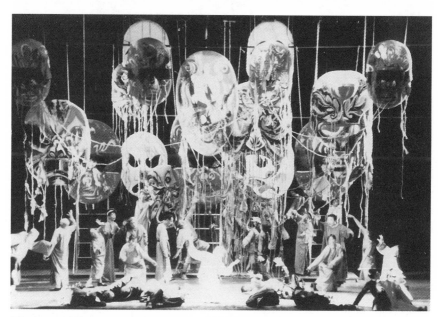

The larger than life, deformed masks which were hung from the flies on ropes in the Third Sichuan Opera Troupe's production of *The Good Person of Sezuan* in Chengdu.

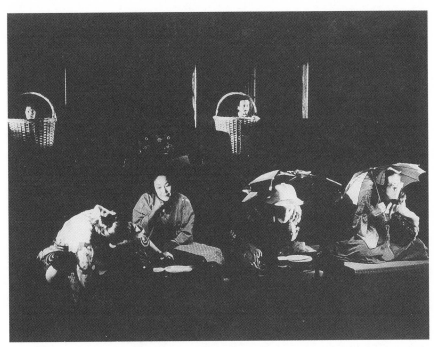

Man 1 and 2 in the two huge wicker baskets in Tadashi Suzuki's *Three Sisters*.

Man 1 and 2, having jumped out of the baskets.

The three sisters' outward appearance in Suzuki's *Three Sisters*.

Ralf Långbacka's *Don Giovanni* at the Royal Opera in Stockholm: the narrow red curtain at the opening of the performance. Photo: Enar Merkel Rydberg.

The demarcation of downstage and upstage areas by pillarlike elements
in the production of *Don Giovanni* at the Royal Opera in Stockholm.
Photo: Enar Merkel Rydberg.

The open stage with its empty center. Photo: Enar Merkel Rydberg.

Kent (Thomas Thieme), Lear (Marianne Hoppe), and the Fool (Andreas Seifert) around the *hashigakari*-like table in Robert Wilson's *King Lear* in Frankfurt. Photo: Abisag Tüllmann.

Lear's cat- and vulturelike daughters, Goneril (Jutta Hoffmann) and Regan (Astrid Gorvin). Photo: Abisag Tüllmann.

Gloucester (Jürgen Holtz) in the cage with Regan (Astrid Gorvin) in front, tearing invisible hair off his beard. Photo: Abisag Tüllmann.

Two Undiscovered Amerindians Visit Covent Garden, London, May 1992. Audience members, after initial shyness, would feed Gómez-Peña and Fusco from outside the cage. Photo: Peter Barker.

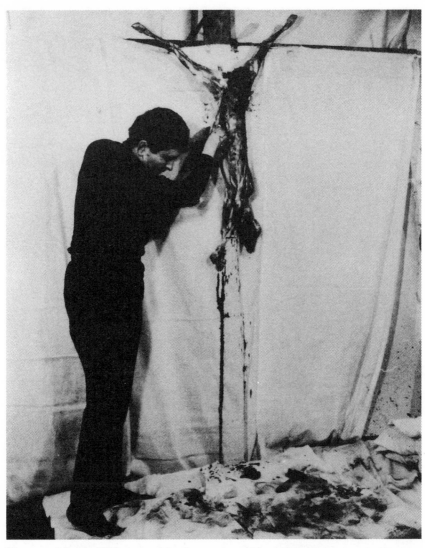

Hermann Nitsch, *Fifth Action*, March 3, 1964, at Otto Mühl's apartment in Vienna.
Photo: L. Hoffenreich.

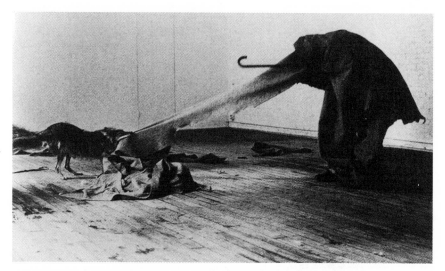

Joseph Beuys, *Coyote*, 1974, at the René Block gallery in New York.

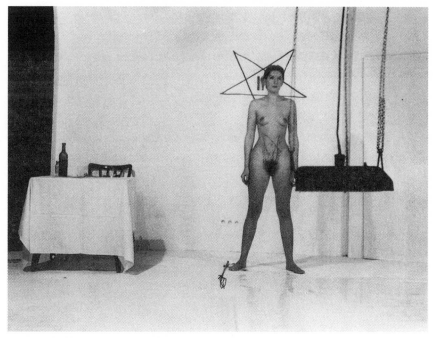

Marina Abramović, *The Lips of Thomas*, 1975, at the Krinzinger gallery in Innsbruck.
Courtesy of the Krinzinger gallery, Innsbruck.

PART III

In the Eyes of Theatre

ALL THE WORLD'S A STAGE
The Theatrical Metaphor in the Baroque and Postmodernism

Performance analysis is still, even today, one of the most neglected areas of academic theatre research. While the analysis of a work in other arts sciences (history of art, literature, and musicology) is attributed a central and dominant position, it has not yet been awarded equivalent rank in theatre studies. Since theatre studies was originally founded on a historical approach, there are good reasons for this phenomenon. For, while I can look at paintings that are centuries old, and read novels that were written in the far distant past, I can only see theatre performances that are taking place now, at this very moment. Thus, I am only able to regard past theatrical events from a theoretical aspect, not an aesthetic one. A performance is indivisibly bound to the actors who perform it and exists only in the brief moment of its creation. Although single elements such as costume, props, and set may last beyond the process of performance and can even be accessible centuries later, all that remains are single elements ripped from their original context, and never the performance from which they are derived. The performance itself can never be handed down to us.

Of course, this may also apply to contemporary productions which we can view aesthetically. A performance does not exist as a material artifact which, in a painting or a novel text, possesses its own determinable, autonomous existence detachable from its creators. The material artifact of a performance only exists in the process of its production and presentation. A determinant, communicable system of notation, however, is indispensable to performance analysis.

As long as there was no fixed method of approach in notating a performance, performance analysis was only practicable in exceptional circumstances (repeated visits to the theatre, a talent for keen observation, notes jotted down during the performance, etc.). With the possibility of presenting relatively reliable documentation in video recordings, as a kind of *aide-*

mémoire, however, the analysis of a work in the field of theatre studies as an arts science has at last been assured more central consideration than ever before.

The general premise that underlies performance analysis is the same as for any analysis of a work. The analysis is carried out as a hermeneutic process which is subjectively conditioned and which is, in principle, nonclosable. Thus, no performance analysis can make any claim to objectivity; nor can it treat its results as definitive. One might think it best to begin with the three stages: description, analysis, and interpretation. But this differentiation has more systematic value than methodological benefit, for I can only describe what I have seen. My perception, however, is influenced and directed by an interpretive hypothesis of rather provisional nature. To this extent, therefore, every description is the result of an interpretive decision, rather than, as one might think, its base. It is a vicious circle which actually represents the precondition of all analyses of works.

An objectively based alternative — true/false — cannot be applied to the experience of performance analysis because it is always subjective and provisional. A more appropriate alternative might be one which is intersubjectively reconstructive — plausible/nonplausible.

One of the cardinal problems of performance analysis, just as in all kinds of analysis, is the question of segmentation. Since a performance cannot be analyzed in its whole, but only through the alternating relations between a whole and its parts, it must be dissected into smaller units more accessible to analysis. In principle, such a procedure opens several possible approaches. One might turn to categories provided by the poetics of drama such as character, plot, situation, space, and time; or one might make a segmentation according to the various sign systems used: linguistic signs, kinesic signs (facial expression, gesture, bodily posture and movement, distance), makeup, mask, coiffure, costume, set, props, light, sound, and music. Or one might integrate various sign systems into groups and investigate the verbal and nonverbal or visual and aural signs individually. The choice of levels of segmentation largely depends upon the kind of performance involved and where the cognitive interests of the analysis lie. In the case of a psychological-realistic production of *Nora*, a segmentation according to character would seem most relevant, while one might choose to dissect Robert Wilson's *CIVIL warS* into visual and aural signs. In interpreting the drama *Macbeth*, character, plot, and space may present practicable units; if, on the other hand, one questions the aesthetic principles of a production, a more appropriate level of examination might be the way different sign systems are used (realistically, symbolically/

stylistically) and how they relate to each other (affirmation/completion, neutrality/contradiction, detachment).

In the following analysis of *Don Giovanni* directed by Ralf Långbacka for the Royal Opera in Stockholm (1989), the method of segmentation is one which implies relatively few preliminary decisions. Both the signs of space and the signs presented by the actor (singer) through appearance and action are individually examined.

AN ANALYSIS OF RALF LÅNGBACKA'S PRODUCTION OF
Don Giovanni AT THE ROYAL OPERA IN STOCKHOLM (1989)

The Signs of Space

As the opening bars of the overture sound, the large red curtain rises on a narrower red curtain which screens center stage and which itself is flanked on both sides by pillarlike structures. In this way, the upstage area is hidden and thus set apart from the downstage area, which is fully in view.

These elements of set can be interpreted as quotations from theatre history. The red curtain functions *pars pro toto* as the absolute sign of theatre. It signals to the audience that the following events on which it rises are to be perceived as theatre within theatre: the stage does not represent the world but a stage.

The pillar structure also suggests various elements from the history of theatre. It alludes to the *scenae frons* of the Renaissance theatre (as in the Teatro Olimpico), the column set so favored in Baroque theatre, and even the boxes of a Baroque theatre auditorium. Thus, the elements used refer partly to the stage and partly to the auditorium of a Baroque theatre.

The separate stage spaces created here — the (visible) downstage area and the upstage area (for the moment hidden)— are also reminiscent of the seventeenth-century theatre and function as a structural element throughout the performance as a whole. In all, three kinds of set are used:

I. the total separation of downstage and upstage areas, whereby the upstage area remains concealed;

II. demarcation of both areas by two pillarlike elements at either side, leaving the center stage area free, though closed at the upstage area by a houselike element;

III. not dividing the downstage and upstage areas in any way at all and forming the whole stage as an undefined area.

The distribution of the three kinds of sets reveals significant differences between the first and second acts:

Act 1: III (1–3); II (4–6); III (7–14); II (15); III (16–18); I (19); III (20).
Act 2: I (1); II (1–6); III (7–10); I (10); III (11); I (12); III (13–15).

In the first act, the whole stage (III) dominates. The proportion of types III, II, and I is 4 : 2 : 1; type III opens and closes the act. This dominance is not carried through to the second act, where, instead, the proportion of III, II, and I is 3 : 1 : 3; type I opens the act, and type III closes it.

The organization and construction of the total stage space allude to Baroque theatre: the buildings onstage are placed quasi-symmetrically at the sides, as flats, as if to provide perspective onstage. They are connected in the center (unlike the painted Baroque backdrop) by an archway.

The basic set is black and brown throughout. It consists of buildings which cannot be ascribed to any specific era (such as the seventeenth century, for example) or to any particular architectural style (Italian Renaissance). Far more, they can be regarded as quotations of architectural elements from different styles and eras: columns, archways, gables, architraves, oriels, balconies, steps, trellises, and even "ruins." The architecture is not imitative or stylistically expressed but achieved through the *mise en scène*. Consequently, the basic set can be described as a row of postmodern houses which are composed in a different way each time.

The frequent cross-references to Baroque theatre, thus, are limited in their potential range of meaning: they are not to be read as historical-realistic elements whose function is to situate the action in the seventeenth century. Rather, they aim to show the era in which the theatrical metaphor dominated and, therefore, function as signs of the process of theatricalization. In this way, the interpretive attitude, suggested by the central red curtain, that this is theatre within theatre is given further definition.

Through the various oriels and balconies, the basic set is furnished with architectural elements which themselves refer to a theatrical activity: looking on. This function is, in fact, only realized in the first act: after the death of the commendatore, onlookers with lanterns appear on the balconies (1.3); and in the Masetto/Zerlina scene (1.7) women throw flowers from the balconies. The oriels and balconies of the basic set divide the characters onstage into two groups: those who act and those who watch the acting from balconies or steps or leaning against the pillars, as theatre within theatre. This division collapses in act 2. The balconies no longer suggest a kind of auditorium, and the stage simply becomes the space of the action.

All three types of set work with the opposition between centralization and decentralization, and here, too, there are significant differences between the two acts. At the beginning and end of act 1, the third type of set (the open stage) is employed. On both these occasions, the center stage remains empty of decoration so that it can be occupied by different characters and alternating constellations of characters. In contrast, during scenes 1.7–14, and 1.16–18, which also use the third set type, the center stage is clearly demarcated by one or other element of the set: in 7–14, by Zerlina and Masetto's garlanded wedding bed, and in 16–18 by a large, green wooden garden bench.

The bed is the scene of Don Giovanni's seduction of Zerlina; Donna Anna sits there as she recounts Don Giovanni's attack in her chamber to Don Ottavio (*Era gia alquanto la notte* . . . It was already quite late at night). Don Ottavio rests against it when he overhears Donna Anna's call for revenge (*Vendetta ti chieddo* . . . I demand revenge of you).

The garden bench is the setting for the reconciliation between Zerlina and Masetto (*Batti, batti, o bel Masetto* . . . Beat, beat, oh handsome Masetto), Don Giovanni's renewed attempt to seduce Zerlina (*Si, ben mio, suo tutto amore* . . . Yes, my dear, I am all in love), and his encounter with Masetto. In this way, the bed and the bench mark the center of the action in such a way that the key emotions of these scenes can be interpreted as love, jealousy, and revenge or more generally Don Giovanni and his desires.

The second type of set (upstage and downstage areas are demarcated but both areas are played) is realized in act 1 in scenes 4–6 and 15. In 4–6, a well stands in the center. Elvira sits at its edge when she complains of Don Giovanni's unfaithfulness (*Ah! chi mi dice mai quel barbaro dov'e?* . . . Ah, who will tell me where the cruel man is?). She also sits here during Leporello's "catalogue" aria while he circles the well, sitting beside her from time to time, copying Don Giovanni's gestures as he does so. Consequently here, too, Don Giovanni's desires occupy the center of the stage, even if they are not directed at Elvira, indeed, despite his lack of desire for her. In 1.15 the well is replaced by a huge wooden bathtub, into which a naked Don Giovanni climbs. Leporello's obscene gestures with the scrubbing brush leave no doubt that the demarcation of the center points yet again to the same phallocentrism. When Don Giovanni is carried off upstage after the champagne aria, the downstage area remains empty.

The first type of set is used only once in act 1. In 1.19 the pillar structures are joined in the middle. The audiencelike function of the boxes within these structures is realized through Don Giovanni and Leporello, who invite the three masked figures, Donna Anna, Donna Elvira, and Don Ottavio, entering at the downstage area to the ball. The center of the stage is not marked at all in this scene. In act 2 the first type of set appears three times: at the beginning of scene 1 and the end of scene 10 and in scene 12. The first scene, which opens with the duet between Don Giovanni and Leporello, takes place before the interval curtain — the central red curtain between the two pillar structures. The centering on the curtain is clearly related to the moment later in this scene when Don Giovanni and Leporello exchange costumes and roles.

At the end of scene 10 Donna Elvira's *recitativo accompagnato* and aria (*In quali eccessi, o Numi* . . . In what excesses, O Gods) are taken from the Vienna score. In this scene the third type of set changes into type I: the pillar walls are positioned halfway toward the middle and, in place of the curtain, there is a wall decorated with a crucifix and candles. A bench is placed in front of it. During her aria, a servant dressed in black and white dresses Elvira in a dark gray robe and she holds a rosary. Thus dressed, Elvira kneels before the bench/altar. The knowledge of Don Giovanni's sins causes a shift of her center toward religion and God. The shift of center in the set thus anticipates her decision in the last scene to enter a nunnery.

In scene 12 a huge painting of a cavalier, possibly the commendatore, hangs in place of the crucifix, and white flowers stand in vases on the floor in an explicit reference to the commendatore. While Don Ottavio consoles Donna Anna again with gesture, mime, and facial expression, she sings the aria *Non mi dir, bell'idol mio* . . . (Do not tell me dear one, that I am cruel to you), turning determinedly away from him. Her gestural behavior directly opposes the text of the aria and, instead, corresponds to the centralization implied by the set. The centering on the father, therefore, anticipates Donna Anna's decision in the final scene to postpone her marriage to Don Ottavio for a year.

In act 2 the second type of set is only employed in scenes 1–6 when the central red curtain is raised after Don Giovanni and Leporello's duet. The well-seat is positioned in the center once again. Here the love scenes between Leporello, dressed as Don Giovanni, and Donna Elvira are acted out, as is the ultimate reconciliation between Zerlina and Masetto (*Vedrai, carino* . . . You'll see, dearest). This demarcation of the center clearly implies a shift of the center away from Don Giovanni. His place is taken by the images of God, the father, and the husband (Masetto).

The third type of set occurs in scenes 7–10, in the cemetery scene (11), and in the finale (13–15). In scenes 7–10, in which Leporello's disguise is exposed, the center stage is empty and remains so during the cemetery scene. The statue of the commendatore is not placed at center stage but stage right on one of the balconies. Only in the banquet scene does a clear demarcation of the center reoccur: a large table, at which Don Giovanni feasts, stands center stage. He leaps onto it to declaim his praise of women and wine to Elvira (*Vivan le feminine, viva il buon vino!* . . . Long live women, long live good wine!) and finally descends with it into hell.

After the demarcated center has shifted away from Don Giovanni, as a result of his resumed sinning, he can at last reclaim both center stage and the focal point of interest with his descent into hell. This he does on the very spot where he killed the commendatore and tried to seduce Zerlina on the bed in the first act. The bourgeois moral order seems once more present: the women, who have been the not always resisting objects of Don Giovanni's desires, find their center in God, the father, and the husband and Don Giovanni is punished in hell for his immoral impulses.

Such an interpretation is, however, too hasty. It takes into account neither the function of the lighting design nor the ending. In the first act light is simply used as the sign of the time of day. Thus, in scenes 1–3 and 9–20 it represents night and in all the other scenes daylight. In the second act, in contrast, the application of light is theatricalized: the act begins with bright light portraying daylight. At Don Giovanni's words (*Già che sia verso sera* . . . Since evening is drawing on) it suddenly dims as if on cue and finally darkens.

Such play on the theatrical nature of light is used once more in the finale. At the entrance of the statue of the commendatore, not only do the doors fly open, but there is a sudden flash of blazing light, like a burst of lightning, before the stage returns to a general darkened state. When Don Giovanni offers his hand to the statue (*Eccola!* . . . Here it is!), the stage blazes with light again. The descent into hell is played with a red light beneath the table and on the cyclorama. After Don Giovanni goes under, there is yet another burst of light.

Light applied in this way, on the one hand, serves the function of theatricalizing Don Giovanni's downfall and portraying his descent into hell as a *coup de théâtre*. On the other hand, it meshes with the system of centralization created by the set: the area ablaze with light is thereby given central focus — the archway, when the statue of the commendatore enters, and later the two figures of Don Giovanni and the statue as they shake hands. This centralizing function of light is carried through to the last scene. While Donna Anna, Donna Elvira, Zerlina, Don Ottavio, Masetto, and Leporello sing *l'antichissima canzon* (the age-old song: *Questo è il fin di chi fa mal! / E de'perfidi la morte / Alla vita è sempre ugual* . . . This is the end o' the evildoer / And the death of wicked men / is always like their lives), the archway is lit bright red and Don Giovanni appears beneath it. Following him, a young girl then a second and a third also enter. Don Giovanni and the three girls stand, arm in arm, beneath the illuminated archway as if framed. The lighting design, like the final apotheosis in Baroque theatre, reveals this image as the new central focus.

The Signs of the Singers (Appearance and Action)

The characters in the opera and their relations to each other can be described in terms of a tight web of oppositions and equivalents. All the makeup and costume used point to the seventeenth century, the age of the *comedias de capa y espada*, indicating thereby the theatrical century *par excellence* and, moreover, the century in which the first Don Juan play was written. A specific historical age (the seventeenth century) is not implied for its own sake, but rather in order to focus on the moment of theatricality *per se*, and this is principally effected by the use of cloaks, hats, masks, and veils.

As far as the frequency of entrances, frequency of costume change, color of costume, and basic characteristic gesture are concerned, Don Giovanni presents a clear opposition to all the other characters. He has the most entrances and is onstage longer than any of the others. This holds throughout the opera, but there is a significant difference between the two acts. In the first act he is onstage in fifteen of a possible twenty scenes (Leporello and Zerlina are in eight; Donna Anna, Don Ottavio, and Donna Elvira in seven; and Masetto in six). The figure is reduced in the second act to ten of a possible sixteen (Leporello, in contrast, appears in eleven scenes, though in part dressed as Don Giovanni; Elvira in nine; Masetto in eight; Zerlina and Ottavio in six; and Donna Anna in only four).

In terms of costume change, however, Don Giovanni is both in opposition to those characters who are provided principally with only one costume which can be worn with various slight modifications (Zerlina, Masetto, Don Ottavio, the peasants and servants) and significantly unlike those who have few or minor costume changes (such as Donna Anna, who puts aside her pink gown for a black one after the death of her father, and Donna Elvira, who puts aside her blue and white gown for a dark gray habit after the change in her center in 2.10).

Don Giovanni wears the most sparkling, glittering colors: his coat and cloak are a glaring mauve and red, though on occasion he wears black; his lilac trousers and frock coat are heavily embroidered in gold and white silver; he wears a black or a purple hat with plumes and shiny black, ornamented boots or shoes with silver heels, and his fingers are heavily bejeweled. His costume seems far more reminiscent of a fake theatrical hero. In addition, especially when he wears the boots, he connotes the figure of the *capitano* from *commedia dell'arte*.

Don Giovanni commonly stands onstage with his legs slightly apart and frequently extends his arms in large gestures. On the one hand, this basic gesture can be clearly classified as one of dominance, yet, on the other hand, it is typical of the operatic heroes of the nineteenth and early twentieth centuries as well as of operetta heroes, who played to their audience with similarly extended gestures. The frequency of costume change, style, color of costume, and basic gestures all suggest that Don Giovanni is an actor playing consciously before his audience.

Don Giovanni is related to the other characters by a series of oppositions and equivalents. Thus, Leporello is brought into relation to him partly through the gaudy yellow-red colors of his cloak and partly through his attempt to imitate the basic gestures of his master during the "catalogue" aria, in the ballroom scene, in the pretended love scene with Elvira, and through the reciprocal role and costume change with Don Giovanni (2.1). His submissive gestures, however, which increasingly prevail in the second half of the second act, place him in sharp opposition to Don Giovanni.

The cut and style of both Don Giovanni's and Don Ottavio's costumes adhere to those of the seventeenth-century fashionable nobility. Don Ottavio, however, wears a subdued gold-brown color throughout, with the exception of a red feather in his hat. Don Ottavio's basic gesture is diametrically opposed to Don Giovanni's: he variously sits (1.13, on the bed, 2.12, on the bench), frequently with head and shoulders bowed. When he stands, his feet remain together and, in general, his hands are clasped at waist height.

The relationship between Don Giovanni and Masetto is exclusively signified by oppositions. Masetto wears the gray-brown costume of a peasant. He stands, sits, or lies stiff and immobile, forcing the others (Zerlina, Leporello, and Don Giovanni) to act. Nevertheless, it is he who finally wins Zerlina.

Even Don Giovanni's relationship to Donna Anna is one marked by oppositions. While Don Giovanni struts across the stage in screaming colors, Donna Anna wears nothing but black after her father's death. Moreover, not one of Don Giovanni's gestures might suggest deep emotions such as sorrow, while Donna Anna's gestures can be interpreted to a great extent as the expression of unendurable grief. During the chase after the seducer (1.1), when she sees her dead father (1.3), and at the sudden discovery of Don Giovanni's identity (1.13), she consistently makes large extended gestures with her arms or her whole body. Thus, she throws herself on the body of her dead father, leaning slightly forward, stretches her right arm out accusingly as she swears revenge (1.13), or puts her hand over her heart in moments of anguish. More prevalent still than these gestures are many smaller ones by which she seeks to appear calm, often with tightly clasped hands.

Donna Elvira is drawn into relation with Don Giovanni principally through her gestures. Musicologists dealing with this opera consistently point out that Elvira's arias are composed in the style of Baroque opera or, more specifically, in the style of G. F. Handel. Since the Stockholm production takes the Baroque theatre as a paradigm for theatricality and theatricalization, this characteristic of the arias might suggest the idea of theatricality in Donna Elvira's behavior. Unlike Donna Anna's, Donna Elvira's large, passionate gestures are in a theatrical manner: she often wrings her hands or puts her hand over her heart; rose in hand and with wide outstretched arms, she pushes herself threateningly on Don Giovanni; during the "catalogue" aria she covers her face with her hands and crosses herself. Her gestures show her to be, like Don Giovanni, of the acting profession. After the costume change and shift of her center toward God, Donna Elvira's gestures also change: she kneels before the bench and exits silently with clasped hands.

Through her red apron, Zerlina is placed in a relationship of equivalence to Don Giovanni. The purposeful movements with which she opens Giovanni's jabot once he has untied her corset serve a similar function. The style of her movements in general, however, are opposed to those of Don Giovanni. While Giovanni focuses his gestures on the theatrical, the "naturalness" of Zerlina's movements is emphasized: she rests one hand against her arm, folds her arms, puts her hands on her hips as she dances round Masetto (1.16), or kicks her heels against the bench. Zerlina is a character who conveys reality rather than theatricality.

In fact, Don Giovanni shows only two distinct ways of relating to these widely different characters: his relationships to women and his relationships to men. His relations to women are defined, on the one hand, through flirtatious advances and, on the other, through flight. The gestures of flirtation used by Don Giovanni are eye contact, hands extended, pressing the hand, kissing the hand, embracing (Donna Anna, Donna Elvira, and Zerlina), kissing (Donna Anna and Zerlina), and attempted seduction (Zerlina). The different approaches he uses do not point to individual differences among the three women, but to the different situations which disrupt his path to conquest at various stages. A similar rule applies to the differences in his various escapes from Donna Anna and Donna Elvira.

Don Giovanni's relations to men are largely defined by his sword. With it he kills the commendatore, compels Masetto leave Zerlina alone with him (1.8), and forces Leporello to invite the statue of the commendatore to supper. His behavior to both men and women is determined by dominance and power. All the women are objects of his desire as all the men are rivals, or at least obstacles to be overcome.

It seems, however, that Don Giovanni does not have this kind of relationship to Don Ottavio. Indeed, from his point of view, there seems to be no relationship to Don Ottavio at all. Although he puts his arms around Donna Anna and Don Ottavio's shoulders in 1.12, to persuade them Donna Elvira is mad, such trusting and companionable gestures are never repeated, and Don Ottavio hardly seems to exist for Don Giovanni anymore. In fact, the reverse is true. It is Don Ottavio who aims the pistol and fires on the fleeing Don Giovanni.

The other characters are the targets of Don Giovanni's desires (Donna Anna, the veiled Donna Elvira, Zerlina), obstacles (the commendatore, Masetto, Donna Elvira), helpmates on his path to satisfaction (Leporello), or spectators of his actions (the peasants and the servants). This constellation changes, however, at the end of the first act. With the exception of Leporello, all the characters unite and block Don Giovanni's exit through the door. Don Giovanni stands alone (in the center at the ramp) opposite all the others (in the archway). His face, however, is not turned to them, as an actor before his public, but his back, as a victim before his hunters. As a result, in the second act the balconies and oriels on the stage no longer function as a place for spectators.

Thus, at the end of the first act relations are defined anew. The empty center stage has already provided a clue as to the possible disintegration of and change in the existing constellation. On the one hand, Don Giovanni loses his central position and, on the other, his audience. The actor has lost his glamor.

The end of act 2 stands in direct opposition to the end of act 1, however. The relationships are clearly renewed, redefined once again. The developments effected in the second act are questioned: in the rosy shimmer of dawn, Don Giovanni stands in the archway arm in arm with three women (a blonde, a brunette, and a redhead) while opposite them, on the ramp, stand the other characters. At first, they face the audience but then they turn and, along with the real audience, face Don Giovanni. Center stage, in the frame of the archway, the actor Don Giovanni seems set in the pose of the famous seducer, while the other characters figure as his audience.

Don Giovanni *and the Aesthetics of Contemporary Theatre*

The ending can certainly be read as a commentary on the opera from a postmodern point of view. It clearly sets out to contradict not only the prevailing tradition of performance (not unexpectedly, demonstratively endorsed in a production at the Salzburg Festival 1987 under the musical direction of Herbert von Karajan), but also elements of the work itself which, in this production, were realized to the full.

On one hand, the ending treats the Christian-bourgeois morality of the story, as it is formulated in the song "This is the end o' the evildoer / And the death of wicked men / is always like their lives," in an ironic manner.

On the other hand, the ending refers back to one of the central elements of the opera which it at the same time negates. The break of dawn in the archway plays demonstratively on the commendatore's words in the cemetery scene, 2.11 (*Di rider finirai pria dell'aurora* . . . You will cease laughing before dawn). Here this prophecy is musically so conveyed that its fulfillment can hardly be doubted. Indeed, Mozart recalls the oracle scenes of the *Tragédie lyrique*. The statuesque nature of the movement, its harmonics and instrumentation (trombone), and the strongly declamatory nature of the singing create a musical topos whose function mainly consists of lending musical evidence to the predestination of fate. From a musical point of view, Don Giovanni's fate seems sealed. In this sense, the ending openly contradicts the music.

This contradiction, which more or less comments retrospectively, is anticipated by a simultaneous contradiction in the punishment scene. The musical form of the downfall and the use of light appear in significant opposition to each other. At the last phrase of the chorus, the orchestra plays a cadenza in D-minor. At the very moment of Don Giovanni's "Ah," instead of the anticipated D-minor, comes a D-major tonic (bar 594). Consequently, it suggests that Don Giovanni's downfall is the decisive event which, for the moment at least, ends the story. For, with the first echo of the original D-major since the beginning of the finale, the circle of action is complete, embracing both the supper and the downfall. Light, on the contrary, shows Don Giovanni's descent into hell as a theatrical spectacle which will ultimately remain without consequence for the protagonist. In this way, the ending colludes with the light rather than with the music.

The commentary suggested by the ending confirms the possibility of human existence as thoroughly amoral, irresponsible, free of obligation, and asocial. It banishes all kinds of metaphysical thinking and the idea of heavenly punishment to the world of theatre and fiction. These days the descent into hell only takes place on the stage.

Thus, the ending can also be read as the self-reflection of theatre through the medium of theatre. Don Giovanni descends into hell accompanied by thunder and lightning every night, just as every night he celebrates his resurrection at the overture. Theatre is the realm of *Wiedergänger* (self-perpetuators) as Heiner Müller wrote in "Bildbeschreibung" (1985; Description of a Picture): the "resurrection of the flesh" is played out every night onstage.[1]

The figure of Don Giovanni has become a myth which theatre, with its daily resurrection and daily descent into hell, can perpetuate into eternity.

As well as reflecting on the capability of theatre to create and hand down myth, the performance also reflects on the constitutive function of the audience. Here the many twists of the metaphor of theatre within theatre find their systematic positions. It is the gaze of the spectator onstage which proves to the spectator in the auditorium that the social life presented onstage is theatre. Similarly, it is the gaze of the characters onstage, representing the spectators in the auditorium, which transforms the image of the seducer Don Giovanni into a myth.

In this way, the production opens a theatrical discourse on the gaze of others as the gaze of the spectator. The gaze of the other is shown to be the origin and also the condition of the possibility of theatre and of theatricality. Thus, Ralf Långbacka's production of *Don Giovanni* might be seen and evaluated in the context of theatrical discourses held today in various cities in Western culture. Giorgio Strehler's production of Luigi Pirandello's *Come tu mi vuoi* (Milan, 1989), for example, reflects on the function of the gaze, as does Ingmar Bergman's production of Yukio Mishima's *Madame de Sade* (Stockholm, 1989) or the above-mentioned theatre text of Heiner Müller's "Bildbeschreibung" (1985). Insofar as the self-reflection in theatre on the conditions of its own potential can be seen as a predominant characterization of contemporary theatre, the Stockholm production of *Don Giovanni* proves to be a quite remarkable, if not totally convincing, example of the aesthetics of the gaze.

PASSAGE TO THE REALM OF SHADOWS
Robert Wilson's *King Lear* in Frankfurt

As Sylvaine Gold noted:

> For years, going to the theatre was about questions and answers. Why has King Hamlet's ghost returned, and what will the Prince do about it? How will Madame Ranevskaya save her cherry orchard? Who is afraid of Virginia Woolf?
>
> In the new theatre, however, questions are neither asked nor answered. Going to the theatre becomes an abstract experience, like going to a symphony, or a Balanchine ballet, or a show of modern art. The audience is offered not thought, but sensation.[1]

Since the late 1960s Robert Wilson, among others, has developed the aesthetic of a new theatre through productions which picked up the program of the historical avant-garde movement — of Appia and Craig, the Bauhaus theatre, and French surrealism — and seemed to fulfill it:[2] the "retheatricalization" of theatre which was to be a radical move away from the literary theatre predominant in Western culture since the eighteenth century. *Deafman Glance* (1971), *Einstein on the Beach* (1976), and *the CIVIL warS* (1983–1984) signified the final evolution of the new aesthetic, the pinnacle of its development.[3]

It is perhaps hardly surprising that Wilson turned toward opera in the mid-1980s — at any rate, many of his productions bear the generic title "opera." In 1984 he directed Marc-Antoine Charpentier's *Medée*, which was one step on from his "work in progress" *Medea* (1980 in Washington, 1982 in New York, 1984 parallel to *Medée* in Lyon); in 1985 Richard Strauss' *Salomé* was to follow in Milan and in 1986 C. W. Gluck's *Alceste* in Stuttgart.

It is surprising to learn, however, that Wilson has now moved on to directing drama: in 1986 he directed Heiner Müller's *Hamletmaschine* (The Hamlet Machine; in New York and Hamburg) and *Quartett* (Quartet; in

Stuttgart). Heiner Müller and Robert Wilson had worked closely together since the early 1980s (Müller was responsible for the text collages in act 4 of the German section of *CIVIL warS*),[4] and it was but a short step from there to a collaboration on one of Müller's own texts. But Wilson was not content to stop there. In 1986 he directed Euripides' *Alcestis* (Stuttgart) parallel to the opera *Alceste*. He followed with Tankred Dorst's *Parzival* in 1987 (Hamburg), Chekhov's *Swan Song* in 1989 (Munich), and Shakespeare's *King Lear* in 1990 (Frankfurt).

With the decision to direct a Shakespeare tragedy, Wilson has unmistakably joined a certain tradition in contemporary theatre: directors such as Peter Brook (Stratford, 1962), Peter Zadek (Bochum, 1974), Ingmar Bergman (Stockholm, 1984), and Klaus Michael Grüber (Berlin, 1985) have all used *Lear* in search of proof that their variously developed theatre aesthetics are capable of unfolding new aspects or even whole new interpretations of the tragedy. This viewpoint is clearly of no small importance to Wilson too; in an interview he confirmed it as "the task of the avant-garde to re-discover the classics."[5] On the other hand, Wilson's notorious denial of any interpretation is more than well known:

> The literary text is important to me, but I find the way in which it is presented on stage utterly dreadful. At home, I can read a play such as *Hamlet*, for example, over and over again and the ever fresh array of meanings and possibilities I find in it gives me great pleasure. In the theatre, on the other hand, I find none of these riches. The actors interpret the text, they enter the stage as if they know everything and comprehend everything, and that is a lie, a swindle, it offends me. I don't believe Shakespeare understood *Hamlet*. Theatre should not interpret, but rather provide the possibility of confronting a work and thinking about it. If one behaves as if one had understood everything, then the work is finished. And *Hamlet* is not finished, it lives, it lives through the multi-layers of forms and meanings. . . . It is not our job to provide answers, but to raise the possibility of asking questions. We must ask questions, then the text will open itself up and that will result in a dialogue between it and the spectator.[6]

In this sense, then, Wilson's aim to "rediscover the ancient classics" most certainly does not mean he will deliver a new interpretation of the tragedy in his version of *Lear*. Nor can it be assumed that he intended to position his production within a certain performance tradition — as is typical in productions of the classics in most European countries, despite the fact that this *Lear* was performed in a German state theatre.

Wilson's productions are — the critics and scholars agree — directed toward international reception. His aesthetic fixes the syntactic of a performance in a total and precise way at the same time as it extensively desemanticizes single elements to create a play-space for different kinds of reception in different cultures. In Wilson's *Lear*, it was apparent that the constituents normally associated with his aesthetic, such as the uncoupling of speech and body or the desemanticization of bodies and objects (i.e., factors which would seem vital to international reception), were not employed with the same degree of consequence as in his previous productions. In *Lear*, Wilson's recourse to Japanese theatre — probably only recognized as such by insiders — only vaguely aimed toward intercultural communication of any kind.[7] Thus, the question arises as to how the production did achieve international reception. An analysis of the performance may reveal possible solutions to this question.[8]

PERFORMANCE ANALYSIS

Structure: Composition

A spectator entering the Bockenheim Depot is confronted with an open picture-frame set, enclosed on both sides by several rows of black wings and at the back by a white canvas, but extending forward in an apron stage covered in black carpet and accessed by ramplike structures to the right and left. A bolt of lightning is depicted on the stage floor in the center, and center front downstage, where the main stage joins the apron stage, stands a thin, upright rod about one meter high which throws a "shadow" of light on the floor downstage left.

As the lights dim, the lightning and shadow disappear and a piercing, whirring sound and drum roll are heard (music by Hans Peter Kuhn). A narrow upright rod of light passes from left to right in the frame of the proscenium arch, dazzling the audience. As the glare subsides, the audience perceives twelve figures spaced out over the whole stage in floor-length royal blue coats. Each slowly mimes a different stylized action of unbuttoning with his or her fingers.

These gestures refer to two precise moments in the *Lear* text which are emphasized in very specific ways: In 3.4, Lear encounters Edgar (as Tom) and comes to the recognition that man "is no more but such a poor, bare, forked animal," continuing with the request, "Off, off, you lendings! Come unbutton here" (ll. 111–112). In 5.3 as Lear comprehends that Cordelia is indeed dead ("Thoul't come no more, / Never, never, never, never, never!" ll.306–307) he begs those around him, "Pray you undo this button" and dies. The unbuttoning mime in prologue A thus calls up two moments in the text when Lear crosses the boundaries of madness and death.

A spotlight focuses on the face of Marianne Hoppe (playing Lear) as she stands at the back right of the group of figures. While the light onstage grows alternately brighter and dimmer and as the music and sounds swell and subside, she recites, immobile, William Carlos Williams' poem *The Last Words of My English Grandmother*.

The poem, which is also printed in the program,[9] contains a multitude of motifs which are picked up on in the course of the performance. The "cry for food": "Gimme something to eat" (l. 9) corresponds to Lear's call for food, "Dinner, ho! dinner!" (1.4.45, in Wilson's version scene 2B). The triple "no, no, no" (l. 12) with which the grandmother objects to being carried off to the hospital is taken up again in scene 12 (4.6) when Lear turns toward the blind Gloucester (l. 179). The words "Let me take you to the hospital, I said" (ll. 14–15) are a pre-echo of the many moments in the performance when a younger character guides or gives an arm to an older character: Kent to Lear in scene 6B (3.4); Edgar to Gloucester in scenes 8 (4.1), 12 (4.6), and 14 (5.2); and Cordelia to Lear in scenes 13 (4.7) and 15 (5.3).

The "stretcher" (l. 23) is picked up again on both visual and textual levels: the shape of Lear's bed in scene 13 (4.7) and Kent's words on Lear's death: "O! let him pass! He hates him / That would upon the rack of this tough world / Stretch him out longer" (5.3.313–315). The line "Is this what you call / making me comfortable?" (ll. 24–25) resounds in Lear's words to Regan in scene 5 (2.4): "thy tender-hefted nature shall not give / Thee o'er harshness. Her eyes are fierce, but thine / Do comfort and not burn" (ll. 173–175) as he offers himself up to Regan's care. The accusation "Oh you think you're smart / you young people, she said, but I'll tell you / you don't know anything" (ll. 27–30) is taken up in Edgar's last words: "The oldest hath borne most; we that are young / Shall never see so much nor live so long" (5.3.325–326). The last elements of reality that the grandmother can relate to, the "fuzzy-looking things out there," the "trees" (ll. 38–39), find visual echo in the tree that stands on the stage in scene 14 (5.2), under which Gloucester dies.

It is not only the unbuttoning mime and the motifs cited from the poem that prefigure elements which later appear in the course of the performance, but also elements of the various systems of props, light, music, and blocking (proxemic signs). The narrow rod stuck in the floor at front stage is actualized as a scepter by Lear in prologue B (1.1) and later, though not as a scepter, by Cordelia in scene 11 (4.6). The flash of lightning returns in scene 6A (3.2) in the storm on the heath. The rod of light stretching to the full height of the proscenium arch which marks the beginning of prologue A makes the reverse passage from right to left after the interval. The drum rolls resound repeatedly in specific intervals in the whole course of the performance. The tableau of characters presented in prologue A closes the whole performance — with somewhat altered blocking and without the blue coats.

From these findings, two general conclusions can be drawn.

1. The performance is built up and structured according to musical principles: many of the leitmotifs introduced in prologue A in the different sign systems (gesture, language, props, music, proxemics) are taken up in the following scenes and echoed or varied in other or partly the same sign systems. The structure of the story, related by the tragedy in five corporate acts, is dissolved into a rhythmic succession of situations, motifs, images. This, in turn, corresponds to the dramaturgical treatment of the text, which transforms the five-act structure into a string of fifteen scenes prefaced by two prologues.[10]

2. The words of the poem, like the gestures of unbuttoning which refer to Lear's words in 3.4 and 5.3, undertake a specific guiding of reception which enables, if not suggests, a first, trial semantification of the material in hand: the theme of "death" is struck — the same theme to which Wilson alluded in his productions of *Death, Destruction & Detroit I* (1979) and *II* (1987) and which he realized to the full in his parallel productions of *Alceste* and *Alcestis* (1986). In *Lear*, however, prologue A directs the theme toward a characteristic variant: it is the transition toward death itself which is marked, the process of dying.

Space

Death is realized in spaces which, because of their high degree of reduction, are reminiscent of the Japanese *no* stage.[11] This is already noted above in the description of the basic stage. While the back wall in the *no* theatre is usually painted with a picture of a pine tree, here the canvas remains blank most of the time. In Edmund's scenes, a starry blue sky is projected on it; at Edgar's escape (scene 4/2.3) red-gray shapes appear on it; at the beginning of the storm on the heath a changing gray projection suggests thunder clouds. On the whole, however, the canvas functions solely as a reflective surface for the constantly changing light scheme. In scene 7 (3.7), the first scene after the interval, where Gloucester is to be blinded, the canvas is draped in black cloth. In moving to the next scene (4.1), the blind Gloucester remains alone on the stage and the cloth suddenly falls down in front of the canvas, throwing out a dazzling light so that the spectators are forced to close their eyes momentarily from the glare.

In the majority of scenes, the main stage remains free of set elements; the wheel on which Kent is tied, scene 5 (2.4), and the beams representing Edgar's hovel, scene 6B (3.4), are set up on the apron stage at stage right. Larger set elements are only found on the main stage in a few scenes: in scenes 2A and 2B (1.3 and 1.4) a long narrow table stands at right angles to the apron, dividing the stage almost in two (it is reminiscent of the *hashigakari*, the entrance bridge in *no* theatre, and is, in fact, used here as a kind of gangway), and the high backrest of the chair looms up in front of the canvas like a guillotine. In scene 6C, Lear's trial scene (3.6), a narrow bench is placed in the middle of the left side of the stage; in scene 13 (4.7) Lear's long narrow bed is downstage left; and in scene 14 (5.2) a tree is set upstage right.[12]

The scene changes are accomplished without interrupting the performance (despite a change in lighting, the music and sounds do not alter and the characters mostly remain onstage) by stagehands who either are dressed like the servants in the play in gray trousers and green-gray shirts or are in black, like Japanese stagehands. The semantification suggested in prologue A clearly allows one to see them in terms of harbingers of death, emissaries from the underworld. Yet it is also legitimate to recognize them solely for their function as stagehands.

The scenes set in Gloucester's castle — scene 1 (1.2), scene 3 (2.1), scene 5 (2.4) — and/or those in which Edmund figures — scene 9 (4.2), the beginning of scene 15 (5.3) — are differentiated from the other scenes by a black screen which is lowered onto the floor of the stage from above, which, together with the front pair of wings, provides the stage with a black frame. In scene 3 (2.1) a second screen is lowered, connecting the second pair of wings. It is considerably higher than the first screen and masks half of the back canvas. In scene 9 (4.2) four further screens are lowered, staggered behind each other as above so that only a thin strip at the very top of the canvas remains visible. The black passageways that are thus created between the screens appear labyrinthine.

In scenes 6 (3.6, Lear's trial scene) and 13 (4.7, Lear's reunion with Cordelia), however, five similarly staggered black screens appear, this time hanging down from above and masking the canvas completely. In this way the screens provide a principal division of the space into three — a space without screens where the main and apron stages are one unit; a space with screens from the floor up dividing the main and apron stages (used for Edmund); and a space modified by screens hanging down from above which do not affect the unity of the main and apron stages (used for Lear at the beginning and end of his madness).

The most significant tool that shapes the space is nonetheless the lighting scheme, which constantly moves between the canvas, the stage, and the characters. These spaces can be seen in a literal sense as light-spaces.

Second to the light-spaces rank acoustic-spaces. The performance is partly structured by the repetitions and variations of the drum and partly by the addition of a wealth of different sounds, noises, and sequences of notes: scintillating sounds which rise and subside can be heard, for example, in prologue B (1.1) and scene 2B (1.4); birds screeching in scenes 1 (1.2), 12 (4.6), 14 (5.2), and 15 (5.3); sounds of the storm in scenes 6A (3.2) and 6B (3.4); distant shouting and general babble of voices in scenes 11 (4.4), 12 (4.6), 13 (4.7), and 14 (5.2); flute music in scenes 6B (3.4), 6C (3.6), 7 (3.7), 8 (4.1), and 9 (4.2); and many others besides. The continual succession and superimposition of sounds are only interrupted by longer moments of silence in two places: in scene 6B (3.4) the sounds of the storm break off at intervals so that silence reigns between Lear's words before, at lines 103ff., the sound of dripping water is added to mark the outbreak of madness; and in scene 7 (3.7) the metallic percussion accompanying Gloucester's torture is repeatedly interrupted by moments of silence. Thus, sound presents very specific sound-spaces crossed and superimposed by light-spaces.

Characters

The characters set into these spaces are placed in certain relation to one another on the one hand through the colors of their costumes. There is no differentiation between the sexes. All the characters wear a suit of one color with either a T-shirt of the same color or nothing underneath. Regan is the only character to wear a skirt instead of trousers and high-heeled instead of flat shoes. Relations between the characters were created by color: Lear's suit is yellow (mustard), Goneril (Jutta Hoffmann) and Albany (Rolf Idler) wear green (petrol), Regan (Astrid Gorvin) and Cornwall (Hans-Jörg Assmann) wear red (aubergine), Cordelia (Alexandra von Schwerin) and the Fool (Andreas Seifert) wear white, Gloucester (Jürgen Holtz) and Edmund (Richy Müller) wear black, Edgar (Christoph Waltz) wears dark blue, Kent (Thomas Thieme) wears brown, and the King of France (Mario Melzer) wears beige. Alternatively, the relations between the characters were defined by different items of clothing: Lear and Gloucester are equivalent insofar as they both wear a coat over their suits. Gloucester's coat is black, to match his suit, but Lear's red coat is a stark contrast to his yellow suit. Indeed, Lear is the only character to wear more than one color. He is further distinguished from the other characters, moreover, in prologue B (the division of the kingdom, 1.1) by a large gold cardboard crown.

As all the critics noted, Marianne Hoppe was not dressed as a man in any way. Clearly, Lear's character is not identified as masculine through costume. Rather, one is unavoidably presented with an old woman who does not make even the slightest attempt on the stage to disguise her own hair under a wig or to transform her impressive face and almost childlike round blue eyes into those of a man by makeup.

On the other hand, the characters are distinguished and placed in specific relations to one another through their various individual gestures. The basic structural opposition between the characters is formed by the opposition of stylized gestures and barely or nonstylized gestures. Barely or nonstylized gestures are principally realized by Lear, though frequently also by Gloucester: when Lear demands food by beating his fist on the table in scene 2B (1.4) or when he shakes his head vigorously in answer to Goneril's arrogance in the same scene or again when he holds the Fool's hand and lays his head on Edgar's shoulder at the end of scene 6C (3.6). All these gestures are directly comprehensible to a spectator from Western culture because they can be recognized from daily life and can be identified as gesture signs which give expression to specific volitional and emotional circumstances — independent of specific marking by any individual subject. Such in this sense "natural" gestures have nothing whatsoever to do with individual psychology and are accorded to the older characters, in particular Lear.

Similarly, Marianne Hoppe does not attempt to reproduce in posture, movement, or gesture any characteristics or behavior patterns that might be classified as typically male. Nothing in her outward appearance suggests that she is acting a man: she looks like an old woman and she behaves like an old woman. This effect was clearly so overwhelming that all the critics remarked on it, describing Hoppe's Lear as "Queen Lear,"[13] as a "tough old lady,"[14] as "the visit of the old lady to a blue castle," or with the words "grandmother's tales of Lear."[15]

The other characters realize strongly stylized gestures. They perform gestures which are either wholly abstract (a slow raising and lowering of an arm or leg, the right hand on the back of the neck, the left hand in the small of the back, to name a few) or show the stylization of intentional gestures (the unbuttoning in prologue A, stabbing with dagger or spear, lifting both arms, holding one's nose, etc.). In terms of these kinds of gestures, all the younger characters are equivalent to one another.[16] In another sense, however, there are significant differences between them which set the characters Goneril, Regan, Albany, Cornwall, and Edmund in principal opposition to the Fool, Cordelia, Kent, and Edgar. As well as the kinds of gesture described above, the characters of the former group execute gestures and facial and physical movements which represent stylized imitations of animal movements. Goneril stretches out on the floor in front of the crown like a cat; with catlike movements she climbs up the high back of the chair and sits on it in scene 2A (1.3); she crouches like a cat ready to pounce before her handkerchief in scene 9 (4.2) and hits it playfully with her "paws." The cat aspect which the character is accorded by the actress in such movements receives clear emphasis on an acoustic level: she enters both scenes with a "miao" and exits similarly.

Regan constantly sticks her neck out like a vulture and spreads her fingers or makes a claw with at least one hand like a vulture's talons. At her exit in scene 4 (2.4) she crooks her arms behind her back so that they look like wings, strutting off with chest, neck, and head protruding in front. Again, the animal aspect is supported by sound: Regan screeches like a bird of prey or bursts into squawkish laughter.

Edmund does two cartwheels like a peacock — in the labyrinth in scene 9 (4.2) and prior to the duel with Edgar in scene 15 (5.3). He does not make any animal noises himself, but his entrances are accompanied by the squawking of birds and a loud, surrealistic insectlike drone.

In scene 9 (4.2), Albany claws the air like a cat or lion, and Cornwall pulls a face in a monster grimace in scene 5 (2.4).

These animal associations release a wealth of possible semantifications which can be understood by both internal and external decoding. They present internal relations to the animal metaphors in Lear's speech in prologue B (1.1), scenes 2B (1.4), 5 (2.4), 6C (3.6), and 12 (4.6).[17] External relations are made possible according to the extent of one's own cultural knowledge and may range from the simple opposition of human/animal to the awareness of the function accorded the cat and the bird in death cults of various cultures. The production itself imposes absolutely no limitation to this interpretation.

Thus, we find three kinds of gesture in the performance which set the characters in relationships of equivalence or opposition: "natural," non- or barely stylized gestures; stylized gestures which remain abstract or which present the stylized imitation of human gestures and activities; and stylized gestures which imitate the movements of animals. The differences in principle in the use of gesture are made particularly clear when the same process is realized by the three different kinds of gesture: Lear dies simply by ceasing to speak, laugh, or move.[18] The servant stabbed by Regan at Gloucester's torture dies by slowly stretching out his arms. With his hands out, he slides slowly to the ground, rolls over in slow motion, and finally remains face down on the floor. The aestheticization of the process is supported by the use of music. Edmund dies by collapsing backward at the knee, falling on his back, and waving his arms and legs helplessly like a beetle on its back before lying motionless, head, arms, and feet on the floor, trunk and thighs pushed up in a bridge.

The classification of the characters into three groups suggested by their use of gesture is supported and confirmed by the ways in which the characters speak the text.

Lear (consistently) and Gloucester (often) present a close relationship between gesture and speech. In the other characters, however, the spoken text is completely detached from the physical movement simultaneously performed.[19] In scene 2B (1.4), for example, when Lear asks Goneril, "Are you our daughter?" (l. 227), Marianne Hoppe bends over slightly and supports herself with her right arm on the table (relationship of affirmation); at the words "Does any here know me?" (l. 234) she turns her head to the right and left in a searching, questioning way (emphasis). In scene 17 (2.4) Regan suggests to Lear that he should return to Goneril and beg her forgiveness. Hoppe, who is sitting behind the screen, dangles both arms over the edge of the screen, lets her head fall, and, drawing single locks of hair in her fingers, speaks the lines: "Dear daughter, I confess that I am old, / Age is unnecessary: on my knees I beg / That you'll vouchsafe me raiment, bed and food" (ll. 155–157; ironic commentary). In scene 12 (4.6)—as a last example—Lear sits on a "tree stump," his legs relaxed, slightly bent, slightly apart. When he threatens his sons-in-law: "And when I have stol'n upon these son-in-laws, / Then kill, kill, kill, kill, kill, kill!" (ll. 188–189) he marks the rhythm of the word "kill" by chopping with both arms down between his knees (illustration). Lear's words and gestures are constantly tightly bound together in this way.

The detachment of spoken text from physical movement employed by the remaining characters is realized in two different ways. The characters of the Fool, Cordelia, Kent, and Edgar (though not as Tom) speak their lines simply and plainly without affectation, without interpretation. At the same time, they stand still or execute movements which do not have any recognizable relation to the text. The figures of Goneril, Regan, Edmund, Albany, and Cornwall, on the other hand, while not attempting to interpret the text, nonetheless give it form. Thus, Edmund recites his lines in a light, singing, declamatory tone; Goneril often speaks in rhythmical repetition of sentences; Regan squawks her lines and in scene 15 (5.5) even reproduces the melodious singsong intonation of the Japanese *kabuki* theatre. At the same time, they perform stylized movements which remain unrelated to the spoken text.

It is well known that the actor's detachment of spoken text from physical movement is an important characteristic, even "trademark," of Wilson's aesthetic. Wilson does not take the detachment as far here as in other productions where the text is simultaneously conveyed by loudspeaker. In *Lear* the detachment gains a different valence, since it is not realized as the only possible kind of relationship between language and movement, but rather as opposition to the closely alternating relationships between the two. The detachment of language from movement and the stylization of gesture can thus function as modes of appearance in which the human surroundings are exposed to the awareness of the two dying old men, Lear and Gloucester, in their transition to another world.

Blocking: Tableaux

The relation between the old characters and the young characters is further qualified by specific forms of interaction. In prologue B (the division of the kingdom, 1.1) it is characterized by a behavior pattern of dominance and submission, which is asymmetrically balanced. Lear realizes almost total dominant behavior; first with his back to the audience, then facing them, he stands erect at center stage at the point where the main stage joins the apron, chin held high. As he curses Cordelia, he raises his arm out threateningly. When Kent contradicts him (1.1.144ff.) he snatches the scepter fixed in the floor at his left and holds it with raised arm toward Kent as a sign of authority.

Lear's excessively dominant behavior corresponds exactly to the submissive behavior of Goneril and Regan. Both declaim their declarations of love from a prostrate position (ll. 55–61, ll. 69–75). Cordelia, on the contrary, rises immediately after prostrating herself briefly on the ground and speaks from a standing position (ll. 95–104).

The behavior model characterized by dominance and submission realized here is not picked up again in this form or to this extent in the later course of the play. It is bound to the crown, to Lear's position of power in the world. The moment Lear relinquishes his power, further demarcation is brought to the theme — the stage suddenly becomes as bright as day. Goneril, Regan, Albany, and Cornwall step forward and with splayed fingers raise their hands behind the crown. They take it and, opening it out flat, place it on the floor at center stage. It reappears there in scene 2A (1.3) and 2B (1.4) highlighted in a beam of light, before disappearing entirely from the world of the play.

The process of Lear's death commences at the close of prologue B. At this point, the old behavior model oriented to Lear's dominance and the submissiveness of others no longer serves a function. Instead, it is superseded by new models: Lear is the last to exit at the end of prologue B. Holding the scepter horizontally at waist height in both hands stretched out in front of her, Hoppe walks erect with chin in the air to upstage right, turns slightly, and moves across the back of the stage parallel to a large white screen (which blocks off the back of the stage) to stage left, where she turns a small half circle as about-face and, passing parallel to the screen again, exits stage right.[20] Halfway along the last part of this walk she suddenly throws the scepter up in a playful way, catching it again in the right hand. At the same time she lifts her left leg testingly in a kind of skip or dance step, before exiting quietly stage right.

The moment of transition to a new state is thus marked by a new movement model — a movement which the audience will be able to interpret to the full in the following scenes as typical of the Fool — the dance. The dissolution of the old status (king — in the sense of holder of political power) makes the function of the behavior model valid till now redundant. The onset of death opens the possibility of new experiences, the trying out of new movements and behavior patterns which in their turn will provoke new behavior models in the other characters.

This is also the case in the transformation of the scepter which, in prologue B, served as the sign of authority. Later in the performance, a rod approximately two meters long replaces it and serves, according to the actors' actions, as either a stick to lead the blind or a spear. The behavior pattern of dominance/submission is dissolved by the transformation of the scepter into two new forms of behavior — caring and cruelty. To the dying, the dominant/submissive behavior patterns are of no use. The others, the young, are now only understood as vehicles or agents of caring or violence. In relation to this, the fundamental division of the character grouping of the young is functionalized: the characters with "human" gestures and language tender their care to the old, while those characters with animal aspects in their gestures, on the contrary, implement force over the old.

The conditions of caring and violence structure the performance from scene 1 to scene 15 through constant repetition and variation: in scene 2B (1.4), for example, the Fool lays his head on the table before Lear, who places his hand over it. In scene 5 (2.4) they sit back to back with their heads leaning against each other. Lear then stands and walks around to the Fool, who still sits, holds his face close to the Fool's face, and says, "O Fool, I shall go mad!" (l. 285). Then he grasps the Fool by the hair and they exit together, locked in this position. In scene 6A (3.2) the Fool kneels behind Lear, leaning his head against him, while Lear puts his hand round his shoulder. Kent walks behind Lear and the Fool with wide outstretched arms as if to protect them from the storm. Slowly, he lowers his arms until they are parallel to the floor, stretched

out toward Lear to guide him into the hut. As he slowly retreats in this position, all three move across the stage to the right in a kind of tableau symbol-
izing protection, caring, and tenderness. A similarly lasting moment is the
frozen image which concludes scene 6C (3.6): Lear leans his head on Edgar's
shoulder and holds the Fool's hand. Before them, Kent crouches on the floor,
his right hand raised. As the light on stage gradually dims, while the music
seems as if it will go on forever, one light remains focused on Kent's hand,
which is the last object to remain visible before the lights totally fade.

Such images of caring and tenderness are set in opposition to those of violence. Lear's ironically intended, playfully pretend-submissive behavior provokes a reaction from the daughters and sons-in-law representing force and
dominance: Kent is tortured on the wheel in Lear's place. In scene 5 (2.4)
Cornwall stands with his back to the audience before the wheel at front stage
right and aims his lance from above at Kent's face. He freezes in this pose for
a few seconds so that the image has a lasting effect on the audience. Lear's
new pattern of behavior in relation to his daughters provokes acts of violence
from them which in turn provide Lear with wholly new experiences. The first
stage of death is thus characterized by a probationary taking on of new
behavior patterns as well as by the new experiences of caring and violence
which these new patterns have provoked. In the next phase, "Lear's madness," scene 12 (4.6), these new patterns of behavior are activated to the full.

In this scene, playful gestures and dance steps are realized naturally alongside gestures of caring and tenderness. All the behavior models which Lear
has tested since the onset of his death are at his fingertips without being explicitly substantiated or negated by the reactions of others (in this case Edgar
and Gloucester).

In scene 13 (4.7) the process of dying seems to have entered a new stage.
Lear lies on a long, narrow bed ("stretcher") and Cordelia kneels by his side.
Slowly, and with obvious effort, Marianne Hoppe sits up: with a smiling face
she says: "Pray you now, forget and forgive; I am old and foolish" (l. 85).
Once sitting, Cordelia moves behind her and holds her left arm up as if it
were a stick—as if she were Charon at the rudder carrying the dead across
the River Lethe in his bark to the underworld. She guides Lear with her right
hand slowly forward. Now the babble and clatter, previously only barely perceived in the background, grow increasingly louder. The noise might be emanating from a canteen or equally the entrance hall of a hospital. The inter-
textual association to the poem of prologue A just evoked by the presence of
the bed thus receives further amplification.

A similar blocking pattern is repeated and varied in scene 15 (5.3). Cordelia holds Lear in her arms. Slowly they walk backward toward the screen,

moving parallel to it before exiting (entering prison) when the group dissolves. The image appears one last time at the end of the performance in characteristic reversal: Lear enters from upstage left holding the (dead) Cordelia in his arms in front of him. The upper part of Cordelia's body leans back against Lear, her arms dangling behind her over those of Hoppe. The pair move slowly toward center stage, where they turn slightly and walk in a straight line to the front. Slowly, Cordelia slides to her knees against Hoppe; both are facing the audience. Lear is in this position when he dies — a moment marked only by an increase of light when Hoppe simply ceases to speak, to laugh, or to move.

A second series of images of caring is provided by Edgar and Gloucester. Edgar leads the blind Gloucester in scenes 8 (4.1), 12 (4.6), and 14 (5.2). In scene 12, for example, both enter at upstage right and move parallel to the canvas. Edgar walks backward, Gloucester, facing him, follows. Edgar is holding a long rod in front of him which touches the floor, igniting a zigzag strip of light on the floor as he does so. Their walk is accompanied by bell-like music which becomes quieter with every change in direction they take, swelling again until the next change of direction. Clearly, sounds are accorded a quite specific function and meaning in Gloucester's scenes after he has been blinded.[21] When Edgar and Gloucester halt, Edgar jams the rod under his arm so that he stands erect, towering above Gloucester. His pose is reminiscent of the Japanese god of death in Tadashi Suzuki's production of Euripides' *Trojan Women* or Cordelia as Charon at the rudder, bearing the dead across the River Lethe. This pose and these movement patterns are repeated again in scene 14, until Gloucester sinks down under the tree and Edgar places the rod in the fork of a branch. The zigzag lines of light are no longer set alight by the rod, however, and the bell-like music is replaced by drum rolls, distant calls, and dogs barking. After Gloucester's death, Edgar takes up the rod — now transformed into a spear — once again. This time he will use it in the duel against Edmund.

Here, too, images of caring are set in opposition to images of violence. In scene 7 (3.7) violence is aimed at Gloucester. Cornwall's servants tie him up, tear his clothes, and shove him into a square of light at center stage while from above a spindlelike cage descends over him. Cornwall strikes him three times with the spear — each time a loud, resounding, metal clang rings out. Regan stands next to him, and, bending over, her left foot lifted graciously behind her, plucks one hair from Gloucester's (nonexistent) beard with a stylized movement, laughing shrilly. Cornwall walks around the cage from behind to the front of the square of light downstage right. At the blinding of Gloucester, Cornwall raises his spear and thrusts it down at an angle toward

Gloucester's eyes. Again, he pauses in this pose, motionless for a few seconds. In the same moment, a glowing red light falls on the caged Gloucester.

The spear is used a last time as instrument and sign of violence in scene 15 (5.3)—with some variations, however. Edgar, now wearing only trousers, enters from upstage right bearing his spear horizontally. He places it so on a stand which the stagehands have set at upstage right. The duel between Edgar and Edmund, the representatives of human youth and animal youth, takes place at and with this horizontally placed spear. Both bare-chested, they take up positions at either end of the spear and raise their right arms vertically in the air. They let their arms fall slowly toward the spear, grasp hold of it, and make a circle with it. They squat down and push the ends of the spear so that it rotates on the stand above their heads, then stand and repeat the whole movement sequence a further two times, changing the direction of the spear each time. When Edmund is hit, a piercing sound is heard; Edmund lifts first one arm then the second and sinks slowly down before he collapses backward.

The image of the duel, interpolated between the deaths of Gloucester and Lear, corrects and concludes the series of images of violence for the audience. It does not, however, have any influence on the death scenes of the two old men and thus remains, in this sense, functionless. The old men experience the human contemporaneity of youth in an ever changing series of acts of caring and violence.

Unlike the younger characters—the servant, Cornwall, Regan, Goneril, Edmund—the old do not die as a result of violence. In the process of death they actually experience others as vehicles and agents of violence who nonetheless do not affect the precise moment of death itself at all. Hoppe thus portrays dying as a *rite de passage*:[22] Death commences with the phase of dissolution where the old status and the former behavior patterns bound to it are relinquished. In the following transitional or liminal phase, new models of movement and behavior which the new experiences release and create are tried out before being adopted and fully activated. Finally, the transformation now enters the last stage of the transition rite—the phase of incorporation. A leader of souls or the dead guides the charge toward admission into the fellowship of shadows in the kingdom of the dead. This last phase is given additional signification in the production: after Edgar's concluding words declaring the tragedy, Cordelia rises and slowly and quietly stands behind Lear. The (dead) Edmund also rises; the other characters enter the stage and together the dead and the living create a single tableau. At center front stands Lear, behind him, Cordelia. Cornwall, Goneril, Edmund, Regan, and Albany are spread out on the right half of the stage, while on the left stand Edgar, Gloucester, the Fool, and, far upstage left, the King of France. The tableau thus highlights specific changes from that of prologue A. The light grows ever dimmer; just before it fades entirely, the characters appear once more contrasted as silhouettes against the screen. When it is completely dark, the music also ceases — incorporation in the fellowship of shadows is complete. The "walls of reality" have opened a "mystical door" to another dimension.[23]

Rites of Passage — An Anthropological Model

Like his previous productions, Wilson's *Lear* is composed along the creative principles of music and fine art.[24] The confrontation with Shakespeare's tragedy has not led to the development of a new aesthetic, but rather is executed in the system of coordinates of Wilson's long-established theatre aesthetic. Indeed, at the beginning of the performance, a far stronger guiding of reception takes place than is usual in his work; this allows the specific semantification of individual characteristics of his aesthetic to exist and be suggested without, however, fixing the audience's attention on these alone. The spectator is free to undertake other semantifications or indeed to reject any semantification at all. The characteristic features of Wilson's aesthetic can be received here *sub specie mortis*. On the one hand, they deal with the *changing awareness* that occurs in dying and, on the other, the *new experiences* released by death.

Real objects are barely seen on this stage; the surrounding space appears to the consciousness far more as a universe of changing light in which the space of the present, the space of the memory, and the space of the future only guessed at are superimposed on one another. However, sounds penetrate the consciousness which are wholly derived from the real surroundings (as at Gloucester's blinding, for example) or rise softly as if from memory, gradually swelling, or are heard for the first time and grow gradually louder. The awareness of space changes according to the perception of the interweaving web of light and sound.

The perception of time changes in similar ways. As the framing of the performance by the two tableaux and the proscenium-high rod of light which moves from left to right at the beginning of the play and right to left after the interval suggests, the whole event seems to take place in the wink of eye, in the moment when "the eyeslit opens between blinks," as Heiner Müller wrote in "Bildbeschreibung" (Description of a Picture),[25] which Wilson used as prologue to his *Alcestis*. The time span of this "wink" expands as far as the time span of memory of the life lived, which in turn is contracted back into the measured real time of the three and a half hours of the performance. Time, seen subjectively, becomes a thoroughly subjective quantity.[26]

Such changed perceptions of space and time only scratch the surface of the real world. And this surface does not propose any meaningful cohesion but rather disintegrates into its single elements: color, movement, words and sentences, tone, sound. These enter the consciousness of the dying as isolated elements *per se*, rather than as fragments of a cohesive unity. In another sense, too, the surface of the real world offers a different perception in dying than that during life: elements which are normally invisible and are only revealed in actions and patterns of behavior now appear directly at the surface, such as the animal aspects in Goneril, Regan, Edmund, Albany, and Cornwall. The surface is not suddenly made transparent, enabling a glimpse of the underlying depths; rather, these components appear far more as directly perceivable surface phenomena.

The onset of death, on the other hand, opens up new experiences. The dissolution of the old status (such as holder of political power) deprives the formerly valid models of behavior of their function. New models must be found and tried out, which themselves will provoke new behavior patterns in others, from which, in turn, will spring the potential of wholly new experiences (such as caring and tenderness or violence). In this sense, the performance of death is executed as a *rite de passage*: the succession of the old identity (as king) begins at the end of prologue B; the liminal or transformation phase is carried out in scenes 1–12. New models of behavior are playfully experimented with and acted out until, the transformation complete, the new identity at the end of scene 12 (4.6) is accepted. Finally, in scenes 13 (4.7) and 15 (5.3) Lear, transformed in this way, is to be incorporated into the fellowship of shadows in the kingdom of the dead.

Death, the theme of this performance, is thus not the death of a specific individual such as Lear or Gloucester. Far more, the theme is played out to the end in all its many variations: prologue A concerns the death of a grandmother in the everyday life of the twentieth century with bed, ambulance, stretcher, and hospital. Certain gestures and sounds allude — so to speak at the opposite end of the scale — to the mythical dimension of death which is associated with animals of death cults such as vultures and cats, as well as those who lead the souls of the dead into the underworld. Embedded between these extremes, and superimposed by them, the deaths of Lear and Gloucester are played out while words of madness, violence, and death are spoken. Death of the individual in a specific sociohistorical situation is thus not the issue here, but death as the ritual transition at the end of a long life into a new condition, a new reality.[27] The structure of the performance follows a basic anthropological pattern: the rite of passage. The rite of passage controls moments of crisis in life and takes on the task of transferring the old identity toward a desired new state (birth, initiation, marriage, childbirth, professional or social advancement, death, etc.). It controls the passage from one kind of life into another. The rite of passage consists of three phases: separation from the usual life; a liminal phase which is the phase of actual transformation; and finally incorporation or reintegration of the transformed person back into society. In basing his production of *Lear* on the anthropological model underlying the rite of passage, Wilson simultaneously fixes the conditions that determine its international (universal) reception.

Thus, Robert Wilson has actually drawn upon a performance tradition that leads back to the beginnings of the European avant-garde. He has accomplished in *Lear* that which Edward Gordon Craig claimed early in this century, in his programmatic article "The Actor and the Übermarionette," to be the goal of theatre as an art form: "to recall beautiful things from the imaginary world" and to make this "ideal world" visible: "that mysterious, joyous and superbly complete life which is called Death . . . the life of shadow and of unknown shapes, where all cannot be blackness and fog as supposed, but vivid colour, vivid light, sharp cut form, and which one finds peopled with strange, fierce and solemn figures, pretty figures and calm figures, and those figures impelled to some wondrous harmony of movement."[28]

In making this "imaginary world" of death visible, Wilson's production of *King Lear* also presents at the same time a specific relationship between its own aesthetic, which creates and accomplishes the visible sense of death, and the Shakespeare tragedy. It is not a realization of a specific interpretation of the tragedy but rather plays through many variations of the theme dealt with by the tragedy. While the Shakespeare tragedy presents changes in awareness with linguistic means — the trial taking on and acting out of new models of behavior and identities resulting in new experiences being opened to the reader[29]—Wilson's aesthetic achieves a similar effect in the performance through the use of different theatrical sign systems based on the anthropological model of the rite of passage. The performance does not exist to provide a new interpretation of the text but rather to "discover it anew" in a quite specific way — as the potential of experiences: the performance aims to create awarenesses and experiences in the spectator similar to those which the contemplative reader might experience in reading the text.[30]

RETURNING THE GAZE
Between Cultural Performance
and Performance Art

Contemporary Western society may be described as a culture which puts itself on display onstage, as a culture of theatricalizations. Individuals and social groups from all social domains compete in the art of putting themselves and their everyday lives most effectively "onstage." Town planning, architecture, and design shape our environment as a kind of theatrical backdrop, against which individuals and groups display themselves and their lifestyles, in ever changing costume, before an audience. Shopping has become a theatrical experience, allowing the consumer to move as a kind of performer through different scenarios devised by clever marketing strategists. The consumer has been turned into "the conspicuous consumer"—the simple act of buying is put on display and represented.

Political events, too, are experienced exclusively as symbolical stagings—when the leaders of two nations stand hand in hand at Verdun on the battlefields of World War I or a minister for the environment swims across a river in order to prove it is clean (as a consequence of his own endeavors). Circumstances such as these have inevitably caused a loss of reality. The eternal sequence of staged/fabricated events seems to suggest that contemporary society has become a culture of experiences and spectacle which can only produce and reproduce itself by staging/fabricating such events. Reality is increasingly experienced as a performance, as a kind of theatre production.

Thus, it would seem appropriate to describe the experience of reality according to a model provided by theatre—that is, a situation in which a performer displays and represents her/himself, another, or something to the gaze of another, in a specifically arranged place and at a particular time, is experienced as reality (theatre). In this sense, reality always appears as theatrical reality.

At first glance, it may seem as though the theatricalization of contemporary everyday life can be perceived as a modern version of the Baroque metaphor of world theatre. But this impression is deceptive. The concept of the *theatrum mundi* or *theatrum vitae humanae* is based on the idea that life is a play performed before the eyes of God, who is author, stage director, and spectator. Since everything is an element of human life, all impulses, emotions, thoughts, words, behavior, and actions are to be seen as elements of this play. Only God alone is in a position to distinguish between the appearance demanded by the role and the true being of the actor, the soul, and to judge a performance adequately and justly. The concept of a theatricalization of everyday life, however, applies to processes of staging reality by individuals and different social groups, as well as processes by which they put themselves onstage. Only that which is made to appear in/by the production and which is perceived by others is regarded as an element of the production as well as the repertoire of techniques and practices employed in order to allow it to appear.

In this way, not only is the Baroque distinction between being and appearance challenged; even the opposition between the "positive" notions of truth, reality, and authenticity and the "negative" notions of appearance, simulation, and simulacrum, so typical of and traditionally valid in Western culture, has become obsolete. This upset was already in the making at the turn of this century. Today it is supported by the so-called new media. The reality represented by the media increasingly absorbs life. Simulations of reality by/in the media, so-called virtual realities, compete with the empirical world as other possible worlds. The simulacrum has become "experience" (*Erfahrungsraum*), and appearance in the media (*Scheinbarkeit*) turns out to be one in which reality — traditionally experienced and defined in opposition to appearance — has dissolved entirely. Thus, the new media contribute considerably to the theatricalization of everyday life and only allow access to a staged/fabricated reality.

In this respect, modern Western culture represents a challenge to the humanities. For even contemporary studies in the humanities continue to privilege texts and monuments and proceed from the assumption that Western culture is predominantly constituted and formulated, even changed and modified, solely through texts and monuments. More recent research, however, has shown the increasing importance of cultural performances such as festivals, political ceremonies, rituals of punishment, funeral rites, games, storytelling, ballad singing, and other concerts in European cultural history.[1]

The term *cultural performance* was coined by the anthropologist Milton Singer in 1959. He used this term to describe such particular instances of cultural organization as plays, dances, musical concerts, etc. According to Singer, a culture articulates its self-image through such performances and thereby represents and exhibits itself to its own members as well as to outsiders. "For the outsider, these can conveniently be taken as the most concrete observable units of the cultural structure, for each performance has a definitely limited time span, a beginning and end, an organized program of activity, a set of performers, an audience, and a place and occasion of performance."[2]

The investigations into cultural performances of all kinds show convincingly that the cultural performance played as important a part in European cultural history as Singer and other anthropologists have demonstrated in different oral cultures.

Contemporary culture, in a way, seems to reshift the focus of Western culture away from texts and monuments to a number of totally new, different kinds of cultural performance. This development does not leave even the arts unaffected. Thus, contemporary art forms seem to privilege the performative mode.

In the field of literature, authors do not restrict themselves to the process of writing a novel, a poem, a story, a documentation, etc. (itself a performative process). The author's activity also includes traveling around and reading works to various eager audiences who have gathered to hear the voice of the poet, novelist, or chronicler and who relish direct contact with the author. Moreover, audiences do not only flock to experience a "live" author. They even assemble in large groups for readings from works of past authors performed by actors, and poetry readings are becoming increasingly popular. One particularly remarkable reading was organized and performed by the group Angelus Novus in Vienna in 1986. In the Vienna Künstlerhaus the members of the group alternately read the 18,000 verses of the *Iliad* in twenty-two hours, nonstop, to an attentive audience. The listeners' attention was attracted to the specific materiality of the reading voices, which was foregrounded as each reader succeeded the next, so that the flow of the hexameters was only interrupted by the sudden changes in vocal quality. At such events, literature is emphatically displayed as a performative mode. It gains life through the voice of the physically present reader and enters the imagination of the physically present listeners via different sensuous channels.[3]

That music is a performative genre is a generally accepted truism. Before the invention of the gramophone, music was played before an audience, although, on rare occasions, the performing musicians were hidden from the eyes of the listeners by a curtain or a wall. Contemporary music foregrounds and stresses the performative characteristic of music in quite a remarkable manner as, for example, in percussion music. In recent times, composition for percussion and, above all, improvisation has widened percussive music to such an extent that it can hardly be categorized any more. The heart and core of contemporary music are to be found in percussion — ranging from "avant-garde," "ethno," and "New Age" to "techno." Percussion generally is to be characterized as a music which is performed and received by the whole body. The aesthetic dimension of this kind of music is permanently bound to a ritualistic or ceremonial one. Here the performative mode is absolutely constitutive.

Concerning the fine arts, one could label them — alongside theatre art — as the place and origin from which performance, as a specific art form, sprang. In the sixties and the early seventies artists such as Joseph Beuys, Wolf Vostell, Yvonne Rainer, and Ann Halprin — to name only the most prominent — promoted and realized a "new" genre of performance art. Even beyond artists such as these, the performing mode is prevalent in contemporary fine art. This is very obvious as far as body art is concerned. For here the live body of the artist is presented and displayed before an audience. Moreover, even in the field of landscape art, light-sculpture, video installations, and other contemporary exhibits the performing mode dominates. For here the beholder is challenged to move around the exhibit and interact with it while other visitors may observe her/him doing so. The roles of performer and spectator alternate accordingly so that a visit to a museum or an art-site nowadays means participating in a performance, partly as performer and partly as spectator.

Theatre, to conclude with this art form, is always a performative genre — *the* performative genre *par excellence*. This statement will arouse passionate protest from some colleagues who attempt to draw a strict dividing line between theatre and performance art, by constructing a clear-cut opposition between the two. In order to establish their argument, they proceed from a very narrow definition of theatre, which they nonetheless pass off as "the essence" of theatre. By totally ignoring its performative dimension, they reduce it to representation, narrativity, and the construction of subjects in physical and psychological spaces. That is to say, they regard only one historical form of theatre which, they claim, defines theatre. This narrow concept of theatre ignores the historic dimension. Until the beginning of the eighteenth century the term *theatre* or *theatrum* was used in most European languages to designate any space where something was taking place which was worthy of being shown and observed. It was employed for a theatrical performance as well as for the *theatrum anatomicum*, for a show of acrobats and clowns in the fairground and the place where an execution was performed; it was used as the forerunner to the museum, as different kinds of collections were displayed in a so-called chamber of art and wonders (*Kunst- und Wunderkammer*), and it was used for the performances by ballad singers performing on a platform (stage), erected in the market square.[4]

However, this concept of theatre excludes all theatrical genres except the genre of dramatic theatre: opera, dance, puppet theatre, most forms of non-

European theatre, the majority of the avant-garde theatre performances in the first decades of our century, as well as many contemporary theatre performances such as Robert Wilson's *Golden Windows* (Munich, 1982).

In line with this narrow concept of theatre, an equally narrow concept of performance is introduced. Performance is defined as denying narrativity and representation. Josette Féral claims that there is "nothing to grasp, project, interject, except for flows, networks, and systems. Everything appears and disappears like a galaxy of 'transitional objects' representing only the failure of representation." Accordingly, she argues that performance "attempts not to tell (like theatre), but rather to invoke synaesthetic relationships between subjects."[5] Even in the sixties and the seventies this definition only applied to a small number of performances. In terms of performances from the eighties and the early nineties, however, it is obvious that the definition given above cannot be applied in most cases. The concept of performance art advocated by Féral and others excludes the majority of performances of the last ten years in Europe and the United States (by Ulrike Rosenbach, Asta Groeting, Eleanor Antin, Whoopi Goldberg, Rachel Rosenthal, or recent performances by Laurie Anderson and Spalding Gray, to give just a few examples).

Thus, it seems wise to renounce any opposition which, necessarily, is built on narrow definitions which only apply to a very small segment of the phenomena in question. Instead of trying to distinguish performance art from theatre, it would appear more promising to proceed in precisely the opposite way. Since the performative mode prevails in many different contemporary art forms, it becomes increasingly difficult to differentiate between them clearly: the borderline separating one neatly from the other seems to dissolve; all art forms seem to merge into one art — a performance art. Thus, it no longer makes sense to draw demarcation lines between the different art forms. If distinctions must be made within the vast range of performance art, they must be based on different criteria. In the context of the cultural developments as sketched above, two questions arise from this state of affairs:

1. How is performance art — in itself a particular genre of cultural performance — related to other genres of cultural performance?
2. What explanations can be found for the prevalence of performance art in postmodern, postindustrial Western cultures? Which functions does performance art fulfill? Which meanings does it generate?

These questions can barely be answered within one essay, so I shall restrict my endeavors to mapping the grounds where these questions might be dealt with properly and exhaustively at a later date.

The point of departure for my argumentation is the performance *Two Undiscovered Amerindians Visit . . .* by the American performance artists Coco Fusco and Guillermo Gómez-Peña. After a "trial run" in the Art Gallery of the University of California, Irvine, the artists first performed in May 1992 in the Columbus Plaza, Madrid, as part of a festival held in commemoration of the so-called Discovery. They continued their tour to London, where they performed in Covent Garden; to Minneapolis, where the performance took place at the Walker Art Center (September); it then went on display at the Smithsonian National Museum of Natural History in Washington (October), at the Australian Museum of Natural History in Sidney (December), and at the Field Museum in Chicago (January 1993). Fusco and Gómez-Peña ended their tour at the Whitney Museum in New York, where they performed for the opening of the biennial (March 1993). The performance was seen by a huge number of people: in Washington 120,000 visitors attended, in Minneapolis 15,000; in both Sidney and Chicago 5,000; and in Irvine 1,000. Exact figures for Madrid and London are lacking, but both the Columbus Plaza and Covent Garden are busy centers of public activity.

At each site, Fusco and Gómez-Peña "lived" for three days in a golden cage as Amerindians from an island in the Gulf of Mexico which the Europeans had somehow failed to discover for five centuries. They called their homeland Guatinau and themselves Guatinauis. They were fancifully dressed as "Amerindians": Fusco wore sunglasses, a necklace of huge teeth, a bra made of fake tigerskin, a grass skirt, and sneakers. Gómez-Peña's face was painted like a tiger in an ironic citation of the mask of the "fierce Mexican wrestler" and his eyes were hidden by glasses; his huge headdress was decorated with ornaments crowned by the picture of an Indian chief with a feather headdress. His shoulders and his chest were covered by a necklace, partly repeating the ornaments of the headdress, partly decorated with pearls. Around his loins he wore a highly decorated girdle, with pearls hanging from it, and a mask of a face directly covered his pelvis. This decoration was repeated in the leg-bands. Both Fusco and Gómez-Peña, in addition to their fanciful necklaces, wore collars. The two guards outside their cage took them to the bathroom on leashes.

Fusco and Gómez-Peña performed what they called their "traditional tasks," which ranged from sewing voodoo dolls, lifting weights, and watching television to working on a laptop computer. In front of the cage there was a donation box indicating that, for a small fee, Fusco would dance (which she did to rap music), that Gómez-Peña would narrate authentic Amerindian stories (which he did in a nonsensical language), and that both would pose with visitors for photographs. The two guards were at hand to speak to the visitors, since the "Amerindians" could not understand or be understood, and fed them sandwiches and fruit.

In front of the cage there were two display boards. The first showed a chronology of highlights from the history of putting non-Western peoples on display in exhibitions. The second was a fake entry in the *Encyclopaedia Britannica*, "Amerindians," with a counterfeit map of the Gulf of Mexico.

The structure and style of this entry copied the *Encyclopaedia Britannica* ironically. Thus, it began with two explanations of the term *Amerindians*. "1) A mythical people of the Far East, connected in legendary history with Seneca and Amerigo Vespucci" and "2) One of the many English terms for the people of Guatinau."[6] The first explanation was elaborated by nonsensical etymological comments on the term and a drawing showing the skeleton of an ape. The second explanation was substantiated by some "general remarks" on the Guatinaui people: "They are a jovial and playful race, with a genuine affection for the debris of Western industrialized popular culture. In former times, however, they committed frequent raids on Spanish ships, disguised as British pirates, whence comes their familiarity with European culture."[7]

The general remarks were completed by a detailed description of "the male and female specimens here on display" and explained, in pseudo-scientific language, the "meanings" of their clothes and ornaments as well as of their gestures, actions, and behavior.

The performance by Fusco and Gómez-Peña explicitly referred to a performance genre that was very popular among European and American audiences in the nineteenth and even the beginning of the twentieth century — the colonial exhibition (*Völkerausstellung*). This genre has been in existence since the fifteenth century, starting with exhibitions of "savages" in fairgrounds, taverns, gardens, and the like as part of freak shows. In the course of the nineteenth century, however, this kind of exhibition moved into a different arena, the zoological garden. The character of such exhibitions also changed insofar as it was now claimed that they served primarily scientific and educational goals and purposes. Display boards as well as introductory lectures commenting on the physical features, behavior, symbols, etc. of the peoples displayed were intended to secure the "educational value" of such exhibitions. Quite often they were accompanied by shows, including prayers, singing, dancing, and wedding processions.[8] In most cases, the "authenticity" of such performances was emphatically stressed. Fusco and Gómez-Peña's performance cited the genre of the colonial exhibition by presenting all the elements constitutive to it and rearranging them in a clearly ironic way. That is to say, they created their performance as art—by quoting a particular genre of cultural performance.

Indeed, many contemporary performance artists proceed from, or draw on, particular genres of cultural performance. While Fusco and Gómez-Peña took recourse to the genre of the colonial exhibition, Joseph Beuys, in his tree-planting performance in Kassel some years earlier, alluded to a particular political ceremony. The British performance group Welfare State refer to the genres of street festival and carnival in most of their performances; the ventriloquist Paul Zaloom, who manipulates milk cartons, boxes, automobile parts, and other trash, the Flying Karamazov Brothers, and the two solo clowns Bill Irwin and Avner the Eccentric all draw heavily on the circus genre. Asta Groeting has quoted figure skating in her most recent performance; Laurie Anderson's performances take recourse to the genre of ballad singing and storytelling, which Spalding Gray also cites. Finally, Karen Finley's performances suggest striptease shows. This consistent playing with explicit references of all kinds to particular genres of cultural performance can be described as a prevalent device among contemporary performance artists.

So it makes sense first to differentiate between performances which allude to a particular genre of cultural performance and performances which do not and second to distinguish the performances which proceed from a particular kind of cultural performance according to the different genres to which they allude. Whatever kind of cultural performance is taken as point of departure, the artistic performance is created as a special transformation of the type or genre of cultural performance. Such artistic transformation may affect the individual traits constitutive of this genre, such as time, place, and occasion of the performance, the kind of program of activity, the set of performers, the arrangement and behavior of the audience, and the particular self-image the culture has encapsulated in the specific performance genre.

In the nineteenth and early twentieth centuries colonial exhibitions and other exhibitions of non-Western people were, in part, organized on the occasion of so-called World Exhibitions (the first was in 1851), where Western culture proudly displayed the achievements of its civilization. Sometimes, however, they were held for no particular occasion all year round. The exhibitions took place either in an especially arranged "natural environment" in the grounds of the World Exhibition or in zoological gardens, panoptica, and the like. They could be visited during the usual opening hours of the respective institution with the exception of special shows which were only performed at prearranged times.

On the one hand, the program consisted of performances of everyday activities, as Carl Hagenbeck describes for the first such exhibition which he organized, the exhibition of a Lapp family in 1874.[9]

On the other hand, special shows were announced where "spectacular" activities drawn from different cultural performances were performed alongside the everyday activities; for example, in the case of Hagenbeck's Kalmuck exhibition (1883) "prayers, singing, dancing, wedding processions, and wrestling,"[10] or, on the occasion of the exhibition of Bella-Coola Indians (1885–1886), chants, games, a shamanistic exorcism, and dances, most prominent of which was the so-called hametzen dance, by which, it was maintained, the Bella-Coola initiated new members into their secret union.

The performers were non-Western people. They performed what the Western organizers, entrepreneurs like Hagenbeck—usually supported by anthropologists such as Rudolf Virchow and Franz Boas—had decided to be an interesting part of their lives to a Western audience.

The audiences which visited this kind of exhibition included members of all social strata and generations. The "educational value" of the exhibition was stressed by pointing to the fact that in former times the experience of a foreign culture was limited to those privileged persons who could afford to travel. The exhibition of a non-Western people made this experience accessible to everybody, particularly as special rates on Sundays were introduced. Thus, it was argued, it became possible for millions of Europeans to "travel" to the foreign worlds of an "Ashanti village," an "Indian town," or a Lapp family. Indeed, audiences poured into the exhibitions in great numbers. Hagenbeck's Ceylon exhibition, which was shown in Hamburg, Düsseldorf, Frankfurt, Vienna, Berlin, London, and Paris, was generally visited by an average of 50,000 to 60,000 people on a Sunday.

The self-image Western cultures formulated and exhibited to their members and non-Westerners through the genre of the colonial exhibition was an image of a "race" and a culture superior to any other. By staging and presenting a comparative relation between "primitive" and "civilized" peoples,[11] such exhibitions seemed capable of suggesting the superiority of the European audiences as "civilized people" over the "primitive races" on display. Such exhibitions were thought an appropriate vehicle for justifying the civilizing mission of the Europeans in their colonial politics. In Germany, for instance, such exhibitions undoubtedly served the function of winning over extensive support for German colonial interests. And in France the colonial exhibition seemed to instill support for a colonial policy which was somewhat controversial because of its doubtful economic profit.

On the other hand, the elements of non-Western cultures presented in a colonial exhibition were also selected and combined in such a way that their presentation would appeal to the suppressed sexual desires and archaic fears of the audiences — to all that had been expelled from official discourse in the late nineteenth and early twentieth centuries. The non-Western people on display incorporated and exhibited the ambiguous image of the "uncivilized Other" in the minds of Western audiences, one who was despised, suppressed, controlled, and at the same time desired as well as feared by them.

Unlike other cultural performances on which contemporary performance artists draw, such as the circus, striptease show, or political ceremonies like tree planting, the colonial exhibition now seems to be an extinct genre. This has to be borne in mind when analyzing the transformation it went through in Fusco and Gómez-Peña's performance.

As mentioned above, *Two Undiscovered Amerindians Visit* . . . was on tour from May 1992 until March 1993. The year 1992, when it mainly ran, was the quincentennial commemoration of the so-called Discovery. Thus, a certain frame was established for the reception of the performance. It clearly related the performance to the history of European colonialism. This frame was only reinforced by the occasion and site of the performances in Madrid and London. Here it was displayed as part of the Edge '92 Biennial, which took place in London and Madrid — in Madrid as part of its quincentennial celebration as the capital of European culture. In both cities, the performance took place in a public arena: the Columbus Plaza in Madrid, where the very name of the square as well as its particular design could be understood as an emphasis of this frame, and Covent Garden in London.

Apart from reinforcing the idea that the performance was related to the history of European colonialism in some way, the occasion at which it was performed brought about an important modification of this frame. It signaled quite outspokenly and unmistakably that the performance was part of an art festival. Thus, the expectation was that the performance would be received as an artistic treatment of the history of European colonialism.

As far as the other performances are concerned, the reference to the year 1992 does not seem to have been constitutive to its framing. Rather, the frame was established by the actual site of performance. In Irvine, Minneapolis, and New York the performances took place in an art gallery, an art center, and an art museum. Thus, it was clearly marked that the audiences were confronted with a piece of performance art. In New York, moreover, this frame was reinforced by the occasion of the opening of the biennial.

In Washington, Sidney, and Chicago the performances were given in natural history museums. Here a particular framing was accomplished by reference to the pseudo-scientific aims of the organizers of colonial exhibitions. The analogies between the exhibition of the different objects in the museum, including the display boards accompanying each item, and the kind of display the two performers had chosen for themselves were intended to trigger a reflexive and critical response.

According to the observations and statements of the performing artists, despite the different places and occasions of the performance and the various different framings which resulted, more than half of the visitors in all cities, except New York, missed and ignored even the plainest and most distinct framing devices and responded to the performance as if it were a specimen of the genre "colonial exhibition" — a genre of cultural performance long since extinct. The transformation of the genre, brought about by the artists through change of place and occasion, thus, was not recognized by the majority of the audience. Despite clear framing devices, signaling that the performance was to be received as a piece of performance art dealing with the history of colonialism or colonial practices and mentality, they somehow managed to believe in the "reality" of the performance and assumed that the exhibition of non-Western people in a cage in a public space or a museum is still "normal" practice in the West — even if they protested against this practice or tried to rationalize it, for instance, with the argument that the "savages" on display might become frightened and attack.

In this way, the transformation of the genre accomplished by the artists revealed the existence and the working of a set of presuppositions concerning the relationship between Western and non-Western peoples which are effective and valid for this group of spectators. These presuppositions enabled them to ignore the framing devices given by the artists and to establish another frame which identified the performance as a colonial exhibition — a frame produced by colonial mentality.

This response from the majority of audiences seems all the more surprising since the program of activities which the performers carried out openly made fun of the proclaimed authenticity of activities shown at a colonial exhibition. The performers maintained the double structure of the program by performing their "traditional" everyday activities all day long and the "spectacular" ones, alluding to particular "traditional" cultural performances like ritual dancing or storytelling, only at "given" times (i.e., whenever a fee was donated).

The performers' activities — as well as their appearance — embodied the most common stereotypes of the "speechless uncivilized Other" whom the

Westerner must civilize, interpret, and make vocal. Nonetheless, the reenactment was structured so as to function as a kind of broken mirror reflecting the stereotypes in a somewhat shattered — and accordingly irritating — manner by incorporating elements which bluntly questioned the stereotype as well as the claim of authenticity. One such example was Fusco's dance to rap music, another was Gómez-Peña's mask, which alluded to another stereotype, the fierce Mexican wrestler, and the fact that the performers worked at a laptop computer.

The ironic reenactment and the program of activities triggered quite different responses in believers and nonbelievers. The believers seem to have missed the irony completely. They speculated at great length in front of the cage as to how the "savages" could possibly run a computer, wear sunglasses and sneakers, and smoke cigarettes. As Fusco reports, the American audience asked neither about Gómez-Peña's made-up language in which he told "Amerindian" stories nor about the legitimacy of the map or the taxonomic information on the signs.

Among the nonbelievers a variety of responses was to be observed. Some seemed to enjoy the spectacle and tried to "join in" by different actions. In London and Madrid, businessmen approached the cage to make stereotypical jungle animal sounds. In New York, a middle-aged man attending the opening of the Whitney Biennial insisted on feeding Fusco a banana. He was told by the "zoo" guard that he would have to pay $10 to do so. He quickly paid, making sure that his picture was taken while feeding Fusco.

Others, mostly other artists and cultural bureaucrats, seem to have felt rather uneasy in front of the cage. As Fusco has explained, they "sometimes have expressed a desire to rupture the fiction publicly by naming us, or they arrive armed with scepticism as they search for the 'believers,' or parody believers in order to join in the performance."[12] Several young artists criticized the fact that the performance was not experimental enough, not really good performance art, or that it was "not critical," for instance, because Fusco was too passive. Reviewers complained that Fusco's dance was not "authentic."

Other visitors, realizing that the people on display were artists, scolded them for being so immoral as to cheat the audience. This reaction occurred quite often in London and also among intellectuals and cultural bureaucrats in the United States. This group of audience members did not wonder how it was possible that people believed in the performance; rather, they reproached the performers for their "dishonesty" in misleading the audience.

Regardless of whether they believed or not, many spectators, both male and female, confronted the performers with sexual challenges, responding to them by taking a clearly voyeuristic stance. Although some men became verbally abusive, talking dirty, taunting Fusco, asking her out, or blowing kisses, no one ever tried to make physical contact with her. Some women, on the contrary, even went so far as to stroke Gómez-Peña's legs, after having asked for rubber gloves, to grab his head, and to kiss him. The erotic appeal of two caged people — whether "savage" or not — thus proved to be quite irresistible to some of the spectators.

All the audience responses described here were reactions by white Europeans and Americans. Other audience members — believers as well as nonbelievers — generally responded differently. Believers often expressed discomfort and a kind of identification with the situation they felt; they explicitly referred to slavery and to the mistreatment of Native peoples and blacks as their own history. Some nonbelievers assured the performers of their solidarity, for instance, by holding their hands. None of them ever attempted — verbally or physically — a sexually charged approach.

I shall not embark here on a detailed evaluation of the audience responses. One might conclude, however, that the reactions of the white Europeans and Americans betray a continuation of a colonial mentality; at least, they proved that the relationship of Westerners to non-Western people is still conditioned and governed by former stereotypes which, officially, have been long since rejected, invalidated, discarded — just like the genre of the colonial exhibition, which has nourished, expressed, mediated, and reinforced such stereotypes. In this respect, one may argue that the transformation of the genre accomplished by Fusco and Gómez-Peña's performance has brought to light how colonial mentality is still deeply rooted in Western culture.

Nonetheless, such an evaluation is not the primary concern here. My interest focuses on the performer-spectator relationship.

The organizers of the colonial exhibition exposed the non-Western performers to the gaze of the Western spectator. Whatever stance the spectators took in such a situation, their gaze always objectified the performers. Not only were the roles of performer and spectator fixed and unchangeable, but, moreover, the relationship between performers and spectators was constituted and ordered by the performance as an irreversible relationship between superior spectators (observers) and inferior, objectified performers (the objects of observation).

At first glance, the situation created by the performance of *Two Undiscovered Amerindians Visit* . . . seems somewhat similar. The performers acted behind the bars of the cage, exposed — albeit voluntarily — to the objectifying gaze of the spectators. The resemblance, however, is restricted to superficial phenomena only. The "deep structure" of the performance reveals quite another arrangement.

First, the spectators were challenged to act themselves if they wanted to see more than the so-called everyday activities. They must pay, literally, a certain price. And this price did not only amount to the fee they had to donate. For in asking the "zoo" guards whether they might feed Fusco a banana, or for rubber gloves in order to touch Gómez-Peña, or if the two people on display mate in public in the cage and by donating the prescribed fee for Fusco to dance or Gómez-Peña to narrate his "stories," the spectators themselves also performed activities. In doing so, they exposed themselves to the gaze of the performers as well as of the other spectators. Second, this holds true for all the other audience responses spoken publicly either to each other (for example, speculation as to how the "savages" might run a computer) or to the performers (such as the sexual harassment or the moral charges of dishonesty, not being critical, or not being authentic).

Whatever the spectators did, however they responded to the performance, under such conditions they themselves turned into players who performed before the eyes of the artists and other spectators in such a way as to reveal their desires, their anxieties, their state of mind. Thus, the roles of performer and spectator were constantly redefined. The spectators, even if unwilling and unaware, adopted the position of the "savages" to be observed and interpreted by others.

In this way, the transformation of the genre of colonial exhibition brought about by Fusco and Gómez-Peña led to a permanent reordering and reconstitution of the relationship between performers and spectators, on the one hand, and between different spectators, on the other. It proved the relationship to be highly unstable and, accordingly, resulted in a reversal of positions and the returning of the gaze. By creating an experimental situation, the performance worked as a critical discourse on the gaze, which observes, surveys, and objectifies the Other.

In this case, the procedure of citing a distinct genre of cultural performance served two different purposes. On the one hand, it exposed the continuing existence of a mentality and ideology which was formerly condensed and manifested in the genre of colonial exhibition and critically commented on it. On the other hand, it reflected that in a postmodern, postcolonial, multicultural society the relationship between its members cannot be ordered and constituted along the lines of such position-fixing ideologies. The spectator of the moment will be a performer the next. The gaze directed at the Other is returned by the Other. There are no stable positions, no nonreturnable gazes anymore. The performance situation (i.e., a situation of direct communication in public) worked here as catalyst to bring these conditions to light, to focus attention as well as to reflect on them.

Of course, performances which draw on other genres of cultural performance will serve other purposes and result in other consequences. There might be affinities, however, with performances which take recourse to striptease shows or particular political ceremonies which designate fixed positions for different groups of participants. But performances which proceed from circus, carnival, street festivals, or ballad-singing and storytelling are probably devoted to other concerns.

Nonetheless, all these performances are very much alike — at least in two respects. First, they share all the characteristics Singer has listed with regard to the cultural performance. Hence, it might be concluded that current performance art, particularly when it quotes a genre of cultural performance, acts as a kind of cultural memory, a reminder of the paramount function that cultural performances also had in Western cultural history, which the humanities have forgotten or marginalized because of the central position accorded to texts and monuments as the privileged expressions of our culture. By privileging the performative mode, contemporary art, on the contrary, emphasizes the importance of cultural performance for Western cultural history and, at the same time, continues its tradition in a particular way.

Second, the performance situation is always a situation of direct communication in public. In the reception of an art form, this condition results in a radical change of reception modes and habits. Instead of contemplating the pages of a book in private or a picture in a gallery for hours, the recipient will respond in public immediately — as is usually the case in a theatre performance or in a concert. Accordingly she/he will realize the act of reception in the midst of a community formed by the audience members. Because this community only exists for the limited time span of the performance, since it recruits its members according to a random principle, it will not exert a particular pressure on its members, nor will it plead forcefully for conformity. Rather, it allows its members to express themselves freely and exchange their impressions, emotions, interpretations. Such an opportunity becomes all the more important and meaningful as, in Western culture, communication increasingly takes place indirectly, as medial communication. Performance art, in response to this development, seems to create and reactivate some of the last residues in contemporary culture that make it possible to communicate directly in public and to act as a member of a community.

Performance art, thus, has far-reaching consequences not only for the arts but for culture in general. These can only be appropriately investigated and dealt with by a strictly interdisciplinary approach that challenges not only the art-related humanities, but all culture-related disciplines as well.

PERFORMANCE ART AND RITUAL
Bodies in Performance

During the summer school at Black Mountain College in 1952, an "untitled event" took place, initiated by John Cage. The participants included, besides Cage, the pianist David Tudor, composer Jay Watt, painter Robert Rauschenberg, dancer Merce Cunningham, and poets Mary Caroline Richards and Charles Olson. Preparations for the "event" were minimal. Each performer was given a "score" which consisted purely of "time brackets" to indicate moments of action, inaction, and silence that each individual performer was expected to fill. Thus, it was guaranteed that there would be no causal relationship between the different actions and "anything that happened after that, happened in the observer himself."[1] The audience was gathered from other participants at the summer school, members of the college faculty and their families, and people from the surrounding countryside.

The seats for the spectators were set out in the dining hall of the college in front of each wall in the form of four triangles whose tips pointed to the center of the room without touching each other. Thus, a large free space was created in the center of the room in which, as it resulted, very little action took place. Spacious aisles between the triangles crossed the room as two diagonals. A white cup was placed on each of the seats. The spectators did not receive any explanation for the cups; some used them as ashtrays. From the ceiling were hung paintings by Robert Rauschenberg — his "white paintings."

Cage, in a black suit and tie, stood on a stepladder and read a text on "the relation of music to Zen Buddhism" and excerpts from Meister Eckhart. Later he performed a "composition with a radio." At the same time, Rauschenberg played old records on a wind-up gramophone with a trumpet while a dog sat beside it listening, and David Tudor played a "prepared piano." A little later, Tudor started to pour water from one bucket to another, while Olson and Richards read from their poetry, in part among the spectators, in part standing on a ladder leaning against one of the walls. Cunningham and others danced through the aisles chased by the dog, who, in the meantime, had turned mad. Rauschenberg projected abstract slides (created by colored gelatine sandwiched between the glass) and clips of film onto the paintings on the ceiling; the film clips showed first the school cook and then, as they gradually moved from the ceiling down the walls, the setting sun. Jay Watt sat in a corner and played different instruments. At the end of the performance four boys, dressed in white, served coffee into the cups regardless of whether the spectators had used them as ashtrays or not.

There can be no doubt that the "untitled event" is to be regarded as a remarkable event in the theatre history of Western culture. And this is as true of the relationship between performers and spectators realized by the performance as it is of the kind of interaction between the different arts.

At first glance, it may appear as though the spatial arrangement favored a focusing of the center. During the performance, however, it became clear that such central focus did not exist. The spectators were able to direct their attention to different actions taking place simultaneously, whether in different parts of the room or joining and overlapping. Moreover, they were in a position that meant that wherever they looked they would always perceive other spectators involved in the act of perceiving. In other words, the actions were not to be perceived in total isolation from each other, nor were they unrelated to the other perceiving spectators, despite the fact that they were not causally related to each other, and the perspective on other spectators was not determined or controlled.

On the other hand, by placing a cup on each seat, one element was introduced that challenged the spectators to act without, however, prescribing how. They could pick it up, handle it, put it on the floor, throw it to another spectator, hide it in their bags, use it as an ashtray. Whatever the case, the cup challenged the spectators to act at the beginning of the performance as well as at the end (after the boys had poured the coffee) without forcing them to make a specific action.

In the performance, different arts were involved: music, painting, film, dance, poetry. They were not united into a Wagnerian *Gesamtkunstwerk* (total work of art)—rather, it seems that their unrelated coexistence very closely approximated Wagner's nightmare "of, for example, a reading of a Goethe novel and the performance of a Beethoven symphony taking place in an art gallery among various statues,"[2] nor was their employment motivated, caused, or justified by a common goal or function; they were only coordinated by the "time brackets." Nonetheless, correspondence did occur in the particular style of their appearance. They all privileged the performative mode: the music was played, the poetry recited, the film shown; painting was performed insofar as Rauschenberg changed his white paintings by projecting the slides onto them, "painting them over," and dance is always realized as an action — or movement. The "union of the arts," the transgression of the borders or the dissolution of the borderlines separating one art from another, was accomplished here because all were realized in a performative mode. The performative function was foregrounded, be it by radically reducing the referential function (for instance, in the unrelatedness of the individual actions, which could not be connected into a story or a meaningful "symbolic" configuration, or by the refusal to give the "*untitled* event" a title) or by emphatically stressing the performative function (for instance, by the arrangement of actions or by the emphasis put on the fact that it was an "untitled *event*").

Thus, one can conclude that the historical relevance of the "untitled event" is founded on its discovery of the performative. That is not to say that European culture had not been performative before the 1950s. Quite the contrary seems to be the case. Going back through the centuries we find that from the Middle Ages to the end of the eighteenth century European culture can most adequately be described as a predominantly performative culture. Even in the eighteenth century, when alphabetization and literacy expanded in the middle-class population, reading was seldom performed as a silent act in isolation from others, but rather as reading aloud to others in different kinds of circles. In this respect, it does not appear to be an exaggeration to state that European culture, at least until the end of the eighteenth century (and in many areas throughout the nineteenth century, too), consisted of different genres of cultural performance to a large extent.

The term *cultural performance* was coined by the American anthropologist Milton Singer. In the 1950s he used the term to describe "particular instances of cultural organization, e.g. weddings, temple festivals, recitations, plays, dances, musical concerts etc."[3] According to Singer, a culture articulates its self-understanding and self-image in cultural performances which it presents and exposes to its members as well as to outsiders. "For the outsider, these can conveniently be taken as the most concrete observable units of the cultural structure, for each performance has a definitely limited time span, a beginning and end, an organized program of activity, a set of performers, an audience, and a place and occasion of performance."[4]

Whereas up to the 1950s a *consensus* existed among Western scholars that culture is produced and manifested in its artifacts (i.e., in its texts and monuments), which, accordingly, have been taken as the proper objects of study in the humanities, Singer drew attention to the fact that culture is also produced and manifested in performances. In this way, he also discovered the performative as a constitutive function of culture and provided another convincing argument for the importance of the performative mode in culture.

The notion of culture as a predominantly material culture (i.e., consisting of and formed by documents and monuments) had become a prevailing concept in the nineteenth century, although it had already been vigorously attacked — as, for instance, by Friedrich Nietzsche. Nonetheless, it was this notion which greatly influenced, if not determined, the development not only of the humanities, but also of other cultural domains. In theatre, for example, in many respects held to be the performative art *par excellence*, the Meiningers foregrounded the literary text of the drama on the one hand — which after many years of adaptation was now no longer open to revision — and the preservable elements of the performance such as the set and the costumes, on the other. Culture, according to nineteenth-century common belief, was manifested by and resulted in artifacts which could be preserved and handed down to the next generation.

It was against this notion of culture that avant-gardist movements such as the futurists, dadaists, and surrealists directed their fierce attacks, proclaiming the destruction of the museums and hailing velocity and ephemerality as the truly culture-creating forces of the future. In this respect, the futurist *serate* and the dadaist soirées as well as other actions they took can be seen as "forerunners" to Cage's "untitled event." But while the futurists and dadaists focused on the destructive forces of their performances in order to shock the audiences — according to their motto "épater le bourgeois" — and to destroy bourgeois culture, Cage's event emphasized the new possibilities opening up not only for the artists but also for the audiences. The performative mode here was applied as a means of "liberating" the spectators in their own perception and acts of meaning constitution.

In the 1950s performativity was discovered anew not only in the arts. As already mentioned, in anthropology the *phenomenon* of the cultural performance came about, in literary theory Roland Barthes focused on *écriture* instead of the static text (as in *Le Degré zéro de l'écriture*, published in 1953), and in philosophy John L. Austin outlined the so-called speech act. At the beginning of the 1950s he developed a philosophy of language, which he presented for the William James Lectures at Harvard University in 1955 in a series under the title *How to Do Things with Words*. Here he explained the pioneering, if not revolutionary, idea that linguistic utterances do not only serve to describe a procedure or to state a fact; the mere uttering of them simultaneously performs an act (for example, the act of describing, stating, promising, congratulating, cursing, etc.). What speakers of language have always known intuitively and practiced accordingly was, for the first time, articulated in a philosophy of language: language serves not only a referential function, but also a performative one.

What Austin's theory of the speech act accomplished with regard to the knowledge of language Cage's "untitled event" realized for theatre. Suddenly, that which theatre artists and spectators had known intuitively and practiced for ages became evident: theatre fulfills not only a referential function, but a performative one too. Whereas, at the beginning of the 1950s, the Western dramatic theatre emphasized the issue of the psychological motivation for the characters' actions, the construction of the plot, the means of scenic arrangements, constellations, and procedures and was seduced, in this way, into ignoring the performative function of theatre, the "untitled event" foregrounded the performative function, recalling its permanent existence in theatre and bringing it back into view.

In order to accomplish this, it strongly opposed not only the contemporary art market, which insisted on the production of objects or artifacts as commodities, but also the contemporary theatre as well. Whereas the contemporary theatre stage usually signified another space —Willy Loman's living room, for instance, or the road where Didi and Gogo wait for Godot— the dining hall in Black Mountain College did not signify any other particular space. One might speculate on whether the specific arrangements of the four triangles formed by the spectators' seats pointed to a figure of the *I Ching* and could be interpreted accordingly. But this is quite another matter. For, first, there was no particular segment in the room delineated for the performers to which a particular meaning should be attributed; second, any meaning derived from the *I Ching* would have to be related to the whole room; and third, reference to the *I Ching* does not provide the prerequisite for being able to follow the actions. Whatever the case, the space was a real space, and it did not necessarily signify another (fictitious) space. Rather, it seems that it provoked a kind of oscillating reception. The spectator who tried to make sense of the event and its single elements/actions became aware that her/his usually applied patterns of constituting meaning did not fit anymore. The usual patterns were not discarded as useless, however, but rather held in suspension, called up, present, and yet somehow inapplicable. The attempt to apply them rather provoked the search for meaning and sense, instead of providing answers. The dining hall was the dining hall — to which the cup as well as the film clip showing the school's cook alluded — and, at the same time, it was refunctionalized: during the time the "untitled event" took place, it was another space, seemingly neither the dining hall nor a particular fictitious space. Nonetheless, the spectator was not prevented from perceiving it as a particular fictitious space, if that occurred to her/him, nor from asking the question "What does this space signify or mean?" In this case, the spectator might have come to the conclusion at the end of the performance that it did not mean anything (in the sense of a referent attributed by the event). That is to say that even space and the perception of it underwent a metamorphosis, a transformation. Accordingly, the search for possible meanings of its single elements like the empty center, the aisles, and the stepladders took the same course.

Similar conclusions can be drawn concerning the sense of time in the performance and the performers. The time of the performance was the real time of its being performed. It did not necessarily signify another time of the day, year, or epoch, nor a time in which a fictitious character performs a particular action or reflection. It was the time that passed during the performance which was structured by the action, inaction, and silences as indicated by the "time brackets" of the score and not necessarily another, fictitious time.

Whereas in the theatre of the 1950s the actors used their bodies in order to signify fictitious characters, to perform actions that were supposed to signify actions by these characters, and uttered words which signified the characters' speeches, the performers of the "untitled event" employed their bodies in order to perform particular actions: to play a gramophone, different instruments, or a "prepared piano," to dance through the aisles, climb a ladder, or operate the projector, etc. When the performers spoke, they either recited their own texts or made it clear that they were reading from texts by other authors. In this way, questions concerning fictitious characters and their histories, actions, or psychological motivations could not arise: real people performed real actions in a real space in a real time. What was at stake was the performance of actions — not the relation of actions to a fictitious character in a fictitious story in a fictitious world, or to one another, so that a "meaningful whole" might come into existence.

In this way, even the role of the spectator was redefined. Since the referential function lost its priority, the spectators did not need to search for given meanings anymore, nor to struggle to decipher possible messages formulated in the performance. Instead, they were in a position to regard the actions performed before their eyes and ears as material and let their eyes wander between the simultaneously performed actions; they were allowed not to search for meanings at all and to accord whatever meaning occurred to them to single actions. Thus, looking on was redefined as an activity, as doing, according to their particular patterns of perception, their associations and memories, and the discourses in which they participated.

At the beginning of the 1950s the artifact in Western culture was held to be the absolute constitutive factor of any art. Dramatic theatre proceeded from a literary text, music composed or interpreted scores, poetry created texts, and the fine arts produced works. Various hermeneutic processes of interpretation proceeded from such artifacts and returned to them in order to substantiate or justify different findings, different interpretations. The artifact dominated the view to such an extent that the performative process of its production (writing, composing, painting, sculpting) or its transformation into a performance (in theatre and concert) as well as the performance itself and its reception totally slipped out of sight.

The "untitled event" dissolved the artifact in performance. Texts were recited, music was played, paintings were "painted over"—the artifacts disappeared into the actions. Thus, the borders between the different arts shifted. Poetry, music, and the fine arts ceased to function merely as poetry, music, the fine arts—they were realized, at the same time, as performance art. They all changed into theatre. Not only did the "untitled event" redefine theatre by focusing on its performative function, it also redefined the other arts. These were realized and described as *performance*. That is to say, the different arts did not "unite" in a Wagnerian *Gesamtkunstwerk*, but in theatre, understood as performative art *par excellence*.

Thus, the "untitled event" not only blurred the borderlines between theatre and the other arts, but also those between theatre and other kinds of "cultural performance." Following Singer, a theatre performance is to be regarded as a particular genre of cultural performance which, by realizing in its own way the features he has listed, partly differs from other genres of cultural performance such as ritual, political ceremony, festival, games, competition, lectures, concerts, poetry readings, film shows, etc., and partly overlaps with them.

The "untitled event" was realized as a theatre performance in the course of which lectures, poetry readings, a film show, a slideshow, concerts, *tableaux vivants* (dog and gramophone, "His Master's Voice"), dance, and a kind of ritual or feast (in the sharing of the coffee) took place. However, these cultural performances were not *represented* as in dramatic theatre, opera, or classical ballet; rather, the performance *was* the realization, or the realization *was* the performance. Since theatre here occurred as a noncausal, nonlinear sequence of individual actions, presented before an audience, its difference from other genres of cultural performance diminished to such an extent that it hardly mattered much anymore—if at all. Performativity turned out to be the most important characteristic of theatre, art, culture. Theatre, art, and culture, thus, were redefined as performance.

From today's viewpoint, the "untitled event" of 1952 appears to have been a revolutionary event in Western culture. The trend toward performativity which has gradually grown since the 1960s in theatre, the other arts, and in culture in general was already unmistakably articulated and uncompromisingly realized in the "untitled event." In this respect, one could state that Cage's "untitled event" and Austin's speech act theory heralded the era of a new performative culture and were its first momentous manifestations.

For such a performative culture, theatre understood as performative art *par excellence*— as realized in performance art— could serve as a model. If theatre is understood as a paradigm of performative art and, in this sense, as the model of performative culture, the question arises as to what, since the 1960s, it has contributed to the development of such a new performative culture. This issue is addressed by drawing on some examples from so-called performance art.

In many respects, performance art takes recourse to the particular achievements of the "untitled event," which it develops further and even radicalizes. Many performances consist of the performance of everyday practices. For instance, in the piece *Cycle for Water Buckets*, first performed in 1962, the Fluxus artist Tomas Schmit knelt in a circle formed by ten to thirty buckets or bottles, one of which was filled with water. Clockwise, he poured its contents from bottle to bottle or from bucket to bucket— until all the water was spilled or evaporated. By taking the action out of all possible everyday context, the search for its intention, purpose, consequence, or meaning was doomed to be as unsuccessful, or at least to remain as undecided, as in the case of the elements in the "untitled event." The focus lay on the very process by which the action was performed. Accordingly, the spectators perceived how Schmit poured water from bottle to bottle or from bucket to bucket; since the context in which such an activity is performed in everyday life was lacking, attributing a particular function and meaning to it— such as preparing to clean the floor, extinguishing a fire, filling a trough, cleaning a bucket/bottle, demonstrating a safe hand, etc.— the action could mean all this, something else, or simply just what it was: pouring water from one bucket/bottle into another.

Other performances allude to or draw on different genres of cultural performance: rituals, festivals, services, carnivals, circuses, shows at a fairground, storytelling, ballad singing, concerts, sports, games, and so on. In such cultural performances, culture always was and is defined and realized as performative. That is not to say that artifacts are not used or do not play a prominent role. Quite the contrary— in many cultural performances some kind of artifacts are needed, are partly even essential for the realization of the performance. However, they only function or are able to display their special power as elements of a performative process, and not as artifacts. Therefore the use of artifacts in a cultural performance by no means entails a reduction of its performativity.

Since cultural performances emphasize the performative character of culture, it seems wise to proceed from performances that refer in one way or another to a genre of cultural performance when embarking on an investigation of theatre's contribution to the development of a new performative culture. In view of the great variety of possible genres of cultural performances referred to by performance artists, however, I shall restrict my explorations to performances which, in one way or another, have taken recourse to a particularly basic genre: ritual.

PERFORMING RITUAL OR THE RITUALIZATION OF PERFORMANCE?
THE SECOND ACTION OF NITSCH'S *Orgy Mystery Theatre*

the walls of the main room are covered in white hessian splashed with paint, blood and bloody water. on a meat hook, on the end of a rope hanging from the ceiling, hangs a slaughtered, bloody, skinned lamb (head down). a white cloth is spread out on the gallery floor, beneath the lamb, and on it lie the blood-soaked intestines. the lamb is swung across the room. the walls, the floor, and the spectators are splashed with blood. blood is poured out of buckets over the intestines and the floor of the gallery. the actor tosses raw eggs against the walls and onto the floor and chews a tea-rose. the bloody lambskin hangs on the blood spattered hessian wall. more blood is splashed over it.[5]

The action lasted thirty minutes and was accompanied by music by the Greek composer Logothetis: loud noises were created by the composer as he drove his hand in rubbing and pressing movements over the taut skin of a drum.

The action was performed by Hermann Nitsch on March 16, 1963, in the Dvorak gallery in Vienna. It was his second action. Nitsch was educated in graphic design and developed the later so-called action art by way of painting actions, in which he poured red color on a canvas in the presence of onlookers. After first attempts at concrete poetry and drama, his second action already contains almost all the elements which are constitutive of his *Orgy Mystery Theatre* and which are constantly repeated regardless of whether the performance lasts thirty minutes, fifteen hours (like his seventh action, which took place on January 16, 1965, in his apartment and studio), or six days (like the play planned for the Prinzendorf Schloß).

All the elements used by Nitsch in a performance are characterized by two main features. They are all highly symbolic, and they cause a strong sensual impression. Nitsch himself has listed a number of symbolic associations that can be presupposed for any of the elements. Concerning the entrails he specifies "slaughterhouse, sacred killing, slaughter, animal sacrifice, human sacrifice, primitive sacrifice, the hunt, war, surgical operation." Among possible sensual impressions he mentions "blood-warm, blood-soaked, malleable, resilient, stuffed to bursting, to puncture, to crush, a stream of excrement, the intensive odor of raw meat and excrement." To the element "blood" Nitsch assigns the symbolic associations "red wine, Eucharist, the blood of Christ, sacrifice, human sacrifice, animal sacrifice, slaughter, primitive sacrifice, sacred killing, life juices" and the sensual impressions "body-warm, warm from the slaughter, blood-soaked, wet, bright, blood-red liquid, to be splattered, poured, paddled in, salty taste, wounding, killing, a white dress smeared with blood, menstrual blood, the stench of blood." With regard to "flesh" Nitsch names the symbolic associations "bread, Eucharist, the transformation of bread into the body of Christ (flesh), sacrifice, animal sacrifice, human sacrifice, sacred killing, slaughter, wounding, killing, war, the hunt." The corresponding sensual impressions he cites as "body-warm, warm from the slaughter, blood-soaked, wet, raw, bright blood red, malleable, resilient, the taste of raw meat, wounding, killing, the stench of raw meat."[6] The "tea-rose," according to Nitsch, provokes the symbolic associations "erotic flower (lust), rosary (Madonna), queen of the flowers" and releases the sensual impressions "scent of tea-roses, the taste of tea-rose petals, the voluptuous opulence of tea-roses, the tea-rose stamen, the pollen of the tea-rose."[7]

It is quite striking that most of the symbolic associations Nitsch assigns to the elements of his actions point to either archaic/mythic or Christian/ Catholic rituals. That is to say they are intended to operate as links between the action/performance taking place here and now (i.e., in the early 1960s) and certain kinds of ritual which still operate in the context of Western culture (i.e., in Vienna in the early 1960s) such as the rituals of the Catholic church or those which we imagine as having taken place — or which still do take place — in ancient Greece and other cultures. This does not necessarily imply that the spectators shared the symbolic associations proposed by Nitsch. But at the very least we can assume that as members of the Viennese culture of the 1960s they disposed of a universe of discourse which was open to the possibility of such associations.[8]

In any case, not only the symbolic associations but also the sensual impressions were accessible to performers and spectators alike. In these actions/performances, the spectators were involved, even acted as performers. They were splashed with blood, excrement, dishwater, and other liquids and were given the opportunity to do the splashing themselves, to gut the lamb, to consume the meat and the wine.

The sensual impressions and the symbolic associations triggered by the different elements of the performance, however, were ordered and structured through reference to one dominant element: the lamb. In Western Christian culture, the lamb can symbolize Jesus Christ and his sacrifice. Insofar, the lamb, as the focal center of almost all performances by Nitsch, opens up a dimension which strengthens the allusion to the above-mentioned rituals to which the possible symbolic actions may refer. Nitsch labels it the "mythical leitmotif of the orgy mystery theatre (mythical expression of the collective need to abreact) the transformation."

communion: TAKE, EAT, THIS IS MY BODY, BROKEN FOR YOU
    FOR THE REMISSION OF SINS . . .
DRINK YE ALL OF THIS, FOR THIS IS MY BLOOD OF THE
    NEW COVENANT; SHED FOR YOU AND FOR MANY . . .
the crucifixion of jesus christ
the tearing apart of dionysus
the blinding of oedipus
ritual castration
the killing of orpheus
the killing of adonis
the castration of attis
ritual regicide
killing and consuming the totemic beast
the primitive excesses of sado-masochism
consuming food:
meat and wine in sumptuous measure[9]

The rituals to which Nitsch refers are scapegoat-rituals, exorcism rituals, cleansing and/or transforming rituals. Like all ritual they do not only signify a particular action but also actually perform it. That is to say, the referential function indicated by the symbols used in the process of ritual is closely linked to, even dominated by, the performative function. The ritual is able to cause the proclaimed effect to which the symbols (objects and/or actions) allude — such as cleansing the community, healing an individual, transforming a group of individuals — only because it is performed in a particular way.

By equating his performances with ancient Greece and Catholic rituals the artist claims that by performing his actions he performs a particular kind of ritual. Such a claim seems problematic in many respects, for it ignores basic differences between rituals that operate within a community and the actions performed by the artist. When, for instance the Holy Communion to which Nitsch refers is performed as a ritual, this procedure is certified as a ritual because an authorized person executes the actions in a particular context and under particular conditions and because the congregation is convinced that she/he is entitled to perform the actions. In this respect the ritual is comparable to a speech act. It can only succeed when it is performed in a particular space, at a particular time, in a particular way, by a person who is entitled to perform it. If someone other than the priest sprinkles water on somebody's forehead and utters the words "Ego te baptisto in nomine Patris et Filii et Spiritus Sancti," she/he has by no means performed a christening — at best, a joke. Or, to give another example, I quote Emile Benveniste's famous statement:

> In any case, a performative statement can only achieve reality when it is confirmed as an action. Outside the circumstances which make it performative, such a statement is nothing more than a mere statement. Anyone can call out in the market square, "I declare general mobilization." But this statement cannot become action because it lacks authority, it is just speech; it is limited to an empty shout, childishness, or madness. A performative statement without action cannot exist. An authoritative action will always be derived from statements made by those who have the right to express them.[10]

Applied to rituals, this means that they will only work when performed by an authorized person. Thus, she/he is part of the particular framing which the ritual needs in order to succeed.[11] As already mentioned, the frame may include a particular occasion, place, time, setting, specific actions; in any case, it will be established by persons who are entitled to perform these actions. Therefore, when an artist like Nitsch proclaims that he is performing a ritual by performing particular actions, the question arises as to what entitles him to perform a ritual — whether in his own eyes or in the eyes of the other participants/spectators.

Another question arises from his claim concerning the relationship between the actions he performs and their possible meaning. If we assume that the action he performs succeeds in causing exactly that effect which it signifies, we have to explain how sign and signified merge. In the rituals to which

Nitsch alludes, this occurs because of either divine or cosmic/magic forces/ energy which the performance releases. What in his performance operates as a substitute for such forces? What can initiate the merging of signifier and signified?

Before embarking on the investigation of these questions — and in order to broaden and strengthen the ground from which to proceed — I shall first briefly describe two other performances which, in one way or another, also allude to ritual: Joseph Beuys' action *Coyote: I Like America and America Likes Me*, which took place in May 1973 in the René Block Gallery in New York, and Marina Abramović's performance *The Lips of Thomas* given at the Krinzinger gallery in Innsbruck in 1975. Both performances were very different from Nitsch's performance as well as from each other and both referred to ritual in very different ways.

COYOTE: I LIKE AMERICA AND AMERICA LIKES ME

Beuys started his action in the plane even before it reached the American continent. He closed his eyes in order not to see anything. At J. F. Kennedy Airport he was completely wrapped up in felt and brought to the gallery by an ambulance. He left America the same way. During his seven-day stay he did not see anything of America other than a long, light room with three windows in the René Block Gallery which he shared with a wild coyote for three days.

The room was divided by a wire screen which separated Beuys and the coyote from the spectators. In the far back corner, straw was put down that arrived with the coyote. Beuys brought along with him as equipment two long felt cloths, a walking stick, gloves, a torch, and fifty issues of the *Wall Street Journal* (to which the current issue was added each day). He presented them to the coyote, who sniffed at and urinated on them.

Beuys placed the two felt cloths in the center of the room. One he arranged as a heap in which he hid the lit torch so that only its light could be perceived. The issues of the *Wall Street Journal* were piled in two stacks behind the wire screen to the front of the room. With the brown walking stick hooked over his arm, he approached the other felt cloth, put on the gloves, and covered himself completely with the felt; all that remained to be seen was the stick poking up out of the felt. In this way Beuys created the impression of a shepherd who then underwent a series of transformations: the stick poked up vertically; bent horizontally, it pointed toward the floor; Beuys squatted down in an upright position, with the stick bent toward the floor. Meanwhile the figure turned constantly on his own axis, according to the movements and changing directions of the coyote. Then, unexpectedly, the figure dropped sideways to the floor, where he remained lying stretched out. All of a sudden Beuys jumped up, letting the felt slip down and hitting the triangle which hung around his neck three times. When the last sound had died away, he turned on a tape recorder placed before the bars, so that for twenty seconds the noise of running turbines was heard. When silence returned, he took off his gloves and threw them to the coyote, which took them in its mouth and mauled them. Beuys went to the issues of the *Wall Street Journal* which the coyote had scattered and torn and rearranged them into piles. Afterward he lay down on the straw to smoke a cigarette. Whenever he did this, the coyote would move toward him.

At all other times, the coyote preferred to lie on the heap of felt. It looked in the same direction in which the light of the torch shone and avoided a position where the spectators would be behind its back. Often it restlessly paced the room, ran to a window, and stared out. Then it would turn to the journals again and chew them, drag them through the room, or shit on them.

The coyote kept a certain distance from the figure in felt. From time to time it circled him sniffing and excitedly jumped at the stick, bit the felt, and shredded it into pieces. When the figure lay stretched out on the floor the coyote sniffed and prodded him, pawed or sat down beside him, and tried to crawl under the felt. Mostly, however, it stayed away, fixing the figure with its eyes. Only when Beuys smoked his cigarette on the straw did it approach him. Having finished his cigarette, Beuys got to his feet, rearranged the felt, and covered himself again.

When three days had passed, Beuys very slowly scattered the straw all over the room, hugged the coyote good-bye, and left the gallery in the same way he had arrived.

It is quite obvious that, in contrast to Nitsch, Beuys mainly used everyday objects — the journals, cigarettes, torch, straw, felt, walking stick, gloves — and performed everyday actions — arranging the journals, smoking a cigarette, switching on a tape recorder. Accordingly, neither the objects nor the actions imply any allusion whatsoever to ritual. Moreover, it is difficult, if not impossible, to ascribe to the objects and actions symbolic associations that may have been shared by the artist and the spectators. However, the elements were accorded a symbolic value by the artist, not in the sense of fixed symbols but of "vehicles of experience, transmitters and communicators. They represent hidden effects and can be made conceivable and transparent."[12]

This is particularly true of the materials and objects. For instance, Beuys established a relationship between the possible implications of the felt and his former actions when he stated that "the way in which felt operates in my action, with double meaning, as insulator and warmer, also extends to imply insulation from America and the provision of heat for the coyote."[13] He used the torch as an "image of energy": "First, the torch houses the energy in concentration, then, the energy disperses throughout the course of the day until the battery has to be renewed."[14] The torch was hidden in the felt because it was not to be presented as a technical object: "It should be a source of light, a hearth, a disappearing sun glowing out from under this gray heap."[15] The brown gloves which Beuys threw to the coyote after each turn represented "my hands . . . , the freedom given mankind through the hands. They are free to do all kinds of things, an infinite range of utensils are at their disposal. . . . The hands are universal."[16] Beuys showed the manifold meanings of the bent walking stick for the first time in his action *Eurasia* (1965): it represented the streams of energy that float in Eurasia from east to west and west to east. The *Wall Street Journal*, on the other hand, embodies "the calcified death-stare of CAPITAL thinking (in the sense of being forced to capitulate to the power of money and position). . . . Time is the measure of the symptoms of the fact that CAPITAL has long been the only artistic concept. That, too, is an aspect of the United States."[17] Even the two sounds produced in the performances, the hitting of the triangle and the noise of the turbines, were accorded such meanings. The noise of the turbines was "the echo of the ruling technology: energy which is never harnessed," while the sound of the triangle is reminiscent of "the unity and the one" and is conceived of "as a stream of consciousness directed at the coyote."[18]

In Nitsch's performance the symbolic associations assigned to various elements by the artist would not necessarily be shared by his spectators. This was ultimately possible, however, insofar as it was assumed that such elements belong to a general universe of discourse. In Beuys' performance this assumption cannot be made. Rather, it is most likely that the American visitors did not share the associations suggested by Beuys at all and, accordingly, made quite different associations when perceiving the objects.

However, there are two aspects which overcome such objections and point to the special status of the performance. First, as already stated, the objects were not linked to the meanings explained by Beuys in the sense of fixed symbols. Rather, they were thought to be able to unfold and realize their potential meanings and effects only in the context of the event that constituted the performance: the meeting of Beuys and the coyote.

The second aspect comes into play regarding this meeting: a certain mythical dimension was accorded both partners. Beuys designed and staged himself as a shepherdlike figure, alluding to the Good Shepherd on the one side and to a shaman on the other — that is to say, a figure which disposes of divine and/or cosmic/magic forces. As his partner in the performance he chose a coyote, which represents one of the mightiest American Indian deities. The coyote is said to be blessed with the power of transformation, being able to move between physical and spiritual states. The arrival of the white settlers changed the status of the coyote. Its inventiveness and adaptability, admired and revered by the American Indians as subversive power, was now denounced as cunning. Thus, it became the "mean coyote" which could be hunted and killed as a kind of scapegoat. Accordingly, Beuys' performance aimed at the "traumatic moment" of American history: "One could say, we should settle the score with the coyote. Only then can this wound be healed."[19] Beuys undertook the action in order to accomplish this goal. It was performed as an "energy dialogue" between man and animal,[20] aimed at triggering the spiritual forces necessary for "healing this wound" in the performer. Beuys acted as a kind of shaman who performs a healing ritual that will save the community by restoring the destroyed — cosmic — order.

Although the participants/spectators were not in a position to share the possible meanings accorded the objects by the performer, it was assumed that they would benefit from the "shaman's" actions as he conjured up or exorcised the hidden potential meanings and effects of the objects employed, thus releasing the "healing forces" (i.e., particular spiritual forces within himself which enabled him to act as a representative of a community) — at least in his own view. In terms of Beuys' performance, the questions formulated above become even more pressing.

THE LIPS OF THOMAS

The third example radicalizes and, thus, focuses an aspect that was similarly constitutive of the two other performances, which has not yet been sufficiently emphasized up to now: the particular use and treatment of the performer's body. In her performance *The Lips of Thomas* Marina Abramović maltreated her own body for two hours in various ways. Before the performance she undressed completely, so that everything she did was performed naked.

Abramović sat down at a table covered with a white cloth and set with a bottle of red wine, a glass of honey, a crystal glass, a silver spoon, and a whip. Slowly she ate the honey with the silver spoon, poured the red wine into the crystal glass, and drank it. After swallowing the wine, she broke the crystal glass in her right hand, hurting herself. Abramović got up, went to the back wall where, at the beginning of the performance, she had fastened a picture of herself and framed it by drawing a five-pointed star around it. She took a razor blade and cut a five-pointed star into the skin of her belly. Then she seized the whip, knelt down under her picture and the star with her back to the audience, and started to flog herself violently on the back. After this, she lay down, arms stretched out, on ice cubes laid out in a cross. A radiator hung from the ceiling was directed toward her belly. Through its heat, the slashed wounds of the star began to bleed copiously again. Abramović remained on the cross of ice for thirty minutes until spectators removed the ice and thus broke off the performance.

No doubt, the most striking aspect of this performance was the self-mutilation performed by Abramović. However, the objects she employed in order to execute the self-mutilation also allow for quite a number of symbolic associations — often very different, even contradictory ones. The five-pointed star, for instance, may be interpreted in various mythical, metaphysical, cultural-historical, and political contexts (even as a fixed symbol of a socialist Yugoslavia). The same holds true for other objects: the whip may point to Christian flagellants, to flogging as punishment and torture, or to sado-masochistic sexual practices; the cross of ice may be related to the crucifixion of Christ — but also to icy prison cells or to winter and to death. Eating and drinking at a table using a silver spoon and a crystal glass may be perceived as an everyday action in a bourgeois surrounding but may equally allude to the Last Supper.

Whatever symbolic associations were triggered by the objects, they were not caused by objects in isolation — the objects as such — but by their particular employment as instruments of self-mutilation. The actions which Abramović performed using these objects structured the performance in such a way that its similarity to a scapegoat ritual in which she played the victim or to a ritual of initiation became obvious. By undergoing a series of clearly perceivable physical transformations such as the intake of certain substances into the body, the mutilations of the body brought about by inscribing the star, by flogging, bleeding, and freezing, in sum, by undergoing an ordeal, the naked performer acquired a new identity. Nonetheless, it seems highly problematic to classify the performance as a ritual — be it a scapegoat ritual or a rite of initiation — for a scapegoat ritual as well as an initiation rite presupposes not only that a *consensus* exists among the members of the community concerning the symbolic meaning of the objects employed but, moreover, that the violations and mutilations conceived of as constitutive elements of the rite are usually inflicted on the victim/initiates by members of the community who are entitled to do so. Here it was the performer who inflicted the pain on herself, and the spectators were the ones to finish the ordeal or break it off by removing the ice.

As in the case of the performances by Nitsch and Beuys, though in other respects very different, the Abramović performance alluded to a particular genre of ritual without actually realizing it.

All these artists introduced or used particular ritual structures in their performances. They followed, for instance, the three phases of a rite which Arnold Van Gennep has described.[21] They started with a clearly marked separation phase: Nitsch, by arranging the environment and by putting on a white garment; Beuys, by letting himself be covered by felt at the airport; Abramović, by setting the environment and by undressing. The actions described above made up the transformation phase. The final incorporation phase at the end of the ritual was indicated by the party or the common meal in Nitsch's performance, by being wrapped in felt and brought back to the airport in an ambulance in Beuys' performance, and by the actions of some spectators in Abramović's performance.

That is to say, the structure and the process of the three performances seem to be derived from rituals. I hesitate, however, to class them as rituals despite each artist's own claims and interpretations. For my question is still unanswered: What is it that entitles the artist to perform a ritual not only in his/her own eyes but also in the judgment of the other participants, the spectators?

THE BODY IN PERFORMANCE

In each of the described performances the artist used her/his body in a striking manner. Nitsch soiled his body with blood and excrement; he dug his own hands into the entrails of the lamb and thus almost literally carried out the lamb's disembowelment himself. He exposed his body to various sensations through contact with blood, wine, paint, dishwater, urine, excrement; and he inflicted violence on the carcass of the lamb with his own hands. It was his own body which appeared to be the actual locus of performance. By using different materials and objects, Nitsch not only changed them but also transformed his own body.

In Beuys' performance the performer's body obviously served a different purpose. By living together with a wild coyote for three days, Beuys created a particular situation. On the one hand, he exposed his body to the risk of being attacked, bitten, or hurt by the coyote. On the other hand, he employed his body in order to communicate with the coyote. The energy of this "dialogue" proceeded from and was received by his body. The spiritual forces which were meant to bring about the "healing" were to be released in and out of his body. And this body, in turn, did not remain unchanged amid all these risks and dangers even if it was ultimately unharmed. The three days shared with the coyote left their imprint.

Abramović abused her body, literally cut into her own flesh, inflicted injuries on it that caused pain and left lasting traces. But she did not articulate her pains, for instance by screaming. She simply performed self-mutilating actions and presented her bleeding, suffering body to the spectators. She exposed the procedure of hurt and its visible traces, but not her pain — this had to be sensed by the spectators. However, obviously this sense became so strong and unbearable that they interfered and put an end to the performer's tortures.

In each of these actions the performer risked her/his body. It was precisely these transformations, threats, and injuries brought about during the course of the performance which legitimized it. Since the performer risked her/his body, the construction of her/his own "fiction"— the mythical dismemberment of a god, the energy dialogue with a coyote, the acquisition of a new identity — was substantiated and, in this sense, transformed into "reality." It was simply the soiled, endangered, violated body that entitled the performer to perform such actions *as if* the performance were a ritual.

This condition clearly marks the difference in principle between an acknowledged ritual and an artist's performance. The traditional rituals originate in collective constructions — such as myths, legends, and other traditions; performing a ritual thus means to resubstantiate them and to reaffirm their effects. The artist's performances, on the contrary, proceed from subjective constructions. Here it is only the soiled body of the artist, the endangered and still unharmed body, the body in pain, which is able to substantiate these constructions for the spectators. The witness of the performers' acting and suffering bodies, thus, may gain the power of evidence of proof in the eyes of the spectators.

However, the spectators do not participate in a ritual as the members of a Catholic congregation at a Holy Communion or the participants at a shamanistic demon exorcism might. For even if the particular use of the body may substantiate the performer's subjective constructions in the eyes of the spectators, it does not follow that they will "believe" in these constructions — that they will be convinced that they are participating in the dismemberment of a god, in the healing of America's traumatic wound, in the birth of a new identity or a sacrifice, respectively. At best, they will sense or even believe that the artist's use of the body manifests and reveals a new attitude toward the body: the attitude of "being my body" instead of only having it, as Helmuth Plessner put it.[22]

Even if the particular employment of the body does not entitle the artist to perform ritual or transform the performance into ritual, it endows the human body with values long since forgotten and ignored in Western culture — values that, at other times or in other cultures, were realized when the rituals were performed to which the artist's performance alludes.

If we come to the conclusion that the artist does not perform ritual, what happens to the relationship between the actions performed and/or the objects used and their possible meanings, to the relationship between the signifiers and the signified?

To begin with, the spectators perceive how the artists perform the actions described above: pouring blood on a white canvas, tearing the entrails from the carcass of a lamb, wrapping oneself in a long felt cloth, arranging journals, smoking a cigarette, drinking red wine, cutting a five-pointed star into the belly, and so on. And since the artists not only perform these actions themselves but as themselves, in their own name (and not in order to represent actions of a particular role figure), the spectators will first ascribe to them this meaning: that Nitsch tears entrails from a lamb's carcass, that Beuys covers himself with felt, that Abramović cuts a five-pointed star into the skin of her belly. In this sense one could state a momentary merging of signifier and signified. On the other hand, all these actions and objects entail an abundance of possibilities which trigger symbolic associations which depend on the universe of discourse of each spectator. This semantic surplus will prevent an actual merging of signifier and signified. However, the performance does not structure the process of perception and meaning-constitution in such a way that particular symbolic associations are emphasized and foregrounded. Therefore the semantic surplus may result in a similar process as the merging: it may draw the spectator's attention away from possible meanings of a gesture — that may mean anything — and focus on its materiality, i.e., go back to the body of the performer. Such focus, at the same time, emphasizes that the action causes certain effects on the performer's body. When Nitsch tears the entrails from the lamb's carcass, he is tainted by them; when Beuys wraps his body in felt, he makes it disappear and creates a particular image (figure); when Abramović engraves a five-pointed star in her belly, it will bleed. Thus, despite the semantic surplus, the semantic dimension is devaluated as secondary. The spectators' attention, in this case, is not directed toward a possible meaning, but focuses on the physical execution of an action on the one side and on the effect it causes on the performer's body on the other side.

While participants in a ritual may take recourse to the collective construction which enables them to assume that performing the ritual exactly causes only those actions which it signifies — the transformation of a wafer into Christ's body, the exorcism of the demon — because the merging of signifier and signified is based on the collective construction, in the artist's performance they fall apart. Though the subjective construction may be substantiated in the eyes of the spectators because of the particular use of the body, nonetheless, the spectators will be able to relate signifier and signified to each other without even considering this construction. The divine/cosmic/magic forces which the collective construction presupposes and whose working the "correct" performance of the ritual will guarantee are replaced in the artist's performance by her/his individual demonstration of being a body and not only having a body (as the common basis of human culture) and the spectators' individual response to it — be it particular sensations, emotions, reflections, or even the execution of certain actions (as in Nitsch's performance) or preventing the performer from continuing her/his actions.

Thus, the performer's body, in many respects, appears to be the basic condition for the "success" of the performance. Its particular use (i.e., its risks and injuries) is able to substantiate the artist's subjective construction in the eyes of the spectators and, in this way, to legitimate her/his performance. It is the artist's physical action which triggers sensations, emotions, and impulses in the spectators to act themselves and which initiates reflections which will allow them to have the experience of being a body, not only having a body.

On the other hand, the reception process is characterized by features that are common to any process of theatrical communication and clearly distinguish it from reception processes in other art forms, which dispose of artifacts. An artifact allows the recipient to attribute ever new meanings to its single elements, the combination of these, and the structure as a whole, and, whatever the meanings may be, it is possible for others to check them by taking direct recourse to the artifact. In a performance, however, the process of meaning production in which a recipient may accord certain meanings to the actions of the performer is closely connected to the fleeting moment of their being physically executed by the performer. Any modification or revision of the meaning constituted during the performance can no longer refer to the actions themselves, nor are others able to take recourse to them in order to check the meaning conveyed to them by a participant. All modifications, revisions, and discussions will necessarily refer to the memory of the participants — any process of meaning-constitution taken up or continued after the performance is over will be performed as a process of recollection. The subjective construction which the performer tends to substantiate through the performance, thus, is brought into relation to and followed by the various subjective constructions which the spectators bring forth as they recall the performance. For them, the only point of reference is their own memory engraved in their own bodies.

Thus, we can conclude that the artist's individual transformation of the genre "ritual" as realized in the performance has considerably shifted the cultural focus. It brings back into view an insight which has long been forgotten and repressed in Western culture — even if never completely: that the basis of any cultural production is the human body and that this body creates culture by performing actions.[23] Here the focus does not center on artifacts that are brought forth by such actions privileged by Western culture in general and the humanities in particular; rather, attention is attracted to the very moment at which the actions are performed.

This moment, in its ephemeral presence, is accorded a time dimension because of its reference to subjective constructions. It is preceded by the subjective construction of the artist who has designed the actions, and it flows into the subjective construction of the spectators who later, in the process of recollection, attribute different meanings to them. While during the performance, for a fleeting moment, signifier and signified seem to merge, before and after it (i.e., in the subjective constructions of the performers and the spectators), they irretrievably fall apart. In this respect, one might even discover a potential utopia in the performance.

Thus, subjective constructions resulting in a physical performance and its recollection appear to be the principal modes of cultural production, and it is only the moment of physical performance that is endowed with the power to transform subjective construction into sensually perceivable realizations that, in their turn, become the point of departure for other subjective constructions. However, a theory of culture that would proceed from the moment of performance, taking this as its pivot, is still to be developed.

Regarding the process of reception, the artists' performances described above question the traditional concept of aesthetic distance in principle. When the spectators' bodies are splashed with blood, when the audience becomes eyewitness to actions by which the artist exposes her/his body to risks and inflicts severe injuries on it, how will they be able to keep aesthetic distance? In such performances, is it still valid to hold aesthetic distance for the "adequate" attitude of reception? A theory of aesthetic perception taking into consideration the body in pain has still to be developed. For it is highly questionable whether the aesthetics of the sublime already deals with this aspect satisfactorily. And such a theory seems all the more desirable since theatre from the 1960s and 1970s on increasingly employs the performer's body in a way which literally risks, endangers, and violates it, whether in the performance of individual artists or of theatre groups.

In the 1960s and 1970s the Viennese artist Rudolf Schwarzkogler, for instance, abused his body with cables and bandages (1960); Chris Burden had himself locked up in a locker measuring 2 feet × 2 feet × 3 feet for five days, nourished only from a water bottle placed in the locker above (1971); in the same year, in a performance entitled *Shooting Piece* he was shot in his left arm by his friend; Gina Pane was cut on the back, in the face, and on the hands and, lying on an iron bed, scorched and burned her body by candles placed underneath.[24] In the 1990s Sieglinde Kallnbach walked on fire and trickled hot wax onto her skin;[25] in *The Reincarnation of the Holy Orlan* the French performance artist Orlan underwent cosmetic surgery to shape her face according to a computer-synthesized ideal that melded the features of women in famous paintings — such as Sandro Botticelli's *Venus*, Leonardo's *Mona Lisa*, François Boucher's *Europa*, *Diana* from the Fontainebleau school, and Jean Léon Gérôme's *Psyche*.[26] The operation was directly transmitted from the operation theatre to a New York gallery.

Since the 1980s, a kind of using the body is to be observed in a number of dance and theatre groups, which includes pushing, kicking, falling down, repeating strenuous exercises endlessly, and so on. Here violence is done to the performers' bodies, injuries and pains are inflicted on them, as, for instance, in the theatres of Jan Fabre, Einar Schleef, Reza Abdoh, Lalala Human Steps, or La Fura dels Baus. And even in productions of Harry Kupfer, Frank Castorf, Leander Haussmann, and others the singers and actors are thrown and fall down.

If the endangered, scorched, pierced, or otherwise injured body is the focus of attention in this way, the question arises as to how this affects aesthetic perception. As Elaine Scarry has shown, pain cannot be communicated:

> So, for the person in pain, so incontestably and unnegotiably present is it that "having pain" may come to be thought of as the most vibrant example of what it is "to have certainty," while for the other person it is so elusive that "hearing about pain" may exist as the primary model of what it is "to have doubt." Thus pain comes unsharably into our midst as at once that which cannot be denied and that which cannot be confirmed.[27]

To perceive pain, thus, means to perceive one's own pain, never the pain of another. The spectators perceive the action by which the performer hurts her/himself but not the pain which she/he senses. They are only in a position to assume that she/he senses pain. Thus, a kind of paradoxical situation comes into being. The fleeting moment in which an action is performed, and, thus, signifier and signified seem to merge, is experienced by the spectators at the same time as the moment when perception and meaning-constitution fall apart and the signified irretrievably separates from the signifier. While the action of hurting her/himself is perceived, the pain which it causes can only be imagined. A gap opens up for the spectators between what is performed *on* the performer's body (i.e., at its surface) and what happens *in* the performer's body, a gap that seems to be bridgeable only by way of imagination. While the performer makes her/his body the scene of violent actions, the spectators will be forced to move the scene into their imagination.

That is to say that the "real presence" of performance is questioned not only by the subjective constructions of the artists and the spectators, but also by the performer's pain. For her/his pain can only gain presence for the spectators in their own imaginations and not in the performance of the action by which the performer hurts her/himself.

Thus, the performance, in a certain respect, turns into a scapegoat ritual. The performer exposes her/his body to risks and injuries against which the spectators aim to protect their bodies; the performer causes her/himself the pains which the spectators seek to avoid. The performer, in this sense, suffers in place of the spectators. She/he saves them from their own physical suffering. The "sacrificial victim" at the torment and death of a martyr, or even at the execution of a repentant Christian up to the eighteenth century, held "a magic power," and the onlookers hoped for "the healing of certain diseases and similar miracles" from the tortured or executed sinner, from "his blood, his limbs, or the rope."[28] While here it was the tortured and violated body of the sinner that seemed to promise and to guarantee the onlookers' own physical integration, in the artists' performance, it is the imagination of the spectators which replaces the magic. Their imagination "saves" them the anxieties of violence and pain directed toward their own body by representing the performer's pain and by attempting to sympathize with it and to sense it themselves.

The aesthetic perception thus initiated, triggered, and provoked by the performance can hardly be described as "disinterested pleasure." On the one hand, the spectators feel shocked and deny what they see; on the other hand, they feel fascinated — fascinated because someone violates her/himself voluntarily, because it is reminiscent of certain taboos such as torture and punishment. They are fascinated as well as shocked because of their own curiosity in a situation where, according to the valid cultural norms, they are supposed to feel disgust or horror. It is this ambiguity in the reception process to which the performance artist Rachel Rosenthal refers: "In performance art, the audience, from its role as sadist, subtly becomes the victim. It is forced to endure the artist's plight empathetically, or examine its own responses of voyeurism and pleasure, or smugness and superiority. . . . In any case, the performer holds the reins. . . . The audience usually 'gives up' before the artist." [29] Here aesthetic perception may be described as a kind of perception which transforms the spectators into involved participants and in this sense into performers themselves by projecting the scene of the body onto the scene of the imagination — an imagination which, however, is tied to the body or is even part of the body (i.e., a physical imagination that causes physical sensations). Therefore, the spectators usually "give up" before the performer; their imaginations have replaced the performer's body with their own and, thus, penetrated into the realm of the incommunicable — to the pain of the other, which now becomes manifest in a physical sensation, a physical impulse, a physical response in the spectators.

As Van Gennep has shown, rituals work in a community in order to secure a safe passage from a given status to a new one at moments of life or social crisis in an individual (such as birth, puberty, marriage, pregnancy, illness, changes in professional positions, death). The performances created by individual artists over the last thirty years alluding to or transforming rituals seek to secure and accelerate the passage of Western culture from the state of a prevailingly material culture to a new performative culture. This passage is also to be understood as a passage from the given order of knowledge, the given sign-concept, as well as semiotic processes, toward a new, undefined order of knowledge. The performances, thus, operate as the signature of a time of transition.

PART IV

Theatre and Theory

AVANT-GARDE AND POSTMODERNISM
Theatre between Cultural Crisis
and Cultural Change

The controversy surrounding postmodernism, which has currently aroused fierce debate in various fields, on different levels, culminates in the persistent question of whether postmodernism has effected a complete break with modernist traditions or whether it has, on the contrary, only radicalized the trends first formulated and pronounced by modernism and extended its conclusions. Both viewpoints are vigorously upheld. This is all the more extraordinary since the ground on which the controversy should be discussed is not yet clearly plotted: Does modernism begin with the *Querelle des anciens et des modernes* or with the Enlightenment? With the industrialization of Western Europe or with Nietzsche? Should one see the historical avant-garde movement as an integral component of modernism (as most European critics seem to do), or should modernism be defined by the exclusion of the avant-garde movement (as many American critics would argue)? In attempting to examine the question of whether the "true" *Epochenschwelle* (threshold of an epoch) is to be termed modern or postmodern, one must first secure agreement on these issues.

The most important arguments so far exchanged in the controversy have been collated in a most informative research report entitled "The Postmodern *Weltanschauung* and Its Relation with Modernism" by Hans Bertens. Rather than repeating those arguments, which in the meantime have become sufficiently well known, I shall take as a starting point those elements which refer to postmodernism in theatre and literature and examine them from a semiotic point of view.

A wealth of argument exists concerning artistic device. Distinctive characteristics of postmodernism have been formulated, the opposites of which are held to be representative of modernism: indeterminacy, fragmentation, montage, collage, intertextuality, hybridization, the carnivalesque (in the sense of M. M. Bakhtin), constructivism, randomness, openness of form, discontinuity, etc. This catalogue, which concentrates on the syntactic level of a work, has yet to be completed.

Most frequently referred to, on the semantic level, are the presentation of possible worlds, the redefinition of the relationship between time and space, and the dissolution of the self and its boundaries. The pragmatic level is conspicuously absent from the argumentation. Here the discussion is concentrated on the shift of the focus away from the work itself and onto the recipient, so that one can only speak, for instance, of a literary object in the strictest sense as the interaction between the reader and the text.

In addition to this, several metasemiotic notions are called upon, such as the shift of the dominant as epistemological question to the dominant as ontological one;[1] from monism to pluralism; from representation to performance; from referentiality to nonreferentiality; or, yet again, the firmly held belief in the self-reflexivity of a work of art and its production. The status of the various arguments and the interconnections between them, however, remain largely unclarified. Must all distinctive characteristics be listed in order to be able to speak of a postmodern work, or would it suffice to specify certain chosen ones and, if so, which? Do they create a structure with one another, within which each fulfills a function, or does one simply enumerate them *ad libitum*? How can one relate the distinctive characteristics found on the different semiotic levels to one another? Does it make sense simply to list specific artistic devices without having analyzed and differentiated their relation to the semantic, pragmatic, or metasemiotic levels?

Apart from these more systematic questions, others arise which stem from the actual methods of procedure. Thus, as verification that it is indeed these distinctive characteristics that differentiate postmodern works from the modern, a literary corpus is created which, despite all its differences in detail, is nonetheless homogeneous in two significant aspects: the examples are predominantly drawn from the narrative genres (short stories and novels) and almost entirely exclude texts from the historical avant-garde. Hence, I should like to elucidate the systematic problem of the distinction between postmodernism and modernism by recourse to a body of literature which principally consists of texts of dramatic literature and which includes those of the historical avant-garde movement as it has recently been foregrounded by Peter Bürger (1983). Texts such as *Sphinx and Strohmann* (Oskar Kokoschka), *Les mamelles de Tirésias* (Guillaume Apollinaire), *Le coeur à gaz* (Tristan Tzara), *Methusalem* (Yvan Goll), *Le serin muet* (G. Ribemont Dessaignes), and Hugo Ball's scripts for the dada soirées are therefore referred to here as examples of modernist literature. Since dada existed at that time, it must also be taken into account. The same, of course, applies to dramas such as *Mysterium buffo* (Vladimir Mayakovsky) or *Pobeda nad solncem* (*Victory over The Sun*, A. Kruchenykh), as well as to futurist texts and constructivist performances.

As a starting point, I have selected a problem which has arisen on the semantic level through which the relation to the syntactic, pragmatic, and metasemiotic levels can easily be established: the area to be examined is the presentation of the individual, the self, in modern and postmodern drama.

By way of introduction, I shall cite a somewhat lengthy passage from Bertens' *Forschungsbericht*:

> For Gerald Graff the celebratory mode of Postmodernism is characterised by a "dissolution of ego boundaries"; for Daniel Bell "the various kinds of postmodernism . . . are simply the decomposition of the self in an effort to erase the individual ego," and Ihab Hassan notes that "the Self . . . is really an empty 'place' where many selves come to mingle and depart." For Hoffmann this movement in the direction of a less defined, less stable identity is even a shift of epistemic proportions: "The perceivable signs of a tendency toward the disappearance of a subjectivity in modern literature become a fact in postmodern works. Thus a radical gap between modern and postmodern literature is reflected in the opposition of two *epistemes*: subjectivity versus loss of subjectivity." The postmodern self is no longer a coherent entity that has the power to impose (admittedly subjective) order upon its environment. It has become decentred, to repeat Holland's phrase. The radical indeterminacy of postmodernism has entered the individual ego and has drastically affected its former (supposed) stability. Identity has become as uncertain as everything else.[2]

Aside from the fact that the boundaries of the individual ego were dissolved as early as August Strindberg's first dream play, *Till Damascus* (1889), it is true to say that modern drama in the early twentieth century was constituted out of the negation of the individual, as the theory here proposes. Pirandello's *Six Characters in Search of an Author*, written and premiered in 1921, for example, can immediately be described as the "*Spiel von der Unmöglichkeit des Dramas*,"[3] since here the possibility of drama is called into question by dramatic characters who no longer have a definable individual ego at their disposal. The "Father" summarizes the problem in the following way:

> My drama lies entirely in this one thing. . . . In my being conscious that each one of us believes himself to be a single person. But it's not true. . . . Each one of us is many persons. . . . Many persons . . . according to all the possibilities of being that there are within us. . . . With some people we are

one person. . . . With others we are somebody quite different. . . . And all the time we are under the illusion of always being one and the same person for everybody. . . . We believe that we are always this one person in whatever it is we may be doing. But it's not true! It's not true![4]

Here we are presented with self-reflection as well as the shift of the dominant from an epistemological question to an ontological one: Since "being" (*Sein*) cannot be known or defined by the individual, the question arises: how can it then be represented in drama?

Pirandello took recourse to the Baroque topos of role-play and the immanent problem of the *Sein-Schein* which he recast in special ways: each individual not only acts but also *is* the different roles without the possibility of being defined either by the set role itself or even as a persona beyond the role. Being (*Sein*) is the "life that ceaselessly flows and changes" and thus one which knows no boundaries. Appearances (*Schein*) are the different roles which, in each case, function as the "form" which seeks to "detain it, keep it unchanging."

The literary devices which Pirandello employs to represent dramatically his concept of the self are, among others, intertextuality, irony, and hybridization. Similarly, another so-called classic author of modern drama, Eugene O'Neill, also denies a bound individual ego. In *Mourning Becomes Electra* (1929–1931), the characters are introduced almost as replicas of replicas of replicas in a never-ending stream back to the source. Individuality no longer exists. This characteristic is true on the emotional level and in the physical development of the action.

All the men in the Mannon family, Abe, David, Ezra, Adam, and Orin, share the same facial characteristics: "an aquiline nose, heavy eyebrows, swarthy complexion, thick, straight black hair, light hazel eyes."[5] The women who marry into the family, such as Marie Brantome and Christine, or those from the family itself, like Lavinia, also share a number of similar physical features: they all have "thick, curly hair, partly a copper-brown, partly a gold, each shade distinct and yet blending with the other," "deep-set eyes of a dark violet-blue," "black eyebrows, which meet in a pronounced straight line above her strong nose," "a heavy chin," and "a large sensual mouth."[6] Furthermore, the male and female members of the Mannon family seem so intertwined that their faces at rest give the impression of a "life-like mask." To these physical similarities, O'Neill ties emotional ones: all the members of the family are driven by incestuous desire. The men all suffer from an Oedipus complex, the women from an Electra or Jocasta complex.

O'Neill uses this system of emotional and physical similarities and equivalents to divest the characters of any individuality: each duplicates the other, who is himself or herself a duplication of yet another. There is no "original" and therefore no individual ego. Each repeats one who is repeating another who is repeating another and so on *ad infinitum*. In fact, they appear not as individual selves and, moreover, seem to be substitutes for someone who is absent — as Orin discovered in the war: "Before I'd gotten back I had to kill another in the same way. It was like murdering the same man twice. I had a queer feeling that war meant murdering the same man over and over, and that in the end I would discover the man was myself! Their faces keep coming back in dreams — and they change to Father's face — or to mine."[7] Equally, the characters act as if they are driven by an "other" or are recalling an action initiated by an "other" in the past. In this way, an earlier action is exactly recalled by others — for example, the small gesture used by Ezra, Adam, and Orin on many occasions to try to smooth Marie, Christine, and Lavinia's hair; alternatively, a whole action sequence is repeated, as in the case of Orin and Lavinia, in the third part of the trilogy.[8] In their nature, their desires, their words and deeds, the characters recall others who came before them; they are neither identical to each other nor to others — they have no individual self, no definable identity. The self is indeed an "empty place where many selves come to mingle and depart." The most important literary device that O'Neill uses is consistently setting the text in its relation to the intertext (Aeschylus' *Oresteia*) and thereby building up a meaning-generating system of differences.

The outstanding feature in both Pirandello and O'Neill of presenting the self as an "empty place" in which widely divergent "roles" (Pirandello) or "others" (O'Neill) can meet is further radicalized in the dada movement. While Pirandello and O'Neill employ, in part, thoroughly "traditional" literary devices, principally in terms of language and dramaturgy, the dadaists turn the play into an antiplay, the theatre performance into an antitheatre; all the traditional devices are parodied, negated, thrown overboard.

In Tristan Tzara's *Le coeur à gaz*, which premiered in 1921 in the "Salon Dada" in Paris, the dramatic characters are Oreille, Bouche, Oeil, Cou, Nez, Sourcil, a dancer, and other characters, who *"entrent et sortent ad libitum."*

While Strindberg questioned the idea of emotional wholeness in a character by introducing the *Doppelgänger* and O'Neill by stressing physical similarities, Tzara fragments the human body and defines these isolated parts as the characters of the action. The self becomes literally the "empty space" between the characters of the action. The dialogue between them proceeds as follows:

> *Oreille:* C'est le printemps, le printemps.
> *Nez:* Je vous dis qu'il a 2 mètres.
> *Cou:* Je vous dis qu'il a 3 mètres.

> *Nez:* Je vous dis qu'il a 4 mètres.
> *Cou:* Je vous dis qu'il a 5 mètres.
> *Nez:* Je vous dis qu'il a 6 mètres.[9]

and so on up to 16 meters.

Alternatively, they confront each other with maxims and proverbs which follow senselessly on from each other:

> *Oreille:* Les hommes simples se manifestent par un maison, les hommes importants par un monument.[10]
> *Bouche:* Non je veux rien dire. J'ai mis depuis longtemps dans la boîte à chapeau ce que j'avais à dire.[11]
> *Sourcil:* "Où," "combien," "pourquoi" sont des monuments. Par exemple la Justice. Quel beau fonctionnement régulier, presque un tic nerveux ou une religion.[12]
> *Cou:* Mandarine et blanc d'Espagne, je me tue Madeleine, Madeleine.[13]

The literary devices employed here can be described as indeterminacy, disconnectedness, randomness, fragmentation, montage, the carnivalesque, hybridization; in short, the whole arsenal of distinctive characteristics belonging to postmodernism finds its realization on a syntactic level.

Similar findings can be confirmed on the metasemiotic level. Indeed, here it is more a question of approaching pluralism — to the point where "anything goes." The trend toward loss of referentiality is also clearly to be seen. In Tzara's *La première aventure céleste de Mr. Antipyrine* we find, for example, the following dialogue:

> *La femme enceinte:* Toundi-a-voua Soco Bgai Affahou
> *Mr. Bleubleu:* Farafamgama Soco Bgai Affahou
> *Pipi:* amerture sans église allons charbon chameau synthétisé amerture sur l'église isisise les rideaux dodododo
> *Mr. Antipyrine:* Soco Bgai Affahou zoumbai, zoumbai, zoumbai, zoum.
> *Mr. Cricri:* il y a pas d'humanité—il y a les réverbères et les chiens dzinaha dzin aha bobobo Tyaco oahiii hii hii héboum iéha iého
> *Mr. Bleubleu:* incontestablement.[14]

Here it is clear that the trend toward performance outweighs that toward representation. This, of course, is also the case, to a certain extent, of the dada soirées and activities, which took place rather like happenings. Raoul Hausmann, among others, has recorded:

> On Sunday, 17 November 1918, Baader attended the morning service at the cathedral in Berlin. As the court chaplain, Dryander, was about to begin the sermon, Baader called out in a loud voice, "Wait! What does Jesus Christ mean to you? Nothing . . ." He wasn't able to go on, there was a terrible tumult, Baader was arrested and a charge of blasphemy held against him. Nothing could be done with him in the end, however, since he was carrying the whole text of his outburst with him in which it continues, "for they do not heed his commands etc." Naturally, all the papers were full of this incident.[15]

In conjunction with the performative character of the dada productions and soirées, the concept of the spectator as an integral component of the performance was deliberately planned. The dada chronicler Walter Mehring, who had himself participated in the sixth performance of the Dada soirée in November 1919, describes how the spectator uprising stage-managed by the dadaists was provoked. Mehring was reciting Goethe's poem *Wanderers Sturmlied* (The Wanderer's Storm Song) in dadaist style

> up to a prearranged cue when the whole Dada tribe burst onto the podium and bellowed "Stop!" "Stop that rubbish!" they roared, and "Walt" snarled Böff, his monocle jammed in place, "Walt, you're not going to throw these — ah — pearls to such swine?" and "Stop!" yelled the Dada chorus simultaneously: "Get out! Ladies and Gentlemen, you are kindly requested to go to hell . . . if you really want amusement, go to the whorehouse, or (said Huelsenbeck) to a Monas Thann lecture!" and they stepped down from the podium arm in arm in a chain to face the enraged stalls.[16]

From here to Peter Handke's *Publikumsbeschimpfung* (Offending the Audience) no longer seems such a giant step.

The literary devices which constitute the syntactic level and the trends realized on the semantic and metasemiotic levels stand in clear relation to the pragmatic level which decides and fixes their respective functions: the intended effect on the reader/spectator is the underlying structural moment. All the dadaist activities were directed at the spectator. Since the founding of the Cabaret Voltaire in 1916 in Zurich, they had utilized newspaper advertisements and leaflets as an important instrument of self-publicity, to draw public attention. While at first they only aimed to "épater le bourgeois," these ventures occurred increasingly in the form of an organized assault on the audience, a "strategy of revolt." The devices shown above were directly aimed at challenging and reexamining the purely passive attitude of expectation and customary practices of spectator reception. In this way, they attempted to dissolve the discrepancies between art and society for the duration of the performance. Theatrical conventions and habits of spectator perception were deliberately abused, indeed utterly destroyed. In the end, it was left to the spectator to decide how to react to the dadaist activities and happenings, how to arrive at a new understanding of "art," and how to create a different kind of receptive attitude: the dadaist performance "work" only existed in the (mostly aggressive) reaction of the audience; it was the product and result of a process of interaction between the agents of the action and the audience.

The dadaist devices operated not only in the pragmatic dimension, but also in the semantic dimension. These devices enabled the presentation of the concept of the world, which they saw as disordered, as chaos.

Reality seemed incalculable and, thus, nonrepresentable. Even if one could admit a fundamental ordering principle to reality, this was in essence beyond human perception. Life was interpreted as a "vital chaos," and the individual as a clown hopelessly trapped within it. Only a work which is random, incoherent, hybrid, indeterminate, and nonsequential can function as an adequate reaction to, or possible way of representing, the condition of the world. The dadaist activities and the techniques and devices employed to achieve them should thus be seen in relation to the so-called culture crisis (*Kulturkrise*) which shook the middle classes in Europe at the beginning of this century. While the majority of the audience which participated in the dada soirées, as members of the educated middle class, still firmly held to the idea of the world and works of art as ordered wholes, the dadaists attempted to "decondition" them by leading them to specific reactions through their actions and thus to force new attitudes on them.

The fundamental perception of a far-reaching crisis in Western culture is also characteristic of the "classic" authors of modern theatre such as Pirandello or O'Neill as well as for the members of the avant-garde theatre before and after World War I such as Craig, Meyerhold, or Artaud: "We are living in probably the most unique era in the history of the world, where the world is passed through a sieve and watches its old values break down. The calcified life is dissolving at its roots. And this, on the moral or social plane, is translated into a monstrous unchaining of appetite, a liberation of instincts most basic, a crackling of burning lives which exposes them prematurely to the flame."[17]

The argumentation so far has led to three general conclusions:

1. The factors that can be called the distinctive characteristics of a postmodern literary work can partly (e.g., Pirandello, O'Neill) or wholly (dada) be found in works dating from the early twentieth century.

2. These factors, which can be related to very different semiotic dimensions, are not separate from each other, but rather create such relations with one another that a structure is formed.

3. This structure is, in its turn, related to the circumstances of the culture crisis, and most particularly to the immanent consciousness of standing at the "threshold of an era" which either will lead to the birth of a new humankind and a new world or will lead to catastrophe.

If, therefore, postmodernism cannot be sufficiently distinguished from modernism by the criteria evidence/absence of certain distinctive characteristics, other criteria must be sought. The conclusions of our examination open at least two possibilities. Postmodernism can be differentiated from modernism on the basis of (1) the relations formed by the distinctive characteristics situated on the different semiotic levels (i.e., on the basis of the structure they form), and (2) the historical, social *Zeitgeist* of the age to which the structure of relations corresponds.

Beckett's later dramas (*Play, Not I, That Time, Ends and Odds*), Heiner Müller's plays after *Germania Tod in Berlin* (Germania–Death in Berlin), and the dramas of Peter Handke and Thomas Bernhard can actually be identified through the very distinctive characteristic (which describes postmodern literature in general) that they are open to the reader/spectator: the disintegration of the dramatic characters on a semantic level, for example, or incoherence, randomness, fragmentation, hybridization on the syntactic level, are leveled at the reader/spectator, who must decide how to deal with the components offered. This can be observed in a very acute way in Robert Wilson's postmodern theatre. In Wilson's mammoth project *CIVIL warS* (1983–1984), separate parts of which were produced and premiered in Rotterdam, Marseilles, Lyon, Nice, Rome, Cologne, Tokyo, and Milwaukee, different ways of treating language were realized and performed. The texts of the characters' speech, for example, might consist of ready-made phrases from everyday life, ("are you all right," "just leave me alone," "oh come on"), phrases which are, on the one hand, presented as set scenes in the process of which the text is disconnected and there is no meaning in the dialogue or, on the other hand, are broken into separate words and phonetic sounds ("are," "you," "all right," "a") and spoken alternately by the dramatic characters many times over.[18]

Here the manifest refusal to employ language in such a way that the sequence of sounds, words, or sentences yields a cohesive dialogue that will make sense is based on yet another device. In act 4 of *CIVIL warS*, for which Heiner Müller was responsible, literary ready-mades, quotes from world literature, were compiled (for example, from *Hamlet, Phèdre, Empedocles*). Single fragments of text were broken away from their original contexts and placed nonsequentially next to one another. In fact, the isolated fragments do yield meaning, not, however, the sequence as a whole.

Another device used to the same effect is employing the text spoken by the actor as an element of a collage of recorded sound which is as much composed of different but simultaneously spoken texts as it is of shreds of music, sound, and speech. In this context, even the single words and speeches are no longer understandable but, instead, are solely identifiable as elements of language. To a large extent they are reduced to the distinctive quality of a sound perceived as noise. In this way, the linguistic sign is more or less wholly deconstructed as sign. At first this seems to be a comparable kind of device to that which we have identified in the constructivist, dadaist, and futurist theatre experiments: language is almost wholly desemanticized and no longer functions as a sign within the context of the performance. However, while this desemanticization of language creates a concentration on the quality of sound, in Wilson's theatre, language is allowed to decay into noise, which because of its multiple and simultaneously transmitted phonetic phenomena can no longer be perceived as a meaningful sign. The desemanticization of language which all three devices considered here effect — in different ways — is even further advanced through the severing of the spoken language, on the one hand, from a "character" and, on the other, from the actor's body. The sounds, words, or texts are spoken by the actor at the same time as they are transmitted on tape through a loudspeaker. In this way, they are disengaged from the body of the actor — the language creates its own acoustic space. In so doing, however, language becomes incapable of functioning as the sign of character: speech is deconstructed not only as part of a meaningful dialogue but also as the sign of character. Speech is presented as phonetic phenomena and fragments of text which can be linked neither to one another nor to the body of the actor in a meaning-generating semiosis.

Alongside the desemanticization of language, Wilson presents the desemioticization of the body. Here again he has developed different devices to achieve it. The most important, and one which is especially typical of Wilson, is that he directs the actors to move so slowly that the impression of a slow-motion picture is created. Through this extremely slow motion the spectator's attention is drawn to the process of the movement itself. The spectator perceives gesture as movement, that is, as part of a moving body, and there is no possibility of perceiving it or interpreting it as the sign for something else (for example, the expression of a role type). The slow-motion technique puts the actor's body on the same level as the objects presented on-stage. The actor's body no longer represents or means anything and finds satisfaction in being presented next to its co-objects. Another device shows the particular use of costume and makeup. Inasmuch as the actor's body can suggest a specific character — as in the German part of CIVIL warS, for example, the character Frederick the Great; his mother, Sophie Dorothée; an angel; a soldier; the tinman; and Lincoln or in the American part Admiral Perry or a Japanese basket-peddler — it is employed as a quotation, so that characters are barely suggested and do not even begin to be built up dramatically.

The separate elements presented by the actor's body such as costume, makeup, gesture, movement in space, and voice do not relate to one another and thus cannot be integrated by the spectator to provide internal relations that will produce any meaning. On the contrary, they create the potential of many random associative external relations which are almost wholly dependent on the spectator's own universe of discourse. A further device consists of simply employing the actor's body on the stage as bearer of an object being presented or prop (for example, the bird in Knee Plays). Although Wilson has adopted this device from the Japanese theatre, where the stagehands dressed in black hold ready the necessary props for the actor or a glass of water, should the actor grow hoarse, or stand ready to light the actor's face when the mime is particularly important, Wilson, in contrast, uses this device to show the unity between the object presented by the actor and the actor's body, thus demonstratively underlining its nonmeaning. The actor's body becomes part of a dreamlike image floating by, in that it contains no semantic cohesion.

The single image can now be received on two levels: (1) on the syntagmatic level of the process onstage which, through the lack of internal relations, is received as an incoherent sequence of ready-made linguistic and bodily quotations, or meaningless sounds and movements, or at best as a chain of information transmitted in bits, in whose sequence it is utterly impossible to discover a coherent meaning, or (2) on the paradigmatic level of the subjectively triggered chain of associations which integrates the single elements into subjectively asserted and structured areas of meaning and thus allows them to change back into subjective carriers of meaning.

The first level of reception can be linked to the flood of communication brought about by mass media in that it allows the words to decay into noise and breaks up the succession of events into incoherent pictures so that they can only be perceived as information in bits whose sequence is meaningless.

The second level of reception, on the contrary, opens the spectators to the possibility of perceiving the process on the stage as they would their own dream images — as a wonderful, unique, at first foreign world, the single elements of which seem wholly familiar without, however, admitting the possibility of being tied to one another into a superior unit of meaning. If the spectators admit the idea of the concreteness of this world, without needing to bring instant interpretation to it, the associative connections which they can now make release them to new experiences and unlock new possibilities of meaning. This level of reception thus initiates new kinds of perception and constitution of meaning and is diametrically opposed to the "consumer habit" promoted by the mass media. Similar to the dada soirées, the work can only be constituted in the interaction between text and spectator.

In the case of dada, such interaction was aimed at a predominantly educated middle-class spectator who was used to tracing specific, if not eternal then at least fixed, meanings in works of art, with the intention of upsetting this expectation and attitude of reception: the spectators must be shocked, attacked, and provoked into aggression to get them to *engage* in any activity at all.

Interestingly, the dada performances did not even achieve the desired effect in an audience composed mostly of workers who did not bring such expectations with them, and it was for this reason that experiments of this kind were discontinued. The audience at which postmodern drama/theatre aims has, on the contrary, long since departed from the expectations and attitudes of reception characterized and fixed by the educated middle classes. It is — as a metropolitan audience — not easily shocked or made aggressive. Consequently the interaction between text and spectator is realized quite differently: either the spectators overlay the single elements and their incoherent sequence with meanings which stem from their own historical, social, and private, autobiographical experience (they know, in this case, that meanings have no fixed, intersubjectively valid values to be conveyed, but that they rather consist of the products of their own imaginative and associative activity) or they refuse to constitute any meanings at all and perceive the bodies, objects, words, and lighting in their concreteness as bodies, words, and lighting without interpreting them as signs of something else, so that, free of the need to bring any meaning to them, they find satisfaction in the very concreteness of the items presented.

On the basis of these changed attitudes of spectator reception (as opposed to those brought about by dada) the distinctive characteristics found on the syntactic, semantic, and metasemiotic levels also take on another function.

Fragmentation and collage should not, for example, shock the spectators into perceiving the world which they assume is interconnected and causal as, in fact, ruled by incoherence and randomness. Rather, the device should encourage spectators already oriented toward the principle of randomness to apply their own meanings to the randomly presented single object, without looking to possible links to the meaning they bring it, or to perceive it simply as an object in its concrete fact.

The dissolution of the boundaries of the self on the semantic level should not shock the spectators, who believe they have an individual personality, by demonstrating the fact that such a supposition of the individual personality is a middle-class fiction, but should rather expose the spectator who is already conscious of the instability of the self to different possibilities of its projection.

The shift of the dominant as epistemological question to the dominant as ontological one does not pursue the goal of sensitizing an essentially rational spectator to the view of the imbalance between the self and the consciousness, but rather confirms to the spectator who has already begun to question rational consciousness and rather more concretely directed perceptions.

Thus, although we can observe the same distinctive characteristics in modern theatre of the early twentieth century as we find in the postmodern, and although in both instances the distinctive characteristics on the syntactic, semantic, and metasemiotic levels only fulfill their function in their relation to the pragmatic dimension, the phenomena we are dealing with are clearly dissimilar. The *Zeitgeist* to which they belong is fundamentally different.

Whether these differences, however, constitute another *Epochenschwelle* in a transition toward postmodernism has yet to be answered. Personally, I believe that the underlying changes on which postmodernism was built had already been fully executed by the end of the nineteenth and beginning of the twentieth centuries: the new perception of time and space, the dissolution of the boundaries of the individual ego, the relativism of rational, logic, causal thinking, which, in their entirety as *conditio sine qua non*, are all evident in postmodern writing and suggest the point of transition into the twentieth century and with it the beginning of modernism.

The essential difference between modernism/avant-gardism and postmodernism seems to lie far more in the fact that the postulate formulated at the beginning of the century as an expression and consequence of a far-reaching culture crisis has long been a reality in the eighties: since the sixties cultural change has occurred *de facto*. Thus, I would, on the one hand, suggest dating the *Epochenschwelle* at the outbreak of the culture crisis in art and, on the other hand, plead not to equalize the vast differences between modernism and postmodernism with reference to their very real similarities. Instead, considering that cultural change has long since been effected, it will prove illuminating to define and judge these differences through a kind of functional examination that has been neglected heretofore.

WALTER BENJAMIN'S "ALLEGORY"

BENJAMIN'S CONCEPT OF "ALLEGORY": A PARADIGM OF AVANT-GARDE ART?

It has often been stated that Walter Benjamin developed his theory of allegory in *The Origin of German Tragic Drama* from his experience of modern art. He himself pointed to this connection in his study of the baroque as well as in conversations with Asja Lacis. Accordingly, there have been several attempts to apply Benjamin's concept of allegory to modern art in order to describe and analyze the particular process of its production, on the one side, and its reception, on the other.[1] Unfortunately, these attempts have to cope with various deficiencies that render it difficult to approve of them. For they either draw ill-defined parallels and similarities between Benjamin's "allegory" and certain features of modern art (for instance, the fragmentary character of both) or try to "translate" Benjamin's hermetic language into one that is understandable and, fitting his concept of allegory into their own theory of modern art, oversimplify Benjamin's theory and thus deprive themselves of those aspects of his theory that seem to be particularly important and promising for this kind of approach.

I am going to add my own, possibly equally futile, attempt to those of the past by reformulating Benjamin's theory of allegory in semiotic terms.

BENJAMIN'S THEORY OF LANGUAGE

Within the framework of Benjamin's theory the concept of allegory is directly opposed to that of the "symbol." And this opposition between symbol and allegory is closely related to the opposition between "name" and "sign."

Whereas the opposition between symbol and allegory is part of Benjamin's theory of art, the opposition between "name" and "sign" forms the basis of his theory of language. While the name points to language as "manifestation," the sign marks language as "instrument."

The Word as "Name"

Benjamin explains this opposition within the framework of an eschatological conception. In the beginning there were only names: "Adam's action of naming things is so far removed from play or caprice that it actually confirms the state of paradise as a state in which there is as yet no need to struggle with the communicative significance of words. Ideas are displayed, without intention, in the act of naming."[2]

This means that the meaning of the thing as the idea that God had in mind creating it and the meaning of the word in the Adamic language coincide in the name. Knowing the name of a thing thus means knowing its idea. For "the idea is something linguistic, it is the element of the symbolic in the essence of any word."[3] The name thus symbolizes the meaning of the thing, the idea.

Consequently, this unity of thing-meaning and word-meaning in the name is given beyond the usage of the word by any individual. Neither the intention of the individual nor his/her subjectivity can reach the name. For it has a particular state of being, "which, in its lack of intentionality, resembles the simple existence of things, but which is superior in its permanence."[4]

The Word as "Sign"

Because of this identity of thing-meaning and word-meaning in the name the realm of names marks the state of paradise. In the historical world after the Fall this identity is lost and gone. Here the meaning of the thing and the meaning of the word fall apart. The objectivity of names which God has given to things and which, accordingly, objectively express the meaning of things, their idea, is lost and replaced by the subjectivity of people who attribute meanings to things arbitrarily. The objectivity of names can only be renewed by philosophical contemplation: "It is the task of the philosopher to restore . . . the primacy of the symbolic character of the word in which the idea is given self consciousness, and that is the opposite of all outwardly directed communication."[5]

"After the Fall" means that after the loss of names things remain mute, for they have become unable to express their own meaning. On the other hand, language has forfeited its symbolic dimension: the loss of nonintentionality in naming causes language to become an instrument of communication. In other words, the communicative function of language is a result of the loss of identity between word-meaning and thing-meaning. The word ceases to be a name and, instead, changes into a sign: "The sign never refers to the thing itself . . . it never refers necessarily to the signified."[6]

This means that words can only be names in Adamic or divine language. The words of historical languages, however, are not necessarily related to the things they denote. Thus, their meaning is created by a subjectively established, arbitrary relation between word and thing.

To constitute meaning in the historic languages, thus, requires three factors: words; things; and a person who relates word and thing to each other.

Consequently, in the historic languages, meaning is constituted when an interpreter relates a sign vehicle to an object, that is in the three-dimensionality of the pragmatic, syntactic, and semantic functions. Hence it follows that meaning is always a semiotic category in the historical languages.

The Redemption of "Language as Such"

Since the semiotic character of historic languages is a consequence of the Fall, language tends to transcend it in the long run of eschatology. Benjamin explains this tendency in "The Task of the Translator." Here he points out that any translation proceeds from difference between languages and aims at its annulment.

Languages differ as regards their mode of intention: "The words *Brot* and *pain* 'intend' the same object, but the modes of this intention are not the same. It is owing to these modes that the word *Brot* means something different to a German than the word *pain* to a Frenchman, that for them these words are not interchangeable, that in the end they strive to exclude each other."[7]

Therefore, it is the task of the translator to complete the mode of intention in his or her language by the mode of intention in the foreign language from which he/she is translating. The completion of all possible modes of intention — as realized in different historical languages — should make the "intended" and the "mode of intention" coincide: the meanings of the things reappear in the meanings of the words; "language as such" would be "redeemed." In this language, words would cease being "signs" and would be changed into "names" again. Thus, the realm of names marks the beginning and the end of eschatology, the state of paradise, as well as the state of messianic redemption, whereas the realm of signs is stigmatized by the Fall.

While the meanings of "language as such" objectively express the idea of the thing as given by God, the meanings of the historic languages are always subjectively determined. They are produced by means of a subjectively established relation between a given thing and a given word. In this way, they revert back to their origin in the Fall, which tore apart the need for unity of word and thing in the name. At the same time, however, they also point forward to the future "language as such," for in any meaning-constituting act — however arbitrary and temporary it might be — some kind of relation between word and thing is always restored.[8]

Bearing in mind the fundamentals of Benjamin's theory of language as represented by the opposition between "name" and "sign," we can now approach his theory of art, which is based on the opposition between symbol and allegory.

Benjamin himself has also pointed to the connection between his theory of language and his theory of art. In "On Language as Such and on the Language of Man" (1916) he writes:

> There is a language of sculpture, of painting, of poetry. Just as the language of poetry is partly, if not solely, founded on the name language of man, it is very conceivable that the language of sculpture or painting is founded on certain kinds of thing languages, that in them we find a translation of the language of things into an infinitely higher language, which may still be of the same sphere. . . . For an understanding of artistic forms it is of value to grasp them all as languages. . . . It is certain, that the language of art can be understood only in the deepest relationship to the doctrine of signs. Without the latter any linguistic philosophy remains entirely fragmentary, because the relationship between language and sign (of which that between human language and writing offers only a very particular example) is original and fundamental.[9]

In "The Origin of Modern German Drama" this relationship is explained as the relationship between symbol and allegory.

The Work of Art as "Symbol"

In order to define the notion of the symbol, Benjamin proceeds from Joseph Goerres' theory of symbols, "which emphasizes the organic, mountain and plant-like, quality of the symbol," and from "Georg Friedrich Creuzer's emphasis of its momentary qualities."[10] Benjamin states: "The measure of time for the experience of the symbol is the mystical instant in which the symbol assumes the meaning into its hidden and, if one might say so, wooded interior."[11] Thus, it is a characteristic of the symbol that it attempts to deny the presence and participation of any meaning-constituting subject because it has taken its meaning into its "interior." That is to say, it has intrinsic meaning.

Even if — as is usually the case — the symbol is created by a subject, here subjectivity tends to vanish, to extinguish itself. Thus, the artistic symbol is described in a way that seems to withdraw it from the meaning-constituting subjectivity of the producer as well as of the interpreter. The symbol created by a subject should imply and express its meaning just as the things created by God imply and express their own meaning. Any symbol thus symbolizes the original identity of thing-meaning and word-meaning in the name: the artistic symbol symbolizes the linguistic symbol, the name.

This is why its meaning appears as neither arbitrary nor produced by a subjectively established relationship between the symbol and the symbolized, but rather as the result of a necessary, objectively given, connection.

Although it originates in the three-dimensionality of sign producer, sign vehicle, and object, the symbol denies its semiotic character and aims at a two-dimensional union of word and thing, excluding and renouncing the participation of any subjectivity.

In this way, the symbol anticipates the future of messianic redemption. As the symbol hides its meaning in its interior, revealing it only in the "mystical instant," nature unveils its secret meaning in the "instant" of redemption. Thus, the symbol implies the end of eschatology because in it "destruction is idealised and the transfigured face of nature is fleetingly revealed in the light of redemption." [12]

In sum, we can characterize the artistic symbol as a particular process of meaning-constitution that tends to annul semioticity in language, that is, to reduce three-dimensionality to two-dimensionality, by eliminating the pragmatic dimension of subjectivity.

The Work of Art as "Allegory"

In opposition to the symbol described above, Benjamin defines allegory "as the earliest history of signifying." [13] Consequently, allegory intends meaning as it is constituted in the historical world. Thus, it proceeds from the sundering of nature and language, from the muteness of nature and, following from this muteness, the human need to attribute meaning to it over and over again. In other words, allegorical meaning is produced as the result of a subjectively established relationship between a thing used as a sign and another thing. Thus, allegory exposes and intensifies a principle which underlies meaning in the historical world: the principle of subjectivity.

Subjectivity in Allegorization

In historical languages, this principle is usually not at once obvious; the long tradition of these languages makes us forget that the connections between words and things are not necessary, but arbitrary. To the common user of a language they seem to be given objectively. It is the comparison between languages that makes the arbitrariness evident: the fact of different signs, meant to denote the same thing, points back to subjectivity as their origin.

Benjamin describes allegory as a process of meaning-constitution which expressly refers to this arbitrariness, to the participation of subjectivity: "Any person, any object, any relationship can mean absolutely anything else." [14] For, in the historical world, things have ceased to have a meaning as such, a meaning of their own. Thus, any given object may be related to any other given object in a signifying relation such that some kind of meaning would be produced. Thus, the allegory symbolizes the linguistic sign.

Historicity in Allegorization

Although allegory reveals subjectivity as the fundamental principle of meaning-constitution in the historic world, it also expressly refers to the historicity of the world. For in it

> the observer is confronted with the *facies hippocratica* of history as petrified, primordial landscape. Everything about history that, from the very beginning, has been untimely, sorrowful, unsuccessful, is expressed in a face — or rather in a death's head . . . this is the form in which man's subjection to nature is most obvious and it significantly gives rise not only to the enigmatic question of the nature of human existence as such, but also of the biographical historicity of the individual. [15]

The movement of history is fixed in allegory; historicity appears as a form. Accordingly, allegory only knows history as history of decline, that is, as a movement directed toward the past, not toward the future:

> This is the heart of the allegorical way of seeing, of the baroque, secular explanation of history as the Passion of the world; its importance resides solely in the stations of its decline. The greater the significance, the greater the subjection to death, because death digs most deeply the jagged line of demarcation between physical nature and significance. But if nature has always been subject to the power of death, it is also true that it has always been allegorical. Significance and death both come to fruition in historical development, just as they are closely linked as seeds in the creature's graceless state of sin. [16]

Thus, allegory is based on the two principles of subjectivity and historicity that imply each other, because they are both understood and explained as resulting from the Fall. Accordingly, they are both related to evil: subjectivity is described as the "absolute, that is to say godless spirituality,"[17] and historicity is described as manifested in transitoriness and decline.

Allegorization as Fragmentation

On the other hand, subjectivity and historicity are pragmatic categories. If they are thought to underlie allegory as the fundamental principles determining the constitution of its meaning, the inevitable consequence seems to be ambiguity. For the things used by the allegorist have no meaning of their own. They are, as such, insignificant. Any meaning that may be attributed to them follows from a subjectively established connection invented by the allegorist. "If the object becomes allegorical under the gaze of melancholy, . . . then it is exposed to the allegorist, it is unconditionally in his power. That is to say it is now quite incapable of emanating any meaning or significance of its own; such significance as it has, it acquires from the allegorist. He places it within and stands behind it. . . . In his hands, the object becomes something different."[18]

Thus, the approach of the allegorist makes the things insignificant and significant at the same time. They are insignificant because the intention of the allegorist's subjectivity does not allow the things to reveal their own meaning given to them by God, and they are significant because, by means of this very act, the allegorist provides them with a new meaning. Of course, in a way, this might be understood as an act of violence directed toward things. But, ultimately, such an act leaves things as they are — it does not actually change them. Moreover,

> with this possibility a destructive, but just verdict is passed on the profane world: it is characterised as a world in which the detail is of no great importance. But it will be unmistakably apparent . . . that all of the things which are used to signify derive, from the very fact of their pointing to something else, a power which makes them appear no longer commensurable with profane things, which raises them onto a higher plane, and which can, indeed, sanctify them. Considered in allegorical terms, then, the profane world is both, elevated and devalued.[19]

By turning the things, the originally signified, into the signifiers, the *signifié* into the *signifiant*, the allegorist creates the particular conditions under which the things will be able to become a *signifié*, a signified in the historical world again. For it is now possible that the things which have become signifiers point to each other as to their signified in a theoretically infinite process.[20]

Since "in the field of allegorical intuition the image is a fragment, a rune," allegory causes "the false appearance of totality [to be] extinguished."[21] Thus, after all, it is allegory that liberates the thing from its imprisonment within a functional context, in which it has a meaning only as part of a whole, as an element of the context, but not in itself. The allegorist breaks the thing out of its context and places it, in turn, in several different new contexts. It is the allegorist's decontextualization and various arbitrary contextualizations which indicate the fact that the meaning a particular context ascribes to the thing — as is the case in any "false totality" — is not its original, its innate meaning, but an arbitrary one. Thus, decontextualization not only causes a desemantization but is also to be understood as the only possible process which highlights the fact that the things had a meaning of their own before being included in any context and that they were once significant as such, not only as structural elements of a context.

In this way, allegory turns back to a far past, the state of paradise and the Fall. Allegorical constitution of meaning can therefore be described as a mode of remembrance. Remembering the past, allegory aims to "rescue" the things from their transitoriness which is caused by the loss of their original meaning, their idea, in language. "For an appreciation of the transience of things, and the concern to rescue them for eternity, is one of the strongest impulses in allegory. . . . Allegory established itself most permanently where transitoriness and eternity confronted each other most closely."[22]

Paradoxically — at least, at first sight — the rescue is attempted in such a way that the intention, the subjectivity of the allegorist, gets hold of the things, tears them out of all their present contexts, and attributes a new meaning to them as fragments. Just as the principle of subjectivity underlying historic languages is exposed and intensified in allegory, the same can be said regarding the principle of historicity underlying the world of things. For allegory is characterized by a strongly "destructive tendency."[23] It strives to destroy even the mere appearance of any perfection — any "false totality" — by presenting things not as parts of a whole but as fragments.

> The word "history" stands written on the countenance of nature in the characters of transience. The allegorical physiognomy of the nature-history, which is put on stage in the Trauerspiel, is present in reality in the form of the ruin. . . . And in this guise history does not assume the form of the process of an eternal life so much as that of irresistible decay. . . . Allegories are, in the realm of thoughts, what ruins are in the realm of things.[24]

The allegorical absorption in the individual thing is intended toward the thing as a fragment — as a thing broken from a whole and pointing back to its being broken. Only as a fragment can it be provided with a new meaning by the subjective arbitrariness of the allegorical act.

This procedure of attributing a meaning to the thing as a fragment is to be understood as the "rescue": without it, the thing would remain meaningless and mute, that is, addicted to transitoriness. The meaning which the allegorist ascribes to a thing has, of course, nothing to do with the original meaning, the idea that it was able to express "before the Fall." But since it is a meaning, the allegorist points — so to speak allegorically — forward to the state of messianic redemption when the things will become language again.

Thus, the decontextualization and fragmentation of the allegorical process turn out to be an allegory by itself. For in allegory "transitoriness is not signified or allegorically represented, so much as, in its own significance, displayed as allegory. As the allegory of resurrection. Ultimately, in the death-marks of the Baroque, the direction of allegorical reflection is reversed; on the second part of its wide arc it returns, to redeem. . . . In God's world, the allegorist awakens." [25]

Because allegory, as a process of meaning-constitution, follows the guideline of exposing and intensifying the principles of subjectivity and historicity, it becomes in itself an allegory in which the "mode of signifying" turns into the signified: as "fixed movement" the allegory signifies the "messianic standstill of history," which Benjamin describes as the messianic redemption at the end of history.

In sum, we can state that Benjamin describes allegory as a particular mode of meaning-constitution which appears under the conditions of the historical world — after the Fall, before redemption — as the only adequate mode of an aesthetic meaning-constitution. For allegory insists on the fact that meaning is always constituted in the historical world as a semiotic category. Accordingly, it expressly declares the pragmatic dimension (i.e., subjectivity and historicity) as the most comprehensive dimension which influences and determines the syntactic and the semantic dimension.

THE ALLEGORICAL PROCESS OF A SEMIOTIC APPROACH

Attempt at a Semiotic Reformulation

Up to now, I have described Benjamin's theory of allegory within the framework of his eschatological conception. For I do not think that it is possible to understand the theory fully with all its implications if the more comprehensive context of eschatology is neglected.

On the other hand, in dealing with Benjamin's theory of allegory, it is very tempting to adopt the part of the allegorist. So why not break his theory of allegory out of its original context of eschatology and place it in another context by reformulating it in semiotic terms?[26]

The allegorical process is performed in a few steps. First, the allegorist breaks one element out of the particular context in which it appears. In this way the element is deprived of its special syntactical dimension as formed by the context. Thus, loss of the syntactical dimension seems to be the first consequence of decontextualization.

Since the element was only able to serve as a sign because of its particular position and function within its previous context, the decontextualization leads to a desemantization of the element in question; as a mere object, it has no meaning by itself and, as a fragment, taken out of its context, it no longer has the meaning ascribed to it by the context. Thus, the loss of the syntactical dimension is followed by a loss of the semantic dimension. In other words, decontextualization and desemantization cause a deconstruction of the element as a sign:[27] the sign is deprived of a function that was only guaranteed by its being an element of a context and is left as an element without a context — i.e., as something without meaning.

Now the allegorist attributes a new meaning to the fragment by placing it into another context. Whereas the first phase of the allegorical process, deconstruction, is completely dependent on pragmatic conditions (because it is up to the allegorist which element is to be broken out of which context) the predominance of the pragmatic dimension becomes even more obvious in the second phase. For the choice of the context into which the fragment is to be placed is wholly determined subjectively. The placing of the element x, taken out of the context A and placed in context B, does not follow any objectively given necessity, but is caused and guided by subjective conditions on the part of the allegorist.

The way that the allegorist places the fragment into the chosen context has several consequences. First of all, it means that the fragment regains a syntactical dimension. Thus, it is to be understood as a contextualization of the fragment that becomes part of a whole, an element of a context again. Moreover, the context itself is reconstructed by this very procedure. It is not only context B plus element x. Since element x becomes an element of context B, the context is changed into context B^1. Consequently, the restoration of a syntactical dimension as regards element x is performed as a contextualization as well as a process of restructuring context B: it is performed as the construction of context B^1.

This construction is followed or accompanied by a semantization: for it is the new context which attributes a new meaning to element x according to its position within the new context and which is dependent on the meanings constituted by the context. However, just as the restoration of a syntactical dimension points back to the two directions of contextualization (in terms of element x) and restructuring (in terms of context B), the same can be said of the restoration of a semantic dimension. On the one hand, the constitution of a meaning of element x is influenced, if not determined, by the meaning of context B. On the other hand, this process of meaning-constitution does not leave the meaning of context B untouched. For Benjamin expressly declares that element x is to be understood as a fragment, that is, as something which is broken out of a whole — which, by its very existence as a fragment, points back to the context from which it is taken. Thus, as a fragment, element x still refers to its previous context. Consequently, its placement within context B establishes some kind of relationship between context A and context B. Hence it follows that the meaning of context B^1 cannot be the same as that of context B.

By placing element x into context B, context B becomes in some way related to context A. In other words, context B^1 refers to context A and intertextuality is produced.[28] And this intertextuality now influences the process by which the meaning of B is reconstituted as the meaning of B^1. In order to construct the semantical dimension of B^1, it is thus necessary to reconstruct the relationship between A and B. Accordingly, the restoration of a semantical dimension as regards element x is performed as a process of construction as well as reconstruction.

In sum, we can state that the allegorical process consists, essentially, of two processes:

1. The process of deconstruction performed as decontextualization and desemantization;
2. The process of construction and reconstruction performed as contextualization and semantization, leading to an intertextuality that is in the change of context B into context B^1.

BENJAMIN'S CONCEPT OF "ALLEGORY": A PARADIGM OF AVANT-GARDE ART

We are now prepared to return to the question we proceeded from: can Benjamin's theory of allegory be appropriately applied to modern art in order to describe and analyze the process of its production as well as its reception?

Production as Allegorization

If we think of works of art such as the early montages by Pablo Picasso or by Georges Braque, it seems obvious that the process of their production can adequately be described by means of the categories developed in delineating the allegorical process. Let us consider, for example, those cases where context A was given as a newspaper and element x as a piece of this newspaper. The first phase of the production was performed as the deconstruction of element x—the piece of the newspaper—as a structural element of the meaningful whole represented by the newspaper: the piece was torn out, thus losing its syntactical as well as its semantical dimension. This piece did not mean anything anymore, particularly since the few lines that it still showed were mere fragments of sentences, not to be restored.

This piece was placed on a canvas, context B. By this very procedure, the piece of newspaper, element x, regained a context and context B was changed into context B^1, the final picture. Since the piece of newspaper points, as a fragment, back to its origin in a newspaper, a certain relationship is established between the picture (context B^1) and the newspaper. As a result a certain intertextuality is created which constitutes the meaning of the picture as well as the meaning of the piece of newspaper as an element of the picture. This means that the semantization of the piece of newspaper and of the picture is performed by a process of reconstruction in terms of the relationship between the newspaper and the painted canvas.

Whereas the categories of deconstruction (as decontextualization and restructuring) seem to be generally valid as regards the process of production, it is doubtful whether the same can be said in terms of the category of reconstruction. For the producer (the painter, composer, author, actor, etc.) may, in fact, perform the process of construction as a process of reconstruction, but not necessarily so. On the contrary, the producer might merely intend a process of construction without aiming at any kind of semantization, thus leaving the reconstruction to the receiver.

Before drawing any general conclusions, let us consider one more example, taken from a different genre and a different age—from the postmodern theatre.

In her production of Shakespeare's *Richard II* Ariane Mnouchkine generally took recourse to the stage codes of different Japanese theatrical forms, especially the *no* and the *kabuki* theatres. In these theatrical forms, all the elements, whether a costume or a movement, an ornament on a mask or a gesture, have a fixed meaning that is as well known by the actors presenting them as by the spectators perceiving and interpreting them.

Taking these elements out of their cultural context means depriving them of their syntactical dimension as formed by a particular theatrical code or language and, consequently, depriving them of their semantic dimension as given by the theatrical language. This procedure is, in fact, realized as a deconstruction of the elements in question. In this case, we have to deal not only with one element x, but with several elements $(x_1, x_2 \ldots x_n)$ that are decontextualized and desemanticized.

These elements $(x_1, x_2 \ldots x_n)$ are broken from the context A_1 (the theatrical code of the *no* theatre) and A_2 (the theatrical code of the *kabuki* theatre) and are placed in context B, Shakespeare's drama *Richard II*.

By this process, the elements regain a context — they now refer to characters, actions, and situations in Shakespeare's play. Moreover, context B, the drama *Richard II*, is transformed into context B^1, as the construction of this particular *mise en scène* of the play. Within the framework of context B^1 the elements $x_1, x_2 \ldots x_n$ taken from contexts A_1 and A_2 are related to the elements $y_1, y_2 \ldots y_n$ which together form the whole of context B. That is to say that the meaning of B^1, the *mise en scène*, and the individual elements $x_1, x_2 \ldots x_n$ is constituted by the particular relations that are established between the elements $x_1, x_2 \ldots x_n$ and the elements $y_1, y_2 \ldots y_n$.

Hence it follows that the construction of B^1 and the elements $x_1, x_2 \ldots x_n$ is not only a reconstruction. Thus, we can state that the phase of reconstruction does not form a necessary, but only a possible, constituent of the process of production, whereas the phases of deconstruction and construction are always realized.

Reception as Allegorization

With regard to the process of reception, Benjamin pointed to a certain parallelism between it and the allegorical process. In the "Theses on the Philosophy of History" (completed in the spring of 1940), he describes the exemplary attitude of a receiver:

A historical materialist approaches a historical subject only where he encounters it as a monad. In this structure he recognises the sign of Messianic cessation of happening, or, put differently, a revolutionary chance in the fight for the oppressed past. He takes cognisance of it in order to blast a specific era out of the homogeneous course of history — blasting a specific life out of the era or a specific work out of the lifework. As a result of this method, the lifework is preserved in this work and at the same time cancelled (*the Hegelian term "aufheben" in its threefold meaning: to preserve, to elevate, to cancel*); in the lifework, the era: and in the era, the entire course of history. The nourishing fruit of the historically understood contains time as a precious but tasteless seed.[29]

Accordingly, the process of reception starts from a phase of deconstruction: the work is taken out of its possible contexts of the lifework, the era, and the homogeneous course of history, insofar as the sum total of these contexts forms, and may be understood as, the particular tradition, determining and even fixing the meaning of the work. If these contexts provide the work with a certain meaning, the work is to be deprived of these contexts as well as of the meaning constituted by them. In other words, it must be deconstructed as a sign, functioning within the context of tradition.[30]

On the other hand, we have to consider that not every given work is presented within the context of a particular tradition and that not every interpreter has to cope with the meanings constituted by tradition since, for example, the tradition may be unknown to him or her. Under these conditions, the phase of deconstruction would, of course, be omitted. Thus, we could define the phase of deconstruction only as a possible, not a necessary, constituent of the process of reception.

However, deconstruction does not only intend the different contexts forming the tradition. On the contrary, it may aim at the particular kind of unity established in the work, context B^1, between context B and the elements $x_1, x_2 \ldots x_n$ taken from the contexts A_1 and $A_2 \ldots A_n$. In this case, the phase of deconstruction is to be regarded as a necessary constituent of the process of reception.

Having deconstructed the unity in question, the interpreter will have to construct the possible relations between the elements $x_1, x_2 \ldots x_n$ and context B, as formed by the sum total of the elements $y_1, y_2 \ldots y_n$. This means that the process of construction (as "contextualization") is performed by establishing the internal relations between the elements $x_1, x_2 \ldots x_n$ and $y_1, y_2 \ldots y_n$ within the framework of the work, that is, within context B^1.

Since deconstruction has marked the elements $x_1, x_2 \ldots x_n$ as fragments, "broken" from other contexts, the construction of the internal relations will be followed by a construction of possible external relations. For even if the elements $x_1, x_2 \ldots x_n$ now function as elements of context B^1, they nonetheless point back to their origin in contexts A_1 and $A_2 \ldots A_n$, in which they functioned as elements before. Thus, the construction of external relations will be performed by reconstructing the contexts A_1 and $A_2 \ldots A_n$. This means that the particular intertextuality of the work, which constitutes its meaning, can only be constructed if the reconstruction intends contexts A_1 and $A_2 \ldots A_n$.

Thus, the semantization of the work is created by simultaneously performing the processes of construction and reconstruction that will establish the possible internal and external relations.[31]

Retracing our last steps, we can state that, as far as the process of production is concerned, the phases of deconstruction and construction are to be considered necessary constituents and that, as far as the process of reception is concerned, the phases of construction and reconstruction seem to be the most important, while the phase of deconstruction is not to be neglected. Thus, we can come to the conclusion that the model provided by Benjamin's concept of allegory has indeed proved itself to be a paradigm of avant-garde art in semiotic terms.

SIGNS OF IDENTITY
The Dramatic Character as "Name" and "Body"

The question of the identity of a dramatic character seems rather easily answered — at least when it is restricted to the question of formal identification. Regarding the written text of the play — the script — every character is to be identified by referring to its name: Oedipus, Jocasta, Hamlet, Polonius, Gertrude, Iphigenia, Orestes, etc. The lines following the name in the script are supposed to be read and understood as utterances of this particular character.

As regards the staging of the play — the performance — the first idential we are usually given is the physical appearance of the actor. It may inform us about the age and sex of the character (old man, young girl), about social status (king, beggar), about social status in a certain epoch (medieval knight, contemporary proletarian), about ethnicity and nationality (Japanese, Indian, English), about the particular type embodied (clown, dandy), or about profession (sailor, police officer). This means that the physical appearance of the actor playing a certain character enables us at first sight to ascribe a temporary identity to this character. On the one hand, this temporary identity shapes our expectations and anticipations regarding the future behavior of this character; on the other, we relate the facial expressions, gestures, and movements the actor performs to this temporary identity, as well as the words the actor utters and the special tone of voice in which they are uttered. This enables us either to affirm the temporarily ascribed identity or to annul it by modifying or even replacing it with another one.

Whereas the name in the script is able to convey only a very vague idea of the identity of the dramatic character — although names like Oedipus, Hamlet, and Mephisto evoke a wealth of associations related to the different contexts in which they may appear — the physical appearance of the actor provides a wider range of predictions and assumptions regarding the identity of the character being played. Nonetheless, the name and the bodily appearance, in a certain respect, fulfill the same function: they both allow the reader/spectator a formal identification of the dramatic character.

Bearing this in mind, most modern theories of identity concern the name as well as the body and identify these as particularly important identials. As David De Levita states:

> The relationship between the name and personality of the bearer has been close in all cultures and times. . . . The magic power of the name is a very general phenomenon. He who knows it has power on the bearer, can damage or benefit him. With the Rotinesians, the child is given a name prior to birth, since it will otherwise not want to be born. With various races the giving of a name to the child is not a naming but an investigation of the name the child has hidden within it.[1]

Hence, it follows that the name cannot be understood as merely a sign of the identity of the person, so that we could easily imagine it to be changed and the person to remain the same. On the contrary, the name must be grasped as an integral part of the person and thus, in a way, can even be taken as an equivalent of the person.

On the other hand, the name is a linguistic sign that some people relate to a certain person — mostly those newborn or just initiated. Insofar as it is a linguistic sign, the name is an element of the symbolical order as formed by language. Being named thus means achieving participation in the symbolical order of language and, moreover, becoming part of the symbolical order of language. Within the system of language the name now functions as the substitute for the person and, conversely, annexes the person to language: rendering that person as an element of the symbolical order as constituted by language.

Insofar as the name is given to the person by others, this act determines the relationship of the individual to the others. By this very act the individual becomes a member of the group. In being named, the person achieves participation in the symbolic order as formed by society; only as a named person can the individual become a member of society. The name is given to the individual by others and is accepted by that individual. From this moment, the individual behaves according to this name. Naming, thus, proves to be a fundamental act of social interaction.

We can conclude that the name must fulfill two basic functions: (1) it makes the named person part or element of a symbolical order — of the language as well as of society; and (2) by this very act it identifies the person as an individual part or element of the symbolical order in question, that is to say, distinguishes that person from, and opposes that person to, all other elements and members of the symbolical order and the symbolical order as a whole. Thus, the name functions as one of the fundamental, most important, and irrevocable identials of a person.

On the other hand, the body is to be seen as no less a fundamental idential than the name. If we proceed from the assumption of a factual body *a priori*, we can state that a self without a body is a contradiction in itself. That means that the body, particularly

the living and lived body, is an element constitutive of the self. Even if (*per impossibile*, I believe) there should be some way of conceiving of the self as existing independently of its body, yet if we do conceive of it having a body we must conceive of it having it essentially. That is, unlike any other of its actual possessions (e.g. its house). There is no way of conceiving of the self independently, of conceiving of its body, if we once conceive of its having a body at all. We can conceive of a person without conceiving of his house, but if we try to conceive of him without his body we can no longer do so. . . . My body is mine and me: it is primordially mine: and it is so just insofar as it is not themacised, not identified as mine. It does not presuppose the independent identifiability of the self which owns it because it is not a simple owned object. As body-subject it is an element constitutive of the self, the subject.[2]

Thus, name and body do not only designate or represent the self but form an integral, constitutive part of it. But whereas the name always proves the self as part of a symbolical order, the body, first of all, shows it to belong to the realm of nature. For as an organism, the body is, in fact, part of nature. As an "in each case different or anismic profile of bodily needs,"[3] the body, moreover, is in each case the specific individual internal nature of a particular human being. This means that the body is part of the natural order and, as such, distinguished from and opposed to all other elements and part of nature.

On the other hand, the human body never exists as pure nature. From the very beginning, the surrounding culture starts its everlasting work upon it — at first, as maternal care. The culture influences not only the development, restructuring, and regulation of the physical needs, but the particular strength of the instinctual drives and the special mode of their articulation as well. It even has an effect on the shaping of the adult body insofar as this depends on culturally determined factors (for instance, nutrition, hygiene, public health on the one hand and the valid ideal body-image on the other). Thus, any human body can be taken to be the result of a reciprocal process or interaction between its individual nature and the surrounding culture. This process starts at the moment of birth and is not finished before death. Its result in each case is a totally different individual body that now participates not only in the natural order but also in the symbolical order of culture. Insofar as the body is part of nature, it is insignificant. Insofar as it forms a part of the symbolical order of culture, it becomes significant. The boundary between the significant and the insignificant actually crosses the body. It is determined by both and participates in both.

Thus, the name and the body function as identials of the self in a very particular way. They form it as a part of a whole — of the symbolic orders of language, society, culture in general, and nature and, at the same time, by this very procedure, as different from all other parts of the whole and from the whole itself: as absolutely individual, as unique.

If we are going to transfer these identials from the sphere of social life to the fictional sphere of dramatic characters, we have to consider that a basic alteration has to be made. In social life, name and body not only represent the self of the person but form an integral, constitutive part of it. As regards the dramatic characters, however, it is quite obvious that "name" and "body" lose this particular quality. For the name in the script is not related to an actual person, but to a fictional character; and the body onstage is the body of the actor and not the body of the fictional character. The actor's body merely functions as a sign pointing to the body of the dramatic character. Thus, we can conclude that "name" and "body" are to be taken as signs of the self and not as its constitutive elements when they refer to dramatic characters.

On the other hand, we can state that the particular identity of a dramatic character is brought forth and constituted by means of the special relationship that is established between "name" and "body" — that is to say: the relationship between the different symbolical orders to which "name" and "body" belong, as language, society, culture in general, and nature. Since this thesis seems to have more immediate evidence as regards the dramatic character onstage, let us first delineate the process by which this particular identity is constituted.

The process starts from the role as laid down in the script. This sounds rather uncomplicated, but in fact entails great difficulty. For, as Georg Simmel remarked quite accurately,

the role of the actor, as it is expressed in written drama, is not a total person. The role is not a man, but a complex of things which can be said about a person through literary devices. The poet cannot give instructions concerning the inflection of language, the tone of voice, or the pace of delivery. He can only project the fate, the appearance, and the soul of a person through the one-dimensional process of poetic imagery.[4]

This means that the role is given as a particular symbolical order as formed by the language of the play. In order to constitute the dramatic character as a particular self, the actor has to "transform" this "one-dimensional" role into the three dimensionality of space: the actor has to reproduce what is given as a symbolical order by means of his or her own individual body. This process will lead in each case to a different result, as Simmel has stated: "Only the autonomous status of the dramatic art explains the strange fact that a poetic role, although conceived as an unambiguous one, can be presenced by a variety of dramatic actors with completely different interpretations, each of which may be fully adequate, and none of which would be more correct or more erroneous than any other."[5]

This will be the case because every actor has to create the dramatic character by means of a totally individual and unique material: his or her own body. In this act, the symbolical order of language and the body meet and work upon each other.

By enacting the role, the actor reproduces a symbolical order as formed by the language of the play, under the particular conditions that are given and determined by the actor's own individual physis. Since the actor's body, partly at least, still belongs to nature, this very procedure leads to a particular desymbolization of the role as a symbolical order: what has been language now becomes — as part of the actor's individual physis — nature. This means that the significance of language is partly canceled and extinguished by the nature of the actor's body.

On the other hand, this process leads to the opposite situation: to a symbolization of the actor's body. For in order to enact the role the actor's body must be transformed — at least insofar as it can be perceived by the spectators — into something significant. The voice and the appearance of the actor's body, every gesture and movement, will become significant elements pointing to the various emotions, psychic states, reflections, actions, etc., of the dramatic character. What may have been nature must be transformed into signs. The enactment can be seen as a process that totally transforms the individual physis of the actor into a symbolical order. Insignificant nature becomes a system of significant symbols. Desymbolization of language and symbolization of the body, thus, imply and cause each other in the process of acting. As a result, the identity of the dramatic character is brought forth as absolutely individual and entirely unique.

In approaching the literary text of the drama, the *script*, we have to face many more difficulties to support our thesis. For although it is quite obvious that the dramatic character onstage is brought forth by the actor's body as well as by language, the dramatic character in the script does not exist beyond the borders of language. How can this dilemma be resolved?

Onstage the symbolical order of language is reproduced by means of the actor's body. In the script, however, the body is reproduced by language. To put it more precisely: the body of the fictional character is brought forth exclusively by the symbolical order of language. Whereas onstage the more comprehensive framework within which language and body meet and work upon each other can be said to be the body, in the script this all-inclusive framework is provided by language. This means that the confrontation between body and language must take place within the symbolical order of language. It is language that establishes certain relations between body and language.

On the other hand, there is no drama which does not establish some kind of relationship between body and language. Moreover, it seems that the fact of this relationship constitutes one of the most fundamental features defining drama as a distinct literary genre. For it is the relationship between body and language, as established by and within the framework of the symbolical order of language in the play, that functions as the *sine qua non* of its production; the body of the dramatic character as brought forth by means of language will be reproduced by means of the actor's body. This is why the actor's body can function as a sign of the identity of the dramatic character.

From the very beginning, the literary genre of drama has been defined by referring to the category of action. In fact, this very category includes physical acts as well as speech acts. This suggests that the category of action implicitly points to a particular relationship between body and language. Although he did not refer to this relationship, Aristotle claimed that the difference between tragedy and comedy mainly is founded, in each genre, on different kinds of action. Whereas the action of tragedy requires "magnitude,"[6] that of a comedy is characterized by means of the "ridiculous."[7] Accordingly, Aristotle determined that the characters of tragedy "shall be good,"[8] while comedy should be "an imitation of man worse than the average."[9]

If we define "action" as a particular relationship between physical acts and speech acts, we can explain the "magnitude" and the "ridiculous" of the action as, in each case, a different relationship between the two kinds of acts. That is to say, the difference between tragedy and comedy is founded on a different attitude toward the body, on the one side, and language, on the other.

In other words: in each genre the tragic and the comic character are constituted by a totally different kind of relationship between body and language.

In tragedy, for instance, the body is referred to by acts of killing or being killed or of wounding or being wounded. This means that the body is introduced as a killing or killed body or a wounding or wounded body. If we interpret and understand the relationship between body and language in drama as a particular realization of the relationship between nature and significance, this seems to be perfectly consistent. For, as Walter Benjamin explained, "death digs most deeply the jagged line of demarcation between physical nature and significance."[10] All tragic heroes kill or are killed, wound or are wounded, plan to kill or to commit suicide. For it is death or the wound that reveals the body as part of nature subjected to the natural order. Significance arises when the symbolical order of language is related to the natural fact of death or of a wound. The identity of the tragic hero, thus, is constituted when the body and language are confronted in sight of death.

Comedy, on the other hand, realizes the harm that may reveal the body as being part of nature only in the mitigated, rather trivial, form of beating or being beaten. Comedy awards the body much more importance than does tragedy. Very often, the comic character is introduced as one who has certain physical peculiarities or qualities. Sometimes the comic character is described in this respect even by the name, which establishes a particular relationship between language and body. As, for instance, in the case of the so-called speaking names, the name often points to its bearer as a person largely determined by bodily features: "Toby Belch" and "Hanswurst" characterize their bearers by expressly reducing them to their corresponding physical utterances or needs.

Quite similarly, the comical character often is determined by certain physical defects or rather unusual features such as a thick belly, a long nose, red hair, a lame leg, etc. On the other hand, the comical person may be introduced as one being totally absorbed in trying to satisfy primary physical needs: while hunting for food, having to cope with digestion, or searching for an opportunity for sexual intercourse.

Thus, the comic character — at least until the rise of bourgeois drama — is presented not only as one having a body, but, moreover, as one who is predominantly characterized or even determined by the body. In each case, the particular identity of the comic character is constituted by the very way in which language is related to this overwhelmingly dominating body.

Therefore, we come to the conclusion that we cannot conceive of the dramatic character without a body, even if the character is conceived while reading the playscript. For language constantly points to the character's having a body and thus forces us to conceive of the fictional characters as subjects having a body and being a body, as subjects who refer to their bodies when referring to themselves.

As stated above, the thetic act that constitutes the identity of the dramatic character by establishing a relationship between body and language is performed onstage within the limits drawn by the actor's body. In the script, however, it is thus carried out exclusively by means of language which brings forth the play as a symbolical order. This thesis can be elucidated in more detail by referring to a concrete example, Sophocles' tragedy *Oedipus the King*, before drawing any far-reaching conclusions.

While in former times this drama was held to be a tragedy of fate, most of the scholars dealing with it nowadays label it a tragedy of identity, emphasizing the way in which Oedipus comes to know the answers to the questions "Who is the murderer of Laius?"; "Am I the murderer of Laius?"; and "Who am I?" My general thesis, on the other hand, makes it necessary to shift the focus from the way of/to knowledge to the thetic act by which body and language are related to each other. Accordingly, I do not aim toward an extensive interpretation of the play, but only to elaborate and stress the specific thetic act that constitutes Oedipus' identity.

In the beginning of the play, Oedipus has two different identities. The first has been ascribed to him by the gods before his birth: it is the identity of a man who kills his father and marries his mother. Apollo revealed this to Oedipus as his future identity, predicted and determined by the gods and therefore unavoidable. Oedipus has rejected this identity. He will by no means accept it as his actual identity and thus has refused to play the part the gods have outlined for him.

The second identity is that of the good king who cares for his city, of the savior of the land, of the responsible democratic ruler. Oedipus has achieved this identity by solving the riddle of the Sphinx and liberating the city from her pressure. This is the identity with which Oedipus fully agrees. It dominates and determines his behavior toward the citizens of Thebes, whom he addresses as "my children," "pitiable children" for whose life and fate he feels responsible.

Although as far as Oedipus knows these two identities are totally dissociated from each other, the plot of the tragedy connects them from the beginning of the play. The plague has befallen the city as a consequence of Oedipus having killed his father, the former king of Thebes. Oedipus (the king and the savior of the land) is asked to help rid the city of the plague. In this way, the two different identities are externally related to each other from the first scene.

The identity ascribed to Oedipus by the gods is exclusively referred to, and affirmed, by acts of his body: he has indeed killed his father and incestuously begotten children with his mother. His body has performed these acts outside his own knowledge, that is to say, outside his language. Thus, his language refers to the murder of his father as a deed to which Oedipus is a "stranger" ("I'll make the proclamation, though a stranger to the report and to the deed," 5.219/220) or as a murder done to a "stranger" ("but if there is a kinship between Laius and this stranger," 5.813/814). Oedipus' language is not able to relate his deed of killing a man to the identity the gods have ascribed to him. Only his body is related to this identity. Oedipus' body actually affirms it as his actual identity without being able to attribute the meaning of identity-constituting acts to its actions. As merely physical acts they remain insignificant.

The identity of the king, in contrast, mainly seems to be realized by means of Oedipus' language: it is brought forth as well as affirmed by his speech acts. He has solved the riddle given by the Sphinx and thus made himself the savior of the city. He has ordered Creon to ask Apollo for help and advice (5.69–72), he commands the citizens to reveal all knowledge of the murder they may have (5.224–226), he curses the murderer and those trying to hide him (5.236–251). Thus, Oedipus' identity of the king is constituted, as well as attested to, by the speech acts he performs.

On the other hand, this identity is acted out in a way that proves it to be a realization of a certain ideal by which the Athenian society of Sophocles' time judged a politician, especially the democratic leader of the polis. It is stressed that Oedipus is deeply concerned about what is happening to the citizens of Thebes ("Pitiable children, oh I know, I know / the yearnings that have brought you. Yes I know / that you are sick. And yet, though you are sick, / there is none of you so sick as I am. / For your affliction comes to you alone, / for him and no one else, but my soul mourns / for me and for you, too, and for the city," 5.58–64). Moreover, he is shown to be no tyrant but a willing listener to the advice of the chorus, even if this seems to be against his own personal interest (as, for instance, when he wants to banish Creon, 5.649–656). Oedipus may be rash of temper, but he never acts despotically, never tries to hide anything from the citizens. Instead, he insists on doing and discussing everything in public (5.93–94). Oedipus' behavior as a king fits in perfectly with the ideal of a democratic leader that was valid in Athens during the fifth century. Since Oedipus seems exclusively determined by this achieved identity, he is characterized in accordance with the prevailing collective identity of the Athenians, which Christian Meier (1983) has explained and defined as a political identity, that is, as an identity constituted in respect to the polis only.

The identity realized and affirmed by the body and the identity acted out and attested to by means of language gradually intertwine as the action of the play continues. The relation between them is established through a process that Oedipus performs by means of language, on the one side, and by means of his body, on the other.

After he has questioned the messenger and the shepherd, Oedipus comes to know that he has killed his father and married his mother. Whereas these acts had been insignificant as merely physical acts before, they are now referred to by Oedipus' language: "I, Oedipus, I am the child of parents who should never have been mine — doomed, doomed! Now everything is clear — I / lived with a woman she was my mother. I slept in my mother's bed, and I / murdered, murdered my father / the man whose blood flows in these veins of mine, / whose blood stains these two hands red" (5.1181–1185). Thus, the physical acts become part of the symbolical order as formed by Oedipus' speech. That is, they become significant as the acts constituting his actual identity. By reperforming them in his own language, Oedipus posits the ascribed identity as his own.

After this, Oedipus walks into the palace and, in the presence of the dead Jocasta, blinds himself using one of her brooches, while cursing his eyes. This physical act, on the one hand, refers to the body as vulnerable nature, since it mutilates it. The blood streaming down over Oedipus' face clearly points to the subjection of the body to the natural order. On the other hand, this very act transforms the body into a symbolic order. For the self-blinding can be seen as a physical act that is intended to be significant and, accordingly, brought forth as a significant physical act, that is, as a sign. Literally, it implies a punishment of a body that has performed highly significant acts as insignificant ones.

Moreover, the self-blinding suggests a symbolic reenactment of the murder as well as of the incestuous sexual intercourse. Whereas earlier Oedipus' body performed these physical acts as if they were insignificant in terms of his identity, the self-blinding is executed as a physical act, a symbolic reperformance of these acts, making them significant as identity-constituting acts. Accordingly, the mutilated body can now function as a sign of Oedipus' new identity brought forth by transforming his body into a symbolic order.

It is to be stressed that this new identity is not the same as either the ascribed or the achieved identity, although it is related to both. The new identity is related to the ascribed identity by consciously adopting it; it is related to the achieved identity in that it shows the mutilated body to the citizens of the polis. The new identity comes into existence through Oedipus' thetic act which transforms the insignificant physical acts into significant ones by naming them, on the one side, and by symbolically reenacting them, on the other.

Thus, a particular relationship is established between the body as a sign of the self and the name as a sign of the self. The name Oedipus can mean "with a swollen foot" as well as "of limping knowledge." It was given to Oedipus because of his swollen feet, that is, because of a particular physical trait that points to his fate. Oedipus renames himself, however, by referring to the second meaning. Since the Greek word οἶδα "I know" originally means "I have seen," the interpretation of the name Oedipus as "of limping knowledge" may be changed to "of mutilated sight." In this way, Oedipus shapes his body according to his name — that is to say, he establishes a new relationship of equivalence between his name and his body. Both now can function as signs of his new identity. Thus, in *Oedipus the King* the thetic act that constitutes the identity of the dramatic character establishes not only a relationship between language and body in general, but also a very specific relationship between "name" and "body."

Are there any aspects of the conclusions drawn from the example of the tragedy *Oedipus the King* that are also valid for drama in general? On the one hand, we have seen that the identity of the dramatic character is constituted by a thetic act which the dramatic character performs, establishing a certain relationship between language and body. On the other hand, we have noticed that the attitude toward language and body underlying the tragedy as a basic prerequisite depends, to a certain extent, on historically determined conditions that are external to the work — for instance, on the collective identity of the society within which the drama was created.

In summing up these general reflections as well as the particular explanations regarding *Oedipus the King*, we can state that the identity of the dramatic character is generally created by means of a thetic act performed by the dramatic character which establishes certain relations between language and body. Since both language and body are determined by historical, as well as social, conditions this definition entails some problems: One is historical, regarding the history of drama with respect to a history of identity; the other systematical, referring to the staging of noncontemporary plays.

In what respect and to what extent is the identity of the dramatic character related to, or even based on, the "collective identity" of society or of the social class within which the play is brought forth?

As regards *Oedipus the King*, we have seen that the personal identity of the dramatic character comes into existence by way of a deviation from the collective identity (which can be defined as an exclusively political identity). Yet the personal identity still remains related to the collective one: the very thetic act that constitutes Oedipus' personal identity fulfills the conditions to which Apollo referred concerning rescuing the polis from the plague. Thus, the personal identity of the dramatic character and the collective identity of the Athenian society appear to be closely entwined with each other. In this way, the drama postulates and posits its own ideal identity.

German and Spanish Baroque dramas, on the contrary, merely seem to revive or to reenact the ideal identity that is already valid within society. *The Magnanimous Prince*, for instance, constitutes an identity that can be adequately described as the identity of an ideal Christian martyr. The significance of this thetic act can only be understood when it is related to the ideal of a Christian martyr that underpins Spanish Christian society of the seventeenth century.

In the nineteenth century, however, the identity of the dramatic character was very often directly opposed to the collective identity of society or of the corresponding social class. The dramatic heroes of Heinrich von Kleist or Georg Büchner, for instance, possess identities that are not only different from those valid within bourgeois society, but quite expressly and rigorously deny the validity of this identity and even its mere possibility. Consequently, it is no wonder that these plays were not staged during the lifetime of their authors.

Thus, we can conclude that in order to determine the particular identity of the dramatic character, not only do we have to reconstruct the thetic act by which that dramatic character relates body and language to each other, but, moreover, we have to relate this thetic act to the collective identity of the society in which the drama was created. However, this will only be possible if we have sufficient material that would allow us to reconstruct what we call the "collective identity" of a society or a social class. I do not think that this problem can be solved satisfactorily by referring solely to the history of ideas, to the *Geistesgeschichte*, or even to the social history of an epoch. Rather, for this purpose, we need investigations like the pioneering work done by Norbert Elias, such as *The Civilizing Process*, for instance, or the research done by the group of historians attached to the journal *Annales: Economies — Sociétés — Civilisations*, who try to elucidate the "mentality" of a group, class, society, and culture. Without such work, the outlined program for historical research cannot be carried out.

From the script of the play one can understand the role as a symbolic order that may be described as a particular historical concept of identity. By enacting this role, the actor onstage reproduces this symbolic order, in which history has engraved its traces sometimes more, sometimes less deeply, by means of the actor's own contemporary body. The enactment, as a partial desymbolization of the symbolic order formed by the language of the play, is performed as an actualization, whereas the symbolization of the actor's body takes place as its historization. Therefore, the identity of the dramatic character onstage, as the result of this process, necessarily points to and participates in two different discourses: that of the culture (epoch/society) within which the play was written and that of the contemporary culture. Thus, the identity of the dramatic character onstage always represents a certain kind of mediation between a former culture and this culture. In order to describe and explain this identity appropriately and satisfactorily, we consequently need a semiotics of the theatrical body that would clarify the "embodied" hermeneutic process or the hermeneutics of "embodiment."

THE QUEST FOR MEANING

The quest for meaning has always been one of the most crucial problems of literary scholarship. Without exaggerating or oversimplifying, we can state that the function and aim of cultural literary studies, theatre studies, and related disciplines for a long time have been defined as the search for a particular meaning of a certain work. Almost unanimously, interpretation was declared to be the heart and touchstone of literary and other art scholarship.

Despite this agreement in principle, there is little consensus regarding the general approach to a work or the particular methods of interpretation. Basically, these are elaborated or chosen depending on, and in accordance with, an underlying concept of art. Since each of these concepts defines art differently, the corresponding approaches vary considerably. Thus, even if we only allow for the fundamental differences between historical concepts of art, we have to distinguish at least four concepts: the mimetic, the expressive, the rhetorical, and the cathartic.

HISTORICAL CONCEPTS OF ART

Scholars proceeding from a *mimetic* concept of art assume that the general meaning conveyed by the work is a representation of reality. This concept determines that the criterion by which a work of art can be judged is its particular ability to represent a reality that is "objectively" given.

Since in the course of history this concept of art has been related to different definitions of "objective reality," the tasks and functions of art have been described differently in each case: art is supposed to represent, for instance, that which is possible; that which is probable; that which ought to be; that which is typical or characteristic; or that which is empirical.

Aristotle, for example, advised the poet not to follow the historian, who is bound to report nothing but the facts, and instead to represent "what might happen, i.e., what is possible, as being probable or necessary."[1] The theoreticians of the eighteenth century, on the other hand, who fully believed in the idea of *imitatio naturae*, proceeded from the assumption that art should represent empirical nature. It should not copy it slavishly but instead beautify and perfect it. The realists of the nineteenth and, partly, of the twentieth century declared that, above all, art should trace the typical features and characteristics of social reality; the naturalists insisted on a detailed and minute copy of facts — be they biological, social, or historical.

Even from this rather short and incomplete survey one can gather that the mimetic concept of art covers a very wide range of theories and conceptions. Nonetheless, despite such variety, all these theories have some important premises in common — besides defining art as imitation. They all hold it possible, in principle, to recognize the reality they intend. They deny the inevitable influence of subjectivity and the symbolic systems which work on the processes of knowledge and insist on the possibility of a pure knowledge of reality instead.

This means that the producer of a work of art (the painter, sculptor, composer, poet, actor, etc.) and the recipient recur to one reality that can be known by them both. In order to create the work, the artist has to represent the "known" reality as perfectly as possible — following, of course, the general rules of copying, beautifying, etc., valid at the time. Thus, in order to interpret and judge the work, the critic must compare the representation of reality as shown in the work to the actual reality that is represented in a similar way, by referring to the general rules of representation.

Accordingly, a scholar who intends to constitute the particular meaning of a work will refer to the reality that is supposed to be represented by it and will establish different relations between the work as a representation of reality and the represented reality. Thus, methods will be chosen or elaborated that are especially appropriate to this end, as is the case, for instance, in a socio-historical approach or various sociological methods. Accordingly, the meaning of a work will be constituted as a specific representation of a particular reality which may be further interpreted as a criticism or affirmation of the represented reality.

The *expressive* concept of art, on the other hand, proceeds from the assumption that it is the task and function of all works of art to express the individual subjectivity of its producer as thoroughly and perfectly as possible. Thus, the meaning of the work is generally described and determined as an expression of the subjectivity of its producer.

This concept was first formulated and followed by the representatives of the so-called Storm and Stress movement. They wanted art to express the originality of the artist. Accordingly, they thought that a work of art could only be created by a genius: whereas the artists of other epochs had to observe certain externally given rules in order to create a work of art, the genius was supposed to bear all valid rules engraved in his/her innermost heart. Thus, it was not necessary to follow any rules other than those given by one's own intuition while creating a work of art.

In terms of the aesthetics of Romanticism, this concept of art became very influential. The reality to which the Romantic artists resorted, and which they aimed to represent in their works, was the reality of fantasy, dream, extreme psychic states, and extraordinary emotions. Creative processes were thought to be triggered by unusual feelings. Accordingly, William Wordsworth defined poetry as the "spontaneous overflow of powerful feelings."[2] The emotions flow, so to speak, from the soul of the artist directly into the work of art. Thus, the work can only be properly understood and judged if it is taken as the expression of the particular individual emotionality of the artist.

Although this concept of art was especially defined by the Romantic movement, it was reformulated by several theoreticians at the beginning of this century, including psychoanalytic theorists such as Sigmund Freud, Carl Jung, and Otto Rank. They defined works of art as being similar to dreams: as manifestations of particular conflicts which determine the subconsciousness of the artist without trespassing the threshold to consciousness.

Thus, the meaning of the work is generally described and defined as the expression of the subjectivity of its producer. In this way, methods must be sought to clarify the particular kind of relationship between the work and its producer and to constitute the meaning of the work. Whereas, in the past, the "objective" approach of biographical research, on the one hand, and the "subjective" method of empathy, on the other, have been thought quite appropriate for this purpose, nowadays, in general, psychological and psychoanalytic conceptions and theories are applied. Such an approach may refer to the "content" of the work as well as to its "modes of representation." In any case, it will aim to constitute the meaning of the work as an expression of the subjectivity of its producer, despite the possibility of considerable differences as to whether such subjectivity is to be understood as unique or as a mere example of the functioning of psychic processes in general.

The representatives of the *rhetorical*, or *aesthetic*, concept of art proceed from the assumption that the meaning of the work is a reality of its own created exclusively by particular symbolic systems employed and the internal relations between the individual elements within the work. This means that any reality outside the work is neglected in the interpretation and judgment of it.

This view was made possible by Immanuel Kant's theory of art, in particular, his introduction of the term *aesthetic pleasure*. Kant defined art as an autonomous field, independent of, and antagonistic to, all other fields of social reality. For social reality is always dominated and governed by concrete goals and purposes, so that we judge any given object and statement according to its usefulness and/or correctness regarding the corresponding goals and purposes. However, a work of art is neither useful nor correct, so it is impossible to judge it in this respect. Hence, it follows that the pleasure-determining aesthetic judgment is not aroused by any concrete interests.[3]

Schiller was the first to refer expressly to Kant's theory, taking it as a basis for his elaboration of an aesthetic theory. As a result, he defined art as "play"; that is, a work of art has nothing in common with actual external or internal reality. It follows different rules which are not derived from reality, which can only be interpreted and judged with respect to its own particular rules.

This view has become especially influential and popular as the basic principle and foundation of the *l'art pour l'art* movements. They radically severed any kind of relationship between art and reality, still considered by Kant and Schiller to be relevant, and declared art to be a totally independent and autonomous phenomenon. A work of art must now be judged according to its ability to purify the material used from all connections with any reality outside the work and to constitute a reality of its own. In other words, the material (language, tones, colors, wood, stone, canvas, etc.) was to function as thoroughly insignificant matter that does not point to any reality or meaning outside the work. The particular order, structure, and configuration formed by the individual material elements are said to constitute the work of art as a reality of its own. The criterion of aestheticity is the extent to which the material used has lost its connection with realities external to the work and, consequently, the realization of self-reference in the work.

Accordingly, scholars proceeding from this concept of art have adopted an approach that is intended to eliminate those factors connecting the work to a reality beyond its borders. The meaning of the work, thus, can be constituted only as a result of the different relations that may be established between the elements of the work. This approach is known as New Criticism among Anglo-American scholars and in Germany as *immanente Interpretation*. In a certain respect, even structuralism can be said to have revived this concept by establishing a system of oppositions that function within the work and deriving the meaning of the work from this very system of oppositions.

The *cathartic* concept of art, by contrast, defines the meaning of the work as the effect or impact it may have on its recipient and, hence, as a specific experience lived by the recipient. Accordingly, scholars referring to this concept stress the particular relationship between the work and its recipient in order to constitute its meaning.

This idea was first formulated by Aristotle. In the *Poetics*, he gives a detailed description of *mimesis* and deals with the effects works of art may evoke in the recipient. He states that tragedy "is the imitation of an action . . . ; with incidents arousing pity and fear, which accomplish the catharsis of such emotions."[4] Thus, he defines the characteristics of tragedy with respect to the particular impact it is supposed to have on the reader/spectator and describes the work's ability to fulfill a certain emotional function in terms of the recipient as one of the most important criteria of aestheticity.

This criterion was thought valid in all poetics dealing with tragedy until the eighteenth century, when Kant introduced the term *aesthetic pleasure* into the theory of art. Whereas the poetics in question — for example, works by Georg Philipp Harsdörffer, or Martin Opitz in the seventeenth and Lessing in the eighteenth century — described and defined the emotional impact as a useful method to induce certain experiences in people and thus to influence and educate them, Kant's theory denounced any emotional impact as a nonaesthetic factor. For he denied that art could serve the concrete goals and purposes of social life. Thus, he silenced the vehement discussion about the possible emotional function of art so persistently that it was not reopened until this century.

Nowadays, on the contrary, the emotional function of art is frequently discussed in all kinds of reader-response theories. The behaviorists, for example, define a work of art as a stimulus to which the recipient responds by producing a certain experience that I. A. Richards has called "the aesthetic experience."

Some psychoanalytic theorists, on the other hand, try to describe the effect of art as an emotional experience by referring to particular ideas and suggestions made by Freud and Ernst Kris.[5] Proceeding from basic assumptions about instinctual drives and, predominantly, the disintegration of the Self into Ego, Id, and Super-Ego, Norman Holland, for instance, defines art as a relief that is brought about by the process of reception. "In the last analysis all art is . . . a comfort."[6]

Thus, the work of art is understood as an experience lived by the recipient, that is to say, as part of the recipient's own subjective reality. Whereas the pre-Kantian *Wirkungsästhetik* described this meaning, generally, as the arousal of emotions, contemporary representatives of this idea attempt to specify the different experiences by applying psychological and psychoanalytic methods. Nonetheless, all agree that the meaning of the work can be understood as the particular experience it evokes in the recipient.

There is no need to deal with the advantages and disadvantages, the consistencies and inconsistencies, of each of these concepts and approaches in particular. They are very well known and have been repeatedly discussed. But we should inquire what are the consequences resulting from these approaches in terms of the process of interpretation as the constitution of a specific meaning. It is quite obvious that each of these four concepts defines the meaning of a work of art so differently that the approaches based on these definitions will inevitably lead to different results. In other words, the application of a certain method implies certain possibilities of meaning, which more or less rigorously exclude others. These meanings depend, to a large extent, on the basic relations that are stressed.

The *mimetic* concept emphasizes the relation between the representation of reality and the represented reality, that is, the semantic dimension of the work. The *expressive* concept focuses on the relation between the work and its producer, that is, on certain aspects of the pragmatic dimension. The *rhetorical* concept is concentrated on the internal relations between the elements of the work, that is, on its syntactic dimension. The *cathartic* concept deals with the relation between the work and its recipient, that is, with certain aspects of the pragmatic dimension.

Accordingly, the meaning of the work is defined as:

1. a representation of reality;
2. an expression of a particular subjectivity;
3. a reality of its own, constructed by the work itself; and
4. an experience lived by the recipient.

Since the general definition of meaning focuses on a different semiotic dimension, or on one aspect of a semiotic dimension, the concrete process of interpretation as meaning-constitution that proceeds from these general definitions will necessarily lead to a different result in each case. In other words: there will be at least four different meanings of the work, none of which is compatible with the other. For, since the underlying concepts of art are all prescriptive and normative, the validity of one excludes the others — or at least two of the others (the mimetic, for example, may be combined with the cathartic, as was the case in Aristotle's theory). Hence, it follows that the application of a method derived from a certain concept of art will be incompatible with the application of methods referring to other concepts of art. From the point of view of one concept, a meaning that is constituted on the basis of another will, consequently, be judged inadequate and false. This explains why every scholar of every epoch who claims the validity of different concepts of art "corrects" the results of predecessors who have determined the "real" meaning in accordance with another concept of art.

The deficiencies of these concepts of art are quite obvious. Each empha-sizes one aspect of the work that may be of some importance to the constitu-tion of its meaning. However, even if this one aspect proves to be most rele-vant, other aspects should not be neglected, since they also contribute to its meaning. In semiotic terms, each of these concepts isolates one semiotic di-mension or one particular aspect of one of the dimensions and assumes and posits the meaning of the work as an exclusive result of the relationship be-tween the two factors defining this very dimension. Thus, the mimetic con-cept only considers the semantic dimension; the rhetorical, the syntactic dimension; both the expressive and cathartic, the pragmatic: one regarding the producer, the other regarding the interpreter. Since meaning can be de-scribed as the result of a semiotic process, all three dimensions will be in-volved. Hence, it follows that the interpretation of a work as the very process that constitutes its possible meanings will have to refer to each of the three dimensions, to varying extents, depending on the work itself.

SEMIOTIC CONCEPTS OF ART

It is characteristic of semiotic theories of art that they consider all three semi-otic dimensions, thus combining the most important features and definitions of the historical concepts of art. Nonetheless, such theories differ from each other in the actual combination realized by each of them, in particular, as regards the particular semiotic dimension held to be especially relevant.

Yury Lotman, for instance, defines art as a secondary modeling system. He explains: "A secondary modelling system is a structure based on a natural language. Later the system takes on an additional secondary structure which may be ideological, ethical, artistic, etc."[7]

As a secondary modeling system art can be understood as a particular mode of knowledge. But whereas knowledge is mostly based on analysis and conclusions, art as knowledge recreates the reality within which we live by its own specific means. It does so not by way of imitation but by shaping a model of reality. This model is substantially different from a scientific model. For the making of a scientific model is always preceded by an analytical act: first, the object is analyzed and recognized, then a model of it is formed. The artist, on the other hand, has a closed idea of the whole perceived and/or imagined object to be reproduced, and it is this whole that will be modeled. This means that any work of art is to be seen as a model of reality. Thus, Lotman stresses the relationship between the work of art and the object or reality it represents, that is, the semantic dimension of the work. However, whereas the mimetic concept of art exclusively considers the semantic dimension, Lotman defines it only as the most relevant one, relating it to the other two. For the work of art as a model of reality is doubly determined: by the subjectivity of the artist who shapes it and by the particular qualities and peculiarities of the symbolic systems used — the language of art, which is, in each case, wholly different.

In shaping the model of an object, the artist inevitably constructs the model in accordance with his or her own view of the world, knowledge, emotionality, and values. Hence, it follows that the structure of the model automatically reflects the structure of the consciousness of the artist who forms it. Thus, the work of art can be seen as a model of two "objects": of reality, on the one side, and of the personality of its author, on the other. This definition considers not only the semantic dimension of the work but its pragmatic dimension as well.

However, this model is determined not only by the subjectivity of its producer but by the qualities of the artistic language which shape it. For any symbolic system disposes of specific structural means in order to express the "same" content. Choosing a particular sign system as artistic language thus means depending on a specific mode of representation. For each sign system is determined by certain restrictions on the object the artist is going to model. Usually, these restrictions are not noticed, but taken for granted. Nonetheless, they bear important consequences for the work.

The artist will shape a model of reality by using one kind of artistic language which forces upon him or her particular ways of modeling which exclude others. Thus, the mode of knowledge made possible by the work is, to a large extent, determined by the symbolic systems used. For "the language of an artistic text is, in essence, an artistic model of the universe . . . artistic language models the universe in its most general categories which, being the most general content of the universe, are the form of existence for concrete things and phenomena."[8] This means that the work of art is not sufficiently described if taken only as a model of reality which is determined by the subjectivity of its producer. Moreover, by using a particular artistic language, the model "reproduces a model of the universe in its most general outlines."[9] Thus, the artist shapes the model of reality by selecting certain objects, "recoding" them in the artistic language with which this artist is working, and combining the resulting constituted sign with others which have been created in a similar way. As a result of this process, a complex aesthetic structure develops which conveys an "information [content]" that "can neither exist nor be transmitted outside this artistic structure."[10] That is to say that the model the artist has constructed is a reality of its own that has no existence outside or beyond the work. It can only be adequately understood if the relations between its individual elements are reconstructed. Thus, Lotman considers all three semiotic dimensions, although he emphasizes the semantic by defining the work as a model of reality.

Julia Kristeva, on the other hand, focuses on the pragmatic dimension. She defines art as an "investigation of the process that constitutes the subject," [11] which she describes as a "subject-in-process" and not as a Cartesian Ego. She explains this particular concept by referring to the psychoanalytic theories of Freud and Jacques Lacan. Kristeva proceeds from the opposition between the "semiotic" and the "symbolic." She defines the "semiotic"—in opposition to the common usage of the term — as the realm of the instinctual drives and their articulation. It has, at least, a contradictory, dual structure, for it is the "birthplace" of the subject as well as the place of its negation, where "its unity gives way to the process of charges and stases that is the one causing this unity." [12]

The "symbolic," on the other hand, is defined as the realm of significance and meaning, that is, "the realm of theses." [13] Without thesis, there is no meaning, and without meaning, the "symbolic" does not exist. Hence, it follows that the "symbolic" has a specific relation to the subject: as the realm of thetic acts, the "symbolic" functions as the basic condition for the constitution of the subject — as a system of intersubjectively valid meanings; the "symbolic," on the other hand, negates the subject, which means that both the "semiotic" and the "symbolic" have a dual structure regarding the subject.

The subject comes into being, according to Kristeva, when the "semiotic" and the "symbolic" meet; for it is exclusively the place of their meeting where "meaning is brought forth." [14] In other words, the subject is only able to constitute the self as a subject within the process of meaning-constitution. Art performs this process in a way that points clearly to the subjective determination of any meaning-constitution. Most of the significative systems are characterized by the attempt of the "symbolic" to repress the "semiotic" as much as possible and to control it by positing and fixing the order of its signifiers. Art, on the contrary, can be defined as "the semiotization of the symbolic." [15] For here the "semiotic" breaks into the order as formed by the denotative language and destructures and/or restructures it.

The "semiotic" thus destroys the intersubjectively valid sign system of the denotative language and transforms it into a new system: that of the poetic language. The work, the result of this process, is therefore "the insignificant." [16] The particular deformation of the denotative language as performed by the poetic language of the work can be taken as an adequate representation of the "subject-in-process." This means that the representation and constitution of the subject by/in the work is determined and effected by the particular order (or disorder) formed by the individual elements of the work through their internal relations: the realization of the pragmatic dimension is based on and determined by the syntactic.

Moreover, the deformation as performed in the work also affects the particular relationship between language and the objects of reality, i.e., the semantic dimension. For even if the subject tries to imitate an object while creating a work of art by reproducing a vocal, gestural, verbal, or other signifier, the subject cannot reach the object, not even by mediation of the "symbolic." This is because the subject "crosses the symbolic" and arrives at the realm of the "semiotic," which is "beyond the social border" and beyond the object.[17]

Although Kristeva focuses on the pragmatic dimension of the work of art by defining it as the place where the subject of its author, as well as of its interpreter, constitutes the self, she also explains its particular relation to the syntactic as well as to the semantic dimension of the work.

Finally, to finish this short and very incomplete survey, Jan Mukařovský defines the work of art as an autonomous sign that may be adequately described and understood as a reality of its own.[18] Thus, he particularly stresses the importance of the syntactic dimension of the work. In this way, he refers to the third model, the rhetorical concept of art. By investigating the particular conditions underlying the specific status of the work, Mukařovský also establishes a certain relationship among all the models of historical concepts of art and, thus, considers all three semiotic dimensions.

Mukařovský proceeds from the opposition between the communicative sign and the autonomous aesthetic sign. Whereas the communicative sign always refers to an actual concrete reality, known to the one who gives the sign and about which the one to whom the sign is given can be informed, the work of art as an autonomous sign has no definite reference. Insofar as it has objects of reality as its theme, it does not represent these objects but uses them as a means to represent another reality. Since the work of art does not serve as any kind of instrument, it cannot be taken as the expression of the emotions of its author either. It is autonomous as regards the reality represented as its theme, as well as regards the subjectivity of its author. Mukařovský explains this peculiarity by referring to the dominance of the aesthetic function that governs all the nonaesthetic functions within the work.

The aesthetic function is not inherent to the work; it is attributed by the beholder. Accordingly, Mukařovský defines the aesthetic as follows:

1. The aesthetic is, in itself, neither a real property of an object nor is it explicitly connected to some of its properties. 2. The aesthetic function of an

object is likewise not totally under the control of an individual, although from a purely subjective standpoint the aesthetic function may be acquired (or, conversely, lost) by anything, regardless of its organisation. 3. Stabilising the aesthetic function is a matter for the collective and is a component in the relationship between the human collective and the world.[19]

This unique quality of the aesthetic function implies a particular relationship between the work of art and reality:

In art . . . the reality about which the work directly provides information (in thematic art) is not the real source of the material connection, but only its intermediary. The real tie in this situation is a variable one, and points to realities known to the viewer. They are not, and can in no way be expressed or even indicated in the work itself, because it forms a component of the viewer's intimate experience.[20]

This suggests that the autonomy of the aesthetic sign is based on the fact that it does not have a semantic dimension of its own to which its statements could be related and thus be verified or falsified. The semantic dimension of the work, on the contrary, comes into existence through the process of reception that is performed according to the particular condition of the structure of the work (its syntactic dimension) and of the recipient (its pragmatic dimension). Thus, the process by which the recipient constitutes the meaning of the work is to be seen as the process that leads to the construction of its semantic dimension. As a result of this process, the work is related to reality: it is not by the work that reality is reconstructed but by the recipient who reconstructs reality by attributing meanings to the work. This means that the work, on the one hand, can be seen as an autonomous sign, forming a reality of its own. On the other hand, the work becomes related to the subjectivity of the recipient as well as to reality in the process of reception. The relation between art and "objective" reality, art and subjectivity, is not established within the work but results from the process of meaning-constitution which the recipient performs. Thus, we must consider that

the realities with which the art work can be confronted in the consciousness and subconsciousness of the viewer are squeezed into the general, intellectual, emotional, and free attitude which the viewer assumes toward reality in general. The experience which surges through the viewer as a result of confronting the work of art spreads to the total image in the viewer's thoughts. The indefinite nature of the material tie of the work of art is compensated by the fact that it is paralleled by the perceiving individual who reacts, not partially but with all aspects of his attitude toward the world and reality.[21]

In this way, Mukařovský stresses the need to consider all three semiotic dimensions, although he particularly emphasizes the syntactic and the pragmatic — and the pragmatic dimension with respect to the interpreter only.

Thus, we can conclude that the semiotic concept of art — independent of the specific semiotic theory of art to which it refers — can be seen as a kind of correction to the historical concepts of art, since it denies and overcomes their onesidedness in the attempt to synthesize their basic definitions. This change of the general approach entails some important consequences regarding particular methods of interpretation. Since they are elaborated depending on and in accordance with a specific concept of art, each is related to a different semiotic dimension. If we proceed from the assumption that any process of interpretation has to consider all three semiotic dimensions, a combination of different methods seems to be the necessary consequence: a structural method will be combined, for instance, with a psychoanalytic one, a social-historical with a genre-oriented approach, an interactional with a linguistic method, and so forth. In other words, the semiotic approach will inevitably lead to a plurality of methods. This may, in fact, challenge literary scholarship to make some important changes. On the other hand, it does not affect the basic consent regarding the definition of its primary function and aim. The quest for meaning can still be carried out as the search for possible particular meanings of the work, even if plural methods may be needed for this purpose.

THE CHALLENGE OF POSTMODERN ART

It is this very premise that is challenged by the works of avant-garde and postmodern art. For if we attempt to constitute their meaning as, for instance, representations of reality, expressions of subjectivity, individual realities, or experiences of the recipient, we shall certainly fail — even if we take into consideration that their meaning may include and realize all of these possibilities. Let us try to find out the reason — or, at least, some reasons — for this fatal state of affairs. For this purpose, I shall consider a concrete example taken from the postmodern theatre, Robert Wilson's production of *The Golden Windows*, staged at the Munich Kammerspiele in 1982.

One of the constitutive factors of dramatic theatre to which interpreters can always refer and from which they mostly proceed when interpreting and judging a production is the category of dramatic character. Onstage a dramatic character is usually created when an actor establishes a certain relationship between the language of the play and his or her own individual body. Thus, the words uttered and the tone of voice in which they are uttered, as well as the facial expressions, gestures, and movements performed, can be taken as signs pointing to the dramatic character being enacted. This means that a dramatic character is always created by a thetic act which the actor performs when establishing a particular relationship between language and body, whether the created character may be meant or interpreted as a psychological, philosophical, actantial, or other unity or as fragmentary, contradictory, incomplete, dissociated. By interpreting the physical acts and the speech-acts the actor performs, we can constitute the meaning of their relationship as a particular dramatic character that (1) represents a fictional character portraying a certain type of character in reality, (2) expresses the subjectivity of a fictional character that may be related to the subjectivity of the producer, (3) constitutes a reality of its own (i.e., the reality of the fictional character), and (4) possibly fulfills a certain emotional function for the spectator, who may identify with the character or project certain images (of parents, brothers, sisters, etc.) into it. In any case, the dramatic character, as the meaning of a particular relationship between several physical acts and speech acts, is revealed as the result of a semiosis which applies this relationship to each of the semiotic dimensions.

Robert Wilson, on the contrary, annuls this very relationship. He totally disconnects language and body, speech acts and physical acts, from each other. The words or lines the actor has to speak are often taped during the performance. This means, on the one hand, that language is separated from the body of the actor: the body has ceased to function as the source and instrument of the words and is replaced by a loudspeaker. Thus, the uttered words are no longer related to the actor's body, which, nonetheless, is present onstage. Since we are used to understanding the actor's body as a sign of the dramatic character (as, in the written play, the name) we are no longer able to relate the spoken language to a dramatic character.

On the other hand, the words now become a part and an element of a sound-collage that combines several words, lines, and phrases, spoken by different actors, as well as various sounds, noises, and musical sequences. It is characteristic of these sound-collages that the linguistic material often points openly to texts and contexts outside the performance — for instance, to well-known commercials and other ready-mades of American mass-media jargon or to various poetic texts, for example, by Gertrude Stein, Kafka, or Beckett.

The gestures and movements of the actor, however, are performed in a way that renders it almost impossible to relate them — and that means the actor's body — to the category of dramatic character. This effect is caused, above all, by a considerable slowing down of the motion; every movement of every part of the body is performed so slowly that it can be compared neither to any "natural" movement in everyday life or in realistic theatre nor to any "artificial" movement as performed in acrobatics, in highly codified theatrical forms (such as the *no* theatre or the Peking opera), or in some avant-garde theatres which draw on different forms and types of Far Eastern theatre. Thus, movement ceases to be a meaningful gesture: instead, the focus is now on movement as a mere process.

On the other hand, the movements of the actors are timed to be synchronized with other movements onstage: movements of objects and, above all, movements of light. They become an element of a movement-pattern that by no means indicates anything we could label a dramatic character.

By disconnecting physical acts and speech acts, the actor's body and his or her language, from each other, Robert Wilson deconstructs the dramatic character as a theatrical category. Any possible relationship between the two is annulled; each is related to other kinds of elements within the performance. We can describe Wilson's method as follows.

1. By separating language and body from each other, he deprives both of the particular context within which they can function as signs of a dramatic character. Thus, he dissolves the syntactic dimension which would be formed by their combination.

2. Since language and body only function as signs of a dramatic character within the context of the specific relationship between them, decontextualization leads to a desemantization: body and language cease to function as signs of a dramatic character, which means that they lose their particular semantic dimension as formed by the reflections, emotions, actions, etc., of a dramatic character.

3. By combining the words, lines, phrases, etc., spoken by one actor with those spoken by another, as well as with sounds, noises, musical sequences, and, on the other hand, by combining the movements of one actor with those of another as well as with object-movements and light-movements, Wilson forms new contexts within which relations are established between different kinds of sounds and different kinds of movements. This contextualization leads to a restructuring of the syntactic dimension.

4. Since the linguistic material of the sound-collages points to texts and contexts beyond the performance, the process of contextualization establishes certain relations between elements of the performance and contexts external

to the performance. Thus, an intertextuality is created. This intertextuality gives rise to a semantization of the elements in question: a semantic dimension is restored.

It is characteristic of this process that it does not emphasize one semiotic dimension, or even different semiotic dimensions in turn, but the permanent shift of the focus from one dimension to another and vice versa: from the pragmatic dimension, which determines that the elements (body and language) are taken out of their context and how this is done, to the syntactic dimension in the process of decontextualization; from the syntactic to the semantic by desemantization; from the semantic back to the pragmatic, which determines in which new contexts the elements will be placed, and from here back to the syntactic dimension again when contextualizing; from the syntactic to the semantic as well as to the pragmatic dimension; for it depends on the pragmatic as to what kind of intertextuality will be produced, what kind of semantic dimension will be construed.

As a consequence of this procedure, none of the possibly established relations seems to be of great importance since, in the next moment, they appear to be annulled. Thus, no one particular meaning of the elements in question (here: spoken language and bodily movement) is stressed, but the process of deconstruction — as regards the dramatic character; construction — as far as the new contexts of sound-collages and movement-patterns are concerned; and reconstruction — with respect to different relations to contexts outside the staging which give rise to intertextuality. In other words, the focus is on the very process of semiosis and not on its results.

This change will affect theatre studies and literary scholarship. The dominant function and purpose of interpretation aim toward the results of the semiotic process; it intends to (re)construct the work as a symbolic object by constituting the meaning(s) of its individual elements, its more complex syntagma, and the work as a whole. If the work is structured in a way that annuls any meaning it might have produced by permanently rearranging and re-establishing the relations between individual elements or more complex syntagmas, it will make little — if any — sense to search for any particular meaning that could be attributed to them. Even if we take into consideration that different meanings may often be possible, nowadays this kind of approach generally appears to be obsolete. For neither the possibility of different meanings nor the actually constituted meanings are of interest, but solely the infinite process by which meaning is deconstructed, constructed anew, or reconstructed and deconstructed again, and so forth. Accordingly, the quest for meaning can no longer be realized as the search for a particular meaning of a certain element or syntagma, but as the reconstruction of the semiotic process.

The shift of the focus from the result — that is, from the meaning that may be constituted — to the semiotic process — that is, to the process by which meaning may be produced — is triggered by avant-garde and postmodern works of art. Nonetheless, it can now be transferred and applied to works that are created in order to constitute certain meanings; they will be analyzed according to the particular process by which they produce meaning. The investigation now aims at the different modes of meaning-production and no longer at the different meanings that might be constituted. In other words, whereas literary scholarship was defined and characterized by its attempts to solve the problem of finding the possible meaning(s) of a work, it now has to deal with the question of how the meaning of a work comes into being. This change constitutes a new paradigm of literary scholarship.

On the other hand, it would be highly erroneous and even ridiculous to proclaim that the new age of theatre studies will be exclusively dedicated to the investigation of different semiotic processes and their specific function in theatre and literature. A thoroughly legitimate need to search for the possible meaning(s) of a work still exists. However, theatre studies and literary scholarship cannot define themselves by referring to the different modes of meaning-production only. Interpretation will invariably remain one of their most important functions and tasks.

This state of affairs need not create a schism in the humanities, in particular the art-related sciences. For both kinds of approaches are related to each other. Reconstructing the semiotic process by restructuring and reestablishing different possible relations between elements of the work, on the one side, and between elements of the work and elements outside the work, on the other, is not exclusive and can be followed or even accompanied by an interpretation of the work that is based on the insights this reconstruction has yielded in terms of the various relations. On the other hand, it hardly seems possible that a meaning will be constituted as the result of certain established relations without having established these relations, which is to say, without having inquired into the semiotic process. Thus, we can conclude that the quest for meaning will be performed as a sequence of thetic acts which establish certain relations which deconstruct, construct, or reconstruct meaning — the one focusing on such processes, and the other on their results.

WRITTEN DRAMA/ORAL PERFORMANCE

THE DRAMA: LITERATURE OR THEATRE?

Theatre in the West is essentially characterized by the tension between written drama and orality. Since Aristotle, there has been much dissent as to whether drama should be considered under literature as writing or under theatre as orality. While Aristotle sharply distinguished drama as literary text from its performance in the theatre because "the effect of tragedy can be felt without the performance or the actor,"[1] drama theorists today tend to classify drama as a "multimedial text."[2] This is a valid approach since literary theory has consistently neglected the dimension of performance. Some conclusions drawn on the basis of such an approach, however, may not always be entirely appropriate.

This is because there are fundamental differences between the performance of a drama and its literary text in terms of both the media and semiotics. Drama, with its fixed, written text, belongs to the class monomedial texts. The performance, on the other hand, which at the very least is communicated by two media — the stage and the actor — belongs to the class multimedial texts. While the literary text consists exclusively of homogeneous linguistic/written signs, and even complex signs (such as character and plot) arise through the combination of linguistic/written signs, the performance is made up of heterogeneous signs which may be verbal or nonverbal (mime, gesture, proxemics, mask, costume, props, set, sounds, music).[3] The literary text of the drama belongs, therefore, to the category writing, the performance of the drama, on the other hand, to orality.

This important distinction between the drama and its performance in media and semiotics has far-reaching consequences in the study of the dramatic dialogue. For the dramatic dialogue primarily represents — even in the fixed, literary text — a face-to-face interaction which, by definition, must fall within the sphere of orality. Second, the language of the dialogue can be constructed so differently that its variants can range across a whole continuum extending between two extremes — a highly elaborate written language and a completely artless spoken language. The tension between writing and orality is thus both constitutive and productive for the dramatic dialogue as much in the literary text of the drama as in its performance.

Our point of departure stems from this unique feature of the dramatic dialogue. The dramatic dialogue is a specific meaning-generating system that is made up of the special alternating relations between writing and orality.

This chapter examines how this system functions. The criteria used to define orality and writing are based on the work of Paul Koch and Wolf Oesterreicher.[4] In the context of our discussion, it is the dramatic dialogue in performance which provides the more interesting and varying functions. Since, however, it is most often based on a literary dramatic dialogue, an introductory systematic of the types of literary dramatic dialogue relevant to our theme is outlined below.

THE LITERARY DRAMATIC DIALOGUE

Every literary dramatic dialogue is — as is the whole text of the drama — organized into "primary" and "secondary" text.[5] The secondary text may be limited to giving the name of the person speaking — and thereby changes in who has the floor — or extended to the provision of detailed information on intonation, mime, gesture, posture, and movement of the speaker or listener. In some cases it may grow into an independent descriptive text of considerable size. Every literary dramatic dialogue thus consists of two different textual systems whose interference produces its particular meaning: one system which constitutes the character's speech and one system which typifies the character's behavior outside the actual dialogue. Thus, we must further distinguish the literary dramatic dialogue according to the extent to which each of the two textual systems is responsible for constituting meaning. Since such a criterion would imply an endless multiplicity of possibilities, we need to make a basic distinction between (1) dialogue whose secondary text is solely restricted to giving the name of the speaker, where meaning is provided through the speech text of the characters and through attribution to their names, and (2) dialogue which, besides listing the names of the speakers, contains a reasonably extensive secondary text offering information not provided in the speech where the meaning is constituted — above and beyond the attribution of speech to name of speaker — solely through the various specific interferences between the speech text and the secondary text.

The dominance of the speech text characterizes, to varying degrees, genres that are as widely different as Shakespeare, classical French or German drama, and the lyrical drama of the *fin de siècle*.

Although there is face-to-face interaction in the lyrical drama of the *fin de siècle*, for example, no other characteristics here indicate orality. There is no explicit reference to the dialogue partner who speaks, the listener, or the situation. Rather, the dialogue is molded by various poetic systems where reflection, decontextualization, density of information, and elaborateness predominate. A situation of direct communication is enacted through the media of elaborate writing.

In German classical drama, the dominance of the speech text operates quite differently. Here the system of turn-taking is acknowledged by the speech text itself. Although, for example, in Goethe's *Iphigenia in Tauris* (1787) all dialogue partners speak in the same style (i.e., cannot be differentiated from one another according to individual styles of speech), the alternating changes between the speaker and the one who responds are so apparent, beyond any change of name in the speech text, that every indication of name for the purpose of ordering the speech and showing the system of turn-taking can be dispensed with. All this can be easily gained from the text itself.

On the one hand, speech is characterized by involvement, context dependency, expressivity, and affectivity. Nevertheless, the dialogue can still operate without a secondary text that would normally describe the various nonverbal signs which would be typical of this kind of situation in direct communication. Instead, all information is provided by a speech text characterized by a wealth of information, compactness, complexity, and elaborateness, based on a specific poetic modeling of the dialogue.

The second dialogue type, whose meaning is constituted by the specific *interference of speech text and secondary text*, always points to a more intense situation of direct communication than does the first type as it explicitly underlines the paralinguistic, mimic, and proxemic signs in the secondary text used by the dialogue partners in the course of the dialogue. Meaning can thus only be accorded to the dialogue when the linguistic signs of the secondary text that point to nonverbal signs are related to the linguistic signs of the speech text. This can be realized in far more different ways than can the absolute dominance of the speech text. If we are aiming toward a useful systematization, it would therefore make sense to limit our discussion to two possible extremes. Either the speech text contributes more to the constitution of meaning in the dialogue than the secondary text or the meaning of the secondary text dominates that of the speech text. Both positions are limited by the absolute dominance of the speech text in one case and by the absolute dominance of the secondary text in the other (as in Beckett's *Actes sans paroles* or Handke's *Das Mündel will Vormund sein* [The Minor Wants to Be Guardian]).

In the German domestic tragedies (*Bürgerliche Trauerspiele*) of the eighteenth century, the secondary text is systematically built up as an integral component of the dramatic dialogue through stage directions referring to the behavior of the characters. In Lessing's *Emilia Galotti* (1772), for example, the speech text and the secondary text complement each other, and this alternating cross-referral constitutes the meaning of the dialogue. The secondary text may list mimic and gestural behavior which strengthens the emotions already expressed in the choice of words or syntax or it may describe deliberate actions which complement the blanks in an incomplete speech text. Nonetheless, the speech text is of considerably greater importance than the secondary text. Through it, the most significant information is communicated, just as the emotions are principally expressed through its specifically linguistic form.

The tension between writing and orality is considerably reduced here in comparison to the first two examples, although not so much that one could speak of a simple — written — notation of a situation of direct communication. The dominant features are spontaneity, involvement, interference of situation, expressivity, affectivity, and an intense sense of process. These arise mainly through the interference of speech text and secondary text. They realize the aesthetic program of creating the illusion of reality, that is, a situation of direct communication.

On the other hand, the features complexity, elaborateness, and construction cannot be overlooked. They point to a conception of character that is determined by the rationality in principle of human beings, whose feelings, however, are natural phenomena given natural physical expression. Since the tension between writing and orality is greatly reduced in comparison to that in French (and German) classic drama, it thus draws attention to explicitly bourgeois values.

In naturalist drama, the tension is, in fact, so reduced that one can speak of simulation — and thereby notation — of a situation of direct communication. Here it often happens that the behavior of a character described in the secondary text does not conform to the speech acts performed by the character in the speech text. The linguistic signs of the speech text and the nonverbal signs carried out in the secondary text appear in undisguised contradiction to one another. While the character's words might portray indifference, for example, or at least disinterest, the character's nonverbal behavior betrays fierce emotional involvement, or vice versa. The meaning of the secondary text thus contradicts that of the speech text.

While in the German *Bürgerliche Trauerspiele* of the eighteenth century the meaning of the secondary text solely intensifies, concretizes, or complements that of the primary text, here it modifies (in the sense of either expansion or dilution) and even stands in direct opposition to the meaning of the primary text. One might summarize the possible relations between the speech text and the secondary text as complementation, concretization, modification (intensification or dilution), and contradiction. In any case, the meaning of the dramatic dialogue can only be constituted by the outcome of the specific relations between the two textual systems.

The dominance of meanings carried in the secondary text over those of the speech text is clear. For they point to the actual feelings and inner thoughts of the character which are neither revealed nor spoken in the speech text. It is only through the secondary text that it is possible to deduce the character's dialogic strategy, which would be completely incomprehensible when drawn from the speech text alone.

Thus, it is the circumstances of communication as much as the strategies of speech in the naturalistic dialogue that point to the features of orality. In this way, on the other hand, an aesthetic program is realized that is comparable to the early bourgeois illusionist theatre inasmuch as it postulates an imitation of reality. Exclusive recourse to orality functions, however, as a sign of a fundamentally changed character conception. It focuses on a split in the character which the frequent contradictions between speech text and secondary text also highlight. It is only through the nonverbal behavior that the appropriate conclusions can be drawn concerning the inner world and thoughts of the character. While solely the physical expression is "true," the words lie, deceive, betray, or are simply inadequate. The character might not even consciously recognize the inner processes thus exposed. They seem to flow without the character's control and are thus removed from consciousness or awareness. Rational decisions are not possible. The character falls victim as much to circumstances as to lack of self-autonomy.

The shifts in the relations between writing and orality thus signalize, on the one hand, the comparability of general aesthetic conception and, on the other, fundamental differences in character conception.

THE THEATRICAL DRAMATIC DIALOGUE

Unlike the literary dramatic dialogue, the theatrical dramatic dialogue not only points to a situation of direct communication, it also represents it. Its realization employs all those sign systems which are characteristic of a situation of direct communication: linguistic, paralinguistic, mimic, gestural, and prox-emic signs. The meaning of the theatrical dramatic dialogue is thus created by the interference of different semiotic sign systems. As a result of this, the the-atrical dramatic dialogue should be systematized according to each specific interference. To do this, it is necessary to begin by distinguishing between the two semiotic systems employed: verbal and nonverbal signs. Either group of signs may occur in various specific relation to the other.

> In the theater, the linguistic sign system, which intervenes through the dramatic text, always combines and conflicts with the acting, which be-longs to an entirely different sign system. All the other components, such as music, scenic sets, and so forth, can be eliminated by the text itself; by the same token, the intervention of the sign systems to which they belong can be reduced to "zero degree," unless they reenter the theatrical struc-ture through the intermediary of the actor. Therefore, the general func-tion of drama in the shaping of the semiotics of theater can be brought out only by means of confronting two sign systems that are invariably present, that is, language and acting.[6]

From this in turn arise two fundamentally different possibilities. Either the verbal signs (language) dominate the nonverbal (performance) or vice versa. Thus, the theatrical dialogue can be systematized according to the dominance of verbal or nonverbal signs. Before examining those two extreme positions separately, I shall offer some preliminary thoughts on the relation between the literary and the theatrical dramatic dialogue and advance a gen-eral survey of the possible interrelations between verbal and nonverbal signs.

THE LITERARY AND THE THEATRICAL DRAMATIC DIALOGUE

From a historical point of view, there is naturally a close correlation between (1) the literary dramatic dialogue, which realizes the dominance of speech text, and the theatrical dramatic dialogue, which is dominated by verbal signs, as there is between (2) the literary dramatic dialogue characterized by the interference between speech text and secondary text and the theatrical dra-matic dialogue in which nonverbal signs predominate.

Goethe's "Rules for Actors," for example, explicitly show that he (living in the classical age) was seeking to secure a clear dominance of the verbal sign in theatre. In paragraphs 1–33 he considers in detail the problems of declama-tion and in particular how to articulate and structure the text in performance.

§22 In order to achieve a proper declamation, one should observe the following rules:

When I first completely understand the sense of a word and feel it completely within, then I must seek to fit it with a suitable vocal tone and deliver it strongly or weakly, quickly or slowly, as the sense of each sentence requires. For example:

"Nations of men shall fade away" must be spoken half loud, murmuring.

"Their names shall toll" must be spoken clearly, ringingly.

"Dark forgetfulness / Spreads her wings, dark as night / Over all mankind" must be spoken in deep, hollow, fearful tones.[7]

The sole purpose of declamation is to make the speech text comprehensible to the spectator. Gesture also serves this goal in that it does not divert attention away from the speech but supports and strengthens it.

§63 In order to attain a proper sense of pantomime and to be able to judge the same properly, one should note the following rules:

One should stand before a mirror and speak what one is to declaim softly or preferably not at all, but only think the words. In this way one will not be distracted by the declamation but rather easily observe every false movement that does not express one's thoughts or softly spoken words. Thus one can select the most beautiful and most suitable gestures and can express through the entire pantomime a movement analogous with the sense of the words, with the features of the art.[8]

Although the theatrical dramatic dialogue as a performed piece of face-to-face interaction clearly belongs to the sphere of orality, Goethe attempts to organize the nonverbal signs relating to orality (the paralinguistic, mimic, and gestural signs) so that the significant features of writing running through the speech text are maintained and also emphasized. The same underlying aesthetic concept forces the literary and the theatrical dialogue into direct relation with one another — the art of acting is subordinate to poetic art, as §83 of the "Rules for Actors" prescribes: "The stage should be considered a figureless tableau for which the actors supply the figures."[9]

Lessing, on the other hand, tried to create the illusion of reality onstage and present individual characters. He saw poetry and performance in quite a different relationship to each other. His aim was to create an art of acting that would be independent of poetry and that would ultimately be able to portray characters without it. Lessing, like Diderot, was convinced that the gestural signs in the art of acting are more capable of conveying emotions than linguistic signs and felt this to be the most important function in the art of acting. Not only do gestural signs realize the secondary text, they also authenticate the truth of the speech. When the actor deliberately reproduces the paralinguistic, mimetic, and gestural signs of anger in the right way, for example,

> the nervous walk, the stomping feet, the raw, sometimes shrieking, sometimes bitter tone, the movement of the eyebrows, the quivering lips, the gnashing of teeth and so on — if he only . . . imitates those things which can be imitated, if you like, and does it well, then without fail a dark feeling of anger will befall his soul which reacts throughout the whole body and produces there those changes which are not simply under our control; his face will burn, his eyes flash, his muscles swell; in short, he will seem to be truly angry.[10]

The true illusion of anger can only be produced by the art of acting. In this sense, according to Lessing, in realizing the aesthetic concept of the theatrical dramatic dialogue, the nonverbal signs are given a certain dominance over the verbal — at least in the case of the portrayal and expression of emotions.[11]

Consequently, an analogy in the formation of the dominants in the dramatic dialogue between the literary text of the drama and its performance in theatre (the dominance of the speech text/the dominance of verbal signs, interference between speech and secondary text or the dominance of the secondary text/the dominance of nonverbal signs) can, as the examples given above show, be historically guaranteed. If these dramas were produced today, on the other hand, such an analogy is not necessarily valid. Goethe's *Iphigenia in Tauris* may, for example, be performed with a clear dominance of nonverbal signs, as Hans Neuenfels demonstrated in his production at the Schauspielhaus in Frankfurt (1979). In this respect, the historically guaranteed analogy must be balanced against a systematic definition of different types of dialogue.

POSSIBLE RELATIONS BETWEEN VERBAL AND NONVERBAL SIGNS

The theatrical dramatic dialogue belongs fundamentally to the sphere of orality. As the historical examples have shown, it can also occur in such a way that it emphasizes the characteristics of writing. It would thus seem necessary to begin by differentiating the basic possible relations between verbal and nonverbal signs.

According to Klaus Scherer,[12] the different functions which the non-verbal signs fulfill in terms of the verbal should be summarized and classified into three categories — the parasyntactic, the parasemantic, and the parapragmatic.

As regards the parasyntactic dimension, the nonverbal signs principally provide structure to the flow of speech. Paralinguistic signs such as these provide emphasis, stress, intonation, and pause, for example. Through emphasis, a particular word can be isolated to underline its significance; a pause might mark the end of a section or theme or its transition to another; intonation might suggest that the person speaking intends to continue the argument or is finishing it; and so on. Certain gestures can also be used in a similar way. A raised eyebrow or a brief, direct stare might emphasize a sentence or indicate that the speaker is reaching the crux of the argument or is ending it. A nod of the head or certain rhythmic hand movements might achieve a similar effect. Gestures such as these are, more than any others, most in a position to accentuate or structure the thought process. They belong to the category of gestures that Paul Ekman termed "illustrators."[13] Proxemic signs, too, may serve the same function: a step toward the person spoken to, for example, might indicate the significance of the words that follow, rhythmical pacing to and fro might structure or outline the thought process, and so on. Consequently, the parasyntactic functions are important for their contribution to a clearer structuring of the spoken text, helping to make it more easily understood.

The parasemantic functions of the nonverbal signs produce certain relations to the meanings of the verbal signs to which they refer. The most significant of these relations are substitution, complementation, modification, neutralization, and contradiction.

Nonverbal signs, coded or noncoded, can stand in place of verbal ones. If a nod of the head is employed as a sign of affirmation, or if a demonstrative gesture takes the place of a spoken instruction, then these signs can be interpreted on the basis of a code that is assumed to be generally known in our own culture. These gestures function as "emblems,"[14] as signs which have a quasi-lexical meaning. If, on the other hand, an entreating look should take the place of a spoken plea, it must be understood intuitively, instinctively (i.e., on the basis of the individual's personal experience).

Nonverbal signs can supplement verbal ones in different ways. A gesture or special intonation might, for example, illustrate the meaning of the linguistic signs by indicating the size, shape, or scale of the person or object being spoken of. Or nonverbal signs might act as repetition of the verbal ones: where the sentence "I feel sad" is spoken with the appropriate paralinguistic signs — for example, with sobbing or quivering voice — while the face adopts a typically sad expression and head and shoulders are lightly inclined,[15] the nonverbal signs constitute the same meaning as the verbal signs: it is repeated and substantiated.

On the other hand, the meaning of the verbal signs might be weakened, strengthened, or slightly altered by nonverbal signs. A sentence which, according to its syntactic structure, may be interpreted as a statement can, for example, be transformed by certain emphasis into a question, an exclamation, a command, an expression of doubt, etc. In order to understand a sentence properly, it requires more than mere understanding of the performative verb and the preposition that follows it — the intonation of the sentence must also be considered. In this sense, for example, a gentle smile or a sympathetic gesture might weaken a command into a friendly request just as a cautionary word can be intensified through relevant emphasis, gesture, or facial expression into a threat.

One special kind of modification is neutralization: the meaning of the verbal sign is so diluted that it loses practically all validity. Where, for example, the sentence "I am so sorry, can I do anything for you?" expressing sympathy and pity is spoken in an indifferent tone and is accompanied by disinterested gestures and behavior, the meaning, though not completely lost, is nonetheless so changed that the sympathy expressed on the verbal level must be understood as purely conventional behavior and not as the expression of a deeply felt emotion.

Where the nonverbal signs not only neutralize the meaning of verbal ones but also constitute a wholly opposite meaning, they thoroughly contradict the verbal signs. If the above example is spoken in a tone that betrays the speaker's secret delight and is accompanied by a radiant — or perhaps stifled — smile, a glint in the eye, shoulders thrown back, etc., a contradiction between the meaning of the verbal and that of the nonverbal sign is produced. The meaning of this contradiction can now only be discovered by reference to the situation, to the relation between the dialogue partners, to the specific circumstances of the speaker, or to the usual predominant sign system of the theatre form in question. A contradiction such as this may function as a sign of the real existence of contradictory feelings in the speaker, as the sign of deliberate, unsuccessful deception, or as the sign of the prevalence of one of the two emotions shown according to the dominance of the sign system: if language is the dominant sign system, then pity outweighs the other emotion in the contradiction. If, on the other hand, the meaning of the nonverbal signs dominates, then the ruling emotion is one of delight.

In considering the parapragmatic functions of the nonverbal signs, two fundamentally different possibilities should be distinguished: (1) the nonverbal signs refer to the speaker, the listener, and the interaction between them; and (2) the nonverbal signs indicate the system of turn-taking.

In the first case, the nonverbal signs may refer to the expression of the speaker and the reaction of the listener and function as the sign of the special relationship between the two within the process of the interaction.

If the nonverbal signs are an expression of the speaker's emotional or mental frame of mind which is constant throughout the dialogue process (for example, joy, sorrow, irritation, aggression, need for moral support, absentmindedness, etc.) then they influence the meaning of the speech as a whole. For signs such as these cannot refer to individual verbal signs, but only to the speech given by the speaker in its entirety.

The nonverbal signs which indicate the reaction of the listener might reveal the degree of attention (as when they show whether the listener is actually listening or not), the evaluation of the other's words as shown through nodding or shaking of the head, smiling, frowning, etc., or the listener's comprehension of the speaker.[16]

If, on the other hand, the nonverbal signs function as an element in the system of turn-taking, then they indicate or prepare for the change of speaker or the continuation of the same speaker. For if the speaker has completed a sentence according to grammatical criteria but employs a continuously increasing intonation, the intention is to continue to hold the floor. However, changes in posture, a step back, lowering of the eyes, etc., signal that the speaker has finished speaking and that the other may now begin to reply. Since such nonverbal signs explicitly show whether the speaker acknowledges the end of the speech or would rather continue, they contribute a great deal to a better understanding of the dialogue process.[17]

In the theatrical dramatic dialogue, the nonverbal signs may, in relation to the verbal signs, fulfill all the parasyntactic, parasemantic, and parapragmatic functions dealt with here. It remains to be seen which of these functions are given priority in the two types of dialogue we have already identified.

THE DOMINANCE OF VERBAL SIGNS

The dominance of verbal signs is based on the general assumption that the speech performed by the characters onstage is the most important meaning-producing system. It must, in any case, be comprehensible. The nonverbal signs acquire their special function as a result of this fact: they help the spectator to comprehend the meaning constituted by the verbal signs better.

This special function indicates a certain choice to be made from all the possible kinds of nonverbal signs: only those signs are chosen which appear particularly appropriate and which allow the meaning of the verbal signs to stand out more clearly.

In this respect, the parasyntactic functions have considerable importance. For it is principally through careful structuring of the flow of speech that the spoken text is given shape and its construction made apparent. One would therefore give preference to those nonverbal signs which are in a position to emphasize and underline single words, expressions, sentences, or phrases or which can provide stress and contour the continuation of the argument. Particularly effective in this are specific paralinguistic signs such as stress, pitch, volume, articulation, rhythm, tempo, intonation, and pauses as well as gestural signs such as certain rhythmic actions of the hand, head, and bodily movements or proxemic signs such as pacing to and fro, walking or remaining still, and so on.

While such parasyntactic functions in this dialogue type are employed to their fullest extent, the parasemantic functions are considerably reduced. This is because any functions which do not synchronize the nonverbal and the verbal signs are, to a large extent, excluded — almost reduced to "zero." Under these circumstances, the most important parasemantic function of the nonverbal sign is that it provides complementation.

Here only those nonverbal signs would be chosen which illustrate or repeat the meaning of the verbal signs, in particular those paralinguistic signs which function as acoustic icons as well as all kinds of mimic, gestural, or proxemic signs which indicate a specific appearance, size, shape, direction, position in space, or scale of an object or person referred to by the verbal signs. One particular category of nonverbal signs are the so-called affect displays which serve to intensify meaning.[18] These signs reveal the affective situation of the persons speaking inasmuch as they refer to single elements of the speech (and not the dialogue as a whole). Such signs repeat the emotion which is currently being spoken of. If a character is speaking of anger, that is, verbally expresses anger, the character can execute nonverbal signs which indicate an angry frame of mind (for example, clenched fists, a deep frown, a rapid pacing). In this way, the nonverbal signs strengthen and intensify the meaning of the verbal signs.

The modification of meaning constituted by nonverbal signs only seems possible to a limited extent. However, a slight weakening/intensification is possible. Or modification might be employed when the speaker's words have a double or multiple meaning: the nonverbal signs can reduce the number of possible meanings and guide the spectator toward deciding on a specific meaning. In this case, the nonverbal signs alter the meanings of the verbal signs by fixing them.

Neutralization and contradiction are functions more or less excluded here. For if the verbal signs constitute the essential meaning of the dialogue, a correct understanding of it will certainly not be achieved by neutralization or by contradiction. When language is the dominating system for producing meaning, the contradictory nonverbal signs are rendered invalid.

Of course, there are exceptions to this — for example, when portraying a conscious plan of deception or in an ironic situation. In such cases, the verbal and the nonverbal signs naturally stand in temporary contradiction to one another. The spectator is never confused, however, as to how this contradiction is to be resolved and interpreted.

The nonverbal signs in this dialogue type serve the function of deepening comprehension of the verbal signs by illustrating the meaning, repeating it, or committing it in a certain direction.

The parapragmatic functions, on the other hand, do not aid the comprehension of single elements of the dialogue but rather create specific preconditions under which a better understanding of the structure of the dialogue as a whole can be achieved. By indicating the mental frame of mind of the dialogue partners and the relationship between them, they characterize the individual situation in which the dialogue arises and thus relate the speech of those who take part to a particular pattern of interaction which underlies the dialogue as a whole. If the spectators can immediately perceive whether the dialogue partners are acquainted with each other, strangers to one another, friend or foe, senior or junior, colleagues, in a good or anxious mood, cheerful or despondent, angry or peaceable, for example, they will be in a better position to comprehend the dialogue that follows than they would be without this information, which might be provided by the verbal signs only at a much later point in the speech. In this way, the communication of meaning is anticipated by the nonverbal signs, and the knowledge they provide is paramount to the understanding of the dialogue as a whole.

Moreover, the parapragmatic functions can, in some cases, emphasize more powerfully than the verbal signs the system of turn-taking. Above all paralinguistic signs such as intonation, mimic signs such as eyes cast down or looking up, gestural signs such as lowering or raising the head, concluding hand gestures or change in behavior, and proxemic signs such as a step toward the partner or a step back indicate to the spectator whether the person speaking intends to finish or continue or whether the listener is about to answer so that the next change of speaker is about to occur. By structuring the dialogue process in this way, the nonverbal signs clarify its composition and thus move the spectator toward a better understanding.

Since the third type of dialogue realizes the interference of the different semiotic systems of verbal and nonverbal signs under the dominance of the verbal, the nonverbal signs are chosen according to their special power to support the meaning of the verbal signs. Thus, the parasyntactic and the parapragmatic functions here outweigh any other, while the parasemantic are considerably reduced to the functions of complementation and intensification (through illustration, repetition, or affirmation). The nonverbal signs are therefore chiefly used to direct the process of reception and to interpret the verbal signs, helping the spectator in the attempt to constitute meaning.

This type of dramatic dialogue is characterized by a powerful tension between writing and orality. For we are dealing here with a case of direct communication. The nonverbal signs are nonetheless employed in such a way as to stress the elaborate written quality of the character's speech, which — in a situation of orality — becomes comprehensible to the spectator.

With some justification, one can say that in European theatre this type of dialogue was dominant, if not exclusively, from the eighteenth century until the beginnings of the avant-garde movement at the start of this century. Theatre was marked as a clearly defined area quite separate from social reality.

In the twentieth century this type of dialogue was identified with middle-class establishment theatre and was severely attacked by all avant-garde movements. Since the 1960s it has rather become an exception in most modern productions, although a few cases recently have shown it to be undergoing a renaissance. In Dieter Dorn's production of *Iphigenia in Tauris* (Munich Kammerspiele, 1981), Peter Stein's *Phèdre* (Schaubühne am Lehniner Platz, 1987), and Patrice Chéreau's production of Bernard Marie Koltès' *Dans la solitude des champs de coton* (Nanterre, 1987) the nonverbal signs were used so emphatically that the dominance of the literary speech text of the characters was explicitly stressed. Whether this is a fundamental change in the aesthetics of contemporary theatre remains to be seen.

THE DOMINANCE OF NONVERBAL SIGNS

The fourth type of dialogue is characterized by the dominance of nonverbal signs. The most extreme case of absolute dominance of nonverbal signs is where the dramatic dialogue passes into pure pantomime.

Insofar as the fourth type of dialogue can be understood as the scenic realization of the second category of the second type of dialogue, on the one hand, it transforms the linguistic signs of the secondary text which refer to nonverbal signs into appropriate nonverbal signs and, on the other, it must resolve the individual interpretation of the blanks, in that it fills the pauses and halts of thought through acoustic or visual signs.

Where the nonverbal signs dominate in the theatrical dramatic dialogue (that is, where they have become the main meaning-producing system toward which the spectator can and should be oriented), the verbal signs, in reverse, lose something of their relevance: in order to understand the dialogue it is far more important to grasp the meanings of the nonverbal signs than the verbal ones. This simple fact results in a wholly different relation between the three semiotic functions which the nonverbal signs are able to fulfill in relation to the verbal signs: the parasyntactic function of structuring the flow of text is subdued to a somewhat secondary function, while the parasemantic is promoted to the most important.

Although, for example, the function of replacement is dispensed with in the third type (for if everything of importance is communicated in words it cannot be replaced by nonverbal signs), it excels all others in significance in the fourth type. This is particularly evident in the second category of the second type. In the literary text, there is a great difference between nonverbal signs which are described in the secondary text and nonverbal signs which may act as replacement for pauses or halt in the thought process or for other signs which imply incompleteness in the character's speech. In the fourth type of dialogue, on the other hand, this difference is irrelevant: the nonverbal signs perceived by the spectator betray nothing of their origins in the speech text or secondary text — rather this differentiation seems totally devoid of function. The only meaning that remains is that created by the difference between the verbal signs and the nonverbal signs that dominate them.

Thus, the parasemantic function of replacement is promoted to the most important position. For it occurs when all nonverbal signs indicated by the secondary or speech text are realized onstage. This may arise through the use of emblems or through other signs which are understood either intuitively (for example, the paralinguistic signs sighing, sobbing, giggling, laughing or mimic signs which convey emotions such as rage, fear, surprise, joy, disgust, sorrow, excitement — the primary affects)[19] or by recourse to another code (gestural signs which point to emotion and intensity of emotion or which indicate intention, doubt, afterthought, decision or proxemic signs which either serve relevant functions or refer to a particular relationship and the possible changes to the relationship between the dialogue partners during the process of the dialogue). The gestural and proxemic signs employed in the theatrical dramatic dialogue can be interpreted either on the basis of a code which — other than a few variations or shading — is broadly valid for the surrounding culture or on the basis of a particularly pure theatrical code. In either case, all kinds of nonverbal signs may be employed which are capable of providing meaning without referring to the verbal signs. The proportion of nonverbal signs might even increase in the course of the dialogue to such an extent that they temporarily become the single meaning-producing system within the interaction, expressing all emotions, attitudes, and thoughts that are contained in words in the third type of dialogue.

In other sections of the dialogue where verbal and nonverbal signs are combined, however, the parasemantic functions of complementation, modification, neutralization, and contradiction outweigh any other. This is because the verbal signs are, to a large extent, elliptical and not explicit, so that the nonverbal signs must develop, define, or extend the meaning through additional information. The nonverbal signs thus complement the verbal ones in that they complete the incomplete speech text. Even in the case where the nonverbal signs might appear more informative than the verbal, their meaning can only be fully grasped according to their direct relation to the verbal signs that they complement.

Since in the fourth type of dialogue the verbal signs are frequently inadequate, in the sense that they are incapable of constituting a clear, precise meaning, they may be slightly modified by the nonverbal signs: while the words may indicate rudeness, the nonverbal signs dilute this meaning in that they signal embarrassment which prevents a more polite expression. In a similar way, the nonverbal signs might go so far as to neutralize the meaning of the verbal signs.

Of particular note in this type of dialogue is the parasemantic function of contradiction. For it is precisely in realizing this function that double meaning in the behavior of the dialogue partner is to be seen. Through particular use of verbal and nonverbal signs, the dramatic dialogue can reveal not only contradictions between one character's true emotions, opinions, attitudes, etc., and those that — for reasons of strategy in the dialogue — the character pretends to have, but also a possible contradiction between the conscious and the subconscious impulses in one character. The contradiction between meanings constituted by the verbal and the nonverbal signs can, in this way, develop into a meaning-producing system of great expressive potential and relevance. The parasemantic function of contradiction proves to be the basis of dramatic dialogue in this century.

The parapragmatic functions of the nonverbal signs — in comparison with those of the third type of dialogue — are similarly extended in the fourth type, if not quite to the same extent as the parasemantic functions. For if the verbal signs only provide somewhat inadequate information on the feelings or frame of mind of the dialogue partners and the relations between them, then the nonverbal signs must undertake the task of defining the relations between them — as much at the very beginning of the dialogue as during the course of it. If the verbal signs do not contain any clues as to the relation between the dialogue partners, then the nonverbal signs become the single meaning-producing system which do express this relationship and which clarify the definition of the relationship for the spectator. The parapragmatic functions of expression and reaction can, in such a case, adopt a guiding function: they inform the spectator of the conditions that underpin the interaction which must be taken into account if the verbal and nonverbal signs and their specific interference in the course of the dialogue are to be appropriately interpreted and understood.

In comparison, the parapragmatic function referring to the system of turn-taking remains somewhat secondary, though certainly not irrelevant. For the system of turn-taking is mostly prepared by the nonverbal signs which give expression to the listener's attempts to take the floor or which announce the speaker's intent to give up or continue holding the floor.

The dominance of the nonverbal sign in the interference of the verbal and the nonverbal in the fourth type of dialogue thus implies a specific choice from all possible nonverbal signs: preference is given to those signs which are able to serve both the parasemantic functions of replacement, complementation, modification, neutralization, and contradiction and the parapragmatic functions defining the relationship and preparing the change in who holds the floor. For it is especially these functions which allow the nonverbal signs either to constitute meaning independently of the meaning of the verbal signs or to provide additional meaning, promoting the nonverbal signs in the process of meaning-producing in the whole course of the dialogue to a leading role.

Even where the nonverbal signs dominate, different relations between writing and orality are evident. In realistic theatre, however, which reproduces situations of direct communication as "true to life" as possible, the tension is reduced to zero inasmuch as the aim here is to create the illusion of "pure" orality.

It must not be overlooked that the dominance of nonverbal signs is often characteristic of nonrealistic, highly stylized forms of theatre. This is particularly true of Far Eastern theatre forms such as Japanese *no* and *kabuki* theatre, Chinese opera, or the Indian dance theatre *kathakali*, and it also holds for isolated examples of European theatre such as *commedia dell'arte* or Baroque theatre. On the one hand, these theatre forms make use of a repertoire of precisely fixed nonverbal signs that can be employed as "emblems" in the sense of Ekman, because their meaning is fixed. The Jesuit Franciscus Lang writes, for example, in his *Dissertatio de actione scenica* (1727):

1. Admiration — Both hands outstretched above the chest and palms towards the audience.
2. Shame — The face turned away over the left shoulder and the hands calmly joined behind the back. This same result can be achieved by just the right hand when it is clenched and unclenched repetitively.
3. Entreating — Both hands upraised with the palms turned to the listener again and again. Also with the arms hanging down. Also with the hands distinctly clutched together.
4. Weeping and Melancholy — Both hands joined in the middle of the chest, either high on the chest or lower about the belt.[20]

On the other hand, these highly stylized nonverbal signs are contrasted with stylized verbal signs of equal importance which have all the characteristics of elaborate writing.

This kind of tension between orality and writing is also typical of Robert Wilson's postmodern theatre. Here visual and aural signs are totally separated from one another. For example, a text of daily speech or elaborate literary quality is spoken through a loudspeaker while at the same time the actors complete specific movements which have nothing to do with it. Not only are the indicators of writing and orality wholly separated from one another, but there is no recognizable relation between them. Their relation is determined by a new — postmodern — theatre aesthetic.[21]

THE DRAMATIC DIALOGUE AS A MEANING-PRODUCING SYSTEM

The dramatic dialogue always represents a face-to-face interaction realized under the general conditions either of writing (in the literary text of the drama) or of orality (in the performance) which can pursue verbalization strategies: these can, in either case, range between the two extreme poles — writing and orality. The dramatic dialogue can, to this extent, be defined as an always different aesthetically modeled orality. This aesthetically formed orality is generally marked by a tension between writing and orality. For the general conditions of communication (literary text vs. performance), the special conditions of communication and verbalization strategies are not usually structured ana-logically. The interference realized in each case between (1) speech text and secondary text (in the literary text of the drama) and (2) verbal and nonverbal signs (in the performance) marks, in employing widely differing variants, ei-ther writing or orality, which is then appropriately functionalized and given additional aesthetic codification.

The dramatic dialogue functions, in this way, as a meaning-producing sys-tem which is capable of creating and realizing any aesthetic or character con-ception. It proves to be an extremely economic system. Since the possible range along the scale between orality and writing is more or less unlimited, the dramatic dialogue constitutes a meaning-producing system that is practi-cally inexhaustible.[22]

THEATRE HISTORIOGRAPHY AND
PERFORMANCE ANALYSIS
Different Fields, Common Approaches?

From its very origins, theatre studies (*Theaterwissenschaft*) has embraced two apparently conflicting approaches: theatre studies was founded as an aesthetic as well as a historical discipline.

At the beginning of this century, theatre studies came into being as an autonomous university discipline through the unique constellation of the history of theatre and the humanities. In a decisive turn away from the historic, positivist school which claimed to direct the humanities according to the model and the standards set up by the natural sciences, Wilhelm Dilthey, in his book *Einleitung in die Geisteswissenschaft* (1883; Introduction to the Humanities), embarked on the pioneering project of working out a systematic foundation for the humanities, whose epistemological and methodological autonomy he sought to secure. Twenty-two years later, in *Das Erlebnis und die Dichtung* (1905; Experience and Poetry), he proposed that scholars in the field of the humanities should focus on the individual artwork, which can only be understood by experiencing it. Thus, he singled out the individual work, the unique event, as the only object deserving the attention of a scholar in the humanities.

This radical change of paradigm in the history of the humanities, in one sense, found its parallel in a change to the paradigm in theatre. In the nineteenth century the status of work of art was only accorded to theatrical performances in terms of how they were able to convey or mediate literary works of art. Despite the fact that even then the idea had been raised, though perhaps sporadically, that a theatrical performance as such might be taken as an autonomous work of art — as, for example, Goethe suggested with reference to the opera in his dialogue *Über Wahrheit und Wahrscheinlichkeit der Kunstwerke* (1798; On The Truth and Realism of Artworks) or as in the case of Richard Wagner, who took up this idea and pursued it further by defining the performance of a musical drama as the only conceivable and valuable artwork of the future (*Das Kunstwerk der Zukunft*, 1849; The Artwork of the Future); however, the majority of Goethe's and Wagner's contemporaries held that the nature of a theatrical performance as art could only be secured by the performed dramatic text. Even as late as 1918, the critic Alfred Klaar wrote in a direct polemic against theatre studies: "Theatre will only succeed in maintaining a position of great importance, when dramatic poetry adds its substance."[1]

The idea of theatre voiced here was sharply attacked by theatre avant-gardists. In the same year as Dilthey's *Das Erlebnis und die Dichtung*, Edward Gordon Craig's book on *The Art of Theatre* was also published. In it, Craig states: "The Art of the Theatre is neither acting nor the play, it is not scene nor dance, but it consists of all the elements of which these things are composed: action, which is the very spirit of acting; words, which are the body of the play; line and colour, which are the very heart of the scene; rhythm, which is the very essence of dance."[2]

Similar statements are to be found in the writings of Vsevolod Meyerhold, Wassily Kandinsky, Lothar Schreyer, Alexander Tairov, and others. Theatre, in such cases, was understood and defined as an autonomous art, with its own material form which is essentially different from the material of any other art form.

Thus, on the one hand, the avant-gardists defined theatrical performance as a work of art *sui generis*, and, on the other hand, Dilthey proclaimed the individual work of art as the only possible object of research in the humanities. It is small wonder that a new discipline sprang up which claimed as its object the theatrical work of art, the performance, which was understood to be essentially different from any other kind of work of art, such as literary works, for example. Consequently, theatre studies was founded as an aesthetic discipline which deals with individual theatrical performances.

At a time when all other disciplines in the humanities were pursued as historical disciplines, it was more or less inconceivable that theatre studies would turn to contemporary theatre (i.e., develop approaches to analyzing and understanding current performances). And since, as is well known, theatre studies is not in a position to deal with past works of art—in a way in which literary history and art history are—Max Herrmann suggested that the object of analysis must first be reconstructed before it can be examined. In order to realize this goal, he drew heavily upon the wealth of material compiled by nineteenth-century scholars who had no other purpose but to collect all available historical documents on theatre. When, in due course, it became clear that the reconstruction of past performances from an epistemological point of view was futile, because it was *a priori* an impossibility, theatre historians restricted their activities to simply continuing to collect and present material. The point of departure, concentrating on the individual performance, disappeared from view.

It was against this academic tradition that a new generation of theatre scholars rebelled in the 1970s and the 1980s. They criticized the current practices not only for their inherent positivism but also for totally excluding performances of contemporary theatre. Thus, various methods of performance analysis were called for and elaborated, mostly within the framework of different kinds of semiotic approaches. In this way, a sharply distinct opposition was construed between the "old" kind of theatre history and performance analysis. One point must be made quite clear, however: such opposition was *never* intended to be an opposition in principle between theatre history and performance analysis. Rather, performance analysis was promoted as a critique of theatre research because the latter totally excluded the only available works of art (i.e., current performances) and pursued history exclusively on positivistic terms. Consequently, it was natural that opposition began to diminish when theatre historians began to explore new approaches to theatre history. In this way, an opposition which was originally deeply fundamental gradually changed into the peaceful coexistence of two different fields of research. Recently, it increasingly happens that scholars are no longer willing to respect the division of the discipline and pursue projects in both fields. This has given rise to the idea that the oft-asserted strict borderlines between the two fields are somewhat fictitious; at the very least, they seem to collapse.

Proceeding from this experience, this chapter aims to explore systematically the relationship between theatre historiography and performance analysis. In the first part I shall describe the researcher's activity in both fields, taking recourse to some epistemological premises. In the second part I shall examine and explain some of the actual methodological problems of both fields.

What are we doing when we pursue theatre historiography? This seemingly simple question is not easily answered. The difficulties in responding to it arise in the very approach to each and every attempt. For there seems to be no reason to suppose that a *consensus* exists among theatre historians concerning the object whose history they claim to explore and to write up. What do we mean when we use the term *theatre*? How can we define what theatre is?

Historians, in particular, are very well aware of the fact that the term *theatre* is culturally and historically determined and that, within Western culture since the sixteenth century, the concept of theatre has consistently changed. Accordingly, the term *theatre* has been applied to quite different cultural, social, and political events, just as it has been employed as a purely aesthetic term in the narrowest sense of the word. At times different usages of the term competed with each other.

At the beginning of the twentieth century, for example, the historical avant-garde movement promoted two quite different usages and meanings of the term *theatre*. On the one hand, they restricted it to a particular art form which, as Craig explained, was defined by its very material as essentially different from the material of any other art. On the other hand, they claimed to close the gap between art and life and to fuse theatre and reality. This demand resulted in a considerable expansion of the concept of theatre. The usage of the term was gradually transferred to the most divergent fields. In the end it was applied to signify any kind of exhibitive, demonstrative, or spectacular event including performances by circus artists, jugglers, clowns, entertainers; dadaist and surrealist "happenings" which took place in streets, cafés, parliaments, churches, and other public places; May Day celebrations, rallies, meetings, union sports days, party conventions; and so on.

In the sixties and seventies, however, the rediscovery of a so-called ritual theatre as well as a newly developing performance culture resulted in an even wider range of the term *theatre*: wherever somebody exhibited her/himself or another, exposed her/himself to the gaze of others, the term *theatre* was applied. This "enormous activation of the semantic field 'theatre'" blurred the borderlines and transitions to a metaphorical use of the term:[3] Michel Foucault conceived his "Theatrum philosophicum," Jean-François Lyotard discussed "the philosophical and political stage," Jean Baudrillard explored "the stage of the body." The term *theatre* is booming across the Western world to an extent that is comparable only to its widespread dissemination during the seventeenth century. Nowadays, however, it seems to be on the verge of declining into inflational currency.

This brief digression into the history of the concept of theatre in our century makes sufficiently clear that there can be no *a priori* consensus regarding the object which is meant when we use the term *theatre*. Quite obviously, this state of affairs results in far-reaching consequences concerning theatre history. For whoever proclaims that she/he is going to explore the theatre history of a given epoch has to define her/his object of investigation, to delineate a particular segment of the vast and multifaceted semantic field *theatre*.

To put it more bluntly, there will be as many objects of historical research into theatre as there are concepts of theatre to be conceived. And since any concept of theatre is based on particular theoretical premises — be they implicit or explicit — the definition of the historian's object is the result of a process of construction which the historian carries out in line with her/his theoretical premises. Each and every theatre historian cannot help but delineate the object of research according to her/his own research interests and theoretical basis and, in this way, construct her/his history of the object thus subjectively chosen.[4]

But even if the subject of our historical research can be so defined, our difficulties are not yet overcome. The term *theatre history* entails two components. So far, we have dealt with the first only. And the second turns out to be no less problematic.

It is nowadays a truism that we cannot presuppose a universal concept of history. Neither do we believe that, in the historical process, G. W. F. Hegel's *Weltgeist* will return to its absolute identity; nor do we detect in it any laws of a development from the stage of an *ur*-community through the stage of class society to a final stage of a classless society; nor do we follow the theory of modernization as elaborated in the Enlightenment, which conceived of the historical process as of a process of never-ending progress and perfection of the human race. Such totalizing teleological historical concepts are long since out of date. The historical disciplines have drawn their conclusions from this state of affairs. On the one hand, they have tried to revive quite traditional strategies of bringing forth historical coherence such as returning to a kind of narrative historiography. On the other hand, competing with this retreat to rather "regressive" attempts, some "transgressive" concepts have been developed, such as the history of everyday life, women's history, and historical anthropology.[5] Notwithstanding their basic and partly crucial differences, all these concepts agree in focusing on microhistorical as well as individual sense-making processes. Instead of macrohistory (i.e., one all-encompassing history of the modern world), microhistory is inaugurated (i.e., many different histories of smaller scale which are all taken as meaningful). In this respect, it seems quite justified to diagnose a resubjectification of the historical sciences. This change has opened up the possibility of formulating totally new questions and of trying out a number of new approaches. Among such newly emerging "schools," in a particularly prominent place is the so-called *Annales* school, which has promoted the project of a history of mentalities since the thirties and has developed quite a series of pioneering studies and revolutionary findings.

The new orientation within the historical disciplines has not caused a dispute among the schools; rather, it has resulted in the conviction that one has to proceed from the fundamental plurality of theories and methods. Any approach, quite necessarily, will be a restricted one insofar as it refers to one particular question, one particular theory only. In this way, the restricted range of any approach was recognized as the *conditio sine qua non* of historiography: each theory explains another kind of aspect of microhistory; each approach refers to another level.

In other words, theatre history can be explored and written down as cultural or social history, as history of thought or ideas, as art history or psychohistory, as historical anthropology or history of knowledge, and so on. Whatever approach is chosen, each case depends on the researcher's interests and theoretical premises and, accordingly, on the issues that are raised and tackled: What are the power relations played out in public life in a given society of a given epoch? What are the role and function of the observer/spectator in a certain event? How does the art of acting in a given society of a given epoch work on the body and discipline it? How do particular theatrical conventions function?—and so on and so forth. Quite consistently, there will be as many histories of theatre as questions to be asked. In any case, the researcher will construct a history of theatre according to her/his own particular interests and theoretical premises. Writing theatre history, thus, means to perform a process of subjective construction, in order to solve a particular problem and to answer a particular question.

Performance analysis, on the other hand, proceeds from a specific concept of theatre or of performance, just as any historical research does. Since the term *performance* can be applied to any event where people perform and are watched while performing, we first have to clarify what kind of performance we are going to analyze: A party political convention or a rock concert? A football game or a circus performance? A Ramlila Festival or Peter Stein's production of the *Oresteia* in the Red Army Theatre in Moscow? In this respect, it does not come as a surprise when I conclude that whatever kind of performance we might conceive can be chosen as the object of performance analysis.

When we have selected our event we have to make another decision: is our analysis intended to refer to the rules underlying and controlling the whole event (regarding performers and spectators, place, time, and reason of the event)? Or shall we restrict it to some or even one of the factors involved (for instance, to the reason behind the event or to the activities of the spectators or those of the performers)? And even if we have chosen a particular focus such as, let us say, the activities of the performers and the spectators—or of only one of these groups—we are absolutely unable to refer to everything performed and displayed by them, since it is performed and displayed in a permanent flow. In order to be able to structure this flow we have to segment it. But any segmentation we carry out depends on certain prerequisites, such as our goal of investigation and our respective theoretical premises.[6] So

before embarking on the enterprise of even choosing a focus we have to formulate the question(s) that we want to tackle in our analysis, such as: What
are the power relations played out in the party convention? What are the role
and function of the observer/spectator at the Olympic Games in Lilleham-
mer? How is violence inscribed in the actors' bodies in Stein's *Oresteia*? What
is the function of the stagehands in Wilson's *Knee Plays*?

That is to say, depending on our research interests and theoretical premises,
we formulate questions concerning a particular performance — of whatever
kind; proceeding from these questions we choose our focus as well as our perspectives and methods of analysis. Since all these conditions and prerequisites
are subjectively determined, the process of performance analysis, quite consistently, is carried out as a process of subjective construction.

In this respect, there seems to be no essential difference between a historical research and a performance analysis. In both cases, we proceed from particular questions and problems that are formulated and inspired by our own
research interests, theoretical basis, and particular concepts of theatre, performance, and history; we embark on the project of working out a solution by
performing a process of, in this sense, a subjective construction. So the question arises as to whether there is any justification for differentiating, in principle, between theatre historiography and performance analysis as between
two distinct fields of research.

One might argue that there is, in fact, a basic difference which legitimizes
the distinction, a difference that is to be found in the point of departure. No
historian will ever have immediate access to the events to which the research
refers, no matter what her/his underlying concept of theatre and history
might be. The events are gone forever, and the questions related to them
spring from documents on the events, not from taking part in the events
themselves, and must be dealt with by taking exclusive recourse to documents. A performance analysis, on the contrary, has its point of departure in
the immediate experience of taking part in the event.

For example, when the event is a performance of theatre as an art form, the
historian will never be able to deal with her/his object — let us say Vakhtangov's production of *Princess Turandot* (1922) — on the basis of an aesthetic
experience. As an aesthetic work the object is not available to the historian:
she/he is bound to deal with documents on it only — the work itself is gone
and lost forever. She/he will rummage through Boris Sachawa's notes, Nikolai Gorchakov's records of the rehearsal process, Vakhtangov's letters; she/he
will examine photographs of the performance to be found in different sources
as well as Vaslav Nijinskij's sketches of the costumes and the stage, even a
model of his stage; she/he will work meticulously on the reviews and descrip-

tions by Fyodor Stepun, Joseph Bromley, Michail Avgustovič Osorgin, and others. All this might result in finding answers to the leading questions of the investigation or even in the emergence of an idea as to how the production might have been, in the imagination of the researcher; but it will never be able to trigger an aesthetic experience such as the performance might have caused in its spectators. The aesthetic experience of the performance is only open — and exclusively so — to its current participants.

Since this is so, we can argue that what distinguishes performance analysis from historical research is the chance of taking part, of communicating directly with the intended object of research, and in this way, sometimes, of creating an aesthetic experience. Thus, in opposition to a historic investigation, performance analysis proceeds from the communicational process of which the researcher her/himself was part and, eventually, from the particular aesthetic experience that the performance aroused in her/him as spectator. Anyone who has attended a performance of, let us say, Wilson's *the CIVIL warS* (the different parts of which were presented in Europe, Japan, and the United States during 1984 and 1986), and who has afterward taken on the painstaking task of analyzing the watched performance can refer to her/his very subjective communicative as well as aesthetic experience as one of the points of departure when starting to formulate the leading questions of the investigation and to design the procedures of analysis.

Having conceded this basic difference, it now seems wise to question its methodological consequences. What are the next steps when we have posed a particular problem, raised a specific question? What are the materials to which we take recourse when carrying out the analysis? Even if we attend a performance several times — which we can only do in the case of theatre productions which run for a certain period and not in the case of other kinds of performances which take place just once — we do not really start the analysis here, let alone finish it. At best, we are able to jot down some notes, to imprint some perceptions in our memory, to allow some ideas to emerge, and, ultimately, to make a video recording. The work of analyzing and reflecting will be done later, and it will be carried out by referring to materials that are not part of the performance, but documents on it, such as programs, reviews, descriptions, interviews, the script, if there is one, our own notes taken during the performance or afterward, photographs, video recordings, and the like. Hence it follows that we do not actually analyze the performance but documents on it. Moreover, having finished our so-called performance analysis, we shall seldom be able to check its results by going back to the performance itself. It is small wonder that the reader of a published performance analysis is not in a position to judge whether the analysis was done by someone who attended the performance or by a researcher who only had access to the same documents (apart from notes made during the performance, of course) and did not proceed from the communicative and aesthetic experience of participating in the event. From the point of view of the reader, who cannot attend the performance because the production has finished its run, the analysis will invariably refer to a historical event.

Thus, when it comes to the question of methodological consequences, the basic difference of having taken part in the performance or not having taken part in it seems to boil down to rather subordinate preliminaries. In both cases, the analysis refers to documents on events that we analyze from the perspective of a particular problem and on the basis of a certain theory. The object of the analysis is never the event itself. That is to say, even in terms of methodology, there is no difference between historical research and performance analysis. What we are used to calling performance analysis is primarily a particular approach made possible by the technology of videotaping or filming a performance. So we should not forget that the very moment the filmed performance is out of the repertoire the film or the video recording that was taped and meant as an *aide-mémoire* by the researcher who made it will become a historical document.

Therefore, I have come to the conclusion that neither from an epistemological nor from a methodological point of view does it make sense to draw a strict borderline between our various research activities, to call the fields we have demarcated from each other by different names — such as theatre historiography and performance analysis — and to assign these two so-called different fields of research to two different kinds of specialists. I have deeply rooted doubts as to whether such a compartmentalizing of our discipline will enable and encourage us to ask the questions that really matter or to tackle problems that are contemporarily relevant. When designing a research project, our point of departure cannot be a specific compartment of the discipline, a so-called field of research, but must be a particular problem. And in order to solve this problem we are not only permitted but actually challenged to cross all the borders between such fields if they obstruct us in our path to a satisfactory answer. Very often, the problem works like a magnifying glass which attracts and focuses quite a number of different aspects and perspectives from various, sometimes apparently quite divergent fields. Dealing with the problem, thus, amounts to interconnecting all the points from which the aspects and perspectives concerned originate — i.e., forming a network. If we restrict our activities, as so-called specialists, to one — in any case arbitrarily delineated — field, we deprive ourselves of the opportunity even to ask innovative questions, let alone to find innovative answers.

To clarify, I shall draw upon the outline of an example based on such an approach which derives from twentieth-century theatre history. In Europe, at the beginning of the twentieth century, a radical change took place in — among other things — habits and modes of perception. A number of factors are commonly thought to be connected with this fundamental change. On the one hand, various technological innovations such as the telegraph, telephone, phonograph, film, photography, the steam railway, and the automobile are held responsible. Even during the course of the nineteenth century, these inventions had already moved time and space closer together than could previously have been imagined. In particular, the high speed of the new transport systems is noted, together with the steady growth of urbanization and industrialization processes, demanding a permanent change of perspective and focus which deeply affected the perceptional modes and habits of everyday life.

On the other hand, the change of perception which occurred is related to some revolutionary advancements in science, principally Max Planck's quantum theory (1900) and Albert Einstein's theory of relativity (1905). The consequence of such theories was that there was no longer reason to believe that "time" and "mass" are factors which are independent of the observer and his or her own movement. Rather, it was shown that time and the mass of an observed body change according to the speed with which the observer moves. Thus the idea of a fixed, external observer who is in a position to measure time and mass objectively by the application of universally valid units had to be abandoned.

A third factor is held to be the revolution in the fine arts, in particular cubist painting and dodecatonic music. Furthermore, since such changes are still occurring, a number of other factors are added which are connected to the third industrial revolution caused by the electronic media.

Within such a framework, the question can be raised: In what ways did the avant-garde theatre serve as part of this radical change in perceptional modes and habits in this century?[7] In the context of this chapter, such a question seems to encompass far too wide a scope. Thus, for the purpose of demonstrating my approach, let us reformulate the question to focus on one element alone, drawing on the examples of two single performances. The first comes from the first half of this century, while the second is more contemporary.

The question now reads: What is the function of the stagehands in Vakhtangov's production of Gozzi's *Princess Turandot* and in Wilson's *Knee Plays* in terms of the changed perceptive modes and habits of European audiences? I shall not deal here with all aspects possibly emanating from the question, but shall push my investigations only as far as it takes to highlight the futility of a fundamental division between theatre historiography and performance analysis.

In *Princess Turandot*, Vakhtangov took great pains to differentiate clearly between the actors serving as stagehands on the one level and those playing the role of a dramatic figure or those playing a mask from the *commedia dell'arte* on the other. They were not only dressed differently, so that they could be identified as different at first glance, but were also supposed to perform differently: "That was the hint: that the Zani do everything that was necessary in the process of the play, and yet remain invisible. . . . The actors who are to play the Zani must be taught to do all that is asked of them onstage in such a way that they do not even seem to be really present onstage at the time. No acting! No mime! *No reaction* to what is happening on stage in front of their very eyes."[8]

Like the stagehands of the Japanese or Chinese theatre, Vakhtangov's stagehands had to provide the actors playing dramatic figures with everything they might need either for their play or for their refreshment. They took off Kalaf's shoes when he lay down to sleep; they procured the dagger Adelma needed for committing suicide. They ground the executioners' axe and carried the heads of the executed suitors offstage.

On the other hand, they dried Barach's and Kalaf's tear-soaked faces with towels and fetched a chair for the actor playing Kalaf so that he could take a rest after having displayed his pain to the point of exhaustion on hearing the bad news of the fate of his parents.[9] That is to say, the stagehands performed exclusively practical actions which did not belong to the fictive world of the play, but instead enabled the actors playing the dramatic figures to continue their play within the frame of the fictive world. Accordingly, they handled the objects solely with regard to their practical functions: they used the towels in order to dry wet faces and procured a chair only so that the actor playing Kalaf could sit down and take a rest. The stagehands changed neither the function of an object nor its meaning. The objects manipulated by them remained objects of everyday life, serving presupposed practical functions: a towel is needed for drying and a chair for sitting down or allowing someone else to sit down.

In this way, an opposition was constructed between the actors playing a figure and the actors serving as stagehands: while the stagehands made use of the generally known practical function of the objects, the actors playing a figure, through their particular acting, transformed them into theatrical signs. By winding a towel around his head, the actor playing Kalaf transformed it into the theatrical sign of a turban; by tying a towel to his chin, the actor playing a sage transformed it into the theatrical sign of a beard; and so on.

Thus, the opposition between the two groups of actors established a particular frame in terms of the process of perception: when the stagehands manipulated an object, the spectators were invited to perceive it as the same kind of object they knew from everyday life and to attribute to it the familiar function and meaning. When, on the contrary, the actors as dramatic figures manipulated an object, the spectators were challenged to perceive the object as a theatrical sign and to attribute ever changing functions and meanings to it depending on the way the actor played with it. In this respect, the introduction of the stagehands served the purpose not only of framing the process of perception but, in addition, of overtly pointing to the fact that the process of perception not only is quasi-automatically determined by the materiality of the presented objects, but, moreover, depends on the particular frame of reference which the perceiver adopts when perceiving.

On the other hand, the particular way in which the stagehands dealt with the objects helped to set off the difference between the actor playing a dramatic figure and the dramatic figure: they did not procure the chair so that Kalaf could sit down on a fictive street, in a fictive Beijing, but so that the actor playing Kalaf could recuperate from his strenuous acting on the stage and then be able to go on playing Kalaf. In this way, the spectators were prevented from following the convention of perceiving the person onstage continuously and quasi-automatically as a dramatic figure — i.e., of accepting the traditional framing of perceptive processes in realistic theatre as "natural" to such an extent that they did not even recognize it as a convention. Instead, two different frames of reference were introduced, thus highlighting the particular conditions under which perception works in the theatre alone.

The same applies to the stage space: by bringing a chair onstage for the actor — and not for the dramatic figure — the stagehands stressed that the stage can be perceived as a theatrical sign of, let us say, a street in Beijing, just as well as the working place of the actors. This aspect was emphasized whenever the stagehands changed the set in front of the audience. They pulled up ropes, flags, flyers, etc., and got them down again, they hung and dismantled backdrops, they made the sun and moon rise and set, and so on. This kind of set change not only informed the audience about the different fictive places and times of day when the action was supposed to take place (such as a street in Beijing at noon, a room in the seraglio by night); it, moreover, permanently and quite demonstratively pointed to the fact that they were sitting in front of a stage, which, depending on a particular frame of reference, could be perceived as the working place of actors, stagehands, etc., or as the theatrical sign of different fictive places.

In the use of the device of stagehands, the production suggested to the spectators that they carry out the processes of perception of the stage space, objects, and actors' bodies from at least two different frames of reference. In this way, it directed their attention to the fact that perception generally depends on a certain framing and that this framing is accomplished by all kinds of conventions of which, in most cases, we are not aware.

By exposing the procedure of framing to the gaze of the spectator as a prerequisite of perception, the production attacked the common and widespread concept of perception of the time, namely, the idea that perception depends on two conditions only: on the existence of a world out there and on the existence of a perceptive apparatus (i.e., the senses). These two conditions having been granted, the process of perception will be executed by everyone in exactly the same way, irrespective of different cultural, historical, linguistic, social, institutional, individual contexts. In opposition to this idea, the production introduced a third condition: the adoption of a particular frame of reference. By multiplying the frameworks, it forced the spectator to perceive the same objects in different ways, depending on different framings. Thus, it made her/him aware of the fact that perception is not only controlled by the senses and the "real" world but, primarily, by a frame of reference which the perceiver adopts or establishes, depending on the particular — cultural, historical, linguistic, social, institutional, individual — context.

In this way, the production denied the concept of perception as a quasi- "natural" process and instead fostered the idea that the process of perception has, in each case, to be carried out by the perceiver depending on, and in line with, the perspective which the particular framing opens up. The transfer of the "foreign" device of stagehands, thus, not only challenged but deconstructed the traditional perceptive modes and habits of European audiences.

In his *Knee Plays*, a series of interludes from his *CIVIL warS*, Wilson introduced, more than sixty years later, not only the property man from the Japanese *no* and *kabuki* theatre but also the puppeteers from the *bunraku*. As in *bunraku*, three puppeteers controlled the puppet of a man and of a lion (in the first knee play) and the puppet of a huge bird (in the fourth knee play). As in the *no* and the *kabuki* theatre, the stagehands procured different kinds of props: they brought in the boat and removed it from the stage; they held some cloth and, by moving it up and down, simulated waves; they lit up the tents, made the baskets dance, fetched the "library," and brought in some laurel branches. In this respect, they fulfilled the same purposes as the stagehands not only in the Japanese theatre but also in Vakhtangov's production.

However, in the *Knee Plays* there was no difference to be noticed regarding the costumes of puppeteers, stagehands, and performers; they were all dressed alike: they wore white trousers, a white jacket, and white shoes. To this uniform costume, some small accessories could be added in order to specify a particular figure such as, for instance, General Perry or the basket seller. Only the dancer Suzushi Hanayagi was singled out by wearing a red robe.

In any case, the uniform of white prevailed. It was worn without any addition in most of the *Knee Plays*: for example, whenever the performers acted as stagehands or puppeteers and procured all the objects which the story about the tree demanded; or when they acted as figures within the fictive world of the story and built a boat, launched it into the water, and so on; or when they performed dances which did not show any recognizable relation to the story, such as the *no* walks. In each of these cases, the audience watched the same performers, wearing the same dress, while, however, serving different functions. In this way, the differences between the functions were not emphasized; quite the contrary, they were rather blurred. The uniform of the white costume, accordingly, seemed to serve as a kind of blank screen on which the spectators could inscribe their own projections.

Thus, the transfer of devices from the Japanese theatre in the *Knee Plays* set particular conditions of perception which differed greatly from those introduced in *Princess Turandot*. While Vakhtangov's production shifted the focus from the so-called objective universal conditions of perception — of a world out there and a perceptive apparatus — to the context-bound conditions of framing, Wilson's production provided no frame at all. It did not seem important that the spectators recognize the different functions to which the "foreign" devices might refer as to their "original" functions. This knowledge was not needed in order to control the process of perception. Here the focus shifted to completely subjective conditions: any spectator might perform her/his own framing depending on her/his own individual subjectivity (i.e., in accordance with her/his individual universe of discourse, imagination, memories, associations, etc.). Each and every spectator would perceive the performers' bodies — the objects, the stage space — within a frame of reference established in her/his mind only and not necessarily onstage. Perception, thus, is declared to be a subjective construction.

I shall break off here because I have reached my goal. I have outlined briefly one possible way to proceed in investigating the contribution of European theatre of this century toward a dramatic change in the perceptive modes and habits of European audiences and, quite tentatively, I have proposed a thesis. This has shed some light on the restricted suitability of traditional distinctions in our discipline — like that between theatre history and performance analysis. In the case of *Princess Turandot*, I took recourse to the different kinds of documents listed above; I have watched the *Knee Plays* myself and afterward carried out my analysis referring to a videotape and some other materials. In both cases, the analysis was undertaken with reference to the question posed. Accordingly, in terms of the problem I identified and the argument I used, it does not make any sense at all to differentiate between theatre historiography and performance analysis.

Thus, I shall conclude that it seems highly advisable to revise the traditional differentiation between fields of research or at least to become aware of the fact that this differentiation does not spring from any *a priori* reason but rather from particular intentions placed on the agenda by certain schools as well as individual researchers within a specific historical context. And if we should discover that such intentions are no longer valid, it will be wise to abolish the differentiation stemming from them. For the so-called distinct fields of research function as specific frames of reference which only permit certain questions and thus advocate and control a specific type of research. Insofar as we proceed from other frames of reference we shall, as a matter of course, ask other questions and carry out other types of research. The debate on a revision is open.

It seems high time that theatre research seriously takes into consideration what productions by Vakhtangov, Wilson, and others have brought to light and that it draws adequate conclusions from these insights as far as its own approaches and procedures are concerned.

NOTES

INTRODUCTION

1. Fischer-Lichte 1990b, vol. 1, 66–76.
2. Fischer-Lichte 1983b, vol. 2, 69–73.
3. Ortega y Gasset 1950. For other examples of such exchange processes in the late fifteenth and early sixteenth centuries, see Greenblatt 1988.
4. Schultze-Naumburg 1902, 144. All translations are by Jo Riley unless otherwise noted.
5. Jaques-Dalcroze 1922, 55.
6. Duncan 1903, 43–44.
7. Nietzsche 1969, vol. 1, 387.
8. Von Hofmannsthal 1979–1980, vol. 7, 465.
9. Concerning the methodological problems, see "Theatre Historiography and Performance Analysis" in this volume.
10. Fischer-Lichte 1993, 81–163.
11. "The Actor and the Übermarionette," 1908, 8.
12. Singer 1959, xii–xiii.
13. Ibid.
14. Ibid.
15. Arvatov 1972, 91.
16. Cf. Klier 1981, 19.

THEATRE AND THE CIVILIZING PROCESS

1. Elias 1982, vol. 1, 224.
2. Ibid., 223.
3. Engle 1968, 107.
4. Elias 1982, vol. 2, 259.
5. Ibid., 259, 271.
6. Kindermann 1956, 12.
7. Lichtenberg 1972, 278.
8. Lessing 1883–1890, 158–159.
9. Engel 1971, vol. 2, 11–12.
10. Meyerhold 1969, 99–100.
11. Artaud 1956–1994, vol. 4, 125.

12. Brecht 1967, vol. 15, 622.
13. Meyerhold 1969, 198.
14. Ibid., 197–198.
15. Ibid.
16. Foregger 1975, 76.
17. Blau 1982, 2.

DISCOVERING THE SPECTATOR

1. Fuchs 1905, 95.
2. Fuchs 1972, 43.
3. Meyerhold 1979, vol. 1, 131–132.
4. Ibid., 135.
5. Ibid. This challenge was first raised by Richard Wagner in *Opera and Drama* (1851). Here he demanded an active spectator who should not just become "an organically participating witness" (Wagner 1887–1888, vol. 4, 192) but also rise to the position of the "vital co-creator of the work of art" (ibid., 186). Meyerhold was familiar with Wagner's writing.
6. Kershentsev 1980, 161. Kershentsev deplored the commercial nature of art in bourgeois society, which denigrated the spectator to a mere consumer. Seventy years earlier Wagner wrote a similar critique in *Art and Revolution* (1849). "Art as it now fills the entire civilized world" has sunk to the level of "merchandise. Its true essence is industry, its ethical goal the gaining of riches, its aesthetic pretext, entertainment. Our art sucks its life juices from the very heart of our modern society, from the very core of the spiral movement of financial speculation on a grand scale . . . enervating, corrupting, de-humanizing everything on which it sheds its venom" (Wagner 1887–1888, vol. 3, 19).
7. Apollonio 1972, 170.
8. Ibid., 174–175.
9. Meyerhold 1974, 45.
10. Eisenstein 1977, 181.
11. Fuchs 1972, 4.
12. Ibid., 3–4.
13. Nietzsche 1967, 74.
14. Cf. Prütting 1971.
15. Artaud 1956–1994, vol. 4, 139.
16. Ibid., 164.
17. Artaud 1970, 63.
18. Ibid., 60.
19. Artaud 1975, 167.
20. Ibid., 132.
21. Kershentsev 1980, 67.
22. Ibid., 58.
23. Ibid.
24. Meyerhold 1974, 22.

25. Here this method of affecting the spectator had its first success in the history of European theatre. In earlier epochs, the ideal of social reality that the spectator should realize in the future was first demonstrated in an exemplary way on the stage. In the Baroque theatre the spectator watched the martyr onstage suffer stoically for Christian beliefs. In the bourgeois theatre of the Enlightenment the spectators watched the tender father and virtuous daughter behaving in line with bourgeois values. Through shock or sympathetic identification, the spectators should come close to the ideal set before them. In the theatre of the avant-garde, however, the "new" being was not to be found onstage but rather discovered in the spectator with the help of specific stratagems that were described as the process of "re-theatricalizing theatre" (Fuchs 1905; cf. "In Search of a New Theatre" in this volume). In opposition to this process, Stalinism in the mid-1930s advocated the doctrine of socialist realism, which demanded the presentation of the highly ideologically determined standard, positive hero so that the spectator could identify with and mimetically emulate heroic values. This was the end of avant-garde theatre in the Soviet Union.

26. Fuchs 1972, 46.

27. Semper 1906, 43.

28. For the purposes of this discussion, Max Reinhardt is particularly of interest because of his almost inexhaustible discovery and exploitation of new spaces for theatre (cf. Huesmann 1983).

29. Piscator 1963, 75.

30. Gropius 1967, 117.

31. Meyerhold 1974, 161–162.

32. Artaud 1970, 75.

33. Ibid.

34. Fuchs 1972, 46.

35. Kershentsev 1980, 187.

36. Feuchtwanger 1911, 82.

37. Meyerhold 1974, 162.

38. Meyerhold 1979, 135–136.

39. Meyerhold 1974, 49.

40. Hausmann 1980, 50.

41. The perspectival view and habits of listening conditioned by tonal music as both were developed in the Renaissance were radically challenged at the beginning of the century in painting as in music. From approximately 1907–1908 (Picasso painted *Les demoiselles d'Avignon* in 1907) the cubists disposed of the perspectively organized picture frame. As early as 1906 Ferruccio Busoni challenged composers in his *Entwurf einer neuen Ästhetik der Tonkunst* (Toward a New Aesthetics of Sound) to advance toward "the infinity of tones" in order to overcome the limitations of tonal music, and in 1908–1909 Schönberg wrote his first atonal work. The theatre of the avant-garde made good use of these developments.

42. Alpers 1977, 55.

43. Brauneck 1982, 100.

44. Here the parallel development of theatre and science is stressed. At the turn of the century, the validity of the physics of the mechanical view of life current since

Galileo was thrown into doubt. In 1905 Einstein published his essay "On the Electro-Dynamically Moving Body," in which he first set forth the theory of relativity by showing that time invades space as a quasi fourth dimension, distorting it. The futuristic multidimensional space-stage sought to realize this through the movement of objects and the use of light and sound.

45. Brauneck 1982, 102.

46. Artaud 1970, 72.

47. Ibid., 38–39.

48. Ibid., 70.

49. Russolo 1986, 28.

50. On the theme of the intercultural trend in postmodern theatre, see "Familiar and Foreign Theatres" and "Changing Theatrical Codes" in this volume. Cf. also Fischer-Lichte et al. 1990a.

51. Aragon 1976.

52. On this particular problem as the general theme of this section, see Fischer-Lichte 1990b, vol. 2, chap. 5, "The Theatre of the 'New' Being."

53. Here, however, in terms of ritual theatre as it developed in the USA in the 1960s, some qualification is necessary. In Judith Malina and Julian Beck's "Living Theatre," for example, or Richard Schechner's "Environmental Theatre" the spectator is to be animated into participation. It was assumed that in experiencing certain rituals (as Richard Schechner gleaned from Arnold Van Gennep's work *Les rites de passage* and directly from the Asmati in New Guinea) the performers and spectators taking part who suffered, on the one hand, from isolation and anonymity and, on the other, from conformity to the community of the masses could be transformed into "communal beings." The reference to the cultural revolution in America as experienced in the civil rights campaign and anti-Vietnam war movements seems to suggest a direct continuation of the goals set by the historical avant-garde in Europe.

54. Müller 1985.

55. Plessner 1966, 1970b, and 1976.

56. Fischer-Lichte 1990b, vol. 1, 3–9.

57. Müller 1985, 4.

58. One might ask how theatre theoreticians and artists of the historical avant-garde could possibly lose sight of this truism. It was overlooked largely because of the special historical and theatrical situation around 1900. With naturalism, theatre had reached the end of a development which began in the mid-1700s with the demand for the emphasis on the literary in the theatre and the presentation of an illusion of reality through theatre (*imitatio naturae*). The representation of reality in minute and precise detail was absorbed seemingly passively by the spectator who sat isolated in the darkness of the auditorium. Neither the representation of reality onstage nor its absorption by the spectator held, in any remote way, a possible solution of the social problems brought together under the heading *Kulturkrise* in Germany. It was only close in the sense that it suggested a connection: the representation of reality in theatre; the passivity of the audience; and the virulence of the crisis in culture. In reverse conclusion, one could deduce that a new nonmimetic, anti-illusionist, retheatricalized theatre and a new active spectator could make a contribution toward overcoming the crisis in culture. In place of the representation of reality, which forced the spectator

into seeming passivity, came the exodus into reality activated by the spectator (see Blau 1990; Carlson 1990; States 1985).

59. Fischer-Lichte 1989d.

FROM THEATRE TO THEATRICALITY

1. Nietzsche 1910, vol. 5, 132–133.
2. Von Hofmannsthal 1952, 133–135.
3. Freksa 1913, 114.
4. Ibid.
5. Fuchs 1906, 13.
6. Ibid.
7. Lequeux 1888, 2.
8. Ibid.
9. Fischer 1900–1901, 502.

10. Both articles by Lequeux and Fischer were widely read. The Lequeux article, first published in 1888 in an issue of *Revue d'art dramatique*, appeared in book form one year later. In 1890 it was reprinted in three languages with numerous pictures added, in *Le Japon artistique*, edited by the art collector Samuel Bing. Fischer's article appeared in a very popular high-circulation journal. In writing on the Japanese theatre, Meyerhold inserts whole passages from Fischer.

11. Fuchs 1905, 38.
12. Fischer-Lichte 1993, 263ff.
13. Fischer 1900–1901, 502.
14. Bie 1910, 24–25.
15. Ibid., 25.

16. New York, February 4, 1912. The Theatre Museum, Vienna, has a number of reviews in its collection from the New York *Sumurun*. Unfortunately, most of them are not identified; some show either the name of the journal or of the critic or give the date. Thus, they are listed in the bibliography and quoted in this truncated form.

17. *New York Review*, January 1912.

18. Joseph Gollomb, "Sumurun." Unidentified review from the archives of the Theater Museum, Cologne.

19. There is no doubt that light and color can be attributed to a particular cultural code (cf. Fischer-Lichte 1992, 110ff.). But since this is not obligatory and since several different codes may exist simultaneously, the outcome of the process of meaning-generating is not predictable: obviously, subjectivity prevails.

20. February 4, 1912, unidentified New York journal, from the archives of the Theater Museum, Vienna.

21. "Why Lot's Wife Could Not Have Sat Out *Sumurun*." Unidentified New York review from the archives of the Theater Museum, Cologne.

22. "Sumurun," *Erie Dispatch*, January 28, 1912.

23. Gollomb, "Sumurun."

24. Mach 1922, 8ff.

25. In the conclusion and argumentation I have drawn on my own theory of meaning (Fischer-Lichte 1979 and 1992) as well as on the theory of Radical Constructivism

(cf. Krohn and Küppers 1992; Maturana and Varela 1984; Schmidt 1988, 1991; Varela 1988; Watzlawick 1981).

WHAT ARE THE RULES OF THE GAME?

1. The term literally means "Exhibition of the Nations or Peoples."
2. Hagenbeck 1909, 96–101.
3. These audiences also included theatre avant-gardists such as Meyerhold and Artaud. In 1910 Meyerhold visited the Samoa Exhibition in Hamburg, and the dances and chants deeply impressed him. On the occasion of the Colonial Exhibition in Paris in 1931, Artaud saw a group of Balinese dancers on which he wrote quite extensively in *The Theatre and Its Double*.
4. Koppelkamm 1987, 356.
5. Goldmann 1985, 64.
6. Goldmann 1987.
7. *Zeitschrift für Ethnologie* (1898), 126; Altenberg 1987.
8. Ibid., 230.
9. Harry Graf Kessler, in the foreword to *Notes on Mexico* (1898), denies that the possibility of experiencing a foreign culture still exists: "Ours is probably the last age where travel is still possible; we barely escape our own civilization; the picture remains extraordinarily similar in one part of the world and the next. . . . Only one whose imagination is great enough to perceive foreign meanings behind the familiar signs, or one who is inspired by strange surroundings and the loneliness of distance to see with new eyes, will regularly, rather than accidentally, experience new things in the other environment" (Kessler 1988, 337).
10. Hagenbeck 1909, 82.
11. Ibid., 95.
12. Lehmann 1955, 39.
13. Ibid., 36.
14. In the spring of 1993 I had an experience which gave me a sense of how these colonial exhibitions must have worked. During my stay at the University of Washington, Seattle, I booked a package tour to Tillicum Village on Blake Island, including a boat trip, dinner, and show by Native Americans of the region. The show started after the visitors had feasted on an opulent salmon meal and were still seated before its remains. A voice announced through a loudspeaker that the Native Americans would present some of their traditional rituals and dances. They were duly performed on an illusionistic stage of the nineteenth century erected in front of the dinner tables. The voice had asked for respect toward the performance because it was traditional and "authentic." To me, this seemed to be an unbearingly disrespectful attitude toward the Native Americans, their traditions, and their culture. Exactly as in the colonial exhibitions, all the elements presented here were taken out of the context of the culture in which they had once functioned as particular meaning-generating elements. Here they were selected and combined in order to be performed on an illusionistic stage as kind of a dessert before an audience that wanted nothing else than to be entertained and accordingly responded especially enthusiastically to the lighting effects of the

illusionistic stage! I had thought that the colonial exhibitions belonged to the past —
yet here was one still doing the rounds.

15. Hagenbeck 1909, 84.

16. *Zeitschrift für Ethnologie* (1898), 66.

17. Eksteins 1989.

18. Material on the London production is available in the archive of the Theatre
Museum, Victoria and Albert Museum in London; material on Lindemann's production including its guest tour to Munich (June 9, 1914–July 12, 1914) and on Reinhardt's production can be found in the archives of the Theater Museum of Cologne
and Reinhardt's "Regiebuch" in the archives of the Vienna Theatre Museum.

19. Hazelton and Benrimo 1913, 1.

20. Ibid., 4.

21. Ibid., 7.

22. Ibid., 23.

23. Ibid., 175.

24. Ibid., 177.

25. Chorus, for example, is a dramatic figure not found on any of the traditional
Chinese stages. This "convention" was created by the authors.

26. Hazelton and Benrimo 1913, 188.

27. Ibid., 190.

28. E. F. S. (Monocle) 1913, 10.

29. E. K. 1914.

30. Elchinger 1914.

31. Koonen 1985, 185.

32. *Breslauer Zeitung*, 1914.

33. Hazelton and Benrimo 1913, 4.

34. Koonen 1985, 185.

35. *Badische Presse*, 1914.

36. Hazelton and Benrimo 1913, 81.

37. Ibid., 83.

38. *Sketch*, 1913, 10.

39. Hazelton and Benrimo 1913, 161–162.

40. *Sketch*, 1913, 10.

41. Turzinsky 1914.

42. *Sketch*, 1913, 10.

43. *Frankfurter Zeitung*, 1914.

44. *Neueste Nachrichten*, 1914.

45. Cf. Schramm 1996.

46. This seems surprising insofar as at least in the cinema people were used to en-
joying the rupture and to allowing meaning to emerge as a result of montage. In the
twenties, however, in many cultural fields, people became used to exploiting the rupture between perception and meaning for pleasure and to producing new discourses
by establishing unexpected relations between perception and meaning. That which
before World War I had been restricted to the theatre, or, to be precise, to the performances of *The Yellow Jacket* and some other performances as well as initially to cinema,
became common cultural practice after World War I.

1. Grotowski 1975, 15.

2. *Theater der Nationen*, 1979, 7.

3. Handke 1976, 53–54.

4. Thus, Leslie Fiedler's cry to "cross the border, close the gap" was answered. Insofar, any discussion on theatre of the last thirty years is also a discussion of postmodernism. Since this aspect cannot be discussed in this context, the relevant literature is indicated here; see among others Hoesterey 1991; Huyssen and Scherpe 1986; Kamper and van Reijen 1987; Weimann and Gumbrecht 1991.

5. Aragon 1976, 3–7.

6. Cf. Fischer-Lichte and Schwind 1991.

7. New computer technologies can apparently make up for this deficit — cyberspace should be able to provide new spatial and bodily experiences. See "Computerwelt als Erlebnisraum . . ." 1992. Even if the computer does succeed in replacing the given perspective with a gaze that moves freely in space, it is nonetheless mostly "autistic" experiences that are created: "there is no stage, no distance, no 'gaze' anymore: it is the end of the spectacle, of the spectacular, all that is left is total, fusionistic, tactile aesthetics and not the aesthetic environment" (Baudrillard 1982, 113).

8. Cf. Rühle 1976, 170–186, and also Rühle 1982 and 1992 for an incomparable history of German theatre after the war with reference to the 1920s; all three are highly recommended. See, moreover, talks and discussions on this era in *Theater heute*. On the happening in general, see among others Kirby 1965; Nöth 1972; and Vostell 1970.

9. Rischbieter 1966, 16.

10. On the Living Theatre, see among others Beck 1972; Beck and Malina 1971; Neff 1970; Silvestro 1971. On audience participation, see also Schechner 1973, where he describes the principles behind the work of his "Performance Garage" and its aims toward audience participation.

11. On this and the productions that follow, see Iden 1982 and *Schaubühne* 1987.

12. On this new concept of space, see among others "Der Raum des Theaters," *Theater heute*, annual vol. (1979), 59–108.

13. Cf. Rühle 1976, 224–233.

14. In addition to the two volumes on the Schaubühne mentioned above, also see Jäger 1974.

15. Cf. Rühle 1980.

16. On Heising's *Stallerhof*, see Michaelis 1972.

17. On Zadek's *Lulu*, see among others Merschmeier 1988b; Rischbieter 1988; Ruf 1988; Zadek and Grützke 1988.

18. On *Othello*, see Canaris 1976b; on the dispute over Zadek's *Othello*, cf. ibid., 21, and Canaris 1976a.

19. Strauß 1969.

20. Rühle 1982, 263.

21. Cf. ibid., 261–266.

22. Schlicher 1987, 129.

23. Grüber, at a rehearsal of *Empedocles*, recounted by Michaelis 1988, 87.

24. At this rehearsal, Grüber quoted a verse from the unfinished *Vaterländischen Gesänge* (Anthems to the Fatherland) from *Mnemosyne*, written at the same time as *Empedocles*, in which Hölderlin wrote: "We are a sign, without meaning" ("Ein Zeichen sind wir, deutungslos"). This holds true in some ways as the key to Grüber's work: he invents puzzling signs to which it is difficult to assign meaning—from which any associative meaning can be drawn.

25. Robert Wilson, in Riewoldt 1987.

26. On Wilson's theatre aesthetic, see among others Brecht 1979; De Smit and Veit 1987; Faust 1979; Fischer-Lichte 1989a and "Passage to the Realm of Shadows" in this volume; Lehmann 1985; Marranca 1983; Pfister 1988a; Rockwell 1984; Willett 1985; Wirth 1991.

27. Danto 1981.

28. Cf. Rötzer 1991.

29. Much of Helga Finter's work has been devoted to this problem. See Finter 1982 and 1989–1990.

30. On Einar Schleef, see among others Auffermann 1987; Eckhart 1989; Merschmeier 1988a and 1990; Rischbieter 1987.

31. Cf. among others Hentschel 1991; Rischbieter 1986.

32. On the production of *Mauser*, see Wille 1991.

33. On the group Angelus Novus, see Lehmann and Schulz 1988.

34. See Finter's comments on trends in Italian contemporary theatre in Finter 1991.

35. Virilio 1986. See also Barck 1988.

36. Müller 1985, 13–14.

37. Cf. Barba and Savarese 1991; Fiebach 1990; Schechner 1982 and 1985. Just as the marking of the materiality of theatrical communication is directly bound to an anthropological interest, both stand in direct relation to the intercultural trend in contemporary theatre. Cf. "Familiar and Foreign Theatres" in this volume; also Fischer-Lichte 1990b and 1990c.

38. Böhme 1991, 483. See also Birringer 1991.

39. Böhme 1991.

40. In the context of this development it is understandable that dance theatre has increasingly come to the fore. See Schlicher 1987; also Bergelt and Völkers 1991.

41. Cf. Finter 1991.

42. Müller and Weimann 1991, 199.

43. Ibid., 200.

IN SEARCH OF A NEW THEATRE

1. The concept was formulated by Fuchs (1905) and subsequently adopted by almost the whole avant-garde movement.

2. This new code should in no way be thought of as one single code. The different orientations and members of the avant-garde were so dissimilar in their programs and artistic and ideological aims that each developed its own theatre form. They shared, however, the features outlined above.

3. By turning to the Greeks, Wagner struggled to annul the chasm between art and life. The Greek theatre seemed exemplary because it was part of a "free and beautiful public" (Wagner 1887–1888, vol. 3, 29); "the people flooded from the state meeting, from the law courts, from the countryside, from ships, from the battlefield, from far distant regions to come together, in order to see the performance of the most profound of tragedies, *Prometheus*, in order to gather before a mighty artistic event, to gather before their own selves, to understand their own actions, to melt into the most intimate of unities with one's whole essence, the whole community, the gods, and thus in the noblest, deepest peace become again *that* which once they were a few hours before in restless excitement and separate individuality. . . . For in tragedy, the noblest part of one's own essence finds itself again, unified with the noblest parts of the whole community, of the whole nation" (ibid., 11–12).

4. The function of the reception of Far Eastern theatre by the avant-garde has remained largely unnoticed in research on the avant-garde. Although the earlier works by Schwartz 1927; Hung 1934; Winters 1956; and Miner 1958 as well as the more recent work by Schuster 1977 provide important material, they are unproductive when it comes to the question of the function of reception in terms of both the methodology and results, for to a large extent they remain descriptive. One exception is offered by Pronko 1967. Pronko examines the Far Eastern theatre forms and their reception in Western theatre, although solely under general theatrical aesthetic aspects, to what extent they are superior to the Western theatre and to what extent the study of Far Eastern theatre could enrich it. The processes of reception are thus described as attempts to enrich Western theatre aesthetics in general. A more accurate determination of the function of reception is to be found in isolated articles and monographs — on Artaud (Innes 1981; Kapralik 1977; Virmeaux 1975), on Brecht (Berg-Pan 1979; Krusche 1980, 340–357; Oba 1984; Tatlow 1977), and on Yeats (Dorn 1984; Mille 1976; Qamber 1974; Taylor 1976).

5. On this concept, see Grimm 1977, 141–142.

6. Principally in the journals *Oriental Review, Japan Magazine, Drama, Mask, Bulletin de l'École Française de l'Extrème Orient, Le théâtre, Mitteilungen der Deutschen Gesellschaft für Natur und Völkerkunde Ostasiens, Westermanns Illustrierte Deutsche Monatshefte, Velhagen und Klasrings Monatshefte, Das Theater, Die Schaubühne.*

7. As, for example, Benazet 1901; Chamberlain 1880; Claudel 1900; Edwards 1901; Florenz 1906; Guimet and Régamey 1886; Hart 1894–1896. From the turn of the century to approximately 1925, a flood of publications appeared on the subject. The most influential in terms of the problematic discussed in this chapter are works by Fenollosa 1916b; Kincaid 1925; and Maybon 1925.

8. Fouquier 1900, 10.

9. *Lecture pour tous* (March 1908); Pronko 1967, 121.

10. *Je sais tout*; cf. Pronko 1967.

11. Blei 1902, 66.

12. September 1900; cf. Pronko 1967, 123.

13. Schickele 1979, 292.

14. Ibid., 291.

15. Cf. Schuster 1977.

16. Meyerhold 1979, vol. 1, 131.

17. Ibid., 107–108.

18. Ibid., vol. 2, 268.

19. Ernst 1974, 92.

20. Ibid., 97–98.

21. Cf. Leiter 1979, 212.

22. Ernst 1974, 111.

23. Meyerhold 1979, vol. 1, 183.

24. Ibid., 187.

25. Ibid., 135.

26. Rühle 1963, 74.

27. Meyerhold 1979, vol. 2, 47.

28. Meyerhold 1974, 162. Cf. "Discovering the Spectator" in this volume.

29. Copeau 1974, 2.

30. Pronko 1967, 89.

31. Copeau 1931, 99.

32. Cf. Arnott 1969 and Barth 1972.

33. From 1890 to 1930 many *no* and *kabuki* dramas were translated into English, French, German, and Russian. Particularly influential were free renderings of some *no* texts by Ezra Pound based on translations by Fenollosa 1916a and collections by Florenz 1900 (2nd edition as early as 1901); Péri 1921; Stopes and Sakurai 1913; Von Gersdorff 1926; and Waley 1921.

34. Pronko 1967, 90.

35. Ibid., 91.

36. Ibid., 92.

37. Copeau 1931, 100.

38. In this work, which was published in Mayakovsky's journal *LEF* (*LEF* 3 [Moscow 1923], 70–75, reprinted in *S. M. Eisenstein* 1964), Eisenstein agreed with Meyerhold that the spectator is the "chief material of theatre" and confirmed the "leading of the spectators in a desired direction" as the task of theatre. He defined an "attraction" in theatre as "each aggressive moment of theatre, that is, each of the elements which has an effect on the spectator's emotion or psyche." The theatre achieves its goal through a new artistic procedure: "the free montage of deliberately chosen, independent effects (attractions)—(even effective outside underlying composition and *sujet*-scene), although, with an exact intention toward a specific thematic end result— the montage of attractions." Eisenstein found this "new artistic procedure" realized in *kabuki* theatre.

39. Eisenstein 1963, 279–280.

40. This concept plays on Boris Eikhenbaum's famous work of 1918, *How Gogol's Coat Was Made* (*Kak sdelana Sinel' Gogol'a*). It is explicitly emphasized that the Russian formalism developed in the same year as the Russian theatre avant-garde (constitution 1915–1916, important works in the 1920s, suppression after the 1930s).

41. Ihering 1961, 95.

42. Ibid., 96.

43. *Bertolt Brecht-Archiv* 1969–1973, 158/44.

1. Goethe 1966, 153.
2. Bruford 1950, 319.
3. January 28, 1812; Goethe 1975 (1901), 206–207.
4. February 4, 1811; ibid., 29–30.
5. Goethe 1989.
6. Goethe 1943, vol. 1.
7. Goethe 1961–1966, vol. 2, 937.
8. On the reception of Far Eastern theatre in the theatre of the European avant-garde movement, see among others: Berg-Pan 1979; Braun 1979; Innes 1981; Kim 1982; Krusche 1980, vol. 2, 340–357; Miner 1958; Oba 1984; Pronko 1967; Qamber 1974; Rudnicky 1969; Schuster 1977; Tatlow 1977; Taylor 1976; Virmaux 1975.
9. Artaud 1970, 72.
10. On performances touring abroad, see in particular Pronko 1967.
11. On the history of *shingeki*, see, among others, Arnott 1969; Barth 1972; Ortolani 1963; Powell 1975; Rimer 1974.
12. On the development of Chinese spoken drama, see Dolby 1976; Eberstein 1983; Häringova 1964; Lau 1970; Mackerras 1980 and 1983.
13. Eberstein 1983, 47.
14. On the reception of Western theatre in India, see, among others, Bharucha 1983; Birendranarayan 1981; Das Gupta 1938–1944; *The Marathi Theatre* 1961; Mathur 1964; Mehta 1960; Ranganath 1982; Rea 1978–1979; Thiems 1966; Yajnik 1933.
15. On the history of African theatre in the twentieth century, see Amankular 1976; Armstrong 1976; Etherton 1982; Fiebach 1986; Graham-White 1974; Ogunbiyi 1981.
16. Soyinka 1978, 75.
17. Soyinka 1976, 177.

CHANGING THEATRICAL CODES

1. On the theatrical code of the Théâtre du Soleil, see in particular Neuschäfer and Serror 1984; Paul 1978.
2. Von Becker 1984b, 15.
3. On the concept of choice, see Gissenwehrer 1990.
4. Grimm 1977, 142.
5. Cf. Lotman 1976 and 1977.
6. On the problems of the code changes in theatre, see Fischer-Lichte 1983b, vol. 2. On code change as a cultural change, see Posner 1989. On the dialectics of code and message (change 2), see Eco 1976.

INTERCULTURAL ASPECTS IN POSTMODERN THEATRE

1. "Nationalliteratur will jetzt nicht viel sagen, die Epoche der Weltliteratur ist an der Zeit, und jeder muß jetzt dazu wirken, diese Epoche zu beschleunigen" (January 31, 1827; Eckermann 1984).

2. Cf. Braun 1979.

3. Cf. Willett 1964.

4. Tairov 1964.

5. Artaud 1956–1994, vol. 4.

6. Arnott 1969.

7. *SCOT* 1985.

8. I had the opportunity to see a performance of this production at the Frankfurt Theatre Festival in September 1985. I have used the English translation of Suzuki's version of the text and the minutes of an interview with Suzuki at the festival.

9. *SCOT* 1985, 6ff.

10. Ibid.

11. Yamaguchi 1985.

12. *SCOT* 1985, 6.

13. Brook 1968.

14. Smith 1974; Von Becker 1985.

15. Fischer-Lichte 1986.

16. Von Becker 1984a and 1984c.

17. Benamou and Caramelle 1977; Schechner 1982 and 1985.

ALL THE WORLD'S A STAGE

1. Müller 1985, 13.

PASSAGE TO THE REALM OF SHADOWS

1. Gold 1985.

2. This relationship is consistently noted by both critics and scholars. See among others Rockwell 1984 and Willett 1985.

3. On Wilson's aesthetic, see among others Brecht 1979; De Smit and Veit 1987; Faust 1979; Fischer-Lichte 1989a; Lehmann 1985; Marranca 1983, 39–45; Owens 1980; Quadri 1984; Riewoldt 1987; Rockwell 1984; Willett 1985.

4. On this point, see Fischer-Lichte 1986, 191–201.

5. Karasek and Jenny 1987.

6. Ibid., 208.

7. The opposite view is held by Pavis 1993.

8. On the principles and methods of performance analysis as they are applied here, see Fischer-Lichte 1992, 173ff.

9. *König Lear*, program to the performance, Schauspiel Frankfurt, 1989–1990 season, May 1990, no page numbers.

10. The sequence of scenes is given at the back of the program to the performance.

11. On Wilson's use of Japanese theatre as, for example, in *Knee Plays*, see Fischer-Lichte 1990b and 1990c.

12. While in *Alcestis* the theme of "death" is portrayed in its mystical dimension by the presence of mummy, temple, and River Lethe onstage, the guiding of reception undertaken in prologue A allows the extensively bare set in *Lear* to function uniquely as a multivariable projection surface.

13. Iden 1990.

14. Stadelmaier 1990.

15. Schödel 1990.

16. This structure of opposition and equivalence describes the main tendency only. The actors were clearly not all capable of achieving it. The actor playing Kent, for example, "suffered" in scene 5 (2.4) on the wheel for a brief moment quite realistically and with heavy personal psychology through sighs and clenched fists. This is not the place, however, to criticize the ability of individual actors, but rather to analyze the performance as a whole in terms of the introductory consideration.

17. Here too the consistently practiced principle of reduction in *Lear* is employed. The animal aspects remain wholly implicit. In *Alcestis*, on the other hand, carrion and lions actually appeared on the stage.

18. The process of dying is accorded a certain modeling — in this case, through light. From the moment of Lear's entry with the dead Cordelia to the moment of his death, the light grows brighter, increasing suddenly in the moment of death. It then grows slowly but noticeably darker.

19. Thus, as in other Wilson productions, no relation is formed between what occurs on the level of linguistic text and on the level of movement performed by the actors. While Lear's gestures support his words — give ironic commentary, illustrate, neutralize, negate, modify, replace, or even explicitly contradict — such a relationship cannot be accomplished where language and gesture are detached from one another. Both systems function and generate meaning wholly independent of the other.

20. It is a characteristic feature of Wilson's aesthetic that the characters mostly move parallel to the apron stage. Only seldom do they turn directly to the audience. In Lear such is the case in only three places. In scene 2B (1.5) the Fool walks forward along the table and Lear walks sideways beside him to the right of the table. At the end of the table, Lear speaks the lines: "Oh! Let me not be mad, not mad, sweet heaven; / Keep me in temper; I would not be mad!" (1.5, 46–47). At the end of scene 7 (3.7) the blind Gloucester walks slowly forward. Finally, at the end of scene 15 (5.3) Lear strides directly forward in the middle of the stage with the dead Cordelia. This seems to imply that the forward direction of movement at center stage is only realized in relation to the passage into a new condition: into madness, blindness, death. These unique moments result in a direct confrontation with the audience. The rest of the time, the passages parallel to the apron are preferred, allowing — less aggressively — the audience a greater opportunity for quiet observation and contemplation of the images put before them.

21. In scene 8 (4.1), which follows directly after Gloucester's blinding, the metal sounds which accompanied the act echo again and again. Gloucester's idea of space is entirely composed of these sounds and Edgar's movements next to him.

22. Cf. Van Gennep 1960.

23. In this sense, Wilson's aesthetic is actually comparable to Richard Wagner's description of his ideal performance in his work "Ein Einblick in das heutige deutsche Opernwesen": "in these elements every factor of scenic life — blocking, painting, lighting, every movement, every transformation brought with it a kind of perfect illusion that wrapped us in a dreaming delusion, a waking dream of things that we have never experienced before" (Wagner 1914, 314). On the other hand, the application

of Wagner's term *Gesamtkunstwerk* to Wilson's aesthetic — which is often taken for granted by some scholars (cf. Lehmann, Marranca, Rockwell, Willett)— can hardly be justified when one seeks to reconstruct the term from a historical point of view. Cf. Fischer-Lichte 1989b.

24. In this sense, Wilson's theatre aesthetic has much in common with Goethe's Weimar theatre aesthetic. For Goethe too, music and the fine arts decidedly formed the underlying principles of his productions, with which he, as Schiller remarked, "declared . . . war openly and honestly on all naturalism in art" (cf. Borchmeyer 1984; Schiller 1965, 818; "for the sake of openly and honestly declaring war on all naturalism in art"). A further correspondence occurs in both directors' love of the tableau. In his *Regeln für Schauspieler* (Rules for Actors), §83, Goethe states, "The stage should be considered a figureless tableau for which the actors supply the figures" (Carlson 1978, 318). (On the theatrical tableau, see Langen 1978b, 292–353.) Thus, it is hardly surprising that Goethe's theatre, encountering an audience used to the realism brought by the Enlightenment, met with rejection and objection from the audience as Wilson's theatre did from the critics. Karoline Herder, for example, spoke for the majority of the audience when she loosed the following invective after Goethe's production of August Wilhelm Schlegel's *Ion* (1802): "The newest rule of the theatre in sway here grows daily more outrageous and shameless. It believes that dramatic art is no more than representation and declamation; the content of the play is rated far below that and may not even be considered as far as the spectator is concerned. We should sit there in the pits like wooden puppets, watch the wooden puppets on the stage and listen to their meaningless declamations, and leave at the end of it empty and disconsolate" (Düntzer and Herder 1861–1862, vol. 1, 301). See a passage from Peter Iden's critique of Wilson's *Lear*: the confusion that some of the audience "experiences stems from the fact that the harmonious and elegant beauty of the *mise en scène*, the unquestionable brilliance in the use of space, light, and the positioning of the actors . . . actually only create a cultivated surface and a monotonously minimal, shining appearance of things — of the tragedy itself, on the other hand, very little is of consequence, except perhaps a slight upset now and then" (Iden 1990, 8).

25. Müller 1985.

26. The perception of time that underlies Wilson's theatre is thus related to the state of modern physics, which argues that in the fourth dimensional "space-time" the idea of absolute, measurable time equivalent for everyone is abolished, and that "each individual has his own personal measure of time that depends on where he is and how he is moving" (Hawking 1988, 33).

27. In this respect, the fact that the role of Lear is played by an actress serves a wholly different function than the same device in earlier eras of theatre history or indeed contemporary transvestite theatre. It is not a question of an actress using her artistic talents to play a man by exposing the typical aspects of man — as is the reverse case in the Japanese *onnagata*, the male actor of female roles in *kabuki* theatre, where the portrayal of the specifically feminine (whatever that may mean) is given fundamental importance. Nor is it a question of the change of sexual identity (note the costumes!). Rather, it is marked by the fact that it deals with a natural death at the end of a long life. (On the question of the special function and effect of the casting of a woman as Lear and on the question of Marianne Hoppe's Lear, see Fischer-Lichte 1991.)

28. Craig 1908, 9.

29. Compare my interpretation of the *Lear* tragedy in Fischer-Lichte 1990b, vol. 1, 133–153.

30. While the criticism ends with the feeling that "Wilson's first Shakespeare" is "actually a flop," that Wilson has "failed as a Shakespeare director" (Schödel 1990, 68), and that "despite all his talent for the artificial, Robert Wilson has not come close to the play itself" (Iden 1990), the results of this analysis do not support such conclusions. True, it is not *Lear* (i.e., it is not an interpretation of the tragedy), but it undertakes the attempt to show similar experiences that are shaped and released by the tragedy. This is a different approach to the text than that which we see not only in state theatres but also in the work of directors such as Peter Brook, Peter Zadek, Ingmar Bergman, and Klaus Michael Grüber, but it certainly is an approach which allows the classic text to be "discovered anew."

RETURNING THE GAZE

1. With respect to festivals, see Biver 1979; CRAR 1994; Davis 1975; Heers 1986; Jacquot 1956–1975; Moine 1984; Roberti 1980; Strong 1991. Regarding political ceremonies, see Apostolidès 1981; Burke 1992; Cannadine and Price 1982; Meyer 1992; Sarcinelli 1987. On punishment rites, see Foucault 1975; Van Dülmen 1988. On funeral rites, see Ariès 1981; Giesey 1960; Huntington and Metcalf 1979. On games, see Bredekamp 1993. On storytelling and ballad singing, see Zumthor 1983 and 1984. On concerts, see Charles 1989.

2. Singer 1959, xii–xiii.

3. Cf. "The Aesthetics of Disruption" in this volume.

4. Cf. the introduction to this volume.

5. Féral 1982, 179.

6. Fusco 1994, 164.

7. Ibid.

8. Lehmann 1955, 39.

9. See the description in "What Are the Rules of the Game?" in this volume.

10. Lehmann 1955, 39.

11. Goldmann 1985, 64.

12. Fusco 1994, 158.

PERFORMANCE ART AND RITUAL

1. John Cage, in Goldberg 1988, 176.

2. Wagner 1887–1888, vol. 4, 3.

3. Singer 1959, xii.

4. Ibid., xii–xiii.

5. Nitsch 1979, 50.

6. Nitsch 1990, 103–104.

7. Ibid., 105–106.

8. This is not the place to investigate the special traditions on which Nitsch

draws — in particular the Viennese tradition. Concerning this question, cf. the study by Stärk 1987.

9. Nitsch 1979, "7. Aktion," 87.

10. Benveniste 1966, 273.

11. Concerning the concept of frame, see Bateson 1955.

12. Joseph Beuys, in Tisdall 1988, 13. (My description of the performance follows the description given by Tisdall.)

13. Ibid., 14.

14. Ibid.

15. Ibid., 15.

16. Ibid., 15–16.

17. Ibid., 16.

18. Ibid., 15.

19. Ibid., 10.

20. Ibid., 13.

21. Van Gennep 1960.

22. Cf. Plessner 1980 and 1970a.

23. Cf. Csordas 1994.

24. *The Conditioning*, part 1 of "Auto-Portrait," 1972.

25. Theater am Turm (TAT), Frankfurt am Main, 1991.

26. New York 1990–1994.

27. Scarry 1985, 4.

28. Van Dülmen 1988, 163.

29. Rosenthal 1981–1982, 24.

AVANT-GARDE AND POSTMODERNISM

1. McHale 1987.

2. Fokkema and Bertens 1986, 46–47.

3. Szondi 1971, 127.

4. Pirandello 1988, 53.

5. *Homecoming*, act 1; *The Hunted*, act 1.

6. *Homecoming*, act 1.

7. *The Hunted*, act 3, ll. 304–305.

8. *The Hunted*, act 2, ll. 355–356.

9. Tzara 1975–1982, vol. 1, 169.

10. Ibid., 159.

11. Ibid., 173.

12. Ibid., 159.

13. Ibid., 158.

14. Ibid., 77.

15. In Huelsenbeck 1984, 226.

16. Mehring 1959, 52.

17. Artaud 1956–1994, vol. 4, 139.

18. *CIVIL warS*, act 1, scene A.

1. Bürger 1983; Masini 1979.
2. Benjamin 1977, 37.
3. Ibid.
4. Ibid.
5. Ibid.
6. Tiedemann 1965, 29, note.
7. Benjamin 1968, 74.
8. Cf. MacCannell 1987.
9. Benjamin 1977, 331.
10. Ibid., 165.
11. Ibid.
12. Ibid., 166.
13. Ibid.
14. Ibid., 175.
15. Ibid., 166.
16. Ibid.
17. Ibid., 230.
18. Ibid., 183–184.
19. Ibid., 175.
20. It is striking to what extent the allegorical process as Benjamin describes it is similar, or parallel to, a process which Derrida explained as "deconstruction of the transcendental signified" approximately forty years later (Derrida 1967a). The allegorist has deconstructed it already.
21. Benjamin 1977, 176.
22. Ibid., 223–224.
23. Benjamin 1972–1981, vol. 1, 690.
24. Benjamin 1977, 177–178.
25. Ibid., 232.
26. This is a procedure that Benjamin himself has applied in his later works about Baudelaire. Here he breaks the concept of allegory out of the context in which he has elaborated it (eschatology) and uses it with regard to a materialistic criticism of capitalism ("Die Entwertung der Dingwelt in der Allegorie wird innerhalb der Dingwelt selbst durch die Ware überboten," 1972–1981, vol. 1, 660).
27. On the concept of deconstruction, cf. De Man 1972; Culler 1983.
28. The term *intertextuality* is used here as Bakhtin has elaborated it (Bakhtin 1981). Moreover, see Kristeva 1977.
29. Benjamin 1968, 265.
30. Regarding Benjamin's late theory of reception, see Fischer-Lichte 1979.
31. Concerning the relationship between internal and external relations of a work, see Lotman 1977.

SIGNS OF IDENTITY

1. De Levita 1965, 172.

2. Wilshire 1982, 158.
3. Lorenzer 1973, 102.
4. Simmel 1957, 169.
5. Ibid., 174f.
6. *Poetics*, ch. 4, 1449a.
7. Ibid., ch. 5, 1449.
8. Ibid., ch. 15, 1454a.
9. Ibid., ch. 5, 1449a.
10. Benjamin 1977, 166.

THE QUEST FOR MEANING

1. *Poetics*, ch. 9, 1–4.
2. Wordsworth and Coleridge (1798) 1963, 240–260.
3. See Kant 1951, 51.
4. *Poetics*, ch. 6, 24–28.
5. Freud reintroduced the term *catharsis* into the theory of art by directly referring to Aristotle.
6. Holland 1968, 174.
7. Lotman 1977, 35.
8. Ibid., 18.
9. Ibid.
10. Ibid., 10.
11. Kristeva 1974, 77.
12. Ibid., 39.
13. Ibid., 53.
14. Ibid., 210.
15. Ibid., 88.
16. Ibid., 75.
17. Ibid., 88.
18. Mukařovský 1970.
19. Ibid., 18.
20. Ibid., 82.
21. Ibid., 82–83.

WRITTEN DRAMA/ORAL PERFORMANCE

1. Aristotle 1964.
2. Pfister 1988b, 6–11.
3. Cf. Fischer-Lichte 1987b.
4. Koch and Oesterreicher 1985.
5. Cf. Ingarden 1960.
6. Veltruský 1976, 114ff.
7. Goethe 1972, vol. 6, 201–202.
8. Carlson 1978, 316.
9. Goethe 1972, vol. 6, 89.

10. Lessing 1948, 246.

11. Cf. Fischer-Lichte 1992.

12. Scherer 1977.

13. Ekman and Friesen 1969.

14. Ibid.

15. Cf. Ekman, Friesen, and Ellsworth 1972.

16. Cf. Schefflen 1972.

17. Cf. Sacks, Jefferson, and Schlegloff 1974; Schlegloff and Sacks 1973.

18. Cf. Ekman and Friesen 1969.

19. Cf. Ekman, Friesen, and Ellsworth 1972.

20. Engle 1968, 107–108. Cf. Fischer-Lichte 1992.

21. See "Avant-garde and Postmodernism" in this volume.

22. Cf. Fischer-Lichte 1979.

THEATRE HISTORIOGRAPHY AND PERFORMANCE ANALYSIS

1. "Bühne und Drama," *Vossische Zeitung,* July 30, 1918.

2. Craig (1905) 1911, 138.

3. Schramm 1990, 206.

4. In referring to a subject who chooses an object of research around which to construct a history, this neither presupposes nor demands that the subject acts as an autonomous individual (such a concept has long been proved invalid). Rather, it is used in the sense of clarifying the fact that the particular choice of object as well as the specific construction of its history will depend on certain conditions intrinsically bound to that particular subject — i.e., the cultural/social context of the subject, the various discourses in which the subject participates, and so on.

5. On "transgressive" concepts, see Rüsen et al. 1988.

6. Concerning such methods of segmentation as well as of performance analysis in general, cf. Fischer-Lichte 1992, 171–253.

7. Cf. the first two chapters in this volume.

8. Wachtangow 1982, 395.

9. Concerning the employment of the device of stagehands in Vakhtangov's production, see Gorchakov 1957; Ivanov and Krivicky 1984; Rudnitsky 1988; Simonov 1959; Smirnova 1982; Smirnov-Nesvitzky 1987; *Sovetskij teatr — dokumenty i materialy: Russkij sovetskij teatr 1921–1926* 1975; Wachtangow 1982; Worrall 1989.

BIBLIOGRAPHY

Adedeji, Joel. 1981. "Alarinjo: The Traditional Yoruba Travelling Theatre." In *Drama and Theatre in Nigeria — A Critical Source Book*, ed. Yemi Ogunbiyi, 221–247. Lagos: *Nigeria Magazine*.

Alpers, Boris. 1977. *Teatral'nye očerki*. Vol. 1. Moscow: n.p.

Altenberg, Peter. 1987. *Ashantee* (1898). In *Gesammelte Werke*, ed. Werner J. Schweiger. 2 vols. Frankfurt/M.: S. Fischer.

Amankular, James U. 1976. "The Traditional Black African Theatre — Problems of Critical Evaluation." *Ufahamu* 4:2, 27–46.

Apollonio, Umbro. 1972. *Der Futurismus: Manifeste und Dokumente einer Künstlerischen Revolution 1909–1918*. Cologne: DuMont Schauberg.

Apostolidès, Jean-Marie. 1981. *Le roi-machine: Spectacle et politique au temps de Louis XIV*. Paris: Editions de Minuit.

Aragon, Louis. 1976. "An Open letter to André Breton on Robert Wilson's *Deafman Glance*." *Performing Arts Journal* 1, 3–7.

Arce, Javier. 1958. *Funus Imperatorum: Los funerales de los emperadores romanos*. Madrid: Aliance Editorial.

Ariès, Philippe. 1981. *The Hour of Our Death*. New York: Knopf.

Aristotle. 1924. *The Works of Aristotle*. Ed. W. D. Ross; trans. vol. 11 (*Rhetorica*) V. Rhys Roberts, (*De Rhetorica ad Alexandrum*) E. S. Forster, (*De Poetica*) Ingram Bywake. Oxford: Clarendon Press.

———. 1964. *Poetik*. Trans. Olof Gigon. Stuttgart: Reclam.

———. 1982. *The Poetics*. London: Heinemann.

Armstrong, Robert Plant. 1976. "Tragedy — Greek and Yoruba: A Cross-Cultural Perspective." *Research in African Literature* 7, 23–43.

Arnott, Peter. 1969. *The Theatres of Japan*. London/New York: Macmillan.

Artaud, Antonin. 1956–1994. *Oeuvres complètes*. 26 vols. Paris: Gallimard.

———.1968–1974. *Collected Works*. New York: International Publications Services.

———. 1970. *The Theatre and Its Double*. Trans. Victor Corti. London: Calder and Boyars.

———. 1975. *Die Tarahumaras: Revolutionäre Botschaften*. Munich: Matthes und Seitz.

Arvatov, Boris. 1972. *Kunst und Produktion*. Munich: Hanser.

Auffermann, Verena. 1987. "Das ist mein Leben — Das ist mein Blut. Das bin ich und das fühle ich. Ich stehe da und bleibe: Beobachtungen nach dem Superdebakel *Die Mütter* in Frankfurt." *Theater heute*, annual vol., 116–120.

Badische Presse. 1914. April 1.

Bahti, Timothy. 1979. "History as Rhetorical Enactment: Walter Benjamin's Theses on the Concept of History." *Diacritics* 9:3 (Fall), 2–17.

Bakhtin, Mikhail. 1981. *The Dialogic Imagination*. Trans. Caryl Emerson and Michael Holquist. Austin: University of Texas Press.

Barba, Eugenio, and Nicola Savarese. 1991. *The Secret Art of the Performer: Dictionary of Theatre Anthropology*. London/New York: Routledge.

Barck, Karlheinz. 1988. "Materialität, Materialismus, Performance." In *Materialität der Kommunikation*, ed. Hans Ulrich Gumbrecht and K. Ludwig Pfeiffer, 121–138. Frankfurt/M.: Suhrkamp.

Barck, Karlheinz, et al., eds. 1990. *Ästhetische Grundbegriffe: Studien zu einem historischen Wörterbuch*. Berlin: Akademie Verlag.

Barner, Wilfried, et al., eds. 1984. *Unser Commercium: Goethes und Schillers Literaturpolitik*. Stuttgart: Cotta.

Barth, Johannes. 1972. *Japans Schaukunst im Wandel der Zeiten*. Wiesbaden: Steiner.

Bateson, Gregory. 1955. "A Theory of Play and Fantasy: A Report on Theoretical Aspects of the Project for Study of the Role of Paradoxes of Abstraction in Communication." *APA Psychiatric Research Reports* 2.

Baudrillard, Jean. 1982. *Der symbolische Tausch und der Tod*. Munich: Matthes und Seitz.

Baumbach, Gerda. 1995. *Seiltänzer und Betrüger? Parodie und kein Ende*. Tübingen: Francke.

Beck, Julian. 1972. *The Life of the Theatre*. San Francisco: City Lights.

Beck, Julian, and Judith Malina. 1971. *Paradise Now*. New York: Random House.

Benamou, Michel, and Charles Caramelle, eds. 1977. *Performance in Postmodern Culture*. Madison, Wis.: Coda Press.

Benazet, Alexandre. 1901. *Le théâtre au Japon*. Paris: Leroux.

Benjamin, Walter. 1968. *Illuminations*. Ed. Hannah Arendt; trans. Harry Zohn. New York: Schocken.

———. 1972–1981. *Gesammelte Schriften*. Vols. 1–6. Ed. Rolf Tiedemann and Hermann Schweppenhäuser. Frankfurt/M.: Suhrkamp.

———. 1977. *The Origin of German Tragic Drama*. Trans. John Osborne. London: NLB.

———. 1978. *Reflections: Essays, Aphorisms and Autobiographical Writings*. Ed. Peter Demetz; trans. Edmund Jephcott. New York: Schocken.

Benveniste, Emile. 1966. *Problèmes de linguistique générale*. Paris: Gallimard.

Bergelt, Martin, and Hortensia Völkers, eds. 1991. *Zeit-Räume: Zeiträume — Raumzeiten — Zeiträume*. Munich/Vienna: Hanser.

Berg-Pan, Renate. 1979. *Bertolt Brecht und China*. Bonn: Bouvier.

Bertens, Hans. 1986. "The Postmodern *Weltanschauung* and Its Relation with Modernism." In *Approaching Postmodernism*, ed. Douwe Fokkema and Hans Bertens, 9–51. Amsterdam: John Benjamins.

Bertolt Brecht-Archiv: Bestandsverzeichnis des literarischen Nachlasses. 1969–1973. 4 vols. Ed. Herta Ramthun. Berlin/Weimar: Aufbau.

Bharucha, Rustom. 1983. *Rehearsals of Revolution: The Political Theatre of Bengal*. Honolulu: University of Hawaii Press.

Bie, Oskar. 1910. "Sumurun." *Die neue Rundschau* 6:21 (June), 24–25.

Birendranarayan. 1981. *Hindi Drama and Stage*. Delhi: n.p.

Birringer, Johannes. 1991. "Erschöpfter Raum —Verschwindende Körper." In *Digitaler Schein: Ästhetik der elektronischen Medien*, ed. Florian Rötzer, 491–518. Frankfurt/M.: Suhrkamp.

Biver, Marie-Louise. 1979. *Fêtes revolutionaires à Paris*. Paris: Presses Universitaires de France.

Blakely, Colin. 1970. "Interview with Colin Blakely." *Drama Review* 13:3, 120–122.

Blau, Herbert. 1982. *Blooded Thought*. New York: Performing Arts Journal Publications.

———. 1990. *The Audience*. Baltimore/London: Johns Hopkins University Press.

Blei, Franz. 1902. "Otojiro Kawakami." *Die Insel* 3:7/8, 66.

Bleiler, Ellen H. 1964. *Don Giovanni*. New York: Dover Opera Guide and Libretto Series.

Böhme, Gernot. 1991. "Für eine ökologische Naturästhetik: Ein Gespräch." In *Digitaler Schein: Ästhetik der elektronischen Medien*, ed. Florian Rötzer, 475–490. Frankfurt/M.: Suhrkamp.

Borchmeyer, Dieter. 1984. "Zu Goethes und Schillers Bühnenreform." In *Unser Commercium: Goethes und Schillers Literaturpolitik*, ed. Wilfried Barner, Eberhard Lämmert, and Norbert Oellers, 351–371. Stuttgart: Cotta.

Braun, Edward. 1979. *The Theatre of Meyerhold*. London: Methuen.

Brauneck, Manfred. 1982. *Theater im 20. Jahrhundert: Programmschriften, Stilperioden, Reformmodelle*. Reinbek bei Hamburg: Rowohlt.

Brecht, Bertolt. 1967. *Gesammelte Werke*. 20 vols. Frankfurt/M.: Suhrkamp.

———. 1975. *Tagebücher 1920–1922*. Ed. Herta Ramthun. Frankfurt/M.: Suhrkamp.

Brecht, Stephan. 1979. *The Theatre of Visions: The Original Theatre of the City of New York, from the mid-60s to the mid-70s*, vol. 1: *Robert Wilson*. Frankfurt/M.: Suhrkamp.

Bredekamp, Horst. 1993. *Florentiner Fußball: Die Renaissance der Spiele*. Frankfurt/M. and New York: Campus.

Brook, Peter. 1968. *The Empty Space*. London: MacGibben and Kee.

———. 1973. "Interview." *Drama Review* 17:3, 45–47.

———. 1987. *The Shifting Point: Forty Years of Theatrical Exploration, 1946–87*. London: Methuen.

Bruford, Walter Horace. 1950. *Theatre, Drama and Audience in Goethe's Germany*. London: Routledge and Paul.

Buck, August, et al., eds. 1981. *Europäische Hofkultur im 16. und 17. Jahrhundert*. 3 vols. Hamburg: Hauswedell.

Bürger, Peter. 1983. *Theory of Avant-Garde*. Trans. Michael Shaw. Minneapolis: University of Minnesota Press (German edition 1974).

Burke, Peter. 1992. *The Fabrication of Louis XIV*. New Haven/London: Yale University Press.

Caldwell, Richard S. 1974. "The Blindness of Oedipus." *International Review of Psychoanalysis* 1, 207–218.

Calinescu, Matei. 1987. *Five Faces of Modernity*. Durham: University of North Carolina Press.

Calinescu, Matei, and Douwe Fokkema, eds. 1987. *Exploring Postmodernism*. Amsterdam: John Benjamins.

Cameron, Alister. 1968. *The Identity of "Oedipus the King": Five Essays on the Oedipus Tyrannus*. New York: New York University Press.

Canaris, Volker. 1976a. "Die Anarchie der Gefühle: Benjamin Henrichs im Gespräch mit Peter Zadek." *Theater heute* 7, 24–29.

———. 1976b. "Was man in England wörtlich darstellen kann, muß man in Deutschland gestisch wiedergeben: Über Peter Hall's *Hamlet* und Peter Zadek's *Othello*." *Theater heute* 7, 12–21.

Cannadine, David, and Simon Price. 1982. *Rituals of Royalty: Power and Ceremonial in Traditional Societies*. Cambridge: Cambridge University Press.

Carlson, Marvin. 1978. *Goethe and the Weimar Theatre*. Ithaca/London: Cornell University Press.

———. 1983. "The Semiotics of Character Names in the Drama." *Semiotica* 44:3/4, 283–296.

———. 1990. *Theatre Semiotics: Signs of Life*. Bloomington: Indiana University Press.

———. 1995. "Theatre History, Methodology and Distinctive Features." *Theatre Research International* 20:2, 90–96.

Carrière, Jean-Claude. 1985. *Le Mahabharata: Adaptation théâtrale*. 4 vols. Paris: Belfond.

Carstensen, Uwe B., ed. 1988. *Klaus Michael Grüber*. Frankfurt/M.: Fischer.

Chamberlain, B. H. 1880. *The Classical Poetry of the Japanese*. London: Trübner.

Charles, Daniel. 1989. *Zeitspielräume: Performance, Musik, Ästhetik*. Berlin: Merve.

Claudel, Paul. 1900. *Connaissance de l'Est*. Paris: Edition du "Mercure de France."

Cohen, Ralph, ed. 1974. *New Directions in Literary History*. Baltimore: Johns Hopkins University Press.

"Computerwelt als Erlebnisraum des Menschen: als akustische Welle durch ein Amphitheater surfen." 1992. *DAS ERSTE: Die Zeitschrift über Fernsehen und Radio* 1 (January).

Copeau, Jacques. 1931. *Souvenirs du Vieux Colombiers*. Paris: Les Etincelles.

———. 1974. "Un essai de rénovation dramatique." In *Registres I: Appels*, ed. Marie-Hélène Dasté and Suzanne Maistre Saint-Denis, 19–32. Paris: Gallimard.

Cowan, Bainard. 1981. "Benjamin's Theory of Allegory." *New German Critique* 22, 109–122.

Craig, Edward Gordon. 1908. "The Actor and the Übermarionette." *Mask* 2, 3–15.

———. 1911. *The Art of Theatre*. London: Heinemann.

CRAR: Centre de Recherche sur les Arts de la Rue. 1994. Rues de l'université, no. 2. *Fêtes, carnavals et artistes de rue*. Paris: Gallimard.

Csampai, Atilla, and Dietmar Holland, eds. 1981. *Wolfgang Amadeus Mozart, "Don Giovanni": Texte, Materialien, Kommentare*. Reinbek bei Hamburg: Rowohlt.

Csordas, Thomas J., ed. 1994. *Embodiment and Experience: The Existential Ground of Culture and Self*. Cambridge: Cambridge University Press.

Culler, Jonathan. 1981. *The Pursuit of Signs*. Ithaca: Cornell University Press.

———. 1983. *On Deconstruction*. Ithaca: Cornell University Press.

Danto, Arthur Coleman. 1981. *The Transfiguration of the Commonplace: A Philosophy of Art*. Cambridge, Mass.: Harvard University Press.

Das Gupta, Gautam. 1988. "The Theatricks of Politics." *Performing Arts Journal* 11:2, 77–83.

Das Gupta, Hemendra Nath. 1938–1944. *The Indian Stage*. 4 vols. Calcutta: Metropolitan Print and Publishing House.

Davis, Natalie Zemon. 1975. *Society and Culture in Early Modern France: Eight Essays*. Stanford: Stanford University Press.

Debord, Guy. 1978. *Die Gesellschaft des Spektakels*. Hamburg: Nautilus.

De Levita, David. 1965. *The Concept of Identity*. Mouton.

De Man, Paul. 1972. "The Rhetoric of Temporality." In *Blindness and Insight: Essays in the Rhetoric of Contemporary Criticism*, 102–141. 2nd ed. St. Paul: University of Minnesota Press.

———. 1979. "Semiology and Rhetoric." In *Allegories of Reading: Figural Language in Rousseau, Nietzsche, Rilke and Proust*, 3–20. New Haven/London: Yale University Press.

Derrida, Jacques. 1967a. *De la grammatologie*. Paris: Minuit.

———. 1967b. *L'écriture et la différence*. Paris: Seuil.

De Smit, Peer, and Wolfgang Veit. 1987. "Die Theatervisionen des Robert Wilson." *Bühnenkunst* 4, 4–29.

Dolby, William. 1976. *A History of Chinese Drama*. London: Elek.

Dorn, Karen. 1984. *Players and Painted Stage: The Theatre of W. B. Yeats*. Brighton, Sussex: Harvester.

Duncan, Isadora. 1903. *Der Tanz der Zukunft*. Leipzig: Diederichs.

Düntzer, Heinrich, and Ferdinand Gottfried Herder, eds. 1861–1862. *Von und an Herder: Ungedruckte Briefe aus Herders Nachlaß*. 2 vols. Leipzig: Dyk.

Eberstein, Bernd. 1983. *Das chinesische Theater im 20. Jahrhundert*. Wiesbaden: Harrassowitz.

Eckermann, Johann Peter. 1984. *Gespräche mit Goethe in den letzten Jahren seines Lebens*. Ed. Regine Otto. Munich: Beck.

Eckhart, Frank. 1989. "Gewalt ist Gewaltsamkeit: Frank Castorf inszeniert *Hamlet*-Assoziationen in Köln, Einar Schleef den *Urgötz* in Frankfurt." *Theater heute* 6, 21–26.

Eco, Umberto. 1976. *A Theory of Semiotics*. Bloomington: Indiana University Press.

Edwards, Osman. 1901. *Japanese Plays and Playfellows*. London: Heinemann.

E. F. S. (Monocle). 1913. "*The Yellow Jacket* in an English Dress." *Sketch*, April 9, 10.

Eisenstein, Sergei. 1963. "Hinter der Leinwand." (1929). In *No — Vom Genius Japans*, ed. Eva Hesse, 264–282. Zurich: Arche.

———. 1964. *S. M. Eisenstein: Selected Works*. In Russian. Vol. 2. Moscow: n.p.

———. 1977. *The Film Sense*. Trans. and ed. Jay Leyda. London/Boston: Routledge and Paul.

E. K. 1914. In *Frankfurter Zeitung*, July 11.

Ekman, Paul, and Wallace V. Friesen. 1969. "The Repertoire of Non-Verbal Behaviour: Categories, Origins, Usage and Coding." *Semiotica* 1, 49–98.

Ekman, Paul, Wallace V. Friesen, and Phoebe Ellsworth. 1972. *Emotion in the Human Face*. New York: Pergamon Press.

Eksteins, Modris. 1989. *Rites of Spring: The Great War and the Birth of the "Modern Age."* Boston: Houghton Mifflin Company.

Elchinger, Richard. 1914. "*Die gelbe Jacke*: Chinesisches Schauspiel bearbeitet von Hazelton und Benrimo: Erste Aufführung im Münchner Künstlertheater am 9. Juli." *Neueste Nachrichten* (Munich) July 11.

Eliade, Mircea. 1965. *Rites and Symbols of Initiation: The Mysteries of Birth and Rebirth.* Trans. V. R. Trask. New York: Harper and Row.

Elias, Norbert. 1982. *The Civilizing Process.* Trans. Edmund Jephcott. 2 vols. New York: Pantheon Books.

Engel, Johann Jakob. 1971. *Ideen zu einer Mimik.* 2 vols. (Berlin, 1785–1786). Frankfurt/M.: Athenäum.

Engle, Ronald Gene. 1968. "Franz Lang and the Jesuit Stage." Ph.D. dissertation, University of Illinois. Ann Arbor: Michigan University Microfilms.

Enninger, Werner, and Richard J. Brunt, eds. 1985. *Interdisciplinary Perspectives at Cross-Cultural Communication.* Aachen: Raader.

Ernst, Earle. 1974. *The Kabuki-Theatre.* 1st ed. New York: Oxford University Press, 1956. Honolulu: University Press of Hawaii.

Etherton, Michael. 1982. *The Development of African Drama.* London: Heinemann.

Evans, Jonathan, and John Deely, eds. 1987. *Semiotics 1983: Proceedings of the 8th Annual Meeting of the Semiotic Society of America.* Bloomington: Lanham/ New York/London: University Press of America.

Exotische Welten: Europäische Phantasien. 1987. Catalogue of the Exhibition, Institut für Auslandsbeziehungen, Württembergischer Kunstverein, Stuttgart/Bad Cannstatt: Cantz.

Faust, Wolfgang Max. 1979. "Tagtraum und Theater: Anmerkungen zu Robert Wilsons *Death, Destruction & Detroit.*" *Sprache im technischen Zeitalter* 1, 30–58.

Fenollosa, Ernest Francisco. 1916a. *Certain Noble Plays of Japan.* Dublin: Cuala.

———. 1916b. *"Noh" or Accomplishment: A Study of the Classical Stage of Japan.* London/New York: Macmillan.

Féral, Josette. 1982. "Performance and Theatricality: The Subject Demystified." *Modern Drama* 25:1, 169–183.

Feuchtwanger, Lion. 1911. "Reinhardt in München." *Die Schaubühne* 30/31, 82–83.

Fiebach, Joachim. 1986. *Die Toten als die Macht der Lebenden: Zur Theorie und Geschichte von Theater in Afrika.* Berlin/Wilhelmshaven: Heinrichshofen.

———. 1990. *Inseln der Unordnung: Fünf Versuche zu Heiner Müllers Theatertexten.* Berlin: Henschel.

Finscher, Ludwig. 1988. "Don Giovanni." *Mozart-Jahrbuch 1987–1988 des Zentralinstituts für Mozart-Forschung der Internationalen Stiftung Mozarteum,* 19–27.

Finter, Helga. 1982. "Die soufflierte Stimme: Klangtheatralik bei Schönberg, Artaud, Jandl, Wilson und anderen." *Theater heute* 1, 45–51.

———. 1989–1990. *Der subjektive Raum.* 2 vols. Tübingen: Narr.

———. 1991. "Ein Raum für das Wort: Zum Teatro di Parola des neuen Theaters in Italien." *Lili: Zeitschrift für Literaturwissenschaft und Linguistik* 81, 53–69.

Fischer, Adolf. 1900–1901. "Japans Bühnenkunst und ihre Entwicklung." *Westermanns Illustrierte deutsche Monatshefte* 89:45, 502.

Fischer-Lichte, Erika. 1979. *Bedeutung: Probleme einer semiotischen Hermeneutik und Ästhetik.* Munich: Beck.

————. 1983a. "Kunst und Wirklichkeit." *Zeitschrift für Semiotik* 5, 195–216.

————. 1983b. *Semiotik des Theaters.* 3 vols. Tübingen: Narr.

————. 1985. "Intercultural Misunderstandings as Aesthetic Pleasure: The Reception of the Peking Opera in Western Germany." In *Interdisciplinary Perspectives at Cross-Cultural Communication,* ed. Werner Enninger and Richard J. Brunt, 79–93. Aachen: Raader.

————. 1986. "Jenseits der Interpretation: Anmerkungen zum Text von Robert Wilsons/Heiner Müllers *CIVIL warS.*" In *Kontroversen, alte und neue: Akten des VII. Internationalen Germanistenkongresses Göttingen 1985,* vol. 11, ed. Wilhelm Voßkamp and Eberhard Lämmert, 191–201. Tübingen: Niemeyer.

————. 1987a. "Die Inszenierung der Übersetzung als kulturelle Transformation." In *Theatralische und soziale Konventionen als Problem der Dramenübersetzung,* ed. E. Fischer-Lichte et al., 129–145. Tübingen: Narr.

————. 1987b. "The Performance as 'Interpretant' of the Drama." *Semiotica* 29, 197–212.

————. 1987c. "Postmoderne Performance: Rückkehr zum rituellen Theater?" *Arcadia* 22:1, 55–65.

————. 1987d. "What is Understanding?" In *Semiotics 1983: Proceedings of the 8th Annual Meeting of the Semiotic Society of America,* ed. Jonathan Evans and John Deely, 361–370. Lanham/New York/London: University Press of America.

————, ed. 1988. *Theatre: Familiar and Foreign.* Forum Modernes Theatre, Schriftenreihe. Tübingen: Narr.

————. 1989a. "Der Körper des Schauspielers im Prozeß der Industrialisierung: Zur Veränderung der Wahrnehmung im Theater des 20. Jahrhunderts." In *Literatur in einer industriellen Kultur,* ed. Götz Großklaus and Eberhard Lämmert, 468–486. Stuttgart: Cotta.

————. 1989b. "Dialog der Künste: Intermediale Fallstudien zur Literatur des 19. und 20. Jahrhunderts." In *Festschrift für Erwin Koppen,* ed. Maria Moog-Grünewald and Christoph Rodiek, 61–74. Frankfurt am Main/Bern/New York/Paris: Peter Lang.

————, ed., 1989c. *Inszenierung von Welt: Semiotik des Theaters. Zeitschrift für Semiotik* 11:1.

————. 1989d. "Wandel theatralischer Kodes." *Zeitschrift für Semiotik* 11, 63–85.

————. 1990a. "Auf der Suche nach einem neuen Theater: Retheatralisierung als produktive Rezeption des fernöstlichen Theaters." *Jahrbuch für Internationale Germanistik* 22:1, 32–55.

————. 1990b. *Geschichte des Dramas: Epochen der Identität auf dem Theater von der Antike bis zur Gegenwart.* 2 vols. Tübingen: Francke.

————. 1990c. "Zum kulturellen Transfer theatralischer Konventionen." In *Literatur und Theater: Traditionen und Konventionen als Problem der Dramenübersetzung,* ed. Erika Fischer-Lichte et al., 35–62. Tübingen: Gunter Narr.

————. 1991. "Between Difference and Indifference: Marianne Hoppe as King Lear in Robert Wilson's *Lear* Production in Frankfurt." In *Gender in Performance,* ed. Laurence Senelick, 86–100. Hanover, N.H.: University Press of New England.

————. 1992. *The Semiotics of Theater.* Bloomington/Indianapolis: Indiana University Press.

———. 1993. *Kurze Geschichte des deutschen Theaters*. Tübingen: Francke.

Fischer-Lichte, Erika, and Klaus Schwind, eds. 1991. *Avantgarde und Postmoderne: Prozesse struktureller und funktioneller Veränderungen*. Tübingen: Stauffenburg.

Fischer-Lichte, Erika, and Harald Xander, eds. 1993. *Welttheater — Nationaltheater — Lokaltheater? Europäisches Theater am Ende des 20. Jahrhunderts*. Tübingen: Francke.

Fischer-Lichte, Erika, et al., eds. 1987. *Theatralische und soziale Konventionen als Problem der Dramenübersetzung*. Tübingen: Narr.

———. 1990a. *The Dramatic Touch of Difference: Theatre Own and Foreign*. Tübingen: Narr.

———. 1990b. *Literatur und Theater: Traditionen und Konventionen als Problem der Dramenübersetzung*. Tübingen: Narr.

Florenz, Karl. 1900. *Japanische Dramen*. Leipzig: Amelang. 2nd ed. 1901.

———. 1906. *Geschichte der japanischen Literatur*. Leipzig: Amelang.

Fokkema, Douwe, and Hans Bertens, eds. 1986. *Approaching Postmodernism*. Utrecht Publications in General and Comparative Literature, vol. 21. Amsterdam: John Benjamins.

Foregger, Nicolai. 1975. "Experiments in the Art of Drama." *Drama Review* 19, 76.

Foucault, Michel. 1975. *Surveiller et punir: La naissance de la prison*. Paris: Gallimard.

Fouquier, Henri. 1900. "Sada Yacco." *Le théâtre* (October 2), 10. *Frankfurter Zeitung*. 1914. July 11.

Freksa, Friedrich. 1913. *Hinter der Rampe — Theaterglossen*, 2nd ed. Munich/Leipzig: Georg Müller.

Freud, Sigmund. 1931. *Totem and Taboo: Resemblances between the Psychic Lives of Savages and Neurotics*. Trans. A. A. Brill. New York: New Republic.

Fuchs, Georg. 1905. *Die Schaubühne der Zukunft*. Berlin/Leipzig: Schuster und Loeffler.

———. 1906. "Der Tanz." *Flugblätter für künstlerische Kultur* 6, 13.

———. 1972. *Revolution in the Theatre: Conclusions Concerning the Munich Artists' Theatre*. Ed. Constance Connor Kuhn. Port Washington, N.Y.: Kennikat.

Fusco, Coco. 1994. "The Other History of Intercultural Performance." *Drama Review* (Spring), 143–167.

Garland, D. 1985. *Punishment and Welfare: A History of Penal Strategies*. Aldershot: Gower.

Gerow, Edwin. 1977. "Indian Poetics." In *A History of Indian Literature*, ed. Jan Gonda, vol. 5, fasc. 3, 245–250. Wiesbaden: Otto Harrassowitz.

Giesey, Ralph E. 1960. *The Royal Funeral Ceremony in Renaissance France*. Geneva: Drosz.

Gissenwehrer, Michael. 1990. "To Weave a Silk Road Away: Thoughts on an Approach towards the Unfamiliar: Chinese Theatre and Our Own." In *The Dramatic Touch of Difference: Theatre Own and Foreign*, ed. Erika Fischer-Lichte et al., 151–160. Tübingen: Narr.

Gissenwehrer, Michael, and Jürgen Sieckmeyer. 1987. *Peking Oper: Theaterzeit in China*. Schaffhausen/Zürich/Frankfurt/M./Düsseldorf: Edition Stemmle.

Gnoli, Raniero. 1968. *The Aesthetic Experience According to Abhinavagupta*. Varanasi: Chowkhamba (1956).

Goethe, Johann Wolfgang. 1943. *J. W. von Goethe's Works: Poetical Works*. 2 vols. London: n.p.

————. 1961–1966. *Sämtliche Werke in 18 Bänden*. Vol. 11. Zurich: Artemis.

————. 1966. *Conversations and Encounters*. Trans. and ed. David Luke and Robert Pick. London: O. Wolff.

————. 1972. *Sämtliche Werke*. Vol. 6. Zurich: Artemis.

————. 1975. *Werke* (ed. for the Großherzogin Sophie von Sachsen). Vol. 22, section 4, 1901. Weimar, 1887. Reprinted Tokyo: Sansyasya/Tübingen: Niemeyer.

————. 1989. *Italienische Reise*. Ed. Herbert von Einem. Munich: Deutscher Taschenbuch Verlag.

Gold, Sylvaine. 1985. In *Wall Street Journal*, March 6.

Goldberg, Roselee. 1988. *Performance Art: From Futurism to the Present*. New York: Harry Abraham, Publishers.

Goldmann, Stefan. 1985. "Wilde in Europa: Aspekte und Orte ihrer Zurschaustellung." In *Wir und die Wilden: Einblicke in eine kannibalische Beziehung*, ed. Thomas Theye, 243–269. Reinbek bei Hamburg: Rowohlt.

————. 1987. "Zur Rezeption der Völkerausstellungen um 1900." In *Exotische Welten: Europäische Phantasien*, 88–93. Catalogue of the Exhibition, Institut für Auslandsbeziehungen, Württembergischer Kunstverein. Stuttgart/Bad Cannstatt: Cantz.

Gollomb, Joseph. "Sumurun." Unidentified review from the archives of the Theater Museum, Cologne.

Gonda, Jan, ed. 1977. *A History of Indian Literature*. Wiesbaden: Otto Harrassowitz.

Gorchakov, Nikolai. 1957. *The Theatre in Soviet Russia*. London: Oxford University Press.

Graham-White, Antony. 1974. *The Drama of Black Africa*. New York/Toronto: Samuel French.

Greenblatt, Stephen J. 1988. *Shakespearean Negotiations: The Circulation of Social Energy in Renaissance England*. Berkeley: University of California Press.

Grimm, Gunther. 1977. *Rezeptionsgeschichte: Grundlegung einer Theorie*. Munich: Fink.

Gropius, Walter. 1967. "Theaterbau" (1935). In *Apollo in der Demokratie*, ed. Hans M. Wingler, 115–123. Mainz/Berlin: Florian Kupferberg.

Großklaus, Götz, and Eberhard Lämmert, eds. 1989. *Literatur in einer industriellen Kultur*. Stuttgart: Cotta.

Grotowski, Jerzy. 1975. *Towards a Poor Theatre*. London: Methuen.

Guimet, Emile, and Félix Régamey. 1886. *Le théâtre au Japon*. Paris: L. Cerf.

Gumbrecht, Hans Ulrich, and K. Ludwig Pfeiffer, eds. 1988. *Materialität der Kommunikation*. Frankfurt/M.: Suhrkamp.

Hagenbeck, Carl. 1909. *Von Tieren und Menschen*. Berlin: Vita Deutsches Verlagshaus.

Handke, Peter. 1976. "Straßentheater und Theatertheater" (1968). In *Ich bin ein Bewohner des Elfenbeinturms* 53–54. Frankfurt/M.: Suhrkamp.

Häringova, Yarmila. 1964. *The Development of T'ien Han's Dramatic Writings during the Years 1920–1937*. Berlin: Akademie Verlag.

Hart, Julius. 1894–1896. *Geschichte der Weltliteratur und des Theaters aller Völker und Zeiten*. Neudamm: Pauli.

Hartman, Geoffrey H. 1980. *Criticism in the Wilderness: The Study of Literature Today.* New Haven/London: Yale University Press (esp. 63–85).

Hausmann, Raoul. 1980. *Am Anfang war Dada.* 2nd ed. Ed. Karl Riha and Günter Kämpf. Giessen: Anabas.

Hawking, Stephen W. 1988. *A Brief History of Time: From the Big Bang to Black Holes.* Toronto/London: Bantam.

Hay, John. 1979. *"Oedipus Tyrannus": Lame Knowledge and the Homosporic Womb.* Washington, D.C.: University Press of America.

Hazelton, George C., and J. H. Benrimo. 1913. *The Yellow Jacket: A Chinese Play Done in a Chinese Manner in Three Acts.* Illustrated with photographs by Arnold Genthe. Indianapolis: Bobbs-Merrill Company Publishers.

Heers, Jacques. 1986. *Vom Mummenschanz zum Machttheater: Europäische Festkultur im Mittelalter.* Frankfurt/M.: Fischer.

Hentschel, Anke E. 1991. "Das Kameraauge im Theater Robert Wilsons— *HAMLETMASCHINE,* eine Bewegung in Zeit und Raum: Analytische Gedanken zur Inszenierung am Thalia Theater Hamburg 1986." *Wissenschaftliche Beiträge der Theaterhochschule Leipzig* 2, 85–142.

Henze-Döhring, Sabine. 1986. *Opera seria, Opera buffa und Mozarts "Don Giovanni": Zur Gattungskonvergenz in der italienischen Oper des 18. Jahrhunderts.* Laaber: Laaber Verlag.

Hesse, Eva, ed. 1963. *No — Vom Genius Japans.* Zurich: Arche.

Hinck, Walter. 1982. *Goethe — Mann des Theaters.* Göttingen: Vandenhoeck und Ruprecht.

Hoesterey, Ingeborg, ed. 1991. *Zeitgeist in Babel: The Postmodernist Controversy.* Bloomington: Indiana University Press.

Holland, Norman Norwood. 1968. *The Dynamics of Literary Response.* London/ New York: Oxford University Press.

Hoover, Marjorie L. 1974. *Meyerhold: The Art of Conscious Theatre.* Amherst: University of Massachusetts Press.

Hößner, Ulrich. 1983. *Erschaffen und Sichtbarmachen: Das theaterästhetische Wissen der historischen Avantgarde von Jarry bis Artaud.* Bern/Frankfurt am Main/New York: P. Lang.

Huelsenbeck, Richard, ed. 1984. *Dada — eine literarische Dokumentation.* Reinbek bei Hamburg: Rowohlt.

Huesmann, Heinrich. 1983. *Welttheater Reinhardt: Bauten, Spielstätten, Inszenierungen.* Munich: Prestel.

Hung, Cheng Fu. 1934. *Un siècle d'influence chinoise sur la littérature française (1815–1930).* Paris: Domat-Montchrestien.

Huntington, Richard, and Peter Metcalf. 1979. *Celebrations of Death: The Anthropology of Mortuary Ritual.* Cambridge: Cambridge University Press.

Huyssen, Andreas, and Klaus R. Scherpe, eds. 1986. *Postmoderne: Zeichen eines kulturellen Wandels.* Reinbek bei Hamburg: Rowohlt.

Iden, Peter. 1982. *Die Schaubühne am Halleschen Ufer 1970–1979.* Frankfurt/ M.: Fischer.

———. 1990. "Queen Lear — mehr 'Vogue' als Wahrheit." *Frankfurter Rundschau* 122 (May 28), 8.

Ihering, Herbert. 1961. *Von Reinhardt bis Brecht: Vier Jahrzehnte Theater und Film.* Vol. 3, 1930–1932. Berlin: Aufbau.

Ingarden, Roman. 1960. "Von den Funktionen der Sprache im Theaterschauspiel." In *Das literarische Kunstwerk,* 403–425. Tübingen: Niemeyer.

Innes, Christopher D. 1981. *Holy Theatre.* Cambridge: Cambridge University Press.

Iser, Wolfgang. 1974. *The Implicit Reader: Patterns of Communication in Prose Fiction from Bunyan to Beckett.* Baltimore: Johns Hopkins University Press.

Ivanov, O., and K. Krivicky. 1984. *Vakhtangov i Vakhtengovzy.* Moscow: Moskovsky Rabochy.

Jacquot, Jean. 1956–1975. *Les fêtes de la Renaissance.* Paris: Editions du Centre National de la Recherche Scientifique.

Jäger, Gerd. 1974. ". . . wie alles sich für mich verändert hat: Über das Antikenprojekt der Berliner Schaubühne." *Theater heute* 14:3, 12–20.

Jaques-Dalcroze, Emile. 1922. *Rhythmus, Musik und Erziehung.* Basel: Schwabe.

Jauss, Hans Robert. 1974. "Literary History as a Challenge to Literary Theory." In *New Directions in Literary History,* ed. Ralph Cohen, 11–41. Baltimore: Johns Hopkins University Press.

Johnson, Barbara. 1980. *The Critical Difference: Essays in the Contemporary Rhetoric of Reading.* Baltimore: Johns Hopkins University Press.

Kamper, Dietmar, and Willem van Reijen, eds. 1987. *Die unvollendete Vernunft: Moderne versus Postmoderne.* Frankfurt/M.: Suhrkamp.

Kant, Immanuel. 1951. *Critique of Judgement.* Trans. J. H. Barnard. New York: Hafner.

Kapralik, Elena. 1977. *Antonin Artaud: Leben und Werk des Schauspielers, Dichters und Regisseurs.* Munich: Matthes und Seitz.

Karasek, Hellmuth, and Urs Jenny. 1987. "Franz Kafka Meets Rudolf Hess: *Spiegel* Interview with Robert Wilson on *Listen, Look, Act.*" *Der Spiegel* 10, 205–214.

Kepplinger, Hans Mathias. 1992. *Ereignismanagement: Wirklichkeit und Massenmedien.* Osnabrück: Fromm.

———. 1993. *Am Pranger: Eine Fallstudie zur Rationalität öffentlicher Kommunikation.* Munich: Fischer.

Kershentzev, Platon. 1980. *Das schöpferische Theater.* Newly edited version of the German translation of 1922 by Richard Weber. Cologne: Prometh.

Kessler, Harry Graf. 1988. *Gesichter und Zeiten.* Frankfurt/M.: Fischer.

Kim, Kisôn. 1982. *Theater und Ferner Osten.* Frankfurt/M. and Bern: P. Lang.

Kincaid, Zoe. 1925. *Kabuki: The Popular Stage of Japan.* London: Macmillan.

Kindermann, Heinz. 1956. *Conrad Ekhofs Schauspieler-Akademie.* Vienna: R. M. Rohrer.

———, ed. 1966. *Fernöstliches Theater.* Stuttgart: Kröner.

Kirby, Michael, ed. 1965. *Happenings.* New York: Dutton.

Kitto, H. D. F. 1958. *Sophocles: Dramatist and Philosopher.* London: Oxford University Press.

Klier, Helmar, ed. 1981. *Theaterwissenschaft im deutschsprachigen Raum.* Darmstadt: Wissenschaftliche Buchgesellschaft.

Koch, Paul, and Wolf Oesterreicher. 1985. "Sprache der Nähe — Sprache der Distanz: Mündlichkeit und Schriftlichkeit im Spannungsfeld von Sprachtheorie und Sprachgeschichte." *Romanistisches Jahrbuch* 36, 15–43.

Koch, Walter A., ed. 1989. *The Nature of Culture*. Bochum: Brockmeyer.

Koonen, Alice. 1985. *Stranicy žizni*. Moscow: n.p.

Koppelkamm, Stefan. 1987. "Das 19. Jahrhundert." In *Exotische Welten: Europäische Phantasien*, 346–391. Catalogue of the Exhibition, Institut für Auslandsbeziehungen, Württembergischer Kunstverein. Stuttgart/Bad Cannstatt: Cantz.

Kotte, Andreas. 1994. *Theatralität im Mittelalter: Das Halberstädter Adamsspiel*. Tübingen: Francke.

Kristeva, Julia. 1974. *La révolution du langage poétique*. Paris: Seuil.

———. 1977. *Polylogue*. Paris: Seuil.

———. 1980. *Desire in Language: A Semiotic Approach to Literature and Art*. Ed. Leon S. Rondiez; trans. Leon Rondiez et al. New York: Columbia University Press.

Krohn, Wolfgang, and Günther Küppers, eds. 1992. *Emergenz: Die Entstehung von Ordnung, Organisation und Bedeutung*. Frankfurt/M.: Suhrkamp.

Krusche, Dietrich. 1980. "Brecht und das Nô-Spiel: Zu den Grundlagen interkultureller Literaturvermittlung." *Fremdsprache Deutsch* 2, 340–357.

Kunze, Stefan. 1984. *Mozarts Opern*. Stuttgart: Reclam.

———. 1988. "Werkbestand und Aufführungsgestalt." *Mozart-Jahrbuch 1987–1988 des Zentralinstituts für Mozart-Forschung der Internationalen Stiftung Mozarteum*, 205–211.

Lang, Werner, et al., eds. 1955. *Von fremden Völkern und Kulturen: Beiträge zur Völkerkunde: Hans Plischke zum 65. Geburtstage*. Düsseldorf: Droste.

Langen, August. 1978a. "Attitude und Tableau in der Goethezeit." In *Gesammelte Studien zur neueren deutschen Sprache und Literatur*, ed. Karl Richter, Gerhard Sauder, and Gerhard Schmidt-Henkel, 292–353. Berlin: E. Schmidt.

———, 1978b. *Gesammelte Studien zur neueren deutschen Sprache und Literatur*. Ed. Karl Richter, Gerhard Sauder, and Gerhard Schmidt-Henkel. Berlin: E. Schmidt.

Lau, Joseph S. M. 1970. *Ts'ao Yü, The Reluctant Disciple of Chekhov and O'Neill: A Study in Literary Influence*. Hong Kong: n.p.

Lazarowicz, Klaus. 1981. "Konzelebration oder Kollusion? Über die Feste der Wittelsbacher." In *Europäische Hofkultur im 16. und 17. Jahrhundert*, ed. August Buck et al., 301–318. 3 vols. Hamburg: Hauswedell.

Lehmann, Alfred. 1955. "Zeitgenössische Bilder der ersten Völkerschauen." In *Von fremden Völkern und Kulturen: Beiträge zur Völkerkunde: Hans Plischke zum 65. Geburtstage*, ed. Werner Lang et al., 31–38. Düsseldorf: Droste.

Lehmann, Hans Thies. 1985. "Robert Wilson, Szenograph." *Merkur: Zeitschrift für europäisches Denken* 39:7 (July), 554–563.

Lehmann, Hans Thies, and Genia Schulz. 1988. "Die Spur des dunklen Engels." *Theater heute* 4, 36–37.

Leims, Thomas. 1990. "Kabuki Goes to Hollywood." In *The Dramatic Touch of Difference: Theatre Own and Foreign*, ed. Erika Fischer-Lichte et al., 107–119. Tübingen: Narr.

Leiter, Samuel. 1979. *Kabuki Encyclopaedia: An English Language Adaptation of Kabuki Jitten*. London: Greenwood.

Lequeux, Alfred. 1888. "Le théâtre au Japon." *Revue d'art dramatique* (April/June), 2.

Lessing, Gotthold Ephraim. 1883–1890. *Lessings Werke*. Ed. Robert Boxberger. Berlin/Stuttgart: Spemann.

———. 1948. *Hamburgische Dramaturgie*, Ed. O. Mann. 3 vols. Stuttgart: Kröner.

Lévi-Strauss, Claude. 1969. *The Raw and the Cooked*. Vol. 1. Trans. J. Weightman and D. Weightman. New York: Harper and Row.

———. 1985. *Le cru et le cuit*. In *Mythologiques 1–4*, vol. 1. Paris: Plon.

Li, Ruru. 1988. "Chinese Traditional Theatre and Shakespeare." *Asian Theatre Journal* 5, 38–48.

———. 1995. "Macbeth Becomes Ma Pei: An Odyssey from Scotland to China." *Theatre Research International* 20:1, 42–53.

Lichtenberg, Georg Christoph. 1972. "Über Physiognomik; wider die Physiognomen." In *Schriften und Briefe*, ed. Wolfgang Promies, 256–295. 3 vols. Munich: Hanser.

Lindner, Burkhardt. 1978. "Links hatte noch alles sich zu enträtseln . . ." In *Walter Benjamin im Kontext*, ed. Burkhardt Lindner, 7–11, Frankfurt/M.: Syndicat.

Lorenzer, Alfred. 1973. *Über den Gegenstand der Psychoanalyse oder: Sprache und Interaktion*. Frankfurt/M.: Suhrkamp.

Lotman, Jury. 1976. *Analysis of the Poetic Text*. Trans. and ed. Barton Johnson. Ann Arbor: University of Michigan Press.

———. 1977. *The Structure of the Artistic Text*. Trans. Gail Lenhoff and Ronald Vroon. Michigan Slavic Contributions 7. Ann Arbor: University of Michigan Press.

MacCannell, Juliet F. 1987. "On Language as Such and on the Language of Man." In *Semiotics 1983: Proceedings of the 8th Annual Meeting of the Semiotic Society of America*, ed. Jonathan Evans and John Deely. Bloomington: Indiana University Press.

Mach, Ernst. 1922. "Antimetaphysische Vorbemerkungen." In *Die Analyse der Empfindungen und das Verhältnis des Physischen zum Psychischen*. 9th ed. Jena: Gustav Fischer.

Mackerras, Colin P. 1980. "New and Old Drama in China." *Hemisphere* 24:2 (March–April), 90–95.

———. 1983. *Chinese Theater from Its Origins to the Present Day*. Honolulu: University of Hawaii Press.

Mailand-Hansen, Christian. 1980. *Mejerhold's Theaterästhetik in den 1920er Jahren — ihr theaterpolitischer und kulturideologischer Kontext*. Copenhagen: Rosenkilde og Bagger.

Marathi Theatre 1843 to 1960, The. 1961. Bombay: Publ. for Marathi Natya Parishad.

Marranca, Bonnie. 1983. "Robert Wilson, Byrd Hoffman School of Byrds." In *The Theatre of Images*, 39–45. New York: Drama Book Specialists.

Marranca, Bonnie, and Gautam Das Gupta, eds. 1991. *Interculturalism & Performance*. New York: PAJ Publishers.

Masini, Ferrucchio. 1979. "Allegorie, Melancholie, Avantgarde: Zum Ursprung des deutschen Trauerspiels." *Text und Kritik* 31/32: "Walter Benjamin," 2nd ed., 94–102.

Matejka, L., and J. R. Titunic, eds. 1976. *Semiotics of Art*. Cambridge, Mass./ London: MIT Press.

Mathur, J. C. 1964. *Drama in Rural India*. New York: Asia.

Maturana, Humberto, and Francisco Varela. 1984. *Der Baum der Erkenntnis: Die biologischen Wurzeln des menschlichen Erkennens.* 2nd ed. Bern/Munich/Vienna: Scherz.

Mauss, Marcel. 1983. *Sociologie et anthropologie.* 8th ed. Paris: Presses Universitaires de France (1935).

Maybon, Albert. 1925. *Le théâtre japonais.* Paris: Laurens.

McHale, Brian. 1987. *Postmodernist Fiction.* New York/London: Methuen.

Mehring, Walter. 1959. *Berlin Dada: Eine Chronik mit Photos und Dokumenten.* Zurich: Arche.

Mehta, Kumud Arvind. 1960. "English Drama on the Bombay Stage in the Late Eighteenth and in the Nineteenth Century." Ph.D. diss., Bombay.

Meier, Christian. 1983. *Die Entstehung des Politischen bei den Griechen.* Frankfurt/M.: Suhrkamp.

Merleau-Ponty, Maurice. 1945. *Phénoménologie de la perception.* Paris: Gallimard.

Merschmeier, Michael. 1988a. "Das Phänomen: Über Einar Schleefs Komödie *Die Schauspieler* in des Autors Urinszenierung am Schauspiel Frankfurt—und über das eintönige Schmerzgeschrei in den Feuilletons." *Theater heute* 6, 16–17.

———. 1988b. "Das Wahre Wede-Kind." *Theater heute*, annual vol., 70–71.

———. 1990. "Faustspiel im Strafraum—*Urfaust* von Einar Schleef und Wolfgang Engel." *Theater heute* 8, 8–11.

Meyer, Thomas. 1992. *Die Inszenierung des Scheins: Voraussetzungen und Folgen symbolischer Politik.* Frankfurt/M.: Suhrkamp.

Meyerhold, Vsevolod. 1969. *Meyerhold on Theatre.* Trans. and ed. Edward Braun. London: Methuen.

———. 1972. *Theater-Oktober: Meyerhold, Tairow, Wachtangow.* Frankfurt/M.: Röderberg.

———. 1974. *Theaterarbeit 1917–1930.* Ed. Rosemarie Tietze. Munich: Hanser.

———. 1979. *Schriften.* 2 vols. Berlin: Henschel.

Michaelis, Rolf. 1972. "Tragödienstadel, Franz Xaver Kroetz' *Stallerhof*, Deutsches Schauspielhaus, Hamburg." *Theater heute* 5, 10–12.

———. 1988. "Jeder Satz eine Katastrophe: Probennächte mit Klaus Michael Grüber zu Hölderlins *Empedokles* 24–29. November 1975." In *Klaus Michael Grüber*, ed. Uwe B. Carstensen, 78–91. Frankfurt/M.: Fischer.

Mille, Liam. 1976. *The Noble Drama of W. B. Yeats.* Dublin: Dolman.

Miner, Earl. 1958. *The Japanese Tradition in British and American Literature.* Princeton: Princeton University Press.

Moine, Marie-Christine. 1984. *Les fêtes à la Court du Roi Soleil 1653–1715.* Paris: F. Lanore.

Morris, Charles. 1981. *Foundations of the Theory of Signs.* Chicago: University of Chicago Press (London, 1938).

Muchembled, Robert. 1992. *Le temps de supplices: De l'obéissance sous les rois absolus; XVe–XVIIIe siècle.* Paris: A. Colin.

Mukařovský, Jan. 1970. *Aesthetic Function, Norm and Value as Social Facts.* Trans. Mark Suino. Michigan Slavic Contributions. Ann Arbor: University of Michigan Press.

Müller, Heiner. 1985. "Bildbeschreibung." In *Shakespeare Factory I*, 7–14. Berlin: Rotbuch.

Müller, Heiner, and Robert Weimann. 1991. "Gleichzeitigkeit und Repräsentation: Ein Gespräch." In *Postmoderne — globale Differenz*, ed. Robert Weimann and Hans Ulrich Gumbrecht, 182–210. Frankfurt/M.: Suhrkamp.

Naeher, Jürgen. 1972. *Walter Benjamins Allegorie-Begriff als Modell: Zur Konstitution philosophischer Literaturwissenschaft*. Stuttgart: Klett-Cotta.

Neff, Renfreu. 1970. *The Living Theatre: USA*. Indianapolis: Bobbs-Merrill.

Neueste Nachrichten. 1914. (Munich) July 11.

Neuschäfer, Anne, and Frédéric Serror. 1984. *Le Théâtre du Soleil*. Cologne: Prometh.

New York Review, 1912. January.

Nietzsche, Friedrich. 1910. *The Complete Works of Friedrich Nietzsche*. Vol. 5. Trans. Anthony M. Ludovici. Edinburgh/London: T. N. Foulis.

———. 1967. *The Birth of Tragedy and the Case of Wagner*. Trans. Walter Kaufman. New York: Vintage.

———. 1969. "Vierte unzeitgemäße Betrachtung" (1876). In *Werke*, vol. 1, ed. Karl Schlechta. Frankfurt/M., Berlin, and Vienna: Ullstein.

Nitsch, Hermann. 1979. *Das Orgien Mysterien Theater: Die Partituren aller aufgeführten Aktionen 1960–1979*. Vol. 1. Naples/Munich/Vienna: Edition Freiborg, Publishers.

———. 1990. "Die Realisation des O.M. Theaters" (1973). In *Das Orgien Mysterien Theater: Manifeste, Aufsätze, Vorträge*, 67–107. Salzburg/Vienna: Residenz-Verlag, Publishers.

Nöth, Winfried. 1972. *Strukturen des Happenings*. Hildesheim/New York: Olms.

Nye, David A. 1984. *Crime, Madness and Politics in Modern France: The Medical Concept of National Decline*. Princeton: Princeton University Press.

Oba, Masaharu. 1984. *Bertolt Brecht und das Nô-Theater*. Bern/Frankfurt am Main/New York: P. Lang.

Ogunbiyi, Yemi, ed. 1981. *Drama and Theatre in Nigeria: A Critical Source Book*. Lagos: *Nigeria Magazine*.

O'Neill, Eugene. 1959. *Three Plays of Eugene O'Neill*. New York: Random House.

Ortega y Gasset, José. 1950. *Papeles sobre Velázquez y Goya*. Madrid: Vda. de Galo Sáez.

Ortolani, Benito. 1963. "Shingeki: The Maturing New Drama of Japan." In *Studies in Japanese Culture*, ed. Joseph Roggendorf, 163–185. Tokyo: Sophia University Press.

Owens, Craig. 1980. "Robert Wilson: Tableaux." In *Art in America* (New York; November).

Paetzoldt, Heinz. 1977. "Walter Benjamin's Theory of the End of Art." *International Journal of Sociology* 7:1, 25–75.

Paul, Arno. 1978. "Ein goldenes Zeitalter des Theaters?" *Theater heute*, annual vol., 86–101.

Pavis, Patrice. 1993. "Wilson, Brook, Zadek: Ein interkulturelles Zusammentreffen?" In *Welttheater — Nationaltheater — Lokaltheater? Europäisches Theater am Ende des 20. Jahrhunderts*, ed. Erika Fischer-Lichte and Harald Xander, 179–203. Tübingen: Narr.

Peirce, Charles S. 1960. *Collected Papers*. Vols. 1–6, ed. Ch. Hartshorne and P. Weiss; vols. 7–8, ed. W. Burks. Cambridge: Harvard University Press (1931–1935).

Péri, Noël. 1921. *Cinq No drames lyriques japonais*. Paris: n.p.

Pfister, Manfred. 1988a. "Meta-Theater und Materialität: Zu Robert Wilsons *the CIVIL warS.*" In *Materialität der Kommunikation*, ed. Hans Ulrich Gumbrecht and K. Ludwig Pfeiffer, 454–473. Frankfurt/M.: Suhrkamp.

———. 1988b. *The Theory and Analysis of Drama*. Cambridge: Cambridge University Press.

Pirandello, Luigi. 1988. "Sechs Personen suchen einen Autor." In *Die Trilogie des Theaters auf dem Theater*, 13–93. Mindelheim: Sachon.

Piscator, Erwin. 1963. *Das politische Theater*. Reinbek bei Hamburg: Rowohlt.

Plessner, Helmuth. 1966. *Diesseits der Utopie*. Düsseldorf/Cologne: Diederichs.

———. 1970a. *Laughing and Crying: A Study of the Limits of Human Behaviour*. Evanston, Ill.: Northwestern University Press (1941).

———. 1970b. *Philosophische Anthropologie*. Frankfurt/M.: Fischer.

———. 1976. *Die Frage nach der Conditio humana*. Frankfurt/M.: Suhrkamp.

———. 1980. *Anthropologie der Sinne: Gesammelte Schriften in drei Bänden*. Frankfurt/M.: Suhrkamp.

Posner, Roland. 1989. "What Is Culture? Towards a Semiotic Explication of Anthropological Concepts." In *The Nature of Culture*, ed. Walter A. Koch, 240–295. Bochum: Brockmeyer.

Powell, Brian. 1975. "Japan's First Modern Theater: The Tsukiji Shogekijo and Its Company, 1924–1926." *Monumenta Nipponica* 30, 67–85.

Pronko, Leonard. 1967. *Theatre East & West: Perspectives towards a Total Theatre*. Berkeley/Los Angeles/London: University of California Press.

Prütting, Lenz. 1971. *Die Revolution des Theaters: Studien über Georg Fuchs*. Munich: Kitzinger.

Qamber, Aktar. 1974. *Yeats and the Noh*. New York/Tokyo: Weatherhill.

Quadri, Franco. 1984. "Robert Wilson: It's about Time." *Artforum*.

Radnoti, Sandor. 1977. "The Early Aesthetics of Walter Benjamin." *International Journal of Sociology* 7:1, 76–123.

Ranganath, H. K. 1982. *The Karnatak Theatre*. Dharwad: Karnatak University Press.

Rea, Kenneth. 1978–1979. "Theatre in India: The Old and the New." Part 3/4. *Theatre Quarterly* 8:32, 47–66; 10:34, 53–65.

Riewoldt, Otto. 1987. "Herrscher über Raum und Zeit: Das Theater Robert Wilsons." *Südfunk* (June 3).

Riley, Jo. 1977. *Chinese Theatre and the Actor in Performance*. Cambridge: Cambridge University Press.

Rimer, Thomas. 1974. *Towards a Modern Japanese Theatre*. Princeton: Princeton University Press.

Rischbieter, Henning. 1966. "Experimenta: Theater und Publikum neu definiert." *Theater heute* 7, 8–17.

———. 1986. "Deutschland, Ein Wilsonmärchen." *Theater heute* 12, 5–16.

———. 1987. "Theater ist Widerspruch: Plädoyer für die umstrittenste Aufführung der letzten Spielzeit: Einar Schleefs Inszenierung von Gerhart Hauptmanns *Vor Sonnenaufgang* am Schauspiel Frankfurt." *Theater heute*, annual vol., 116–120.

———. 1988. "Der wahre Wedekind: Lulu Furiosa." *Theater heute* 4, 8–14.

Roberti, Jean-Claude. 1980. *Fêtes et spectacles de l'ancienne Russie*. Paris: Editions du Centre National de la Recherche Scientifique.

Rockwell, John, ed. 1984. *Robert Wilson: The Theatre of Images*. New York: Byrd Hoffman Foundation.

Roggendorf, Joseph, ed. 1963. *Studies in Japanese Culture*. Tokyo: Sophia University Press.

Rose, Arnold M., ed. 1962. *Human Behaviour and Social Processes: An Interactional Approach*. London: Routledge and Paul.

Rosen, Charles. 1977. "The Ruins of Walter Benjamin." *New York Review of Books* 24:17, 3–10; 18, 30–38.

Rosenthal, Rachel. 1981–1982. "Performance and the Masochist Tradition." *High Performance* (Winter).

Rötzer, Florian, ed. 1991. *Digitaler Schein: Ästhetik der elektronischen Medien*. Frankfurt/M.: Suhrkamp.

Roubine, Jean-Jacques. 1980. *Théâtre et mise en scène 1880–1980*. Paris: Presses Universitaires de France.

Rudnicky, Konstantin. 1969. *Režissër Mejerkhol'd*. Moscow: n.p.

Rudnitsky, Konstantin. 1988. *Russia & Soviet Theatre: Tradition & the Avant-Garde*. London: Thames and Hudson.

Ruf, Wolfgang. 1988. "Nicht nur ein Zugtier vor dem Pflug: Lulu und andere Frauen." *Deutsche Bühne* 4, 12–16.

Rühle, Günter. 1976. *Theater in unserer Zeit*. Frankfurt/M.: Suhrkamp.

———. 1980. "Das Lehrstück und das Lernstück: Hans Neuenfels inszeniert Goethes *Iphigenie* in Frankfurt." *Theater heute* 8, 8–11.

———. 1982. *Anarchie in der Regie*. Frankfurt/M.: Suhrkamp.

———. 1992. *Was soll das Theater?* Frankfurt/M.: Suhrkamp.

Rühle, Jürgen. 1963. *Theater und Revolution: Von Gorki bis Brecht*. Munich: Deutscher Taschenbuch Verlag.

Rüsen, Jörn, et al., eds. 1988. *Die Zukunft der Aufklärung*. Frankfurt/M.: Suhrkamp.

Russolo, Luigi. 1986. *The Art of Noises*. Trans. Barclay Brown. New York: Pendragon.

Sacks, Harvey, Gail Jefferson, and Emanuel Schlegloff. 1974. "A Simplist Systematics for the Organization of Turn-Taking for Conversation." *Language* 50, 696–735.

Sarcinelli, Ulrich. 1987. *Politikvermittlung: Beiträge zur politischen Kommunikationsstruktur*. Schriftenreihe der Bundeszentrale für politische Bildung. München-Landsberg: Bonn Aktuell.

Scarry, Elaine. 1985. *The Body in Pain: The Making and Un-Making of the World*. New York: Oxford University Press.

Schaubühne am Halleschen Ufer, am Lehniner Platz 1962–1987. 1987. Frankfurt/M. and Berlin: Propyläen.

Schechner, Richard. 1973. *Environmental Theatre*. New York: Hawthorn Books.

———. 1982. *The End of Humanism: Writings on Performance*. New York: Performing Arts Journal Publications.

———. 1985. *Between Theatre and Anthropology*. Philadelphia: University of Pennsylvania Press.

Schefflen, Albert. 1972. *Body Language and Social Order*. Englewood Cliffs, N.J.: Prentice-Hall/University of Illinois.

Scherer, Klaus. 1977. "Die Funktionen des nonverbalen Verhaltens im Gespräch." In *Gesprächsanalysen*, ed. D. Wegner, 275–297. Hamburg: Buske.

Schickele, René. 1979. "Hanako." In *Vollständiger Nachdruck der Jahrgänge 1905– 1918*, 291–293. (1908). Königstein/Ts.: Athenäum.

Schiller, Friedrich. 1965. *Sämtliche Werke*. Ed. Gerhard Fricke and Herbert G. Göpfert. Vol. 2. 4th ed. Munich: Hanser.

Schlegloff, Emanuel, and Harvey Sacks. 1973. "Opening Up and Closings." *Semiotica* 8, 289–327.

Schlicher, Susanne. 1987. *Tanz Theater, Tradition und Freiheiten: Pina Bausch, Gerhard Bohner, Reinhild Hoffmann, Hans Kresnik, Susanne Linke*. Reinbek bei Hamburg: Rowohlt.

Schmidt, Siegfried J. 1988. *Der Diskurs des Radikalen Konstruktivismus*. Frankfurt/M.: Suhrkamp.

———, ed. 1991. *Gedächtnis: Probleme und Perspektiven der interdisziplinären Gedächtnisforschung*. Frankfurt/M.: Suhrkamp.

Schödel, Helmut. 1990. "König Licht." *Die Zeit* 23 (June 1), 68.

Scholes, Robert. 1982. *Semiotics and Interpretation*. New Haven: Yale University Press.

Schramm, Helmar. 1990. "Theatralität und Öffentlichkeit: Vorstudien zur Begriffsgeschichte von 'Theater.'" In *Ästhetische Grundbegriffe: Studien zu einem historischen Wörterbuch*, ed. Karlheinz Barck et al., 202–242. Berlin: Akademie Verlag.

———. 1995. "The Surveying of Hell: On Theatricality and Styles of Thinking." *Theatre Research International* 20:2, 114–188.

———. 1996. *Karneval des Denkens: Theatralität im Spiegel philosophischer Texte des 16. und 17. Jahrhunderts*. Berlin: Akademie Verlag.

Schultze-Naumburg, Paul. 1902. *Die Kultur des weiblichen Körpers als Grundlage der Frauenkleidung*. Leipzig: Diederichs.

Schuster, Ingrid. 1977. *China und Japan in der deutschen Literatur 1890–1925*. Bern/ Munich: Francke.

Schwab, Heinrich W. 1971. *Konzert: Öffentliche Musikdarbietung vom 17. bis 19. Jahrhundert*. Leipzig: Deutscher Verlag für Musik.

Schwartz, William L. 1927. *The Imaginative Interpretation of the Far East in Modern French Literature*. 1800–1925. Paris: Champion.

Scone, Gregory P. 1962. "Appearance and the Self." In *Human Behaviour and Social Processes: An Interactional Approach*, ed. Arnold M. Rose, 86–118. London: Routledge and Paul.

SCOT: Suzuki Company of Toga. 1985. Ed. Suzuki Company of Toga. Tokyo: n.p.

Seeck, Gustav Adolf, ed. 1979. *Das griechische Drama*. Darmstadt: Wissenschaftliche Buchgesellschaft.

Semper, Manfred. 1906. *Das Münchner Festspielhaus: Gottfried Semper und Richard Wagner*. Hamburg: A. Kloss.

Senelick, Laurence, ed. 1991. *Gender in Performance*. Hannover, N.H.: University Press of New England.

Silvestro, Carlo. 1971. *The Living Book of the Living Theater*. Cologne: M. DuMont Schauberg.

Simmel, Georg. 1957. "Der Schauspieler und die Wirklichkeit." In *Brücke und Tür*, 168–175. Stuttgart: Koehler.

Simonov, Reuben. 1959. *S Vakhtangovym*. Moscow: Iskusstvo.

Singer, Milton, ed. 1959. *Traditional India: Structure and Change*. Philadelphia: American Folklore Society.

Skura, Ann Meredith. 1981. *The Literary Use of the Psychoanalytic Process*. New Haven: Yale University Press.

Smirnova, N. I. 1982. *Evgenij Bagrationovich Vakhtangov*. Moscow: Znanie.

Smirnov-Nesvitzky, Yury. 1987. *Vakhtangov*. Leningrad: Iskusstvo.

Smith, Antony C. H. 1974. *Peter Brook's "Orghast" in Persepolis*. London: Eyre Methuen.

Smith, Rowland, ed. 1976. *Exile and Tradition*. London: Longman and Dalhousie University Press.

Sophocles. 1970. *Oedipus the King*. Trans. Thomas Gould. Englewood Cliffs, N.J.: Prentice-Hall.

Sovetskij teatr — dokumenty i materialy: Russkij sovetskij teatr 1921–1926. 1975. Ed. A. Ya. Trabsky. Leningrad: Iskusstvo.

Soyinka, Wole. 1976. "Drama and the African World View." In *Exile and Tradition*, ed. Rowland Smith, 173–190. London: Longman and Dalhousie University Press.

———. 1978. *Death and the King's Horseman*. London: Methuen.

Stadelmaier, G. 1990. "Königingroßmutter der Nacht: Marianne Hoppe spielt, Bob Wilson inszeniert Shakespeares *Lear* in Frankfurt." *Frankfurter Allgemeine Zeitung* 122, May 28, 33.

Stärk, Ekkehard. 1987. *Hermann Nitsch, Das Orgien Mysterien Theater und die Hysterie der Griechen: Quellen und Traditionen zum Wiener Antikenbild seit 1850*. Munich: Fink.

States, Bert. 1985. *Great Reckonings in Little Rooms: On the Phenomenology of Theater*. Berkeley/Los Angeles/London: University of California Press.

Stopes, Marie C., and Joji Sakurai. 1913. *Plays of the Old Japan: The "No."* London: Heinemann.

Strauß, Botho. 1969. "Das schöne Umsonst." *Theater heute* 5, 13.

Strong, Roy. 1991. *Feste der Renaissance 1450–1650: Kunst als Instrument der Macht*. Trans. Susanne Höbel and Maja Ueberle-Pfaff. Freiburg/Würzburg: Ploetz.

"Sumurun." 1912. *Erie Dispatch*. January 28.

Suzuki, Tadashi. 1985. "Culture Is the Body!" In *SCOT: Suzuki Company of Toga*, ed. Suzuki Company of Toga, 6–7. Tokyo: n.p.

———. 1986. *The Way of Acting*. Trans. Thomas Rimer. New York: Theatre Communication Group.

Szondi, Peter. 1971. "Spiel von der Unmöglichkeit des Dramas." In *Theorie des modernen Dramas 1880–1950*, 127–135. Frankfurt/M.: Suhrkamp.

Tairov, Alexander. 1964. *Das entfesselte Theater*. Cologne: Kiepenheuer und Witsch.

Tatlow, Antony. 1977. *The Mask of Evil*. Frankfurt am Main/Bern/New York: Lang.

Taylor, Richard. 1976. *The Drama of W. B. Yeats: Irish Myth and the Japanese Nô*. New Haven/London: Yale University Press.

Terayama, Shuji. 1971. *Theater contra Ideologie*. Trans. and ed. M. Hubricht. Frankfurt/M.: S. Fischer.

Theater der Nationen, 1979. April 26–May 13. Hamburg: n.p. *Theater heute*, 1962–1996.

Theye, Thomas, ed. 1985. *Wir und die Wilden: Einblicke in eine kannibalische Beziehung*. Reinbek bei Hamburg: Rowohlt.

Thiems, Paul. 1966. "Das indische Theater." In *Fernöstliches Theater*, ed. Heinz Kindermann, 21–120. Stuttgart: Kröner.

Thomsen, Christian W., ed. 1985. *Studien zur Ästhetik des Gegenwartstheaters*. Heidelberg: Winter.

Tiedemann, Rolf. 1965. *Studien zur Philosophie Walter Benjamins*. Frankfurt/M. Suhrkamp.

Tisdall, Carolin. 1988. *Joseph Beuys Coyote*. 3rd ed. Munich: Schirmer-Mosel (first ed. 1976).

Turzinsky, Walter. 1914. In *Breslauer Zeitung*, April 1.

Tzara, Tristan. 1975–1982. *Oeuvres complètes*, 5 vols. Ed. Henri Behar. Paris: Flammarion.

Van Dülmen, Richard. 1988. *Theater des Schreckens: Gerichtspraxis und Strafrituale in der frühen Neuzeit*. 3rd ed. Munich: Beck.

Van Gennep, Arnold. 1960. *The Rites of Passage*. Trans. Monika Vizedom and Gabrielle Caffee. Chicago: University of Chicago Press.

Varela, Francisco J. 1988. *Kognitionswissenschaft—Kognitionstechnik: Eine Skizze aktueller Perspektiven*. Frankfurt/M.: Suhrkamp.

Veltruský, Jiri. 1976. "Dramatic Text as a Component of Theatre." In *Semiotics of Art*, ed. L. Matejka and J. R. Titunic, 94–177. Cambridge, Mass./London: MIT Press.

Virilio, Paul. 1986. "Geschwindigkeit—Unfall—Krieg: Gespräch mit Virilio." *TAZ* 2 (May 3), 12–13.

Virmaux, Odette. 1975. *"Le théâtre et son double": Antonin Artaud: Analyse critique*. Paris: Hatier.

Von Becker, Peter. 1984a. "Die Sonnenkönigin des Theaters: Ariane Mnouchkine und ihr Théâtre du Soleil." *Theater heute*, annual vol., 12–19.

———. 1984b. "Die Theaterreise zu Shakespeare: Aufbruch in das ferne fremde Land, das wir selbst sind: Ein Gespräch mit Ariane Mnouchkine nach Abschluß ihres Shakespeare-Zyklus." *Theater heute*, annual vol., 13–19.

———. 1984c. "So schön, um wahr zu sein—über Ariane Mnouchkines Shakespearezyklus und *Heinrich IV* im Théâtre du Soleil." *Theater heute* 4, 15–17.

———. 1985. "Der Sommernachtstraum des *Mahabharata*—Peter Brook dramatisiert das größte Epos der Welt: Neun Stunden Theatergeschichte beim Festival in Avignon." *Theater heute* 9, 6–11.

Von Gersdorff, Wolfgang. 1926. *Japanische Dramen für die Deutsche Bühne verarbeitet*. Jena: Diederichs.

Von Hofmannsthal, Hugo. 1952. *Hugo von Hofmannsthal*. Trans. Mary Hottinger et al. New York: Pantheon.

———. 1979–1980. *Gesammelte Werke in 10 Bänden*. Frankfurt/M.: Fischer.

Vossische Zeitung, 1918. July 30.

Voßkamp, Wilhelm, and Eberhard Lämmert, eds. 1986. *Kontroversen, alte und neue: Akten des VII. Internationalen Germanistenkongresses Göttingen 1985*. Vol. 11. Tübingen: Niemeyer.

Vostell, Wolf, ed. 1970. *Aktionen, Happenings und Demonstrationen seit 1965.* Reinbek bei Hamburg: Rowohlt.

Wachtangow, Jewgeni B. 1982. *Schriften: Aufzeichnungen, Briefe, Protokolle, Notate.* Berlin: Henschel.

Wagner, Richard. 1887–1888. *Gesammelte Schriften und Briefe.* 2nd ed. 10 vols. Leipzig: E.W. Fritzsch.

———. 1914. *Richard Wagners Gesammelte Schriften.* Ed. Julius Kapp. Leipzig: Hesse und Becher.

Waley, Arthur. 1921. *The Noh Plays of Japan.* London: Allen and Unwin.

Watzlawick, Paul, ed. 1981. *Die erfundene Wirklichkeit: Wie wissen wir, was wir zu wissen glauben? Beiträge zum Konstruktivismus.* Munich/Zurich: R. Piper und Co.

———, ed. 1984. *The Invented Reality. How Do We Know What We Believe to Know?: Contributions to Constructivism.* New York: L. L. Norton.

Weber-Schäfer, Peter, ed. 1986. *Vierundzwanzig No Spiele.* 2nd ed. Trans. Peter Weber-Schäfer. Frankfurt/M.: Insel (1961).

Wegner, D., ed. 1977. *Gesprächsanalysen.* Hamburg: Buske.

Weiler, Christel. 1994. *Kultureller Austausch auf dem Theater.* Marburg: Tectum.

Weimann, Robert, and Hans Ulrich Gumbrecht, eds. 1991. *Postmoderne — globale Differenz.* Frankfurt/M.: Suhrkamp.

"Why Lot's Wife Could Not Have Sat Out *Sumurun.*" Unidentified New York review from the archives of the Theater Museum, Cologne.

Wille, Franz. 1991. "Das Rad der Geschichte dreht durch: Heiner Müller inszenierte Heiner Müller —*Mauser* und manches mehr am Deutschen Theater in Berlin." *Theater heute* 10, 2–7.

Willett, John. 1964. *Brecht on Theatre.* Trans. John Willett. New York: Hill and Wang.

Willett, Ralph. 1985. "The Old and the New: Robert Wilson's Traditions." In *Studien zur Ästhetik des Gegenwartstheaters,* ed. Christian W. Thomsen, 91–98. Heidelberg: Winter.

Wilshire, Bruce. 1982. *Role Playing and Identity: The Limits of the Theater as Metaphor.* Bloomington: Indiana University Press.

Wilson, Robert. 1982. *Die goldenen Fenster (The Golden Windows).* Munich/Vienna: Hanser.

———. 1984. *the CIVIL warS, a tree is best measured when it is down.* Frankfurt/M.: Suhrkamp.

———. 1985. *the Knee Plays from the CIVIL warS: a tree is best measured when it is down.* Frankfurt/M.: Theater der Welt.

Winters, Lee E. 1956. *The Relationship of Chinese Poetry to British and American Poetry of the Twentieth Century.* Berkeley: University of California Press.

Wirth, Andrzej. 1991. "Interculturalism and Iconophilia in the New Theatre." In *Interculturalism & Performance,* ed. Bonnie Marranca and Gautam Das Gupta, 281–291. New York: PAJ Publishers.

Wohlfarth, Irving. 1978. "On the Messianic Structure of Walter Benjamin's Last Reflections." *Glyph* 3, 148–212.

Wolin, Richard. 1981. "From Messianism to Materialism: The Later Aesthetics of Walter Benjamin." *New German Critique* 22, 81–108.

Wordsworth, William, and Samuel Taylor Coleridge. 1963. *Lyrical Ballads by Wordsworth and Coleridge.* The text of the 1798 edition with the additional 1800 poems and the prefaces. Ed. R. L. Brett and A. R. Jones. London: Methuen.

Worrall, Nick. 1989. *Modernism to Realism on the Soviet Stage: Tairov — Vakhtangov — Okhlopkov.* Cambridge: Cambridge University Press.

Wundt, Wilhelm. 1973. "Die Gebärdensprache." In *Völkerpsychologie,* vol. 1, 131–243. Den Haag: Mouton (Stuttgart, 1900).

Yajnik, R. K. 1933. *The Indian Theatre: Its Origins and Its Developments under European Influence, with Special Reference to Western India.* London: Allen and Unwin.

Yamaguchi, Masao. 1985. "The Provocative and Privileged Space and People in Japan." Paper read at the International Summer Institute for Semiotic and Structural Studies Conference in Bloomington, Indiana.

Zadek, Peter, and Johannes Grützke. 1988. *Lulu — eine deutsche Frau.* Frankfurt/ M.: Athenäum.

Zeami. 1954a. *Blumenspiegel, Zweiter Teil: Die zwölf Themen. OAG Report,* vol. 34, sec. A (I).

———. 1954b. *Buch der No Gestaltung. OAG Report,* vol. 34, sec. D.

———. 1961. *Schriften der dritten Schriftenperiode des Meisters. OAG Report,* vol. 41, sec. C.

Zeitschrift für Ethnologie: Verhandlungen der Berliner Gesellschaft für Anthropologie, Ethnologie und Urgeschichte. 1898.

Zumthor, Paul. 1983. *Introduction à la poésie orale.* Paris: Seuil.

———. 1984. *La poésie et la voix dans la civilisation médiévale.* Paris: Presses Universitaires de France.

INDEX

avant-garde, (*continued*) theatre, 28, 34, 39, 57–58, 72, 94, 116, 130, 159, 222, 268, 316, 347, 355
avant-gardism, 273
avant-gardists, 17, 34–38, 57–58, 62, 64–65, 106–107, 138, 159–160, 339, 358

Balinese theatre, 54, 136, 159
ballet, 7, 200, 239
barong, 116
Baroque, 11, 28–29, 39, 50, 59–60, 126, 187, 189, 190, 194, 196, 218–219, 264, 275, 283, 301, 336, 355; drama, 301; theatre, 11, 28, 126, 189, 190, 194, 196, 336, 355
Bauhaus, 53, 88, 200
Bayreuth festival theatre, 46, 115
behaviorists, 307
behavior pattern, 9, 31, 39, 207, 210–212, 214, 216
Berlin Schaubühne, 91, 97–99, 103–104, 332
biographical research, 305
bio-mechanics, 37, 54, 128
Black Mountain College, 233, 237
Bockenheim Depot, 202
bodily practice, 5, 111
body: a priori, 292; art, 15, 221; being a, 252–253, 297; having a, 252–253, 292, 296–297; image, 5, 292; as material, 101–102; in pain, 251, 254; in performance, 250; subject, 292
bourgeois theatre, 28, 33–34, 41–43, 51, 53, 55, 119, 136, 156, 323, 355
box-set stage, 21, 45–46, 51, 56, 65, 72, 81, 89, 98–99, 120, 142
Bungei Kyokai (Literary Society), 137, 159
bunraku, 108, 139, 350
Bürgerliches Trauerspiel, 322–323

Cabaret Voltaire (Zurich), 267
canticum triumphale, 1
Cantonese opera, 77
carnivalesque, the, 261, 266

catharsis, 307
central perspective, 2–3, 21
Chamber of Art and Wonders. See *Kunst- und Wunderkammer*
charivari, 16
Charleston, 7
Chinese: drama, 136; opera, 116, 133, 148–149, 152–153, 155, 336; stage, 78, 81; stage convention, 78; theatre, 35, 78–82, 89, 133, 148, 151, 348
civilizing process, 10, 25, 28–30, 33–34, 36, 38–40, 112
classical ballet, 7, 239
classless society, 342
collage, 8, 107–108, 139, 148, 201, 261, 270, 273, 315–317
collage of cultures, 139, 148
collective identity, 298, 300–301
colonial exhibition. See *Völkerausstellung*
colonialism, 74–75, 77–78, 142, 149, 227–228
comedias de capa y espada, 194
commedia dell'arte, 53, 56, 116, 128, 151, 194, 336, 348
communicative sign, 276, 312
compactness, 321
concept of art, 31, 303–306, 308–310, 312, 314; cathartic, 303, 306, 308; expressive, 303–304, 308; mimetic, 303–304, 308–310; rhetorical, 303, 308, 312; semiotic, 309, 314
concert party, 142
concrete poetry, 8, 241
conditional theatre, 120, 124
constructing reality, 72
construction, 8, 10, 45, 48, 53, 69, 70, 71, 72, 165, 190, 221, 237, 251, 253, 254, 284, 285, 286, 287, 288, 289, 313, 317, 322, 330, 341, 343, 344, 351, 372; process of, 71, 72, 285, 286, 288, 341; of subjects, 221
constructivism, 261
constructivists, 37, 38, 52, 263, 270
contemplation, 276, 366
contemporary theatre, 22, 56, 57, 69, 106, 110, 111, 138, 139, 145, 149,

335; level, 45, 56, 70, 91, 262–263, 267; rule, 115, 128, 156

primary text, 320, 323

productive reception, 115–116, 123–124, 126, 128, 131–132, 150, 154–157

proletarian theatre, 42, 44, 46, 48

proletcult movement, 50

property man, 350

proscenium, 21, 46–49, 51, 56, 124, 141, 202, 204, 215

puppet and marionette theatre, 116

Querelle des anciens et des modernes, 261

Ramblers' Association, 6

randomness, 261, 266, 269, 273

reader-response theory, 307

ready-mades, 108, 270, 315

realism, 81, 89, 118, 355, 367

realistic theatre, 79, 81, 89, 115, 119, 124, 136–138, 148, 160, 316, 335, 349

realist movement, 34

reconstruction, 285–289, 317–318, 339

rediscovery: of the human body, 111; of language, 111

referential function, 235, 237–238, 243

referentiality, 262, 266

Renaissance, 5, 26, 28, 44, 61, 70, 189–190, 355

Renaissance theatre, 189

representation, 8, 25, 29–30, 33, 39, 64, 66, 69–71, 95, 138, 140, 167, 221–222, 262, 266, 303–305, 308, 310–311, 356, 367; of emotions, 29

retheatricalization, 62, 71–72, 107, 115–116, 118, 128, 136, 138, 200

revolutionary theatre, 43

revolution of theatre, 94

rhythm, 5, 7, 37, 63, 70, 107, 128, 209, 330, 339

rhythmical space, 52

rite, 2, 16, 18, 36, 44–45, 53, 144, 214–217, 219, 249–250, 356; of May, 16; *de passage,* 44, 214–217

ritual, 1–2, 11, 16–17, 19, 38, 44, 51, 116, 143–144, 148, 165, 216, 219,

228, 233, 239–246, 248–254, 256–257, 341, 356, 358; healing, 248; of initiation, 249; scapegoat, 243, 249, 256; theatre, 341, 356

ritualization, 241

Romanticism, 305

Romantic movement, 305

Russian constructivists, 37

Russian formalism, 363

Salon Dada (Paris), 265

scenae frons, 189

Schein, 50, 71, 264

Scheinbarkeit, 219

script, 21, 78, 290, 293, 295, 297, 301, 345

secondary modeling system, 309

secondary text, 320–324, 326, 333, 337

segmentation, 10, 188–189, 343; levels of, 188

Sein, 264

self-reflection of theatre, 94, 109–110, 198

self-reflexivity, 262

semantic: dimension, 252, 268, 283–285, 287, 308–310, 312–313, 316–317; function, 277, 327, 329–330, 332–335; level, 70, 262–263, 269, 272–273; rule, 115, 128, 156

semantization, 284–286, 289, 317

semiosis, 57–58, 270, 315, 317

semiotic, 311; approach, 283, 314, 340; dimension, 269, 308–309, 311–312, 314–315, 317; function, 86–87, 333; level, 70, 262–263, 266–267, 269, 272–273; process, 257, 309, 317–318; system, 61–62, 64, 69–71, 324, 332

semiotics, 21, 25, 147, 302, 319, 324

semiotization, 38–39, 311; of the body, 38; of the symbolic, 311

separation phase. *See* phase of dissolution

serate, 236

Shakespearean stage, 34

shichisan, 121–122

Shimmy, 7

theory: of art, 275, 278, 305, 307, 314; of modernization, 342
thesis, 293, 295, 297, 311, 351
thetic act, 297, 300–301, 311, 315, 318
threshold of an epoch. *See Epochen-schwelle*
total theatre, 46–47, 156
total work of art. *See Gesamtkunstwerk*
Tragédie lyrique, 198
transfiguration of the commonplace, 105
transformation phase. *See* liminal phase
transgressive concepts, 342
transitional phase. *See* liminal phase
transvestite theatre, 367
tripartite stage, 46

universal concept of history, 342
universality, 150
universal language, 10, 141, 145, 147–148; of theatre, 141, 145, 148
uslovnost (conventionality), 155

Verfremdung, 35, 37, 108, 152
Verfremdungseffekt, 37, 136, 151
vernacular play, 1–2
video installation, 15, 221
Vienna *Volkstheater*, 116
Viennese actionists, 15
virtual reality, 219
Völkerausstellung, 11, 16, 73–77, 224–228, 230–231, 358–359
Volksgemeinschaft, 44
Vor-schein, 146
voyeur, 123

Wandervogel movement, 5
Weimar theatre, 135–136, 158, 367
Weltgeist, 342
Weltliteratur, 134–135, 158, 270, 364
Werkbund Theatre (Cologne), 46
Wirkungsästhetik, 307
Wooster Group, 22
word as "name," 275, 278, 293, 300
word as "sign," 104, 275
world: culture, 145–146; theatre, 93,

126, 130, 146, 158, 164, 166–168, 218. *See also Weltliteratur*

Yoruba theatre, 134, 142–144, 147, 155

zapping, 110
Zeitgeist, 269, 273
Zen yoga, 101

NAMES

Abdoh, Reza, 255
Abramović, Marina, 11, 245, 248–252
Aeschylus, 22, 25, 49, 98, 265
Aillaud, Gilles, 100
Alexandre, Arsène, 118
Alpers, Boris, 52
Anderson, Laurie, 222, 225
Antin, Eleanor, 222
Apollinaire, Guillaume, 262
Apostolidès, Jean-Marie, 18
Appia, Adolphe, 17, 52, 200
Aragon, Louis, 57, 94
Arce, Javier, 18
Arroyo, Eduardo, 100
Artaud, Antonin, 17, 35, 37–38, 44, 47, 54–55, 101, 106, 136, 138, 146, 159, 268, 358, 362
Arvatov, Boris, 17, 19
Assmann, Hans-Jörg, 206
Attar, 140, 166
Austin, John L., 236–237, 240
Avner the Eccentric, 225

Baader, Johannes, 50–51, 267
Bakhtin, Mikhail, 261
Balanchine, George, 200
Ball, Hugo, 8, 55, 262
Barba, Eugenio, 17, 92, 148, 167
Barthes, Roland, 236
Baudelaire, Charles, 370
Baudrillard, Jean, 341, 360
Baumbach, Gerda, 17
Bausch, Pina, 104
Beck, Julian, 356

STUDIES IN THEATRE HISTORY AND CULTURE